P9-BVM-926

Reprints of Economic Classics

BRITAIN'S COMMERCIAL INTEREST

Explained and Improved

TWO VOLUMES

VOLUME II

BRITAIN'S

COMMERCIAL INTEREST

EXPLAINED AND IMPROVED

In a SERIES of

DISSERTATIONS

ON Several Important BRANCHES of

HER TRADE AND POLICE

BY

MALACHY POSTLETHWAYT

TWO VOLUMES

VOLUME II

[1757]

REPRINTS OF ECONOMIC CLASSICS

AUGUSTUS M. KELLEY · PUBLISHERS
NEW YORK 1968

First Edition 1757

(London: Printed for D. Browne, *without Temple-Bar*; A. Millar, *in the Strand*; J. Whiston & B. White, and W. Sandby, *in Fleet-street*, 1757)

Reprinted 1968 by

AUGUSTUS M. KELLEY · PUBLISHERS

NEW YORK NEW YORK 10010

LIBRARY OF CONGRESS CATALOGUE CARD NUMBER

68-22376

PRINTED IN THE UNITED STATES OF AMERICA
by SENTRY PRESS, NEW YORK, N. Y. 10019

BRITAIN's COMMERCIAL INTEREST EXPLAINED and IMPROVED;

In a SERIES of

DISSERTATIONS

ON

Several Important BRANCHES of her TRADE and POLICE:

CONTAINING

A Candid ENQUIRY into the *secret Causes* of the *present Misfortunes* of the *Nation*.

WITH

PROPOSALS for their REMEDY.

ALSO

The great Advantages which would accrue to this Kingdom from an Union with IRELAND.

BY

MALACHY POSTLETHWAYT, Esq;

AUTHOR of the

UNIVERSAL DICTIONARY of TRADE and COMMERCE, &c.

VOL. II.

LONDON:

Printed for D. BROWNE, without Temple-Bar; A. MILLAR, in the Strand; J. WHISTON and B. WHITE, and W. SANDBY, in Fleet-street. M DCC LVII.

TO THE

RIGHT HONOURABLE

THE

MARQUIS of GRANBY,

Major-General of His Majeſty's Forces, and one of the Knights of the Shire for the County of CAMBRIDGE.

MY LORD,

IT is the duty of every true friend to his country to exert himſelf to the utmoſt, according to his talents, in the public ſervice, in ſuch perilous times as the preſent are. Though my talents

lents are cut out only for writing for the intereſt and honour of the nation, they may not be leſs neceſſary and uſeful to the ſtate than the abilities of thoſe who are formed to ſerve it in any other capacity.

Your Lordſhip, as well as His Grace your father, having honoured me with your patronage of my Dictionary of Commerce, and the following political Diſſertations, corroborating and extending many parts of what is therein urged, they have a ſort of claim to Your Lordſhip's countenance and protection: nor could I, conſiſtent with that high regard and veneration that I have profeſſed for your noble family, have addreſſed thoſe diſcourſes to others.

There are other motives too, My Lord, for requeſting Your Lordſhip to accept of this freſh teſtimony of my regard. Your Lordſhip, like the noble duke your father, is eſteemed and beloved by all parties; and as this treatiſe tends to promote an happy union

union amongſt any miniſtry that ſhall be appointed, Your patronizing of this work will convince the adminiſtration that Your Lordſhip is a friend to that union, concord, and harmony that are ſo neceſſary at preſent to the proſperity and glory of the nation.

THIS work, My Lord, may be conſidered as a kind of *political chart*, whereby the rulers of the kingdom may ſteer clear of thoſe rocks and ſhoals whereon their predeceſſors have unhappily ſtruck.

I WILL not preſume to tell Your Lordſhip that the chart is complete. If it ſhall be found pretty correct, as far as I have extended it, I may be excited to make further efforts to render the ſame as perfect as I am able; and I aſſure Your Lordſhip that I have great materials for the purpoſe; ſome of which I have had the honour to ſhew you; and Your Lordſhip knows that I do not want application, and I hope my health will permit me to ſpend the remainder of my life for the intereſt of my country.

But there are many things, which the courſe of my ſtudies has led me to, that are by no means proper to be made public, they giving the enemy advantage over us; for that, Your Lordſhip well knows, which will do great public ſervice, may be converted to do no leſs public injury. Theſe things I reſerve, as being fit only to be laid before the adminiſtration in manuſcript; and I hope Your Lordſhip will act in concert with His Grace your father, that my good intentions may produce the deſired effect. I am, with the higheſt veneration,

My Lord,

Your Lordſhip's

Moſt humble and

Obedient ſervant,

Malachy Postlethwayt.

CONTENTS

TO THE

SECOND VOLUME.

DIS-

CONTENTS.

DISSERTATION XXV.

DISSERTATION XXVI.

DISSERTATION XXVII.

DISSERTATION XXVIII.

DIS-

CONTENTS.

DISSERTATION XXIX.

DISSERTATION XXX.

DISSERTATION XXXI.

DISSERTATION XXXII.

DIS-

CONTENTS.

DIS-

CONTENTS.

DISSERTATION XXXVI.

DISSERTATION XXXVII.

POLI-

POLITICAL DISSERTATIONS ON THE British trade, and commerce, and other interesting subjects, &c.

DISSERTATION XX.

The system of policy pursued by France, from the year 1701, *to the present time, in relation to her* AMERICAN AFFAIRS; *whereby it will appear by what steady measures that nation has become so powerful in that part of the world; being an abridgment of their statutes, with respect to those colonies; extracted from their royal ordonnances, edicts, and arrets; with suitable observations thereon, interesting to these kingdoms.*

HAVING, in our preceding dissertations, delineated with all brevity the formidable views of France in America, it will be necessary to point out the gradual steps whereby those mighty things are proposed to be accomplished

pliſhed by the French court; for when all theſe things are *connectedly* laid properly before us, with their whole conjunctive force, we ſhall be the better capable of defeating thoſe deſtructive deſigns, wherewith this nation is at preſent threatened.

THAT we may have the requiſite evidence before us, whereby a right judgment may be made of the matter, it will be proper to take a retroſpect of the ſtate of the French iſlands and other colonies before 1701; and we can depend on no accounts thereof more authentic than thoſe given by the French board of trade themſelves, in their memorial to the royal council; which is as follows, viz.

" WHEN once, ſays the board, this commerce ſhall be well eſtabliſhed [meaning that of the ſugar iſlands] and our colonies ſhall be ſufficiently ſtocked, it will not be difficult for us to imitate the Engliſh of Jamaica in the traffic they have with the Spaniards. We may, by the way of St. Domingo, trade in negroes: by favour of that trade, we might vend great quantities of our goods and manufactures to the Spaniards of the neighbouring iſlands, and on the coaſt of the continent, and might get of them a great deal of gold and ſilver in exchange *. The grand occur-

* In conſequence hereof, before the peace of Utrecht, the French had the Aſſiento for ſupplying the Spaniſh Weſt-Indies with negroes; which proved the means of introducing immenſe

occurrence of the union of France and Spain gives us hopes of an open commerce, and

---

immense quantities of the French manufactures into Spanish America. But when they had greatly enriched themselves thereby, and so overdone this trade as to render it good for nothing to any successor, they very wisely transferred the Assiento, by the treaty of Utrecht, to our English South-Sea company; and what the company and the nation got by it, as it was modelled and conducted, is too well known to need explanation. But here it may be needful to prevent a mistake in the reader, lest he should apprehend, that our obtaining a proper Assiento from Spain; and that conducted as it ought to be, must necessarily prove a disadvantageous contract. On the contrary, it might easily be shewn to be quite otherwise, as well to the crown of Spain as Great Britain, and might prove the cement of great friendship between those two kingdoms. And before the late peace of Aix la Chapelle was concluded, and the affair of the South-Sea company were settled, I was desired by a certain person of distinction to state the nature of such a new Assiento, in order to lay before a certain great man; which I did, and the consequence thereof will appear in my memoirs of the transactions of that certain great man.

To such a degree did the French trade in the South-Seas, by virtue of their Assiento, that they were enabled, by a computation made from the several registers in Spain, and remittances otherwise made (according to authentic intelligence now lying before me) to import into the French dominions TWO HUNDRED AND FOUR MILLIONS OF PIECES OF EIGHT; which reduced the Spanish West Indies to such a degree of misery, as obliged the viceroy of Peru to present a memorial to his Catholic Majesty, representing the grievances under which the trade laboured, by the French being permitted and encouraged in the carrying on such a destructive trade in the South-Seas; which had, according to the words of the Spanish memorial, occasioned—The whole trade to be at a stand—The treasure of the kingdom to disperse different ways—All commercial negociations to be embarrased—The merchants to be ruined—The subjects to be miserable—The quinto's (or king's duties of one-fifth) to be decreased—The duties in general to be misapplied—The public revenue in general dissipated—The traders in general to become beggars—And the French reaping all the benefit.

an

an eaſy correſpondence, which may enable us *to undertake any thing*. We have a great many ſhips which lie uſeleſs in our ports, and are rotting for want of employment. The intendants of the maritime provinces can atteſt this truth: it is grievous to the king's ſubjects to ſee their ſhipping periſh thus, while they might make good uſe of them, had they the liberty which they deſire.

THEN follow the meaſures preſcribed by this board, in order to eſtabliſh the ſugar-trade of France, and divers other things eſſentially neceſſary to their general commerce.

" IT is neceſſary to repreſent, continue the board, that the duties which were ſettled by the arrets of the 20th of June, 1698, on the white ſugars imported from the iſlands, at 15 livres, over and above the 3 per cent. duty to the domaine of the weſt, are too high, and prejudicial to the commerce of France, and advantageous to the trade of foreigners, for the reaſons following:

I. THE Portugal ſugars, which are imported into France, pay but 15 livres the hundred weight, and are exempted from the duty of 3 per cent. of the weſtern domaine, which thoſe of our colonies pay.

II. HIGH duties hinder great conſumption; the dearer any thing is, the more ſparing are people in uſing it; this is contrary to the deſign of improving the colonies. Beſides, it it is certain, that when ſugars come to ſink in their price, they cannot bear ſo high a duty: it will, therefore, be expedient to reduce the duty of 15 livres to 8, and the duty on brown from 3 livres to 30 ſols; for, at this very time, white ſugars are worth but from 25 to 30 livres the hundred weight, and the brown from 12 to 13 livres.

III. WHEN the crop of ſugars ſhall be in any degree plentiful, the enterpoſt ought to be allowed, to favour the vending of it, and carrying of the over-ſtock to foreigners. In Holland the brown ſugars pay but 20 ſols, and the white but 30 ſols; it would therefore be convenient to reduce the duties in France to ſuch a foot, that our ſugars might be carried out with the ſame advantages as thoſe of other nations.

THE royal council ſeems to have deſigned to remedy theſe inconveniences, by the arret of the 28th of June, 1698, which allows the carrying directly to foreign parts clayed and refined ſugars, paying only the 3 per cent. duty of the weſtern domaine.

BUT the execution of this arret would be prejudicial to the ſtate, becauſe the French ſhips, going directly from the American iſland to foreign ports, are neceſſitated, after they have unladen, to refit; this creates expence, money muſt be laid out in ſubſiſting the ſhips companies, and in revictualling to return to France. This is conſuming foreign commodities; our carpenters, ſail-makers,

makers, rope-makers, and other mechanics, who work to the ſea, are deprived of the profits, which they would reap, if the ſhips made their voyage directly back to France.

THE crews oblige the captains to pay them their wages, it cannot be avoided, the cargo being a ſecurity for the wages of the ſeamen; this money is diſſipated among foreigners in debauchery, and their families, which are in France, are deprived of their ſubſiſtence: in a word, this practice will ruin our navigation, inſtead of increaſing it.

IV. THE miſmanagement of the clerks (or agents) of the farmers, is very prejudicial to the commerce; they make a difficulty to return the duties (or pay the drawbacks) which they are obliged to do, when the ſugars refined in France are ſent out of the kingdom: they take advantage of their authority, and of the protection with which the council honours them; the length and charge of the proceedings diſcourage the merchants.

V. PROVISION ſhould be made by proper regulations, againſt the frauds which the inhabitants of the iſlands are apt to commit. Care has been already taken to correct thoſe which they uſed in making of ſugars, by ordering every one to put his mark on the caſks with a hot marking-iron, in order to diſcover and proceed againſt the culpable: it is neceſſary to oblige every one of the inhabitants to keep in his houſe a good beam and ſcales, with weights of lead or iron, marked according to the ſtandard, and to forbid them to make uſe of ſtillards and weights of ſtone. It is likewiſe neceſſary to oblige the director, who was paid a duty for weighing after the rate of one per cent. for all goods, though he does not weigh them, to ſend every year an expert maſter-weigher, with braſs weights, and other neceſſaries, for aſcertaining, and marking according to the ſtandard, all the weights of the inhabitants, making them pay for the materials added to defective weights, and this for remedying the frequent abuſes which are committed by falſe weights.

THE deputies are obliged to obſerve further to the royal council, that, for three or four years paſt, a duty is levied at St. Domingo of two ſols per livre on indigo ſhipped off there. This novelty is the more pernicious, becauſe that drug ſerves for dying our manufactures in blues or blacks, and becauſe we make a conſiderable traffic thereof to the north. It is of great importance for the royal council to be pleaſed to take off this duty, which is capable of ruining the cultivation of this drug, which is very near as good as that of Guatamala.

VI. IT might be proper to add to the regulation by which the council enjoins every ſhip to carry a certain number of lads or fellows, who hire themſelves to ſervice for augmenting the colonies, which might be taken

out

out of the Hotel Dieu, and maids brought up to, and expert in manufactures, to be married to the hired men-servants after they have served out their times; and to forbear sending the common prostitutes, who are more likely to corrupt and infect the country, than to people it; and, as there are abundance of beggars in France able to work, who live in perfect idleness, it would be essential to order the justices to cause numbers of them to be taken up, and shipped off to our colonies.

VII. Lastly, it would be convenient to establish four consular jurisdictions, in the islands of St. Domingo, St. Christopher, Martinico, and Guardeloupe, in the nature of those established in France: they might be composed of one judge and four consuls, who might decide sovereignly all causes to the sum of ——, and for the greater sums, give a liberty of appeal to the sovereign court of the place.

About forty years ago the French were little versed in commerce, and little skilled in navigation. In those days it was necessary to form companies, and to grant them privileges, in order to engage them to beat out, for the king's subjects, tracks of commerce which were unknown to them. It is expedient and very beneficial to the state to act in the like manner, as often as new settlements of colonies, clearing and cultivating of new discovered places, or new inventions are pro-

posed;

posed; yet, in these cases, the privileges ought not to be granted but for a certain number of years: but, unless on such occasions, nothing is more destructive to a state than exclusive privileges."

No man of sense, can read these sentiments of the French deputies of commerce, which they laid before the royal council, but must applaud them, they being so well adapted to the advancement of colonies, especially, in their infancy, as it were: nay, we find, from the sense of these deputies themselves, that the whole trade of France was then but in it's infant state; for they acknowledge, that, about forty years before this, the French were little versed in commerce, and little skilled in navigation: and, although England has had the start of them in trade and navigation by some ages, yet we experience, that they have already overtaken us. Could they have possibly effectuated these great things, if the laws and regulations of their trade, and the encouragements they have constantly given within this century, were not exquisitely well calculated to answer the end proposed? They had the advantage, indeed, of our laws for their guidance; and they have shewed as much sagacity in imitating the best, as in rejecting the worse: whereby they have, in many respects, improved in their laws and regulations of commerce and navigation upon ours; and, if there is any thing importantly useful to be borrowed

from

from them in our turn, it is to be hoped, that we ſhall not be ſo unwiſe as to condemn it, becauſe it is of French production.

Regulations concerning hired ſervants, and fire-arms, exported by merchantmen to the French colonies in America and New France. November 16, 1716, regiſtered in parliament.

Of hired or articled ſervants.

ARTICLE I.

ALL captains of merchantmen that ſhall go to the French colonies of America, and New France, or Canada, excepting thoſe in tho negro trade, ſhall be obliged to carry thither hired ſervants, viz. a ſhip of 60 tons, and under, ſhall carry three hired ſervants; from 60 to 100, four ditto; and, from 100 and upwards, ſix hired ſervants.

2. The terms of carrying theſe ſervants ſhall be mentioned in the permiſſion given by the admiral to the captain for ſailing.

3. Thoſe ſervants ſhall be between the age of 18 and 43, none leſs than four feet in ſtature, ſtrong, fit to work, and ſhall ſerve three years.

4. Such ſervants ſhall be examined by the officers of the admiralty at the port from whence the ſhips ſhall ſail, and thoſe ſhall be rejected who are not qualified according

to

to the preceding article, and of a good conſtitution.

5. The particular characteriſtics of the ſervants ſhall be minuted in the ſhip's book.

6. Such of them that are handicrafts-men and mechanics, uſeful to the colonies, ſhall be accounted as two, and the trade each is of ſhall be ſpecified.

7. The captains of ſuch merchantmen, as ſoon as arrived, ſhall deliver them to the commiſſary appointed for the purpoſe, who ſhall examine whether they anſwer the deſcriptions required, and are the identical perſons who embarked.

8. The captains and inhabitants of the colonies ſhall agree upon the price; but, if they cannot agree, the commiſſaries ſhall oblige thoſe inhabitants that have not the number of hired ſervants required by the ordinances, to take them, and ſettle the price.

9. The captains ſhall bring a certificate from the commiſſioners, teſtifying the ſaid ſervants to be the ſame as embarked.

10. The captains, on their return to France, ſhall produce the ſaid certificate to the officers of the admiralty

11. The captains and owners of ſhips ſhall be abſolutely condemned in the penalty of 200 livres for every ſuch articled ſervant not carried to the colonies, without appeal.

Of fire-arms.

Article I.

All captains of merchantmen who ſhall ſail to the iſland colonies in America, and New France, or Canada, except thoſe who are concerned in the negro-trade, ſhall be obliged to carry thither in each veſſel four buccaneer-guns, or four fuſees for hunting, mounted with braſs.

2. The condition upon which theſe guns may be carried, ſhall be inſerted in the permiſſion given by the admiral for ſuch ſhips to ſail.

3. Theſe buccaneer-guns ſhall be four feet four inches long, light, and carry balls of 18 to the mark pound weight.

4. The fuſees for hunting ſhall be four feet long, and light.

5. The ſaid captains ſhall, on arrival in the colonies, depoſit the ſaid arms into the king's arſenal where they ſhall land, in order to be examined and proved in the governor's preſence.

6. If any piece ſhall not hold in the proof, the captain ſhall be fined 30 livres.

7. The ſaid 30 livres ſhall be immediately laid out by the governor in buccaneer-hunting-guns, and diſtributed to the poor inhabitants.

8. The ſaid captains ſhall leave the ſaid arms till they are ſold, or till the governor

ſhall

ſhall have diſtributed them among the companies of the militia; in which caſe he, in concert with the intendant or commiſſary, ſhall order payment for the ſame.

9. The captains ſhall take a certificate from the governor, atteſted by the intendant, of the ſending back ſuch guns, and of the ſum paid on account of not ſtanding proof.

10. They ſhall alſo be obliged, on their return to France, and in making their declaration, to carry with them the ſaid certificate to the officers of the admiralty.

11. The captains and owners of ſuch merchantmen ſhall be condemned by the officers of the admiralty in 50 livres fine for every ſuch gun that they ſhall omit to carry into the colonies, without appeal.

Of proſecutions and fines.

ARTICLE I.

ALL proſecutions, occaſioned in diſregard to the ſaid regulations, ſhall be undertaken by the king's ſollicitor of the admiralty.

2. The fines made to the admiralty ſhall belong to the admiral; and thoſe made by the marble-table, the one half ſhall go to the admiralty, the other to the king, according to the ordinance of 1681.

THE governors, intendants, or commiſſaries in the colonies, ſhall jointly tranſmit an account every half-year to the council of marine,

rine, of the number of articled ſervants and guns that every merchant ſhall ſend to the colonies, of the ſums paid for defective arms, and how the arms have been employed.

In conſequence of which, letters patents were granted by the king, in the manner we have before given inſtances of, to cauſe the ſaid regulations to be duly obſerved in his dominions.

It is obvious enough, from the leaſt reflection, that, (1) The intention of the preceding regulations is, to people the French colonies with a number of whites proportionate to that of blacks, that the latter might not be an over-match for the former, and diſturb the plantations with inſurrections. (2) That, by ſending over French workmen, as articled ſervants, is to render labour cheaper in the plantations, and ſo far to inſtruct the negroes in ſuch workmanſhip as may render them the more ſerviceable to the planters. And, (3) To accuſtom the people to the uſe of arms, as well to defend their colonies at the leaſt expence to the crown, as to train them to hunting, and that not only to ſupply them with food at the leaſt expence, but for the ſake of the peltry trade in New France, or Canada, which is the eſſential article of that commerce.

Marine laws to be obſerved in all the ports of the iſlands and French colonies, wherever ſituated. Of January the 12th, 1717.

Of the judges of the admiralty, and their juriſdiction.

ARTICLE I.

THERE ſhall be, for the future, judges appointed, well ſkilled in MARITIME AFFAIRS in all the French colonies, and in all places where the French have ſettlements, called officers of the admiralty, diſtinct from the civil ones, who ſhall conform themſelves according to the ordinances made in 1681, and other marine laws.

THE king's * lieutenants and ſollicitors cannot be admitted till 25 years of age; if they are not graduates, yet that ſhall be diſpenſed with, provided they have a competent knowledge of the maritime laws and ordinances, in which they ſhall undergo an examination before admittance.

Of the methods of proceeding in the courts of admiralty and their judgments.

DEMANDS for the payment of part, or all a ſhip's cargo, ready to ſail to France from

* A lieutenant, in this ſenſe, is a magiſtrate that preſides in the courts of admiralty, to ſee that the royal edicts, ordinances, &c. are duly put in execution.

the

the colonies, ſhall be tried *ſummarily*, and executed, notwithſtanding an appeal, and the detainers of ſuch merchandiſes ſhall be compelled by the ſail of their effects, and even by the detention of their perſon, to diſcharge their obligation, &c.

Of granting permiſſions for ſailing, and reports relating thereunto.

NO veſſel ſhall ſail from the ports and havens of the colonies, and other French eſtabliſhments, either to return into France, or to paſs from one colony to another, without permiſſion or licence from the admiral, on pain of confiſcation of ſhip and cargo, &c.

THE maſters of ſhips whoſe ordinary navigation lies in carrying ſugars, or other merchandiſes, from one port to another in the ſame iſland, as alſo thoſe who navigate from iſland to iſland, and go from Martinico to the iſlands of Guardeloupe, Grenade, Grenadins, Tobago, Mary Galante, St. Martin, St. Bartholomew, St. Alouzie, and St. Vincent, St. Dominico, and thoſe that go from the iſland of Cayenne to the province of Guiana, to the coaſt of St. Domingo, and to the iſland of Tortuga, ſhall take licences from the admiralty, which ſhall be granted to them for one year.

THOSE who carry on trade from the Iſle Royal, or Cape Breton, from port to port, or who go to the adjacent iſlands, as the iſland of Sable to that in the gulph of St. Laurence,

rence, and to the coaſts of the ſaid gulph, ſhall likewiſe take out licences from the admiralty, which ſhall be granted them for one year; but, if they come to Quebec, they ſhall take out a new licence.

THE maſters of the ſaid ſhips, before receiving their licences, ſhall give ſecurity not to go into any iſland, or to any foreign coaſt, on pain of confiſcation of ſhip and cargo, and a fine of 300 livres.

THE maſters of ſhips, who ſhall trade in the river and gulph of St. Lawrence, ſhall alſo take licences from the admiral, which ſhall be granted them for a year; and thoſe that ſhall go from Quebec to Cape Breton ſhall do the ſame.

LICENCES for fiſhing ſhall not be granted without the conſent of the governors, who ſhall take cognizance of that branch of trade, that it is not abuſed by trading with foreigners.

ALL maſters of ſhips arriving in the colonies and other French ſettlements, ſhall be obliged to make their report to the lieutenant-general of the admiralty, 24 hours after their arrival, on pain of ſuffering an arbitrary fine.

EXCEPTING only thoſe, who arriving at Cape Breton on the fiſhery account, for they may enter into the ports and havens where there is no admiralty; in which caſe they ſhall make their report at the neareſt place where there is a court of admiralty, and that

within

within one month or more from the time of their arrival, under the ſame penalty.

His majeſty forbids all maſters of ſhips from unloading any merchandiſes before making their report, unleſs in caſe of imminent danger, on pain as well of corporal puniſhment, as confiſcation of the merchandiſes ſo unloaded.

The king's ſollicitor of every court of admiralty ſhall be obliged, at the end of every year, to ſend to the admiral a ſtate of the officers of the admiralty of their juriſdiction, and of whatever has occurred of importance, as likewiſe a liſt of the ſhips arrived there, with the day of their arrival, and of their departure, according to the manner that ſhall be preſcribed them.

All merchants, maſters, and captains of ſhips, are forbid navigating in the American ſeas, to carry on any commerce with foreigners or to land with this intent on the coaſt or iſlands of their ſettlements, under pain the firſt time, of confiſcation of ſhip and cargo, and, in caſe of repetition, the maſters and ſailors ſhall be ſent to the gallies.

The maſters and pilots, in making their report, ſhall repreſent their licences, declare the time and place of their departure, and the loading of their ſhips, the courſe they have ſteered, the hazards they run, the accidents happened to their veſſel, and every circumſtance relating to their voyage.—They ſhall alſo repreſent the journal of their voyage, which ſhall

ſhall be returned to them, if deſired, by the officers of the admiralty, within eight days, and without any expence, after they ſhall have extracted whatever is requiſite to render the ſaid navigation more ſecure *, of which they ſhall take care to give an account to the admiral every three months.

THE captains and maſters of ſhips who arrive from the French colonies in the ports of France, ſhall be obliged, in making their report, in what manner they were received in the colonies, how juſtice was adminiſtered to them, and what charges and averages they were obliged to pay from their arrival to their departure: his majeſty commands the officers of the admiralty to interrogate the maſters and captains upon theſe particulars; to receive the complaints of the paſſengers and ſailors, who have any to make †, and to direct a verbal proceſs thereof, which ſhall be made, in order to be ſent to the admiral of France.

Of the viſiting of ſhips.

ON the arrival of ſhips, the officers of the admiralty ſhall viſit them, according to the edict of 1711. They ſhall take account with

* This is certainly a very judicious regulation, and tends greatly to the ſecurity of navigation.

† This alſo is mighty well calculated for the regulation of navigation.

what merchandiſes they are laden, what ſailors they have, what paſſengers they have brought, and they ſhall ſignify the day of the ſhip's arrival, and ſhall verbally give an account thereof.

THE viſitation of ſhips intended to return to France, ſhall be made before their loading is taken in, by the officers of the admiralty, with an approved carpenter, and in preſence of the maſter, who ſhall be obliged to aſſiſt therein, under pain of an arbitrary fine, to examine if the veſſel is in fit condition for the voyage intended.—They ſhall likewiſe examine into all the ſhip's tackle, and every thing thereunto belonging, excepting the ſailors and the proviſions, and this before one or two captains appointed for that purpoſe by the officers of the admiralty, in order to know whether the ſhip is fit for the voyage in all reſpects; and the maſters of ſhips who are preparing for their loading ſhall be obliged to apprize the officers of the admiralty thereof, two days before they begin ſo to do, under the penalty, for diſregard hereof, of the expence of unloading the ſaid ſhip, and reloading of another *.

THEY ſhall alſo take the declaration of the maſter, with regard to the quantity and quality of the proviſions, in order to judge whe-

* Is not this exquiſite policy, for many reaſons that will naturally occur to the judicious reader?

ther

ther they are competent to the length of the voyage, and the number of ſailors and paſſengers.

If two thirds of the ſailors make declaration againſt the maſter of the ſhip and the purveyor, that the proviſions are not of good quality, or that there is not the quantity mentioned in the maſter's declaration, the officers of the admiralty ſhall teſtify the ſame: and, in caſe the declaration proves falſe, the maſter and the purveyor ſhall be each condemned in the fine of 100 livres, and to take the proviſions themſelves as ſhall be ordered, which ſhall be proſecuted by the ſollicitor of the admiralty, and of another *whom the ſailors ſhall nominate*,, &c.

The officers of the admiralty ſhall prepare a verbal proceſs of the condition of the ſhip, of the tackle and the proviſions; a copy of which ſhall be delivered to the maſters, who are obliged to repreſent the ſame to the admiralty at the place of their return, under the penalty of an arbitrary fine.

Then follow letters patents of the ſame date, ratifying the foregoing, and ordering the ſtrict execution thereof; of the nature of which, as we have given inſtances before, we ſhall not repeat the ſame.

The

THE king's letters patent, concerning the regulations for the commerce of the French colonies, of the month of April, 1717.

ARTICLE I.

THE armaments of ſhips intended to ſail to the ſaid iſland colonies, ſhall be made in the ports of Calais, Dieppe, Havre, Rouen, Honfleur, St. Malo, Morlaix, Breſt, Nantes, Rochelle, Bourdeaux, Bayonne, and Cette.

2. MERCHANTS, who ſhall fit out ſhips in the ports of the cities aforeſaid, for the French iſlands and colonies, ſhall give ſecurity to the ſecretary of the admiralty, whereby they ſhall be bound under the penalty of ten thouſand livres to cauſe their ſhips to return directly from the colonies into the ſame port from which they ſailed, unleſs otherwiſe compelled by ſtreſs of weather or ſhipwreck; and the merchants ſhall cauſe ſuch ſecurities to be depoſited in the farmer of the revenue's office.

3. All proviſions and merchandiſes, either of the production or fabrication of the kingdom of France, even ſilver plate, wines and brandies of Guyenne, or other provinces, deſigned to be exported to the French iſland colonies, ſhall be exempted from all duties of exportation and importation, as well from thoſe of the provinces of the five great farms, as of thoſe reputed foreign provinces; and likewiſe from all local duties, in carrying mer-

chan-

chandiſes from one province to another, and in general from all other duties, which tend to our advantage, thoſe only excepted, which relate to the general farm of aids, &c.

4. All warlike ammunition, proviſions, and other things neceſſary, bought in the kingdom for the victualling and fitting out of ſhips appointed for the French iſlands and colonies, ſhall enjoy the ſame exemption from duties.

5. The proviſions and merchandiſes of the kingdom, appointed for the French iſlands and colonies, and coming from one ſea-port to another in the kingdom, ſhall be, upon their arrival in the ports, where intended to be landed in the ſaid iſles and colonies, warehouſed, and not be moved from ſhip to ſhip, on pain of confiſcation, and a thouſand livres penalty.

6. Merchants who ſhall have brought proviſions and merchandiſes of the kingdom into the port, appointed for embarkation, ſhall be obliged to declare, at the cuſtom-houſe of the place of their unloading, if there is any one, if not, at the neareſt to the ſaid place, the quantity, quality, weight and meaſure of the proviſions and merchandiſes deſigned for the French iſles and colonies, in order to have them viſited, leaded, or marked, by the commiſſioners of the farms, to have their ſecurity diſcharged, and be obliged to return, within three months, a certificate of their being taken from the depoſitory

warehouſe for embarkation, as before declared; but ſuch embarkation may be made without warehouſing of proviſions and merchanchandiſes brought by land or river-carriage.

7. Carriers ſhall be obliged to repreſent, and cauſe to be examined, thoſe diſcharges of ſecurity by the commiſſioners and directors of the farms in the cities, wherever they are eſtabliſhed; and the ſaid commiſſioners ſhall teſtify, without any delay or expence, the number of tons, caſes, &c. included in the ſaid diſcharge, and obſerve if the leads and marks affixed, &c. are entire and undefaced, without minutely examining into the ſaid proviſions and merchandiſes, or opening the tons, bales, or caſes, &c. unleſs the leads, &c. ſhall be broken, defaced, or changed. —And if, on examination, any fraud appears, the goods ſhall be confiſcated, and the offenders condemned in 500 livres penalty.

8. The ſaid proviſions and merchandiſes ſhall, before their embarkation, be viſited and weighed by the commiſſioners of the farm, in order to aſcertain the quantity, quality, weight, and meaſure thereof, and they ſhall not be laden in any veſſel without the ſaid commiſſioners being preſent.

9. Merchants ſhall give ſecurity to the officer of the farms at the port of embarkation, to report, in a twelvemonth or more, a certificate of the diſcharge of the ſaid proviſions and merchandiſes in the French iſlands and colonies; and the ſaid certificate ſhall be wrote

wrote on the back of the difcharge of the fecurity, and figned by the governors and intendants, or by the commandants and commiffioners fubdelegated in their refpective diftricts, and by the commiffioners of the farms of the weftern domaine, on pain of paying four times the duties.

10. Provifions and merchandifes coming from foreign countries, whofe confumption is allowed in the kingdom, even thofe which come from Marfeilles and Dunkirk, fhall be liable to the duties of importation due to the firft office of farms, by which they fhall enter into the kingdom, notwithftanding they fhall have been declared to be intended for the French iflands and colonies; but, when they fhall be exported to the faid iflands and colonies, they fhall be entitled to the exemptions mentioned by the third article.

11. We permit, notwithftanding, to come from foreign countries, into the ports beforementioned in the firft article, falt beef, to be fent into the faid iflands and colonies, and the fame fhall be free from all duties of importation and exportation, on condition that it fhall be warehoufed as aforefaid, on pain of confifcation.

12. Merchants of our kingdom fhall not load for the French iflands and colonies, any foreign merchandizes whofe importation and confumption are prohibited, on pain of confifcation, and 3000 livres fine, which fhall be impofed by the officers of the admiralty.

13. The ſilk, and other merchandizes of Avignon, and the county of Venaiſine, which ſhall be declared for the french iſlands and colonies, ſhall pay the duties required at importation, and be exempt from all duties of exportation, and all others, thoſe excepted which depend on the general farm of aids and domaines.

14. Swiſs linens that are free from all duties of importation, ſhall not be allowed the exemptions mentioned by article the third, although deſigned for the French iſlands and colonies.

15. Merchandizes and proviſions of all ſorts, of the produce of the French iſlands and colonies, ſhall be warehouſed at their arrival in the ports of Calais, Dieppe, Havre, Rouen, Honfleur, Rochelle, Bourdeaux, Bayonne, and Cette; to the end that, when they are unhouſed to be exported into foreign countries, they ſhall be entitled to the exemption of duties of importation and exportation; even to thoſe belonging to the farms of the weſtern domaine, with a reſerve only of three per cent. to which they ſhall be liable, &c.

16. Merchants of the cities before-mentioned, who ſhall export by ſea merchandizes which come from the ſaid iſlands and colonies, ſhall be obliged to make a declaration at the office of farms eſtabliſhed in the port from whence they ſhall depart, of the place where they are intended to be ſent into foreign coun-

countries, and to give ſecurity, within ſix months, or longer, to report a certificate in proper form of their unloading, ſigned by the French conſul; and, in caſe of his abſence, by the judges of the place, or other public perſons, on pain of paying four times the duties.

17. Merchants belonging to the ports mentioned in the firſt article, ſhall be allowed to ſend by land, into foreign countries, raw ſugars, indigo, ginger, rocou', and cacao, which come from the French iſlands and colonies, and cauſe them to paſs, by tranſit, through the kingdom, without payment of duties of import or export, nor other duties, except thoſe depending on the general farm of aids and domaines, on condition of declaring to the office of farms, at the port of their departure, the quantities, qualities, weights, and meaſures, and of having them viſited and leaded, and taking the diſcharge of their ſecurity, and promiſe, within four months or later, to produce a certificate of the ſending ſuch merchandize out of the kingdom; which certificate ſhall be wrote and ſigned on the back of the ſaid diſcharge of the ſecurity, by the commiſſioners of the laſt office of farms at their going out of the kingdom, after the ſaid commiſſioners have allowed the leads, and viſited the ſaid merchandizes; and the carriers ſhall be obliged to cauſe the ſaid diſcharges to be inſpected by the ſaid commiſſioners

ſioners of the farms of that rout, and by the directors of the farms, where ſuch are eſtabliſhed: all which muſt be done and performed on pain of paying four times the duties, and confiſcation of the carriages and horſes of ſuch who ſhall neglect or offend as carriers.—Theſe precautions taken, the ſaid merchandizes ſhall not be opened, and the ſaid directors and commiſſioners ſhall verify, without any delay or expence whatever, the number of tons, caſks, bales, &c. and examine if the leads thereunto affixed are whole and entire; but, in caſe the ſaid leads are broke or altered, or any way defaced, then they are to viſit the ſaid merchandizes, and ſeize them in caſe of the laws being violated, the goods to be confiſcated, and the offenders condemned in 500 livres fine.

18. The five following ſorts of merchandizes, which ſhall be ſent by tranſit into foreign countries, ſhall go out of the kingdom by no other places than thoſe hereafter named, viz. thoſe appointed for the ports of Spain, ſituate on the Mediterranean-Sea, by the ports of Cette and Agde.

19. Thoſe which ſhall go out of the kingdom by the land for Spain, by the office of farms, from Bayonne, by the way of Beobie, Aſcaing, and Dainhoa.

20. Thoſe deſigned for Italy, by the ſaid ports of Cette and Agde.—Thoſe for Savoy and Piedmont, by the office of Pont de Beauvoiſin, and of Champarillan.—Thoſe for Geneva

neva and Switzerland, by the office of Seiſſel and Coulonges.—Thoſe for Franche Comte, by the office d'Auxonne.—Thoſe deſigned for the three biſhoprics, and Lorrain and Alſace, by the office of St. Minehould and Auxonne.—And thoſe deſigned for the Low Countries, belonging to foreign nations, by the office of Liſle and Maubeuge.

21. We abſolutely forbid the ſaid merchandizes going out of the kingdom by other ports and offices, when they paſs by tranſit, with exemption of duties, on pain of confiſcation of merchandizes, carriages, and horſes, and liable to 3000 livres penalty.

22. The merchandizes hereafter ſpecified coming from the French iſlands and colonies, and allowed to be conſumed in the kingdom, ſhall pay, for the future, for duties of importation in the ports of Calais, Dieppe, Havre, Rouen, Honfleur, Rochelle, Bourdeaux, Bayonne, and Cette; viz.

Muſcavado, or raw ſugars, the hundred weight, 2 livres 10 ſols; 33 ſols, 4 deniers of which, ſhall be appropriated to the farmer-general of the weſtern domaine revenue, and 16 ſols 8 deniers to the farmer-general of the five great farms.—The clay or caſſonade ſugars, 8 livres per hundred weight; 2 of which ſhall be appropriated to the farmer-general of the five great farms.—Indigo, 100 ſols per hundred weight.—Ginger 15 ſols per hundred weight.—Cotton-wool, 30 ſols per hundred.—Rocou, 2 livres 10 ſols per

100 weight. Sweet-meats and preſerves, 5 livres per hundred weight.—Caſſia, 1 livre per hundred weight.—Cacao, 10 livres per hundred weight.—Dry raw hides, 5 ſols a piece.—Tortoiſe-ſhells of all ſorts, 7 livres per hundred weight.

23. The ſum total of the duties on the ſaid nine laſt ſpecies of merchandize ſhall be appropriated to the farmer-general of the five great farms of the revenue.

24. The merchandizes ſpecified in the preceding article, which ſhall be carried by ſea into the ports of St. Malo, Morlaix, Breſt, and Nantes, may not be brought into the other provinces of the kingdom to be conſumed, but upon payment of the ſame duties.

25. All merchandizes coming from the French iſlands and colonies ſhall pay, upon their arrival in the ſaid ports of Bretagne, above and beſides the ordinary duties, thoſe of provoſtſhip, ſuch as are done at Nantes, without any drawback thereof, when the ſaid merchandizes ſhall be exported to foreign countries, nor any diminution of the duties declared by the 19th article, when they are brought into the provinces of the five great farms, or other provinces of the kingdom.

26. White unrefined ſugars coming from the colony of Cayenne, and entering by the ports of Calais, Dieppe, Havre, Rouen,

Honfleur,

Honfleur, Rochelle, Bourdeaux, Bayonne, Cette, and intended for home-confumption, fhall only pay 4 livres per 100 weight, in conformity to the arrets of the 19th of September, 1682, and the 12th of October, 1700. And, with regard to thofe which fhall be carried into the ports of Bretagne, they fhall there pay the fame duties as the clay fugars coming from the other French colonies; viz. at their arrival, the duties of the provoftfhip of Nantes, and other local duties; and, at their paffing out of Bretagne to go into the province of the five great farms, and other provinces of the kingdom, for confumption, the 8 livres mentioned in article 19.

27. Merchandizes coming from the French iflands and colonies, and not mentioned in the 19th article, fhall pay the duties fixed by the tariff of 1664, in the provinces of the five great farms, and the local duties, as has been heretofore done in the provinces reckoned foreign; excepting refined fugars coming from the faid iflands and colonies, which fhall pay, at every entrance of the kingdom, even in the ports of the province of Bretagne and Bayone, 22 livres 10 fols per 100 weight, conformably to the arrets of the 25th of April, 1690, and the 20th of June, 1698.

28. The duties required by the faid arret of the 25th of April, 1690, upon foreign fugars

ſugars of all qualities, ſhall be alſo paid in all the ports of the kingdom, even in the ports of Bretagne, and in thoſe of Marſeilles, Bayonne, and Dunkirk, notwithſtanding all privileges and exemptions before granted: and the ſaid ſugars need not be warehouſed, as required by the ſaid arret of the 25th of April, 1690, or other ſubſequent arrets, which ſhall be made null and void; except nevertheleſs with regard to the caſſonade ſugars of the Brazils, which ſhall be warehouſed in the ports only of Bayonne and Marſeilles, and ſhall not go out of the warehouſe with exemption from the duties required by the arret of the 25th of April, 1690, but to be exported into foreign countries, &c.

29. All merchandizes of the production of the French iſlands and colonies ſhall pay to the farmer-general of the revenues of the weſtern domaine, at their arrival in all the ports of the kingdom, even in the free ports, and in thoſe of the provinces reputed foreign, once for all, 3 per cent. ad valorem, when they ſhall be declared to be exported into foreign countries.

30. We expreſly forbid all the inhabitants of our iſlands and colonies, and all the merchants of our kingdom, to export from the ſaid iſlands and colonies, into foreign countries, or into the foreign neighbouring iſlands, any merchandizes of the produce of the French

French iſlands, on pain of confiſcation of ſhip and merchandize, and of 1000 livres penalty; which ſhall be inflicted by the officers of the admiralty, and the captains and maſters of ſhips to be anſwered in their own name, beſides impriſonment for a year, and alſo to be declared incapable of commanding or ſerving in the quality of an officer aboard of a ſhip; wherefore all captains ſhall be obliged to repreſent, at their arrival in France, a ſtate of the merchandizes that ſhall have been loaded at the ſaid iſlands, ſigned by the commiſſioners of the weſtern domaine.

31. We prohibit alſo, under the like penalties, all merchants of our kingdom, captains and maſters of ſhips deſigned for the French iſlands and colonies, from taking or loading in any foreign country, even in the iſland of Madeira, any wines, or other proviſions and merchandizes, to be carried into the ſaid colonies.

32. All ſorts of ſugars and ſyrups of the French iſlands and colonies ſhall be declared at their arrival in all the ports of the kingdom, by the quantity of the caſks, without the merchants, captains or maſters of ſhips, being obliged to declare them by weight; but the declaration of other merchandizes ſhall be made according to cuſtom, by the quantity, quality, and weight; nor ſhall any merchandizes be unloaded but in the preſence

ſence of the commiſſioners of the farms of the revenue.

33. The warehouſe wherein to depoſit the merchandizes and proviſions of the kingdom, intended for the French iſlands and colonies, as alſo thoſe of the produce of the ſaid iſlands, of ſalt beef from foreign countries, and of caſſonade ſugars of the Brazils, ſhall be choſen by the merchants themſelves, at their own expence, and locked up with three different keys; one of which ſhall be given to the commiſſioners of the great farms of the revenue, the other to the commiſſioner of the farm of the weſtern domaine, and the third into the hands of an overſeer appointed by the merchant himſelf.

34. The eaſineſs of the duties of importation, by theſe preſents laid upon all raw and muſcavado ſugars, coming from the French iſlands and colonies, the taking off the duties impoſed by the arrets of the council of September, 1688, and the 1ſt of September, 1699, upon the footing of 9 livres, and 6 livres 15 ſols, ſhall remain, for the future, regulated at 5 livres, 12 ſols, 6 deniers per 100 weight of refined ſugar, in the cities of Bourdeaux, Rochelle, Rouen, and Dieppe, which ſhall be exported into foreign countries; and of the ſaid 5 livres, 12 ſols, 6 deniers, there ſhall be reſtored 3 livres 15 ſols by the farmer-general of the weſtern domaine, and 1 livre, 17 ſols, 6 deniers, by

by the farmer-general of the five great farms."

On April the 3d, 1718, a royal ordinance was made, prohibiting all captains of ſhips who ſhall carry negroes to the French iſlands, againſt landing them, or any of their cargo, without leave had and obtained from the governors, in order to prevent any contagious diſtemper being ſpread among the inhabitants.

" Royal letters patents, containing regulations of trade between Marſeilles and the French iſlands of America, given at Paris in the month of February, 1719.

ARTICLE I.

The fitting out of veſſels deſigned for the French iſlands and colonies of America, ſhall be done in the port of Marſeilles as in the ports mentioned by our letters patents of the month of April, 1717.

2. Merchants, who fit out ſuch ſhips, ſhall be obliged to apply to the ſecretary of the admiralty of Marſeilles, to oblige themſelves, under the penalty of 10,000 livres, to cauſe ſuch ſhips to return directly into the port of Marſeilles, unleſs compelled by ſhipwreck, or other inevitable accident, juſtifiable by verbal proceſs. The merchants ſhall give ſuch obligation into the office of farms, and ſhall not embark in the ſaid ſhips any proviſions

ſions and merchandizes without permiſſion firſt had and obtained in writing, and in preſence of the commiſſioners of the farms of the revenue, under pain of confiſcation of the ſaid proviſions and merchandizes, and a penalty of 3000 livres, which ſhall be laid by the officers of the admiralty.

3. All proviſions and merchandize of the produce or fabrication of the kingdom, even ſilver plate, wines, and brandies, of Provence, Guyenne, or other provinces of our kingdom arms and ammunition, and all neceſſaries of our kingdom for the victualling and fitting out of ſhips, which ſhall come into the port of Marſeilles to be exported to the French iſlands and colonies, ſhall be exempted from all duties of export or import, as well as thoſe of the provinces of the five great farms, as thoſe reputed foreign provinces; and likewiſe from all local duties, in paſſing from one province to another, and generally from all other duties, which are to our advantage, except thoſe depending on the general farm of aids and domains, which exemption the merchants of Marſeilles cannot be entitled to, without obſerving what is hereafter ordained.

4. The proviſions and merchandizes mentioned in the preceding article, coming by ſea from another port of the kingdom into that of Marſeilles, ſhall, at their arrival, be put into the warehouſe of entrepoſt, and ſhall not be moved from ſhip to ſhip, on pain of confiſcation, and of 1000 livres penalty.

5. Mer-

5. Merchants who ſhall cauſe to be brought to Marſeilles, either by ſea or land, the ſaid proviſions and merchandizes deſigned for the French iſlands and colonies in America, ſhall be obliged to declare, at the office of farms at the place of their unloading, if ſuch office be there; if not, at the neareſt there is, the quantities, qualities, weights, and meaſures, to cauſe them to be viſited and leaded by the commiſſioners of the farms, to take their diſcharge of ſecurity, and to ſubmit to report, within three months, a certificate of their unloading into the warehouſe of the entrepoſt, on their arrival at Marſeilles: we will and decree, that, in ſix months from the regiſtering of theſe preſents, the merchandizes manufactured in different provinces and places of our kingdom, except thoſe in the city and territory of Marſeilles, ſhall be reputed as foreign merchandizes, and ſhall not be ſhipped upon veſſels which ſhall depart from the port of Marſeilles for the French iſlands and colonies, without paying the duties that ſhall be hereby decreed, if, in the place the neareſt to their unlading, declaration has not been made, that they are intended for the ſaid iſlands; and if, upon their arrival in Marſeilles, they have not been put into a warehouſe of entrepoſt.

6. The land-carriers ſhall be obliged to repreſent, and cauſe to be examined, their diſcharges of ſecurity by the commiſſioner of the

the office of farms, and by the directors of the farmers of the revenue, in thoſe cities wherein they are eſtabliſhed, through which the ſaid proviſions and merchandizes paſs; and the ſaid commiſſioners and directors ſhall certify, upon the ſpot, and without delay or expence, the number of tons, caſks, and bales, &c. contained in the ſaid diſcharge of ſecurity, and ſhall inſpect whether the leads affixed thereunto be whole, undefaced, and unchanged, without viſiting the ſaid proviſions and merchandizes, or opening the ſaid tons, caſes or bales, unleſs the leads are broken or altered: and, if on examination any fraud appears, the merchandize ſhall be confiſcated, and the offenders condemned in 500 livres penalty.

7. The ſaid proviſions and merchandizes ſhall be, before their embarkation, viſited and weighed by the commiſſioners of the farms, in order to certify the quantity, quality, weight, and meaſure thereof, and they ſhall not be loaded in any veſſel, but in the preſence of the ſaid commiſſioners.

8. Merchants ſhall make at the office of farms their report, within a twelvemonth or more, a certificate of the unloading of the ſaid proviſions and merchandizes in the French iſlands and colonies; and the ſaid certificate ſhall be wrote on the back of the diſcharge of the ſecurity, and ſigned by the governors and intendants, or by the commandants or commiſſaries, ſubdelegated by the

the commiſſioners of the office of farms of the weſtern domaine eſtabliſhed at Marſeilles, on pain of forfeiting four times the duties.

9. Proviſions and merchandiſes coming from foreign countries, the conſumption of which is allowed in the country, and which ſhall be received in the port, city, or territory of Marſeilles, ſhall not be embarked to be exported to the French iſlands in America, till declaration has been made at the office of farms, of their quantity, quality, weight, and meaſure, and that the ſame duties have been paid at the office as required, when they were firſt imported into the kingdom.

10. Foreign proviſions and merchandiſes, which ſhall be conſumed in the kingdom, and which, after having paid the duties of import at another office of farms, and brought into the ſaid city of Marſeilles, to be exported into the French iſlands and colonies of America, ſhall be entitled to thoſe exemptions contained in article the 3d, by obſerving the ſame regulations, which have been before preſcribed for the original merchandiſes of the kingdom.

11. We allow to be brought from foreign kingdoms into the ports of Marſeilles ſalt beef, in order to be exported to the ſaid iſlands and colonies, and it ſhall be exempt from all duties, even that of 40 ſols, which is known by the farm of the gabelles, or exciſe duty, on condition that on it's arrival it ſhall be

houſed

housed in an entrepost, till embarkation, on pain of confiscation.

12. There shall not be loaded in the port of Marseilles, for the French islands and colonies, any merchandises, which import and consummation shall be prohibited in the kingdom, on pain of confiscation, and a penalty of 3000 livres, that shall be inflicted by the officers of the admiralty.

13. The silk and other merchandises of Avignon and the county of Venaissine, which shall be declared for the French islands and colonies, and which shall have paid the duties of the custom-house of Lyons, with which they are charged in going out of the said county, to come into the kingdom, shall be exempt from all duties, as well upon their entrance into the territory of Marseilles, as on their embarkation; provided, on their arrival at Marseilles, they shall be housed in a warehouse of entrepost, till their embarkation; and the same shall be observed, for the rate of the said merchandises, as has been before decreed in regard to those fabricated in our kingdom.

14. Swiss linens, which are exempted from all duties at importation into the kingdom, shall pay to the offices of farms, upon the confines of the territories of Marseilles, the ordinary duties of export, although designed for the French islands and colonies.

15. Merchandises and provisions of all sorts, coming from the French islands and colonies, shall

ſhall pay, on their arrival at Marſeilles, once for all, the duty of 3 per cent. ad valorem to the farm of the weſtern domaine, and that when even they ſhall be intended to be exported into foreign countries.

16. The merchants of Marſeilles may tranſport by land, into foreign countries, clay and caſſonade ſugars, ginger, and racou, coming from the French iſlands and colonies, and cauſe them to paſs by tranſit acroſs the kingdom without paying any duties at importation and exportation, nor any other duties, excepting thoſe depending on the general farm of the aids and domaines; on condition of declaring, at the office of farms, the time of their departure, the quantity, quality, weight, and meaſure, in order to be viſited and leaded, to take a diſcharge of the ſecurity, and be obliged to report, within four months or longer, certificates of the exportation of the ſaid merchandiſes out of the kingdom; which certificates ſhall be wrote and ſigned on the back of the ſaid diſcharges of ſecurity, by the commiſſioners of the laſt office of farms at the ſaid exportation, after the ſaid commiſſioners have inſpected the leads and viſited the ſaid merchandiſes; and the land carriers ſhall be obliged to cauſe to be inſpected the ſaid diſcharges of ſecurity, by the commiſſioners of the offices of farms lying in the rout, and by the directors of the farms, where any are eſtabliſhed; the whole here-

hereof to be done and performed on pain of paying four times the duties, and of confiſcation of the carriages and horſes of the carrier ſo offending; which precautions being taken, the ſaid merchandiſes ſhall not be opened, and the ſaid directors and commiſſioners ſhall certify only, without any delay or expence, the number of tons, caſes, or bales, and examine if the leads thereunto affixed be whole and entire: in caſe the ſaid leads ſhall be broke, altered, or defaced, we do permit the ſaid commiſſioners, to viſit the ſaid merchandiſes, and to ſeize them in caſe of violation of the laws, to be confiſcated, and the offenders condemned in 500 livres penalty.

17. The ſaid three ſorts of merchandiſes which ſhall be ſent by land from Marſeilles by tranſit into foreign countries, ſhall not be ſent out but by way of the places hereafter named; viz. thoſe deſtined for Savoy and Piedmont, by the office of farms at the bridge of Beauvoiſin and Champarillan.—Thoſe deſigned for Swiſſerland or Geneva, by the office of Seiſſel and Coulonges.—Thoſe for Franche Comte, by the office of Auxonne.—Thoſe for the three biſhoprics, Lorrain, and Metz, by the office of St. Menehoult and Auxonne.—And thoſe deſigned for the low countries, under foreign dominion, by the office of Liſle and Maubeuge.

WE exprefly prohibit the faid merchandifes from going out of our kingdom by any other offices, when they fhall pafs by tranfit with exemption of duties, on pain of confifcation of merchandifes, carriages, and horfes, and a fine of 3000 livres.

18. Merchandifes hereafter fpecified, coming from the French iflands and colonies, and which, after their arrival in the port of Marfeilles, fhall be brought into the kingdom, accompanied with certificates of the commiffioners of offices of weights, &c. fhall after pay only for the duties of entry, viz.

RAW, or mufcovado fugars, the hundred weight, 2 livres, 10 fols; 30 fols 4 deniers of which fhall be appropriated to the farmer of the weftern domaine; and 16 fols 8 deniers to the farmer-general of the five great farms.

CLAY, or caffonade fugars, 8 livres the hundred weight; two livres whereof fhall be appropriated to the farmer of the weftern domaine, and fix livres to the farmer-general of the five great farms.

INDIGO, 100 fols per hundred weight.—Ginger, 15 fols per hundred weight.—Cotton in the wool, 30 fols per hundred weight.—Rocou, 2 livres 10 fols per hundred weight.—Sweet-meats, 5 livres per hundred weight.—Caffia, one livre per hundred weight.—Hides, raw and dry, 5 fols a-piece.—Tortoife-fhell of all forts, 7 livres per hundred weight.

THE fum total of the duties upon the faid nine laft forts of merchandifes fhall be raifed for

for the benefit of the farmer-general of the five great farms.

Cacao, indigo, cotton-wool, and hides raw and dry coming from the French islands and colonies, shall be liable to those easy duties before decreed, only on condition that they are housed, on their arrival at Marseilles, in a magazine of entrepost, from whence they shall not be moved, but in the presence of the commissioners of the revenue-farms, to whom they shall deliver their certificates; in default whereof, the said merchandises shall pay, at their importation into the kingdom, the same duties as foreign merchandises do.

19. Cacao, and indigo, produced in the said islands and colonies, and which, on their arrival, have been housed in a magazine of entrepost, and taken thence in presence of commissioners of the farms, may be sent into foreign countries, and pass, by transit, over the kingdom, in observing what is required by the 16th and 17th articles.

20. White and unrefined sugars of Cayenne, which shall be warehoused as aforesaid, on their arrival in the port of Marseilles, and which shall afterwards be brought into the kingdom, shall pay only 4 livres per hundred weight.

21. Merchandises coming from the French islands and colonies, and not mentioned in the 18th article, shall pay, at entrance into the kingdom, such duties as before known and usual

uſual, except refined loaf ſugar, which ſhall pay at every place of entrance into the kingdom (when even they are intended for the conſumption of the city and territories of Marſeilles) 22 livres 10 ſols per hundred weight, in conformity to the arrets of our council of the 25th of April 1690, and 20th of June 1698.

22. The duties required by the ſaid arret of the 25th of April 1690, on foreign ſugars of all ſorts, ſhall be paid in the port of Marſeilles, notwithſtanding all privileges and franchiſes before granted to that city; and the ſaid ſugars ſhall not be intitled to the benefit of the entrepoſt, granted either by the ſaid, or other ſubſequent arrets; excepting, however, the caſſonade ſugars of the Braſils, which ſhall be warehouſed in the port of Marſeilles, and ſhall not be taken out of the ſame with exemption of duties required by the ſaid arret of the 25th of April 1690, unleſs to be exported into foreign countries.

23. We expreſsly forbid the inhabitants of theſe iſlands and colonies, and all merchants of Marſeilles, to export from the ſaid iſlands and colonies into foreign countries, or into the neighbouring foreign colonies, either on French or foreign bottoms, any merchandiſes of the produce of the French iſlands, on pain of confiſcation of ſhip and merchandiſe, and a fine of 1000 livres penalty; which ſhall be laid by the officers of the admiralty, and againſt

againſt the captains and maſters of ſhips, to anſwer the ſame in their own perſon, to ſuffer a year's impriſonment, and be rendered incapable of commanding, or ſerving again as an officer on ſhipboard: wherefore, all captains ſhall be obliged to repreſent, at their arrival in France, an account of the merchandiſe they have loaded in the ſaid iſlands, ſigned by the commiſſioners of the weſtern domaine.

24. We expreſsly prohibit alſo, under the aforeſaid penalties, all merchants of Marſeilles, captains and maſters of ſhips, bound for the French iſlands and colonies from lading, in any foreign country, even in the iſland of Madeira, any wines or other proviſions and merchandiſes to carry them into the ſaid colonies.

25. The duties of import which ſhall be paid upon merchandiſes of the iſlands and colonies, ſhall not be drawn back, when even they ſhall be ſent to foreign countries, and they ſhall be liable to the duties of exportation; excepting, nevertheleſs, ſugars of all ſorts, indigo, ginger, caſſia, rocou, cacao, drugs, and ſpiceries.

26. Sugars of all ſorts, and ſyrups of the French iſlands and colonies, ſhall be reported at their arrival, by the quantity of caſks or caſes, without ſubjecting the merchants, captains and maſters of ſhips, to report them by weight; but the report of other merchandizes ſhall be made according to ordinary

dinary uſage, by the quantity, quality, and weight; nor ſhall any merchandize be unloaded, but in the preſence of the commiſſioners of the farms.

27. Warehouſes ſerving for the entrepoſt, required by the articles 4, 5, 6, 10, 11, 13, 18, 19, 20, and 22, ſhall be choſen by the merchants themſelves, at their expence, and locked with three different keys; one of which the commiſſioners of the five great farms ſhall have, another the commiſſioners of the weſtern domaine, and the other any overſeer appointed by the merchants.—Thus we order and decree, &c.

A royal ordonnance, forbidding all governors, and lieutenant-generals, all particular governors, and intendants of colonies, from having plantations.—Paris, 7 November, 1719.—By the king.

His majeſty being informed, that, among the governors and lieutenants-general, particular governors and intendants of the French colonies in South-America, there are ſome who poſſeſs plantations of ſugar, indigo, cacao, and other proviſions and merchandizes of the ſaid colonies; and that ſome intend to ſettle new ones, which being inconſiſtent with his majeſty's ſervice, and, beſides, their reſidence in the ſaid colonies being only for a time, this may prove injurious to them in the conſequences, when his majeſty ſhall require them elſewhere for his ſervice: his majeſty

majeſty has, with the advice of his uncle the duke of Orleans, regent, ordered, and does hereby order for the future, that no governors, or lieutenants-general, &c. ſhall purchaſe, or otherwiſe eſtabliſh, any plantations of ſugar, indigo, tobacco, cacao, cotton, ginger rocou, or other proviſions or merchandizes of the ſaid colonies: his majeſty, notwithſtanding, permits them to have gardens for fruits, pulſe, and herbage, for their own uſe only; and, with reſpect to thoſe who have plantations already, his majeſty forbids them to make any increaſe thereunto, upon any pretence whatſoever, &c.

A royal ordonnance, iſſued againſt captains and ſupercargoes of merchantmen, who ſhall carry on foreign trade to the French iſlands in America. Paris, 26 November, 1719. By the king.

His majeſty being informed, that, notwithſtanding the great attention and care that he is deſirous of taking to prevent foreigners trading to the French iſlands of America, the captains and factors of the ſhips of his ſubjects that go to the ſaid iſlands, receive on board their veſſels, in the roads, proviſions and merchandizes, that are brought to them by foreign boats, and that they purchaſe them, either with ready money, or with French or Indian proviſions, from the facility they have to unload and ſell them to the

the inhabitants: it being of importance to prevent a contraband trade ſo prejudicial to the commerce of the kingdom, that it hinders the ſale of the merchandizes and proviſions brought from France, retards the vent of the cargoes of the ſaid ſhips, prolongs their ſtay in the iſlands, which occaſions mortality among the ſailors, and great expence to the merchants: all which being neceſſary to put a ſtop to, his majeſty, with the advice of the duke of Orleans, regent, forbids all captains, factors, or ſupercargoes of French ſhips, from carrying on any commerce, directly or indirectly, with foreigners, on pain of the offenders being ſent to the gallies for ever. His majeſty orders and commands Monſ. the count of Toulouſe, admiral of France, and all governors and lieutenant-governors of the ſaid iſlands, all particular governors and officers of the ſuperior courts of the colonies, and other officers belonging thereto, to pay ſtrict obedience hereunto, &c.

Regulations by the king, concerning foreign or contraband commerce carried on in the French colonies.—Paris, July 23, 1720.

THE king being informed that commerce with foreigners continues to be carried on in ſome of his colonies, notwithſtanding the prohibitions to the contrary that have been made by divers

divers ordinances and regulations, and eſpecially by that of the 20th of Auguſt, 1698. And being deſirous to prevent the continuance of this diſorder, and to ſecure to his ſubjects the *whole commerce* of all his colonies, his majeſty has judged it neceſſary, by and with the advice of Monſ. the duke of Orleans his uncle, regent, to make the preſent regulations.

ARTICLE I.

His majeſty orders all officers and captains of ſhips to ſeize all veſſels, barks, and others, as well French as foreign, carrying on contraband commerce with his colonies in America, and to reduce them by force of arms, and bring them into the neareſt iſland where the prize was taken.

2. His majeſty permits all his ſubjects to ſteer the proper courſe for the taking of the ſaid ſhips and veſſels carrying on foreign commerce; and orders that, for the future, it ſhall be inſerted in the commiſſions of ſhips of war and merchantmen, that ſhall be granted by the admiral of France, that the bearers thereof ſhall be permitted to run upon thoſe ſhips, barks, and other veſſels, as well French as others, carrying on a foreign commerce to the French colonies of America, to reduce them by force, and carry them into the iſlands neareſt to the place where they were taken; the ſaid commiſſions,

ſions, however, ſhall not be granted without the ſame ſecurity being given as in times of war.

3. The prizes thus made, either by his majeſty's ſhips, or thoſe of his ſubjects, ſhall be judged of by the officers of the admiralty, conformably to the ordonnances and regulations made for that purpoſe, without appeal to ſuperior courts; except in time of war, when the proceedings ſhall be ſent to the ſecretary-general of the marine, to be judged by the admiral as uſual; and, if the prize be condemned, one tenth ſhall go to the admiral, according to the ordonnance of 1681.

4. The produce of the prizes made by his majeſty's ſhips ſhall be divided, after the one-tenth part thereof appropriated to the admiral, viz. one tenth to the commander of the ſhip that took the prize, one tenth to him who commanded the ſquadron, one tenth to the governor and lieutenant-general of the colony whither the prize ſhall be carried in, one tenth to the intendant, and one half of the ſurplus moiety to the ſailors, the other to the commiſſioners of the treaſury of the marine, for the maintenance of the colonies, according to his majeſty's orders.

5. Prizes made by the ſhips of his majeſty's ſubjects ſhall be adjudged to him who took them; except the one tenth to the admiral, and upon the ſurplus of the produce there ſhall be raiſed one fifth; one half

whereof ſhall be depoſited in the hands of the commiſſioners of the treaſury of the marine in the colonies, in order to be employed for the maintenance of the hoſpitals of the ſaid colonies, according to his majeſty's pleaſure; and the other moiety ſhall be divided thus, two thirds to the governor and lieutenant-general, and the other third to the intendant of the colony, where the ſaid veſſel making the capture ſhall have been fitted out: and, with regard to thoſe prizes, which ſhall be made by ſhips fitted out in France, the ſaid moiety ſhall be divided, as aforeſaid, between the governor and lieutenant-general, and the intendant of the colony where the prize ſhall be carried in.

6. His majeſty orders, that the particular governors of the colonies of Cayenne and Cape Breton ſhall enjoy, for the prizes which ſhall be brought into the ſaid colonies, either by his majeſty's ſhips, or by thoſe of his ſubjects, as alſo by thoſe fitted out in the ſaid colonies, ſuch proportions as ſpecified in article the 4th and 5th of the preſent regulation made for the governors and lieutenants-general, and the commiſſioner of the ordinances of the ſaid colonies ſhall be entitled to thoſe parts allotted to the intendant.

7. His majeſty requires that the preſent regulation ſhall be executed according to its form and tenor, notwithſtanding all ordinances and regulations to the contrary, which

his

his majeſty hereby makes null and void. His majeſty orders and commands Monſ. the count of Toulouſe, admiral of France, to have a ſtrict regard to the execution of the preſent regulations, to cauſe them to be made public wherever needful, &c.

The king's declaration, with regard to merchandiſes of the French colonies.—Paris, 14 March 1722.

LEWIS, by the grace of God, king of France and Navarre, greeting—Whereas by the 26th article of our letters patent of the month of April 1717, containing regulations for the commerce of the French iſlands and colonies, we have expreſsly forbid the inhabitants of the ſaid iſlands and colonies, and the merchants of our kingdom, to export into foreign countries, or into foreign neighbouring iſlands of the ſaid colonies, either by the means of French or foreign veſſels, any merchandiſes of the produce of the French iſlands, on pain of confiſcation of ſhips and cargoes, and a penalty of 1000 livres: and, beſides the captains and maſters of ſuch ſhips being obliged to anſwer the ſaid confiſcation and penalties in their own perſon, to ſuffer a year's impriſonment, and alſo to be declared incapable of command, or of ſerving in the capacity of an officer on ſhipboard again: in conſequence whereof, the captains are obliged to repreſent, on their arrival in France, a

ſtate,

ſtate, ſigned by the commiſſioners of the weſtern domaine, of the merchandiſes which they have laden at the ſaid iſlands and colonies. Although the laſt diſpoſition of the ſaid article is eſſential, and the greateſt ſecurity that can be taken againſt ſuch foreign trade, by the certification that ſhould be made of merchandiſes, on the arrival of ſhips in France, from the ſtate of the loading made in the iſlands; yet we are informed, that the greateſt part of the maſters of ſhips returning from the ſaid iſlands, are diſpenſed with, in regard to their report of a ſtate of their loading, according to the form required; and that the commiſſioners of our farms in the ports of France cannot ſubject them thereunto, nor proceed ſecurely againſt them, apprehending that our judges will not have due regard thereunto, by reaſon that the ſaid 26th article of the regulations of 1717 does not inflict any penalty againſt thoſe, who ſhall neglect to make ſuch report, ſigned by the commiſſioners of the weſtern domaine, but only againſt thoſe who ſhall carry on foreign trade; which renders the prohibitions in regard to this commerce ineffectual, from the impoſſibility of knowing in France, whether all the merchandiſes which have been loaded in the ſaid iſlands are faithfully reported, at the ports of their return, and whether no part thereof has been unloaded in foreign countries: whereupon we judge neceſſary to remedy

remedy the ſame, by a certain diſpoſition which declares the penalties inflicted by the regulation of 1717, againſt the maſters of ſhips, who ſhall carry on foreign commerce; that the ſame penalties ſhall be incurred by thoſe, who ſhall neglect to report the ſtate of their loading, ſigned by the commiſſioners of the French iſlands and colonies, &c.—For theſe and other reaſons us hereunto moving, with the advice of, &c. &c.—We have, by theſe preſents, ſigned with our hand; and we decree, will, and ordain, &c. that the 26th article of our letters patents of the month of April 1717, ſhall be executed, according to the due form and tenor thereof, and, in conſequence of the ſame, that maſters of ſhips, returning from the French iſlands and colonies, ſhall be obliged to repreſent, on their arrival in France, a ſtate, ſigned and certified by the commiſſioners of the weſtern domaine, of the merchandiſes which they ſhall have loaded at the ſaid iſlands and colonies.—We decree, that on failure of the ſaid maſters making a report within 24 hours of their arrival in the ports of France, to the commiſſioners of the office of our farms, the ſaid ſtate of their ſhips loading; or on failure of reporting the merchandiſes agreeable to the ſaid ſtate, ſuch maſters of ſhips ſhall be looked upon as having carried on a commerce at theſe iſlands with foreigners; in conſequence whereof their ſhips and merchandiſes ſhall be confiſcated, the owners of the ſaid merchandiſe and the

cap-

captains and mafters of the faid fhips condemned in the whole fine of 1000 livres, and be liable to the other pains and penalties inflicted by the faid 26th article of our letters patents of the month of April 1717. Thus we give and command, &c.

Letters patents, upon the arret, which fixes the time of a year of the entrepoft of merchandifes coming from the French iflands and colonies into the ports therein mentioned, and of thofe which fhall be declared by the entrepoft for the faid iflands.—Verfailles, May 23, 1723.

LEWIS, by the grace of God, &c.—— Whereas, by our declaration of the 19th of January laft, we have, for the caufes and confiderations therein given, in confirmation of our letters patents of the month of April, 1717, for regulating the commerce of the French iflands and colonies, ordered, that the merchants proprietors of the provifions and merchandifes which fhall be houfed according to the entrepoft, and defigned for the faid iflands and colonies, fhall be obliged, after one year's entrepoft, to declare to the offices of farms at thofe places, the quantities, qualities, weight, and meafure of the faid provifions and merchandifes, which fhall remain in warehoufes, which declaration fhall be certified by the adjudicatory commiffioners of our farms, and, in cafe of neglect, and falfe declaraclaration, that the merchants proprietors of the ſaid proviſions and merchandiſes ſhall be condemned in 500 livres penalty, beſides the payment of the duties of the merchandiſes which ſhall be found wanting in their declaration: and, in caſe of the ſale of the ſaid merchandiſes ſo warehouſed, the merchants proprietors thereof ſhall be obliged to diſcharge the duties thereupon, one month after ſale, on pain of the like penalty, and of 500 livres.—And being informed that it is yet neceſſary to limit the time of entrepoſt, as well for the proviſions and merchandiſes declared and intended for the commerce of the French iſlands and colonies, as thoſe which come from the ſaid iſlands and colonies; in order to prevent the abuſes introduced, and which will always encreaſe, by reaſon of thoſe entrepoſts, if they ſubſiſt for an unlimited time: we have provided, by an arret made in our council of ſtate, we being preſent, the 3d of the month and year of the date hereof, for execution of which, what we have ordered is requiſite.—For theſe reaſons, with the advice of our council, who have conſidered the ſaid arret hereunto annexed, under the counter-ſeal of our chancery, &c. we have decreed and ordained, and by theſe preſents, ſigned with our hand, we decree and ordain, that the time of the entrepoſt, as well with regard to merchandiſes, which ſhall come from the French iſlands and colonies into the ports of Calais,

Dieppe,

Dieppe, Havre, Rouen, Honfleur, Rochelle, Bourdeaux, Bayonne, Cette, Marſeilles, and Dunkirk, as thoſe which ſhall be declared and intended for the ſaid iſlands and colonies, and warehouſed in the ſame ports, and in thoſe of St. Malo, Morlaix, Breſt, and Nantes, ſhall be and remain fixed, for the future, to one year, to be accounted from the day that the ſaid merchandiſes and proviſions ſhall have come into port. And, with reſpect to thoſe which are actually warehouſed, they ſhall be intitled to the benefit of the entrepoſt for one year, from the day of the publication of the ſaid arret, and of theſe preſents; after which time, the ſaid merchandiſes ſhall be liable as follow, viz.—Thoſe declared and houſed for the French iſlands and colonies, to the ſame duties as they ſhould have paid, had they not been declared for the iſlands; and thoſe that come from the ſaid iſlands and colonies, ſhall be ſubject to the duties regulated according to our letters patents of the month of February, 1719, and according to thoſe of the month of October, 1721.—Thus we command, &c.

An arret of the king's council of ſtate, revoking thoſe permiſſions before granted to the merchants of the kingdom, to carry to Cadiz, Genoa, Leghorn, and Naples, directly from the French iſlands of America, merchandiſes of the produce of the ſaid iſlands. June 14, 1723. Extracted from the regiſters of the council of ſtate.

THE king having been informed that to facilitate, during the time of the plague with which the city of Marſeilles, and ſome other places of the kingdom, have been afflicted, the exportation of merchandiſes of the French iſlands of America into Spain and Italy, where the admittance of French ſhips coming directly from the ports of France was refuſed; it was allowed to all merchants of the kingdom, to ſend merchandiſes to Cadiz, Genoa, Leghorn, and Naples, of the produce of the French iſlands of America, without putting them into entrepoſt warehouſes, required in the ports of France by virtue of the 15th article of letters patents of the month of April, 1717. But, the motives to this toleration ceaſing, it becomes neceſſary to re-eſtabliſh the execution of the 2d article of the letters patents of the month of April, the intent of which is very important for the ſecurity of the duties of the farms, and to prevent the contraband exportation of the merchandiſes of the French iſlands

iſlands of America into foreign countries: againſt which his majeſty being willing to provide, and being preſent in council, and having heard the report of the Sieur Dodun, counſellor in ordinary to the royal council, and comptroller-general of the finances, hath revoked and annulled the ſaid permiſſions granted to the merchants of his kingdom, to carry to Cadiz, Genoa, Leghorn, and Naples, directly from the French iſlands of America, merchandiſes of the produce of the ſaid iſlands: wherefore his majeſty orders and decrees, that all ſhips which ſhall depart from the ports of France, deſigned, according to the firſt article of the ſaid letters patents, for the commerce of the French iſlands and colonies in America, as likewiſe thoſe which ſhall depart from the ports of Dunkirk and Marſeilles, in order to ſend the merchandiſes of France to the ſaid French iſlands and colonies of America, ſhall be obliged to make their return directly into the port of their departure; and, to this end, the merchants who ſhall fit out the ſaid ſhips, ſhall make the ſubmiſſion required by the 2d article of the letters patents of the month of April, 1717, to the ſecretary of the admiralty, which ſhall be executed, for the time to come, according to their form and tenor. Done at the royal council of ſtate, held at Meudon, the 14th day of June, 1723.

A royal

A royal ordinance, declaring Gilles Robin, captain of the ſhip St. Michael, of Havre, incapable to ſail, for the future, in any ſhip intended for the colonies, for having carried on a contraband trade at St. Domingo. The 25th of July, 1724. By the king.

His majeſty being informed that, in violation of the prohibitions ſo often made and repeated, to prevent carrying on a contraband commerce with foreigners in the iſlands of America, ſeveral captains and traders have occaſioned the loſs of their ſhips, by foreign merchandizes, which have been brought to them by foreign veſſels in the roads of the ſaid iſlands, which is not only contrary to the trade of the kingdom, but cauſes the ruin of thoſe who fit ſuch ſhips out, theſe captains conſuming, by the long ſtay they make in the colonies, in carrying on this fraudulent traffic, the advantages the proprietors might have reaped, if their voyage was ſhorter: the above named Gilles Robin, commanding the ſhip called the St. Michael, of Havre, fitted out for Leogane, upon the coaſt of St. Domingo, was ſurprized in the month of February laſt, carrying on, in the night-time, contraband or foreign trade, with a ſmall Engliſh ſhip; upon which, he being tried in the court of admiralty of the ſaid place, his merchandizes were confiſcated, and the ſaid Gilles Robin condemned in the

penalty

penalty of 2000 livres, and ſix months impriſonment. His majeſty thinking it neceſſary to ſuppreſs the like abuſes, by examples which may include in their conſequence captains of merchantmen, who may fall under the like circumſtances, he hath declared, and does hereby declare, the ſaid Gilles Robin incapable of ſailing for the future in any ſhip bound for the colonies.—His majeſty orders and commands Monſ. the count of Toulouſe, admiral of France, the governors and lieutenant-governors of America, intendants of the marine officiating in his ports and colonies, &c. to have ſtrict regard to the due execution of the preſent ordinance, which ſhall be regiſtered by the ſecretaries of the admiralties at the ports which have permiſſion to fit out ſhips for the ſaid iſlands and colonies; and alſo read, publiſhed, and fixed in the ſaid ports, &c.—Done at Chantilly, the 25th of July, 1724.

Royal letters patents, in the form of an edict, concerning the foreign or contraband commerce to the iſlands and colonies of America.—Given at Fontainbleau, in the month of October, 1727.

LEWIS, by the grace of God, &c.—The care that the late king, our moſt honoured lord and great-grandfather, took for the advancement of the commerce of our iſlands and colonies, that which we alſo have taken by by his example, ſince our acceſſion to the crown, the expence that has hitherto been for this purpoſe, and that we ſtill annually continue, have only in view the ſecurity and the increaſe of the trade and navigation of the ſaid iſlands and colonies: and herein we have had all the ſucceſs that could be expected; our ſaid colonies *being very greatly augmented, and in condition to carry on a conſiderable trade and navigation,* by the ſale of negroes, proviſions and merchandizes, carried thither by the ſhips of our ſubjects, in exchange for ſugars, cacao, cotton, indigo, and other productions of the ſaid iſlands and colonies. But we have been informed, that a fraudulent contraband commerce has been introduced, which, beſides diminiſhing the commerce and navigation of our ſubjects, may prove of dangerous conſequence to the ſupport of our ſaid colonies.—The juſt meaſures we take that they may be ſupplied from France, and from our other colonies, with the negroes, proviſions, and merchandizes they need, and the protection we owe to the trade of our ſubjects, have determined us to fix, by a certain law, ſuch precautions, and lay ſuch ſevere pains and penalties upon the offenders, as may put a ſtop to ſuch fraudulent traffic: for theſe, and other reaſons us hereunto moving, with the advice of our council, and of our certain knowledge, full power, and royal authority, we have,

by

by theſe preſents, ſigned with our hand, decreed and ordained, that there ſhall not be received, into the colonies ſubmitted to our obedience, any negroes, effects, proviſions, and merchandizes, unleſs carried thither in French ſhips or veſſels, which ſhall take in their lading in the ports of our kingdom, or in our ſaid colonies, and which ſhall belong to our ſubjects born in our kingdom, or our ſaid colonies: In conſequence whereof we will and decree as follows, viz.

Of ſhips carrying on foreign or contraband commerce.

ARTICLE I.

WE forbid all our ſubjects born in our kingdom, and in our colonies, to cauſe any negroes, effects, proviſions, and merchandizes to be brought into our ſaid colonies from foreign countries, or foreign colonies, except ſalt beef from Ireland, which ſhall be brought in French ſhips, and which have taken their loading in the ports of the kingdom, on pain of confiſcation of ſhip and cargo, and 1000 livres penalty againſt the captain, who ſhall alſo be condemned to the gallies for three years.

2. We forbid, under the ſame penalties, all our ſubjects to export from our ſaid iſlands and colonies any negroes, effects, proviſions, and merchandizes into foreign countries, or

into

into foreign colonies: we permit, neverthe-leſs, our French merchants to carry directly from our iſlands of America into the ports of Spain, ſugars of all ſorts, excepting raw ſugars, together with all other merchandizes of the produce of the ſaid iſlands, according to the regulations made by the arret of our council of the 27th of January, 1726.

3. Foreigners ſhall not land with their ſhips, or other veſſels, in the ports, roads, or havens of our iſlands and colonies, not even in our UNINHABITED iſlands, nor navigate their ſhips within a league round thoſe iſles and colonies, on pain of confiſcation of their ſhips and veſſels, and alſo of their loading, and 1000 livres penalty, &c.

4. We order all our officers, captains, commanders of our ſhips, &c. to purſue all foreign ſea veſſels which they ſhall find within the ſaid latitude, and even thoſe belonging to our own ſubjects carrying on foreign or contraband trade, and reduce them by force of arms, and bring them into the iſland neareſt to the place where ſuch prize has been taken.

5. We permit all our ſubjects to purſue the ſaid ſhips and ſea veſſels, and thoſe belonging to our own ſubjects carrying on foreign or contraband commerce; and we decree, for the time to come, it ſhall be inſerted in the commiſſions granted, either for war or commerce, by the admiral of France, that thoſe who bear ſuch commiſſions may

purſue

purſue the ſhips, and other ſea veſſels, which they ſhall find under the before-mentioned circumſtances, and reduce them by force of arms, and bring them into the iſland neareſt the place where the prize has been made; but theſe commiſſions ſhall not be delivered to them without giving the ſame ſecurity as is done in time of war.

6. Prizes made on theſe occaſions, either by our ſhips, or thoſe of our ſubjects, ſhall be adjudged by the officers of the admiralty, conſiſtently with the ordinances and regulations iſſued on this occaſion, without appeal to the ſuperior council of the iſlands or colonies where the prize ſhall be adjudged; with this exception, that, in time of war, the proceeding of the court, with regard to the prizes made upon thoſe nations with which we may be at war, ſhall be ſent to the ſecretary-general of the marine, in order that the caſe may be adjudicated by the admiral, as uſual on thoſe occaſions; and one tenth of the produce of thoſe prizes determined lawful, ſhall be appropriated to the admiral, according to the ordinance of 1681.

7. The produce of prizes made by our ſhips ſhall be divided, after deduction of the admiral's tenth. viz. one tenth to the commander of the veſſel which makes the prize; one tenth to the governor or lieutenant-general of the colony whither the prize ſhall be carried in; one tenth to the intendant; and the ſurplus of the moiety to the ſailors; and the

the remaining half part ſhall be depoſited in the hands of the commiſſioners of the treaſury of the marine in the ſaid colony, to be appropriated according to our orders, &c.

8. Prizes made by the ſhips of our ſubjects ſhall be adjudged to him who made them, except the tenth to the admiral, and he ſhall be entitled to one fifth upon the ſurpluſage of the produce, the half whereof ſhall be depoſited in the hands of the commiſſioner of the treaſury of the marine in the colonies, to be employed as we ſhall judge proper; and the other half ſhall be divided, two thirds to the governor, our lieutenant-general, and the other third to the intendant of the colony where the ſhip taking the ſame ſhall have been fitted out: and, with reſpect to prizes made by ſhips fitted out in France, the ſaid moiety ſhall be divided, as before ſaid, between the governor, our lieutenant-general, and the intendant of the colony whither the prize ſhall have been carried in.

9. The particular governors of the colonies of Cayenne, Guardaloupe, and Cape Breton, ſhall be entitled for prizes carried in thither, either by our ſhips, or thoſe of our ſubjects, fitted out in France, or in the ſaid colonies, to thoſe proportions ſettled by the 7th and 8th articles of the preſent edict, to the governor our lieutenant-general; and the commiſſioners of the ordinances of the ſaid colonies

lonies ſhall be entitled to thoſe appropriated to the intendant.

10. We command all officers of our troops, or militia, commanding in the different parts of our colonies, even the captains of militia in their diviſions, to arreſt ſuch foreign veſſels as ſhall be found in the ports, roads, and havens of their diſtrict, and alſo French ſhips carrying on a contraband trade in thoſe places: and $\frac{1}{10}$ of the produce thereof ſhall belong to the admiral, and $\frac{1}{3}$ to the officer who made the price, $\frac{1}{3}$, which ſhall be divided in halves, between him that commands the detachment, and the ſoldiers or inhabitants who have compoſed the ſame. The remainder of the whole, ſhall be depoſited in the hands of the commiſſioners of the treaſury of the marine, to be employed according to our order, &c.

11. Ships, or other foreign veſſels, either of war or merchantmen, which by ſtorm, or other urgent neceſſities, ſhall be forced into our colonies, ſhall not water, on pain of confiſcation of merchant's ſhips and cargo, except in ports or roads where we have garriſons, viz. in the iſland of Martinico, Fort Royal, in the borough of St. Pierre, and à la Trinité; in the iſland of Guardaloupe, at the road of La Baſſe Terre, at Little Cul-deſac, and at Fort Lewis; at Grenade, in the chief port, as well as at Marie Galante; and, in the iſland of St. Domingo, at Petit Guave, Leo-

Leogane, St. Louis, St. Marc, Port de Puisé, and Cape Francois: at which places they shall not be stopped, provided they make appear they were not intended for our colonies; and, upon this appearing, all desireable succour and aid shall be given them. We order the governor, our lieutenant-general, or other commanding officers, to send a detachment of four soldiers and a serjeant on board the said ships and vessels, to prevent the embarkation and debarkation of negroes, effects, provisions, and merchandises, under any pretence whatever; which detachment shall remain on board such vessels, at the expence of the proprietors thereof, so long as they shall remain in the ports and roads of our colonies.

12. Captains of the said vessels thus at liberty, who shall have occasion for provisions, rigging, or other utensils, to enable them to continue their voyage, shall be obliged to ask permission of the governor, our lieutenant-general, or commander, in his absence, and of the intendant, to embark them; which permission shall not be granted till their request is communicated to the director of the domaine; and these shall be granted by the said governor, our lieutenant-general, or commander in his absence, and an ordinance made importing the said permission; and, in case the director of the domaine should oppose the same, his motives for so doing, as well as those of the governor, lieutenant-general, or commander in his absence, and the inten-

intendant ſhall be tranſmitted, with a copy of the ſaid ordinance, to the ſecretary of ſtate for that department of the marine, to give us an account thereof: we require, however, that the ſaid ordinance be proviſionally executed, &c.

13. If it is abſolutely neceſſary to refit or careen the ſhips of foreigners thus at liberty, to unlade their effects, proviſions, and merchandiſes, the captains thereof ſhall be obliged to aſk permiſſion of the governor, our lieutenant-general, or commander in his abſence, and of the intendant; which permiſſion ſhall not be granted till the requeſt be communicated to the director of the domaine; and there ſhall be granted an ordinance importing the ſaid permiſſion. And, in caſe the director of the domaine oppoſes the ſaid permiſſion, his motives, as well as thoſe of the governor, our lieutenant-general, &c. ſhall be repreſented, together with a copy of the ordinance, to the ſecretary of ſtate of the marine, to acquaint us of the ſame: we require, however, that the ſaid ordinance be proviſionally executed; and, in caſe of the landing of the ſaid merchandiſes, there ſhall be given a verbal account, in preſence of the director of the domaine, containing the quantity and quality thereof, ſigned by the captain of the ſhip, and by the ſaid director of the domaine; which account ſhall be ſent to the ſecretary of ſtate of the marine; and the ſaid governor, our lieutenant-general, or commander in his abſence,

abſence, ſhall place a centinel at the gate of the warehouſe where the ſaid merchandiſe ſhall be depoſited, to prevent any being taken out, or ſold in the ſaid colonies; and, while the ſaid merchandiſe ſhall remain in the ſaid warehouſe, which ſhall be ſhut with three locks, one of which keys ſhall be given to the intendant, another to the director of the domaine, and the other to the captain of the ſaid ſhip. We require alſo, that, in caſe he has landed negroes, he ſhall draw up a liſt, wherein they ſhall be exactly characterized, who ſhall be ſequeſtered in the hands of ſome reſponſible perſon, that they may be reſtored again, &c. the whole hereof muſt be performed on pain of confiſcation of the value of the ſaid negroes, and alſo the ſhip and cargo.

14. The expence of ſuch ſhips or veſſels in our iſlands and colonies ſhall be made there, and paid in caſh or bills of exchange: and, in caſe the captain has not money, nor can find any one in the ſaid iſlands and colonies, who will anſwer for the payment of the ſaid bills of exchange, permiſſion ſhall be granted by the governor, our lieutenant-general, or the commander in his abſence, and the intendant, on the requeſt of the captains of the ſaid ſhips (which ſhall likewiſe be communicated to the director of the domaine) for the ſale of a certain number of negroes and merchandiſes, to make good the ſaid expence ONLY; and an ordonnance granting the ſaid per-

permiſſion ſhall be made, ſignifying the ſaid expence, together with the quantity and quality of the negroes, and merchandiſes ſold: and, in caſe the director of the domaine ſhould oppoſe ſuch ſale, his motives, together with thoſe of the governor, our lieutenant-general, or commander in his abſence, and the intendant, ſhall be repreſented to be ſent, with a copy of the ordonnance, to the ſecretary of ſtate of the marine: and we require that the ſaid ordonnance ſhall be executed proviſionally, and that the ſale, ſo permitted, ſhall not exceed the amount of the expence incurred, under any pretext whatſoever.

15. We require, that as ſoon as the ſaid foreign ſhips ſhall be at liberty, and in condition to take in again their loadings of negroes and merchandiſes ſo landed, there ſhall be a re-examination of the ſame, ſigned by the director of the domaine, a copy whereof ſhall be ſent to the ſecretary of ſtate for the marine, and after the ſaid embarkation the ſaid veſſels ſhall put to ſea.—We require alſo, that thoſe which ſhall be thus at liberty, depart the firſt favourable opportunity, after being in a condition for ſailing, on the penalty againſt the captain of 1000 livres, and confiſcation of ſhip and cargo: the governors, our lieutenant-governors, particular governors, or other officers commanding in our colonies, ſhall not permit the ſaid ſhip to make any longer ſtay, than what ſhall be abſolutely neceſſary to fit them for ſea.

16. We

16. We forbid the captains of the ſaid foreign ſhps, ſupercargoes, and others thereunto belonging, to land or ſell any negroes, or other merchandiſes brought by the ſaid ſhips, nor to ſhip any negroes or merchandiſes of the French colonies, on pain of confiſcation of the ſaid ſhips and loading, and 1000 livres penalty beſides, which ſhall be paid without abatement by the captains and ſailors.

Concerning negroes, effects, proviſions, and merchandiſes, found on the ſea-ſhores, and in the ports and havens, brought as well in French ſhips carrying on contraband trade, as in foreign ones.

ARTICLE I.

NEGROES and merchandiſes found on the ſhores, ports, and havens, brought by French ſhips carrying on unlawful commerce, ſhall be confiſcated, together with the ſhip and loading, and a penalty of 1000 livres laid on the captain, beſides being condemned to the gallies for three years; the moiety of which penalty ſhall go to the informer.

2. Negroes and merchandiſes ſo found upon the ſhores, and in the ports and havens brought by foreign ſhips, ſhall alſo be confiſcated, together with the veſſel from whence they were unloaded, and the cargo and the captain condemned in 1000 livres penalty, which ſhall be

be paid without deduction by him and the sailors, and one moiety thereof shall go to the informer.

3. The said confiscations, pains and penalties, shall be adjudged by the officers of the admiralty, without appeal to superior courts.

Of negroes, effects, provisions, and merchandises, found on land, coming as well in French ships carrying on contraband commerce, as in foreign ones.

ARTICLE I.

NEGROES and merchandises found on land, brought by ships belonging to our subjects, carrying on illicit trade, shall be confiscated, together with the ship and cargo, and the captain condemned in the penalty of 1000 livres, and sent to the gallies for three years.

2. Negroes and merchandises which shall, in like manner, be discovered, landed, brought by foreign ships, shall also be confiscated, together with the ship and cargo, and the captain condemned in the penalty of 1000 livres, which shall be paid without abatement, by him and the sailors.

3. Those in whose possession such negroes and merchandises shall be found, brought by French ships carrying on illicit trade, and by foreign ships, shall be condemned in 500 livres penalty, and be sent to the gallies for three years.

4. One moiety of the ſaid fines and confiſcation ſhall go to the informer, the other to the farmer of the revenue of our domaine.

5. Proſecution of ſuch offenders ſhall be made before the judges in ordinary, without appeal to ſuperior courts.

Of appeals in regard to ſentences paſt, as well with reſpect to French ſhips carrying on contraband commerce, as foreign ſhips doing the ſame.

ARTICLE I.

APPEAL lodged in ſuperior courts, with reſpect to ſentences paſſed in the ordinary courts of law, or in thoſe of the admiralty, on occaſion of contraband trade being carried on by French ſhips and foreign ones, ſhall be adjudged in the following manner:

2. Our ſuperior courts ſhall continue to aſſemble after the uſual manner.

3. The ſittings which they commonly hold, and during which all cauſes are diſpatched that are ready to be heard, ſhall be divided into two parts.

4. At the firſt ſitting there ſhall be heard as well civil as criminal cauſes, which concern individuals, and others that concern foreign or contraband trade, or have any relation thereunto, as foreign ſhips, &c.

5. All cauſes which concern the ſaid foreign or contraband trade, or have any relation

there-

thereunto, and likewiſe all thoſe concerning foreign ſhips, ſhall be heard at the ſecond ſitting, which ſhall be held immediately after the firſt.

6. The governor, our lieutenant-general, the intendant, major, officers; thoſe only ſhall aſſiſt at the ſaid ſecond ſittings, and alſo five counſellors that we ſhall name for this purpoſe, the ſollicitor-general and the ſecretary: we require, that in caſe any of the ſaid counſellors ſhould not be at the ſaid ſittings, either by abſence, ſickneſs, or any other lawful cauſe, ſentence ſhall be paſſed, when there are but three of the ſaid counſellors only.

Of merchandizes coming in foreign ſhips, and brought by means of French veſſels.

ARTICLE I.

MERCHANDIZES coming in foreign ſhips, that ſhall be found in ſhips belonging to our ſubjects, ſhall be confiſcated, and the captains of the ſaid veſſels, factors, &c. fined in three thouſand livres penalty without deduction, and moreover the captains to be ſent three years to the gallies, and the factors, &c. ſuffer ſix months impriſonment; the ſaid confiſcations and penalties ſhall go, the one half to the informer, and the other part ſhall be depoſited in the hands of the commiſſioner of the treaſury of the marine in our colonies, to be employed as we ſhall direct, either for the increaſing or maintaining hoſpitals,

tals,

tals, buildings, or other neceſſary works of the ſaid colonies.

2. The ſaid captains, factors, &c. ſhall be obliged to juſtify by invoices, manifeſtoes, charter-parties, bills of lading, &c. in regular form, and this before the intendant at the firſt requiſition, that the merchandizes ſold are the intire produce of thoſe laden in France; and, for want of thoſe, they ſhall be cenſured and reputed to have ſold merchandizes coming in foreign ſhips, or French ſhips trafficking in foreign or contraband trade, and as ſuch ſhall be condemned in the penalties contained in the preceding article.

3. We refer the cognizance of cauſes that may require expedition, to the intendants of our colonies, and thoſe we forbid to be tried in other courts.

4. We require, that, in caſes where the ſaid captains ſhall be convicted of the ſaid offence, the ſaid intendants ſhall place ſome reputable perſon on board ſuch ſhips, in order to be carried into France to their owners.

5. We require, that all perſons of what rank or condition ſoever, who ſhall be convicted of contraband commerce by veſſels belonging to them, or that they have hired ſhips on freight that have favoured ſuch trade in foreign veſſels, or who have ſent, into foreign countries or colonies, negroes, effects, proviſions, or merchandizes of our colonies, may be cendemned, beſides the penalties impoſed

posed by these articles, to the gallies for three years.

6. We require, that such foreigners who carry on foreign commerce, and import negroes, and foreign merchandizes into our colonies, and likewise those who send negroes and merchandizes into our colonies, and likewise those who send negroes and merchandizes from our colonies into foreign countries, shall be liable to prosecution for the same, five years after commission, and that the proof thereof may be made within that time.

7. All contests of this kind, either as plaintiffs or defendants, shall be referred to the jurisdiction and cognizance of the intendants of our colonies, and we forbid all other courts and judges from trying the same.

8. We impower our commissaries of ordonnances, and our first counsellors in the islands and colonies, where there is no intendant, to supply their place.

Of foreigners settled in the colonies.

ARTICLE I.

FOREIGNERS settled in our colonies, even those who are naturalized, or who may be so hereafter, shall not act as merchants, brokers, and agents, in affairs of commerce, in any manner whatsoever, on pain of 3000 livres penalty to the informer, and be banished

niſhed for ever from our ſaid colonies; we permit them only to purchaſe lands and plantations, and to deal ſolely as planters in commodities produced therefrom.

2. We grant, to thoſe who are at preſent engaged in trade, three months time, from the day of regiſtering theſe preſents, to lay the ſame aſide, and the offenders ſhall be condemned in the penalties laid by the preceding article.

3. We forbid all merchants and traders in our colonies, from having any agents, factors, book-keepers, or other perſons concerned in this commerce, who are foreigners, although they be naturalized: we require them to be diſmiſſed within three months at the fartheſt, from the day of regiſtering theſe preſents, on the penalty of 3000 livres inflicted on ſuch merchants and traders, and againſt the ſaid agents, factors, book-keepers, or other perſons who ſhall be engaged in their affairs, and to be baniſhed for ever from the ſaid colonies.

4. We enjoin and command our ſollicitors-general, and their ſubſtitutes, to attend duly to the execution of theſe three preceding articles, on pain of anſwering the ſame in their own perſons.

Thus we require and command all our faithful friends who enjoy ſuperior poſts in the ſaid iſlands and colonies, that theſe preſents may be known, publiſhed, and regiſtered, and the contents hereof ſtrictly obſerved

ſerved according to their form and tenor, notwithſtanding all edicts, declarations, arrets, and ordonnances, to the contrary, which we have by theſe preſents made null and void: For ſuch is our pleaſure. And, to the end that this may be for ever in force, we have hereunto affixed our ſeal. Given at Fontainbleau in the month of October, in the year 1727, and in the 13th year of our reign.

An arret of the royal council of ſtate, containing regulations on the point of conteſts between the admiralty of France and the farmers-general of the revenue, with regard to contraband and prohibited commerce, made as well at ſea, and in the ports, havens, and water-ſide of the kingdom, as in the French iſlands and colonies of America.—Of the 25th of May, 1728. Extracted from the regiſters of the council of ſtate.

THE king being in council, and the memorials preſented as well by the admiral of France, as by the adjudicatory of the united body of farmers-general of the revenue, on the ſubject of controverſies ariſen between the admiralty of France and the ſaid farmers-general, in regard to contraband and prohibited commerce, &c. And, in regard to the application of the penalties and confiſcations made, which have occaſioned conteſts between

between the judges of the admiralty and the judges of the ſaid adjudicatory of farmers-general: his majeſty, to put an end to thoſe conteſts at preſent, and to prevent others for the future, having determined by a certain regulation what are the rights that belong to the one and the other, hath attended to the report of the Sieur Le Peletier, counſellor of ſtate in ordinary, and to the royal council, and comptroller-general of the finances; and his majeſty, being in council, has decreed, and doth decree, &c. what follows, viz.

ARTICLE I.

THE knowledge of offences committed, and diſcovered in France, on the veſſels and in the ports, roads, coaſts, and ſhores of the ſea, with reſpect to contraband and prohibited commerce, carried on by importation and exportation of merchandizes, ſhall appertain to the Sieurs intendants, and commiſſaries, reſident in the provinces and generalities of the kingdom, in conjunction with the officers of the admiralty, without appeal to the council in civil affairs, and ſhall be the dernier reſort in criminal caſes, &c.

2. The produce of the penalties and confiſcations ſhall belong to his majeſty, or to the adjudicatory of his farms, at whoſe requeſt and expence all proſecutions ſhall be carried on, without the admiral of France pre-

pretending any thing thereto, under any pretext whatſoever.

3. The officers of the admiralty ſhall have cognizance in the firſt inſtance of offences in regard to foreign commerce, as well in regard to affairs of a civil as criminal nature, and contraband or prohibited merchandizes, which ſhall be diſcovered to be carried on by ſhips, and in the ports, roads, coaſts, and ſhores of the ſea in the French iſlands and colonies, with appeal to ſuperior courts, except thoſe offences contained in title 5 of the letters patents of the month of October, 1727; the cognizance whereof ſhall belong to the intendants and officers of the admiralty, in calling to their aſſiſtance, if need be, the number of graduates, or officers, required by the ordinances in caſes of pronouncing corporal puniſhment.

4. The produce of the penalties and confiſcations ariſing from ſuch offences which ſhall be diſcovered by the commiſſioners of the weſtern domaine, in the ports, coaſts, and ſhores of the ſea in the French iſlands and colonies, ſhall be remitted to the account of caſh of the domaine, and belong one moiety to his majeſty, or to the adjudicatory of his farms, and one moiety to the informers, and employed by the domaine that ſhall have contributed to the diſcovery and the capture.

5. The

5. The cognizance of ſuch offences as ſhall be diſcovered on land by the officers of the domaine to the ſaid iſlands and colonies, ſhall belong to the intendants, without appeal to the council, except where corporal puniſhment is inflicted; in which caſe, the cognizance in the dernier reſort ſhall be left to the ſaid Sieurs intendants, in calling to their aſſiſtance the number of graduates, or officers, required by the ordinance; and the produce of the penalties and confiſcations that ſhall ariſe, as well in civil as criminal caſes, ſhall be remitted to the caſh-account of the domaine, one moiety whereof ſhall belong to his majeſty, or to the adjudicatory of the farms, the other moiety to the informers, and the ſervants of the domaine who have contributed to the diſcovery and capture.

6. The product of the penalties and confiſcations which ſhall ariſe from the prizes at ſea by the pinnaces and commiſſioners of the farm, authorized by the commiſſions from the admiralty of France, ſhall be remitted to the domaine, and be appropriated (one tenth belonging to the admiral being deducted) one moiety to his majeſty, or the adjudicatory of his farms, the other moiety to the informers, and thoſe employed by the domaine who have contributed to the capture.

7. The penalties and confiſcations, with regard to affairs undetermined in France and America, ſhall belong to his majeſty, or to the

the adjudicatory of his farms, according to articles 4, 5, and 6 of the preſent regulations.

8. Effects and merchandizes ſeized, as well in France as in the French iſlands and colonies, by the commiſſioners of the adjucatory of farms, ſhall be depoſited only in the office of farms; and, with relation to prizes taken at ſea (one tenth of which fall to the admiral of France) the adjudicatory of farms, or their commiſſioners, ſhall be obliged to ſecure them in a warehouſe, under two different keys, one of which ſhall remain with the officers of the admiralty, and the other with the receiver of the depoſitory of farms, till definitive judgment be given.

9. And, to indemnify the admiral of France for thoſe rights which may be pretended to belong to him, as well in reſpect of contraband trade in France, as that in the French iſlands and colonies, and to put an end to the litigations which ſuch pretenſions may occaſion, there ſhall be paid to him annually, on the firſt day of the year, by the adjudicatory of farms, to commence from the preſent year 1728, the ſum of 20,000 livres; which, for the future, ſhall put an end to all pretenſions of this nature in the preſent admiral and his ſucceſſors; nor ſhall the farmers of the revenue interfere with the determinations of the officers of the admiralty,

ralty, with reſpect to confiſcations, nor any thing which does not immediately concern contraband and prohibited trade, and the care of the duties of the farms.

10. The farmer of the revenue, under pretence of care thereof, be it either for the loading of ſalt, and to prevent contraband trade, or for whatever other reaſon, ſhall not have, or put to ſea, any veſſel of what ſize ſoever, without leave and commiſſion from the admiral of France, regiſtered at the admiralty of the place, under the penalty contained in the ordinance of 1681; except, however, ſmall boats requiſite to viſit ſhips in creeks, ports, and roads. With reſpect to the loading of ſalt, there ſhall be permiſſions granted for ſuch ſhips every voyage: and, in relation to veſſels and pinnaces that are always on the ſea for the ſervice of his majeſty's farmers of the revenue, their leave and commiſſion ſhall be granted them annually.

11. The adjudicatory of the farms ſhall be allowed to have upon the ſea, and at the mouths or entrances of rivers, armed veſſels, pinnaces, and ſhallops, on condition of the ſaid veſſels tranſmitting, every ſix months, to the ſecretary of the admiralty of the province, an account, certified by the commiſſioner-general of the farms, of the ſur and chriſtian names of all perſons therein employed.

12. The

12. The adjudicatory ſhall be permitted to fit out the ſaid veſſels, and to chuſe their ſailors, provided they are not in the ſervice of the royal marine.

13. Licences ſhall be granted them from the admiral of France for ſuch veſſels and pinnaces which they may judge requiſite for their purpoſe, in order to be armed upon the coaſts of the kingdom; and theſe licences ſhall remain in force for one year, and be renewed annually at their expiration, under the penalties contained in the ordinance of 1681.

14. With relation to thoſe pinnaces, boats, or other veſſels that the farmers of the revenue may think neceſſary to arm at the iſland-colonies in America, to go within the extent of the limits preſcribed by the regulations made in regard to veſſels carrying on contraband commerce, they ſhall be obliged to take out a commiſſion of the admiral of France, as required by article the 5th of the letters patents of the month of October, 1727, which commiſſion ſhall remain in full force for one year only.

15. If any veſſel, carrying on contraband commerce on the coaſts of the iſlands of America, ſhould be attacked by any armed veſſel commiſſioned by the admiralty of France, and alſo by a veſſel armed by the farmers of the revenue, under the like commiſſion from the admiralty, the prize ſhall be divided between them, according to the num-

number of ſailors and cannon in the reſpective armed veſſels, conformably to the ordinance of 1681.

16. There ſhall be no innovations made with regard to prizes and offenders, which concern damaged ſalt and tobacco, in the ports, and on the coaſts of the kingdom; the full power to judge of which remaining in the officer of the gabelles, and others who have cognizance thereof, according to the regulations iſſued for that purpoſe; all which ſhall be executed according to their form and tenor, without deviating from the preſent arret.

17. Upon this occaſion, our letters patents of the month of October, 1727, ſhall be taken into conſideration, as likewiſe other regulations concerning contraband and prohibited merchandizes. His majeſty enjoins the Sieur intendants and commiſſaries throughout the provinces and generalities of the kingdom, and the ſaid French iſlands and colonies, to be vigilant in the execution of the preſent arret, which ſhall be executed, notwithſtanding any obſtructions thereunto; of which, if any ariſe, the cognizance thereof ſhall be left to his majeſty in council, and all courts and ordinary judges are hereby forbid to interfere in theſe caſes.—Done at the royal council of ſtate, his majeſty being preſent, held at Verſailles the 25th of May, 1728.

LEWIS,

Lewis, by the grace of God, &c.—To our faithful friends and counſellors, concerned in our councils, maſters of requeſts of our houſhold, Sieurs intendants and commiſſaries throughout the provinces and generalities of our kingdom, and our French iſlands and colonies in America, greeting, &c.—We command and injoin you, by theſe preſents, ſigned with our hand, to be vigilant and attentive, each in his reſpective ſtation, to the due execution of the arret, the extract whereof is hereunto annexed, under the counter-ſeal of our chancery, iſſued this day in our council of ſtate, we being preſent, for the reaſons therein contained.—In the firſt place, we order and command our ſerjeant, on this requiſition, to ſignify and publiſh the ſaid arret, to all whom it may concern, that no one may be ignorant thereof, and to take all requiſite meaſures to put our commands in execution, without other permiſſion, notwithſtanding any impediments hereunto; the cognizance of which we reſerve to ourſelves and our council, and forbid all other courts or judges any way to interfere therein.—We will and ordain, &c."

Upon the 3d of October, 1730, a royal declaration was iſſued, concerning the regulation and collection of the capitation-tax at the Windward iſlands of America: and, on October the 4th, 1731, inſtructions were alſo iſſued, to facilitate the execution of the ſaid declara-

declaration. In regard to the firſt of theſe, although there is every thing done that could be, to prevent the evaſion of the tax, and all frauds in the collection, yet there does not ſeem leſs judgment in joining moderation with rigor and ſeverity. Example: in article the 9th of the ſaid declaration it is ſaid, "That ſuch who ſhall break up freſh land in the French iſlands and colonies ſhall be exempted, for two years, from the ſaid tax of capitation, not only for their own perſons, but for their domeſtics and negroes employed therein.—Likewiſe thoſe who ſhall eſtabliſh new plantations, either for cacao or indigo, ſhall be intitled to the ſame privileges."—Theſe being the chief particulars which relate to traffic, we ſhall take no other notice of the before-mentioned declaration than to obſerve that the latter, viz. the inſtructions for execution of thoſe of October the 4th, 1731, contain ſuch plain and intellgible rules for the execution of every diſtinct article of the former, that it is not poſſible either for the officers of the crown to miſtake their duty, or the people the intention of the legiſlator.

THE next eſſential particular that occurs, according to the order of time, with regard to the laws of France, in relation to their American iſlands and colonies, is a royal regulation with reſpect to the wheat-meal of Canada, which was iſſued by the king the 18th of May, 1732; and which is introduced with the following preamble:

"HIS

"HIS majeſty being informed, that the meal ſold in Canada, and which is exported thence to Cape Breton, and other of the French iſlands in America, is frequently of a bad quality, thre being mixed therewith meal of other grain than that of wheat-corn, and that the ſame is barrelled up too moiſt, or in caſks not ſufficiently dried: his majeſty deſirous to prevent a continuation of the like abuſes, which will abſolutely ruin and annihilate the ſaid commerce of meal, which is highly beneficial to the ſaid colony of Canada: his majeſty has ordered, and does order, &c. as follows, viz."

ARTICLE I.

MERCHANTS and manufacturers of wheat-meal in the colony of Canada ſhall be obliged, from the day of the publication of the preſent ordinance, to mark with fire both ends of the barrels wherein ſuch meal ſhall be packed, before the ſail or embarkation of the ſaid barrels, on pain of three livres penalty for every barrel not ſo marked, that ſhall be offered to ſale, be ſold, or embarked.

2. Merchants and others ſhall be obliged, on pain of 20 livres penalty, to depoſit the image or impreſſion of the ſaid fire-mark which they uſe (viz. thoſe merchants and other manufacturers of meal reſiding in the city of Quebec, or under it's government) in the rolls of the admiralty eſtabliſhed in the

ſaid

ſaid city ; and thoſe dwelling in the cities of the three rivers, and at Mont-Real, or under the government thereof, ſhall be depoſited in the rolls of the royal juriſdictions of the city, within the diſtricts of their habitation.

3. Thoſe who ſhall embark the ſaid barrels, if meal, ſhall be obliged to mention, in their invoice of the ſaid barrels, the diſtinct mark thereof, and to mention the ſame likewiſe in the bills of lading, on pain of 20 livres penalty for every offence.

4. The captains of thoſe ſhips on which the ſaid barrels of meal ſhall be laden, ſhall be obliged, before their loading, to certify whether the ſaid barrels be marked ; and, in caſe they are embarked without marking, they ſhall be condemned in the penalty of three livres for every barrel ſo embarked.

5. Meal barrelled and offered to ſale in Canada, which ſhall be found to be of bad quality, ſhall be confiſcated, and the proprietor thereof condemned in four livres per barrel penalty.

6. Meal ſent from Canada to Cape Breton, and to other of the French iſlands in America, which ſhall be found to be of bad quality, ſhall likewiſe be confiſcated, and the proprietor thereof condemned in a penalty of 4 livres per barrel.

7. Cognizance of offences committed in Canada againſt the preſent ordinance, on account of barrels of meal being expoſed to ſale on the land, and before having been embarked,

ed, and which barrels ſhall not be marked, and on default alſo of not depoſiting the ſaid mark with the ſecretaries of the royal juriſdiction, together with the bad quality of the ſaid meal; ſhall belong to the intendant of New France, or to his ſubdelegates in his abſence; but, if the ſaid offences ſhall be diſcovered in any other places than on the keys, and in the ſhips and veſſels, or in the warehouſes wherein they ſhall be put from the firſt time of their landing; and, in caſe the ſaid fire-mark hath not been duly depoſited, in conformity to the preſent ordinance, in the rolls of the admiralty of Quebec, the officers of the ſaid court ſhall take cognizance of the ſaid offences.

8. The officers of the admiralty of Quebec, and thoſe of Cape Breton, and of other French iſlands in America, ſhall take cognizance, each within the extent of his diſtrict, of offences committed by neglect of the fire-mark required at both ends of the ſaid barrels, and alſo of the bad quality of the meal, provided the offence be diſcovered upon the keys, or in the ſhips or other veſſels, or in the warehouſes where they ſhall be depoſited for the firſt time of their being landed: they likewiſe ſhall take cognizance of the default, in omitting to mention the mark of the ſaid barrels in the invoices and bills of lading of the concerned.

9. The officers of the admiralty of Cape Breton ſhall be obliged to direct a verbal proceſs,

ceſs, with reſpect to the bad meal; which proceſs ſhall be ſent to the intendant of New France, in order to be tranſmitted to the officers of the admiralty of Quebec: on which account the proprietors of the ſaid meal ſhall be condemned in the penalty of 4 livres per barrel, as aforeſaid.

10. The officers of the admiralty of the other French iſlands in America ſhall, in like manner, be obliged to direct a verbal proceſs, with regard to the bad meal; which proceſs they ſhall ſend to the ſecretary of ſtate, having there the juriſdiction of the marine, to be tranſmitted by him to the officers of the admiralty of Quebec, to the end that the proprietor may be condemned in the penalty of 4 livres for every barrel of bad meal.

11. Cognizance of offences committed againſt the preſent ordinance, which ſhall be diſcovered after the landing of the ſaid meal at Cape Breton, or at other French iſlands in America, and after they ſhall have been bought up from the keys or warehouſes wherein they may have been put, ſhall belong to the intendant of the iſland where they ſhall have been landed, and, in his abſence, to his ſubdelegate.

12. The intendants of the ſaid iſlands, or their ſubdelegates in their abſence, ſhall be obliged to direct the like verbal proceſs, in relation to bad meal; which proceſs they ſhall ſend to the ſecretary of ſtate for that juriſdiction

riſdiction of the marine, to be tranſmitted by him to the intendant of New France, to the end that the proprietors may be condemned in the penalty of 4 livres per barrel, which ſhall be found bad.

13. Theſe verbal proceſſes, made on account of the bad quality of meal arriving at Cape Breton, and other the French iſlands in America, ſhall ſignify the quality and condition in which the meal ſhall be found, together with the mixture of what other grain ſhall be therein made; they ſhall mention likewiſe to what the bad quality of the ſaid meal is to be attributed.

14. The penalties and confiſcations which ſhall have been adjudged by the intendant of New France, ſhall belong (viz. for offences committed in the government of Quebec) to the general hoſpital of the ſaid place; for thoſe committed in the government of the three rivers, to the Hotel-Dieu of the ſaid city; and, for thoſe committed in the government of Mont-Real, to the Hotel-Dieu there eſtabliſhed.

15. The penalties and confiſcations decreed by the judge-commiſſary of Cape Breton, ſubdelegated by the intendant of New France, ſhall belong to the hoſpital of the ſaid iſland; and thoſe decreed by the intendant of the other French iſlands of America, or their ſubdelegates, ſhall be appropriated to the neareſt hoſpital.

16. The

16. The penalties and confiscations decreed by the officers of the admiralty, ſhall belong to the admiral of France.

His majeſty orders and commands Monſ. the count of Toulouſe, admiral of France, and the governors, his lieutenant-general, and intendants in America, to keep a vigilant eye, every one in his own perſon, to the due execution of the preſent ordinance, which ſhall be read, publiſhed, and fixed up in every place where needful, and regiſtered in the rolls of the admiralty of the reſpective colonies wherein they have juriſdiction.—Done at Compeigne, the 18th of May, 1732.

Upon the 21ſt of May following the count of Thouloufe, admiral of France, iſſued his orders to all concerned, to have ſtrict regard to the execution of the preceding ordinance.

An arret of the royal council, forbidding all privateers and merchants, carrying on trade in the French iſlands and colonies, to ſend ſtuffs or painted linnens of the Indies thither, or thoſe of Perſia, China, or the Levant.—May 9, 1733. Extracted from the regiſters of the council of ſtate.

The king cauſing to be laid before him the letters patents of the month of April, 1717, touching the regulation of the commerce of the French iſlands and colonies of America, by the 12th article of which it is declared,

declared, that the merchants of the kingdom ſhall not ſhip for the ſaid iſlands and colonies any foreign merchandiſes, whoſe import and conſumption in the kingdom are prohibited, on pain of confiſcation, and a penalty of 3000 livres, which ſhould be decreed by the officers of the admiralty: alſo other letters patents, of the month of February, 1719, including regulations of trade from Marſeilles to the ſaid iſlands and colonies, the 12th article of which contains the ſame diſpoſition: alſo thoſe of the month of October, 1721, by which his majeſty granted to the city of Dunkirk the privilege and liberty to carry on trade to the ſaid iſlands, and ordained, by article 14, that the general regulation of the month of April, 1717, ſhould be executed in whatever was not repugnant to the diſpoſitions made by thoſe laſt letters patents: and his majeſty being informed that the merchants who carry on the commerce of the ſaid French iſlands and colonies, might export thither ſtuffs and painted linens of the Indies, Perſia, China, or of the Levant, under pretence that theſe ſorts of merchandiſes (whoſe uſe and importation are nevertheleſs prohibited) are not expreſsly comprehended in the ſaid 12th article of the general regulation of 1717; againſt which his majeſty deſiring to provide, and conſidering the advice of the deputies of council of commerce, heard the report of the Sieur Orry, counſellor of ſtate, and counſellor in ordinary to the royal council, and comp-

comptroller-general of the finances, the king, being present in council, has ordained, and and does hereby ordain, that the letters patents of the month of April, 1717, of February, 1719, and October, 1721, shall be executed according to their form and tenor. In consequence of which, his majesty expressly forbids all privateers and merchants, carrying on trade to the French islands and colonies of America, to carry thither stuffs or painted linens of the Indies, of Persia, China, or the Levant, under what denomination soever, on pain of confiscation, and a penalty of 3000 livres, and to be EXCLUDED from being concerned in the said commerce for the future.—The like prohibitions are made to all captains, master-pilots, marine officers, sailors, passengers, and others who make up the crews of ships designed for the said islands and colonies, to carry thither, in any shape whatsoever, any of the said stuffs and painted linens, on pain of confiscation, and of 3000 livres penalty against the captains, master-pilots, marine officers and passengers, besides their being rendered incapable of commanding and serving in any vessel whatsoever; and, with respect to sailors, and others whereof the ship's crew consists, on pain of one year's imprisonment, or more, according to the case: his majesty commands and enjoins the Sieurs intendants and commissaries in the marine provinces of the kingdom, and the officers of the admiralty, and likewise the governors

vernors and intendants of the ſaid French iſlands and colonies, or all commanders and commiſſaries ſubdelegated, to have a ſtrict regard, each for himſelf, to the execution of the preſent arret, which ſhall be read, publiſhed, and fixed up, wherever needful. Done at the king's council, his majeſty being preſent, held at Verſailles the 9th of May, 1733.

Lewis, by the grace of God, &c.—To our friends and faithful counſellors, concerned in our councils, the Sieurs intendants and commiſſaries, diſperſed, for the execution of our orders, throughout our maritime provinces, and to the officers of the admiralty, alſo to the governors and intendants of the French iſlands and colonies, or to the commanders and commiſſaries ſubdelegated in their diſtricts, greeting: we command and enjoin, by theſe preſents ſigned by us, to have a ſtrict regard, every one in his own perſon, to the execution of the arret hereunto annexed, under the counter-ſeal of our chancery, this day given in our council of ſtate, we being there preſent, for the reaſons therein contained, &c.

An arret of the royal council of ſtate, which grants the merchants of St. Jean de Luz, for their whale and cod fiſheries at Canada and Cape Breton, the ſame rights, privileges, and exemptions granted by letters patents of the month of April, 1717, for the trade of the French iſlands and colonies of America. —July 20, 1734. Extracted from the regiſters of the royal council of ſtate.

Upon a petition preſented to the king in council, by the merchants of St. Jean de Luz, containing, that as yet, with regard to the cod and whale fiſheries, which is the only commerce of that city, they are under the neceſſity of ſending ſhips, as well to the iſland of Terra Nova, which makes part of the French colonies of America, as to Davis's Streights in North America; notwithſtanding they have never enjoyed an exemption of duties on merchandiſes deſigned for the French colonies, with reſpect both to the cargo or the victualling of their veſſels; of which they have always refuſed the acquittance of ſecurity at Bourdeaux, under pretence that there is no warehouſe of entrepoſt eſtabliſhed in their port; and that in the letters patents of the month of April, 1717, containing regulations for the commerce of the French colonies, which ſignify the ports where veſſels are to be fitted out, that of St. Jean de Luz hath been omitted: and, as that omiſſion makes it

impoſ-

impoſſible for them to carry on the commerce of the colonies upon an equality with other merchants of the kingdom, included in the ſaid letters patents, they being liable to theſe duties, from which others are exempt: which have proved ſo burthenſome, that they have ſuſtained conſiderable loſſes, for ſome years paſſed, in their cod and whale fiſheries: for theſe reaſons they requeſt, that his majeſty would pleaſe to order the eſtabliſhment of a warehouſe of entrepoſt in the ſaid city of St. Jean de Luz, for fitting out ſhips for the French colonies of America, and that they may enjoy thoſe exemptions of duties, and other privileges and advantages, granted to the merchants, contained in the letters patents of the month of April, 1717. His majeſty having ſeen the ſaid petition, heard the ſentiments of the deputies of commerce, and the report of the Sieur Orry, counſellor of ſtate, and comptroller-general of the finances, and the king being preſent in council, hath granted, and doth grant, to the merchants of St. Jean de Luz, for their whale and cod fiſheries at Canada and Cape Breton, the ſame rights, privileges, and exemptions which are granted for the commerce of the French colonies, to the merchants of the kingdom, included in the letters patents of the month of April, 1717; to which end, his majeſty orders that there may be eſtabliſhed, in the ſaid city of St. Jean de Luz, a warehouſe, wherein the merchandiſes and proviſions deſigned

ſigned for the victualling of ſhips fitted out for the ſaid fiſheries, ſhall be lodged, according to the entrepoſt, and in conformity to the 30th article of the ſaid letters patents.—Done at the council of ſtate, held at Verſailles, the 20th of July, 1734.

An arret of the royal council of ſtate, and letters patents in conſequence thereof, concerning the entrepoſt, as well in reſpect to merchandiſes intended for the French iſlands and colonies, as thoſe which come from thence.—Of the 6th of May, 1738. Regiſtered in the council of aids.

THE letters patents of the month of April, 1717, being repreſented to the king in council, containing regulations for the commerce of the French colonies, by which his majeſty hath ordered, by articles 5, 6, and 30, that the proviſions and merchandiſes of the kingdom intended for the ſaid colonies, together with thoſe alſo of the ſaid colonies, ſhall be warehouſed, according to the entrepoſt in the ports therein deſigned, and that the warehouſes for that purpoſe ſhall be choſen by the merchants, at their expence, and locked with three different keys, one of which ſhall be depoſited with the commiſſioner of the five great farms, another with the commiſſioner of the weſtern domaine, and the third with the

the overſeer appointed for that purpoſe by the merchants: the declaration of his majeſty, of the 19th of January, 1723, which orders that the merchants, the proprietors of the proviſions and merchandiſes deſigned to be warehouſed, and intended for the French iſlands and colonies, ſhall be obliged, after one year's entrepoſt, to declare, at the offices of farms of thoſe places, the quantities, qualities, weights, and meaſures of the ſaid proviſions and merchandiſes, which ſhall remain in the entrepoſt warehouſes; which declaration ſhall be certified by the commiſſioners of the adjudicatory of the farms; and, in caſe of offending there-againſt, by a falſe declaration, the merchants proprietors of the ſaid interpoſed merchandiſe ſhall be condemned in the penalty of 500 livres, and likewiſe obliged to the payment of the duties of the merchandiſes which ſhall be found wanting according to their declaration: and laſtly, in caſe of the ſale of the ſaid merchandiſes, the merchants proprietors thereof ſhall be obliged to diſcharge the duties one month after ſale, on pain of the like penalty of 500 livres. The arret of the council of the third of May, 1723, and letters patents, in conſequence thereof, of the 21ſt of the ſaid month, by which his majeſty hath fixed the time of entrepoſt, as well with reſpect to the merchandiſes of the iſlands and colonies, as of thoſe declared and deſigned for the ſaid

iſlands

islands and colonies, shall be for one year, reckoning from the day that the said merchandises shall have been so warehoused; which time being expired, they shall be liable to duties. And his majesty being informed, that, in the cases where the farmer of the revenue, on account of the difficulties which attend warehouses under keys, permits the merchants to make the entrepost in their own warehouses, many of whom lodge the said merchandises, or change the warehouses, without making any declaration thereof to the farmer, which hath occasioned divers abuses: his majesty, being resolved to remedy the same, by adding to the abovesaid regulations fresh precautions, which may, in in some measure, supply the default of the keys, which, in the terms of the letters patents of April 1717, should be deposited with the farmer of the revenue, &c. The king having heard the report of the Sieur Orry, counsellor of state, and comptroller-general of the finances, being present in council, hath ordered, and doth hereby order, that, in case where the farmer of the revenue shall permit merchants to put merchandises in their own warehouses, the said merchants shall be obliged to declare, to the commissioners of the farms, the warehouse wherein they design to place them, and to give to tho officer of farms security to represent them in the same quality and quantity, at the time required,

quired, under the pains and penalties hereafter mentioned.—His majeſty forbids the merchants to take out the ſaid merchandiſes from the warehouſes wherein they ſhall be depoſited, or even to ſhift them from one warehouſe to another, till they have made a declaration thereof to the ſaid office, and taken out a licence for that purpoſe, &c. His majeſty orders, that, in caſe of fraud, the ſaid merchants ſhall be condemned to the confiſcation of the value of the merchandiſes wanting, and beſides in the penalty of 500 livres, &c. and, in caſe of a change of warehouſe without declaration made thereof, they ſhall be deprived of the benefit of the entrepoſt, and liable to the payment of all the duties, &c.

Then follow letters patents to inforce the ſame.

MAY the 21ſt, 1741, was iſſued an arret of the royal council of ſtate, permitting privateers for the French iſlands and colonies to load ſalt in Bretagne, or in other parts where cuſtomary, to be employed at Cape Verde, for the ſalting of beef deſigned for the ſaid iſlands, without paying any duties, &c.

ON July the 19th, 1742, a royal ordinance was made, forbidding all captains of ſhips diſarmed in the ſaid iſlands of America,

rica, from paying in the ſaid iſlands the balance due to their ſhip's crew, and injoining them to make the diſcounts in the preſence of the officers charged to take an account of ſeveral claſſes of the ſailors, and regulating the peculiar forms requiſite upon thoſe occaſions, &c.

JUNE the 24th, 1743, an arret of the royal council of ſtate was iſſued, ordering that the merchandizes of the produce of the French iſlands of America, intended for Cape Breton, ſhall be diſcharged, to the 1ſt of January, 1747, of the duty of weight of 1 per cent. and that thoſe merchandizes of the produce of the ſaid iſlands, deſigned as well for Cape Breton as for Canada, ſhall be diſcharged, during the ſaid time, of the duties of 3 per cent. of the weſtern domaine, together with the duty of 40 ſols per 100 weight upon ſugars of the ſaid iſlands, which ſhall be ſent there.

OCTOBER the 29th, 1743, an arret of the royal council of ſtate was iſſued, ordering that the merchants and privateers of Marſeilles ſhall be obliged to bring to the office of the weſtern domaine all merchandizes coming from the French iſlands of America, ſo well as thoſe which ſhall be embarked for the ſaid iſlands, to be there viſited, and the duties diſcharged.

APRIL

April the 20th, 1744, an arret of the royal council of ſtate was made, ſuſpending, during the late war, the execution of the ſecond article of the letters patents of the month of April, 1717, concerning the commerce of the French iſlands of America.

On the 22d of December, 1750, an arret of the royal council of ſtate was declared, containing an exemption of the duty of 3 per cent. of the weſtern domaine, on cottons brought from the French colonies of America, for home-conſumption, and to ſubject them to the ſame duties of exportation that they paid before the arret of the 12th of November, 1749. Alſo ordaining that the duty of 3 per cent. of the weſtern domaine ſhall continue to be collected upon cotton of the French colonies exported to other nations; and that the duty of one half per cent. eſtabliſhed by the declaration of the 10th of November, 1727, ſhall continue to be collected upon the cotton of the ſaid colonies, in the ſame manner as collected upon other merchandizes which come from thence.

On the 17th of Auguſt, 1751, an arret was iſſued by the royal council of ſtate, fixing at 8 livres per 100 weight the duties on the exportation of cotton-wool out of the kingdom, coming from the French iſland colonies, and thoſe on cotton-yarn at 10 livres

livres per 100 weight, as well for the duties of the five great farms, as for thoſe of the weſtern domaine; ordaining alſo, that the duty of one half per cent. augmentation of the weſtern domaine ſhall remain to be collected at importation in the kingdom, upon cottons coming from the ſaid iſlands.

We have dwelt the longer on the laws eſtabliſhed in France for the regulation of the trade of their American iſlands and other colonies, becauſe theſe things ſeem to be little known in this kingdom, and becauſe they point out the meaſures which that nation has taken, from the year 1701 to the preſent time, for the advancement of the commerce of their colonies. And, as the ſucceſs and proſperity of this neighbouring nation, in theſe iſlands and colonies, have been ſo remarkable and conſpicuous to the whole world, within half a century, a knowledge of thoſe laws, whereby ſuch great things have been effected, one ſhould ſeem to think, muſt be acceptable to all who would enter into the cauſes of ſuch unparalleled conſequences.

That our readers may form a right judgment of theſe laws and regulations, we ſhall obſerve the following particulars, viz.

1. That they are grounded on the repreſentations of the deputies of commerce, made, from time to time, to the royal council

cil of ſtate: that thoſe deputies of commerce are perſons well ſkilled and experienced in thoſe branches of trade about which they lay their ſentiments before the royal council.

2. THAT theſe laws and regulations, in general, are derived from a very exact and circumſtantial ſtate of the commerce, as carried on by the practical merchants and traders; which indicate that the legiſlators in all countries cannot be too well informed of all the various methods and arts made uſe of by traders in the proſecution of their reſpective branches, the better to enable them ſo to adapt and conform their laws to the nature of peculiar branches, that the national proſperity cannot fail of being promoted.

3. THAT the fines and penalties made on traders violating thoſe laws are very rigorous and ſevere; and that the French nation are no leſs ſtrict in the execution of thoſe laws, than they are circumſtantial and deliberate in the enacting them: witneſs the caſe of captain Gilles Robin, for carrying on illicit trade with an Engliſh veſſel at St. Domingo.

4. THAT the laws of trade in France ſhould ſeem, ſuitably to the nature of the conſtitution of their government, to be wiſely accommodated to preſerve the whole trade of their iſlands and colonies to themſelves, in order to render them abſolutely ſubſervient to the proſperity of their mother-kingdom.—That,

to this end, we find them, by their laws, extremely vigilant to prevent all contraband trade from being carried on with foreign nations in their colonies, they judging it highly detrimental to the intereſt of their colonies, as well as of the kingdom of France in general.

5. THAT, ſince the laws of France in general are ſo well calculated to prevent ſuch contraband trade, we may preſume that, whenever this nation permits ſuch trade with their American colonies, they are certain to be gainers by it; otherwiſe we may reaſonably enough believe, that they would ſoon put an effectual ſtop thereto, as the due execution of their laws could not fail of being effectual to that purpoſe.

6. THAT as the French encourage a trade being carried on between the Britiſh northern colonies and the French ſugar-iſlands in America, as is taken notice of in theſe papers, it is to be feared that the French are too ſenſible of the advantages ariſing from that trade, or they would as little admit of that in particular as any other; and, if that proves a gainful branch of trade to the French, does it not become the wiſdom of Great-Britain ſo thoroughly to examine into this commerce with the French colonies, as to determine whether a commerce beneficial to France can be ſo in its conſequences to Great-Britain?

7. THAT

7. THAT the French take all proper care to promote a trade between Canada, or New-France, and their iſland colonies; and that it ſhould not ſeem to appear bad policy in Great-Britain to promote, as much as poſſible, the commerce of our North-American colonies, with our own ſugar-iſlands, rather than to permit them to carry on a trade to the French ſugar-iſlands.

8. THAT the French have ſurpriſingly increaſed in their ſugar-trade, as well as in every other part of the commerce of their iſlands and colonies in America, is a fact uncontrovertable; and that their maritime power, in general, has augmented, in the like proportion, is as little to be diſputed.

THE number of prizes that were taken from the French in the late war, and the frequent arrivals of their numerous fleets, have rouzed and opened the eyes of many that would not be convinced before: and, ſince our indolence is at length awakened, our ſecurity alarmed, and every breaſt ſeems to be filled with thoſe paſſions which are inkindled by the love of our country, is it not full time to exert our whole ſtrength, to reduce this nation within bounds, if poſſible?

IN order to anſwer ſo deſirable an end, it will be neceſſary to ſearch narrowly into the preſent ſtate, laws, eſtabliſhments, and rules of commerce, as well foreign as domeſtic, and to retrench what is ſuperfluous and inconvenient

convenient in our own laws, and to ſupply what is inſufficient by prudent regulations. But, above all, does it not behove Great Britain ſeriouſly to think of making ſuch foreign alliances, as will enable us to humble this eternal diſturber of Europe once for all? For this I will preſume to ſay may be done: and now or never ſeems the time!

DIS-

DISSERTATION XXI.

The ſyſtem of the French with regard to their African trade; wherein will appear, by what meaſures they have become ſo ſucceſsful therein, and they have had ſo greatly the advantage over us.

THE African trade is eſtimable to the French, as well as other European nations, who have a ſhare in it, on account of the gold, the ivory, and the ſlave trade. Though the commerce of this country, as it has hitherto been carried on, affords but few articles, in compariſon to that of others, yet it is valuable and important; and the more ſo, in that it is ſo neceſſary a trade to the Europeans, as they are at preſent circumſtanced. For

THIS commerce is not only profitable to the reſpective Europeans, in the direct way of trading from their ſeveral countries to the African coaſt, but is ſo much the more ſo to thoſe nations, which have colonies and plantations to ſupport by the dint of negro-labour, for want of a competent number of whites, for the cultivation of ſugars, tobacco's baccoes, and all other plantation-productions.

How greatly beneficial this traffic has proved to the French nation in this reſpect, we may judge from the extraordinary encreaſe of their ſugar colonies. It is not above half a century ſince they did not employ above 100 ſail of ſhips for the ſupply of their own kingdom for ſugars; but in the late war it was diſcovered, that they employed above ſix hundred ſail. This is one of the great nurſeries of trade and ſeamen, that has rendered the French no leſs formidable in America than Europe.

By what means theſe mighty things have come to paſs, cannot be ſo effectually repreſented, as by the authentic ordonances and arrets; which ſhews the real ſpirit of their laws.—We need trace theſe no farther back than the year 1716.

The king's letters patent for the liberty of trade upon the coaſt of Africa, publiſhed at Paris, January 1736.

[The preamble runs thus, which I ſhall note with all brevity, for the ſake of ſome uſeful obſervations.]

Lewis, &c—To all, greeting.—By letters patent of the late king, dated January 1685, there was eſtabliſhed a company by the name of the Guinea Company, to continue for the ſpace of 20 years, excluding all others

others the trade of negroes, gold duſt, and other merchandize trafficked in upon the coaſt of Africa, from the river Searraleone to the Cape of Good-Hope; and likewiſe granting to this company divers privileges and immunities; and, among other grants, exempted them from half the duties of all merchandizes, brought from all places within their diſtrict and iſles of America upon their own account, although the time limited by theſe letters patents ſhould be expired.—The late king, &c. thought good, on account of engagements this company had made, in order to ſupply the Spaniſh Weſt-Indies with negroes by the Aſſiento contract, to continue to them the ſame privileges and immunities, under the title of the Aſſiento treaty, until the month of November, 1713.—The merchants of our kingdom having repreſented how much it tended to the benefit of trade in general, and in particular to the improvement of the French iſlands in America, that the commerce of the Guinea coaſt ſhould be free and open to all his majeſty's ſubjects; the late king did not think it proper to form a new company, though there were many perſons ready to offer themſelves, and enter into ſuch an aſſociation; and, as we are willing to encourage the freedom of commerce, and deal favourably with the merchants and traders, who ſhall undertake this traffic, and afford them every thing neceſſary to render it more conſiderable than it has

has been, and by that means to provide for our ſubjects of the French iſles in America a ſufficient number of negroes, for improving the cultivation of their lands: for theſe and other reaſons moving us hereunto, we have thought fit, by the advice, &c. And have declared, reſolved, and ordained, &c. That

ARTICLE I.

WE have permitted, and do permit, to all the merchants of our kingdom for the time to come, to have a free trade for negroes, gold duſt, and all other merchandizes that may be brought from the coaſt of Africa, from the river Searralyonne to the Cape of Good-Hope, provided their ſhips are fitted out in the harbours of Rouen, Rochelle, Bourdeaux, and Nantes.

2. The maſters and captains who trade to the coaſt of Guinea, ſhall be obliged to declare at the ſecretary's of the admiralty office, eſtabliſhed at the place of their departure, and give ſecurity at the receipt of cuſtoms, to oblige them to return into one of the ports of Rouen, Rochelle, Bourdeaux, and Nantes; except, nevertheleſs, thoſe ſhips which ſhall go out from Rouen, Rochelle, and Bourdeaux, ſhould be drove, at their return, into Nantes, or St. Malo.

3. The merchants of thoſe ſhips that ſhall tranſport to the French iſles of America negroes bought upon the coaſt of Guinea, ſhall pay, upon the arrival of their ſhips in the ports

ports of Rouen, Rochelle, Bourdeaux, and Nantes, into the hands of the treaſurer-general of the marine in being, the ſum of 20 livres for every negro that ſhall be carried to the ſaid iſlands, for which they ſhall give ſecurity to the ſecretary of the admiralty, on their being permitted to take their leave of our moſt dear and truly beloved uncle, Lewis Alexander of Bourbon, count of Thoulouſe, admiral of France, &c. and as to thoſe merchants, whoſe ſhips ſhall only trade for gold duſt, and other commodities upon the ſaid coaſt, they ſhall likewiſe be bound, upon the arrival of their ſaid ſhips in the ſaid ports, to pay into the hands of the treaſurer of the marine the ſum of three livres for every ton his ſhip's burden ſhall contain; which twenty livres aforeſaid, and three livres, ſhall be employed, by order of the council of marine, for the keeping in repair the fortifications, factories, and cuſtom-houſes, which are or ſhall be ſettled on the ſaid coaſts of Guinea, which expences we will defray for the time to come.

4. Nevertheleſs, the payment of the ſaid three livres per ton duty is excuſed during the three next following years, from the day and date of theſe preſents, to all our ſubjects, whoſe ſhips ſhall trade to the Guinea coaſt for gold and other merchandizes, ſlaves only excepted.

5. Be it enacted by the authority aforeſaid, that all manner of merchandizes that ſhall

be

be brought from the coaſt of Guinea by our ſubjects, directly to the ports of Rouen, Rochelle, Bourdeaux, and Nantes, we exempt from one half the duties of importation, that are farmed, or may be farmed; likewiſe our will is, that all ſugars, and other merchandizes, of all our ſubjects that ſhall be brought from the French American iſlands, ariſing from the ſale and truck of negroes, be equally exempted from the ſaid half duties of importation, on their producing a certificate from the ſuperintendant of the iſles, or commiſſary-governor, or commiſſioner of the cuſtoms in the Weſt-Indies, that the goods ſhipped at the ſaid iſlands aroſe from the ſale and barter of negroes, which the ſaid ſhips had there unloaded, the ſaid certificate ſpecifying the ſhips names, number of negroes that ſhall be ſhipped to the iſlands, and lodged in the receivers office, who ſhall grant to the captains and maſters a duplicate of the ſame, without any expence.

All our receivers, commiſſioners, or deputies, are forbid to take more duties, upon pain of four times the value.

6. Linens of all ſorts, toys, mercery, glaſsware wrought and plain, iron-bars, plate-iron, guns, ſwords, and other arms, gun-flints, being the manufacture of this kingdom, ſhall be free from all duties of exportation, uſual both in our receiver's office, and all the offices in their paſſage, and the ports they are bound to, on condition it is proved they are

are intended for the Guinea trade; until which is confirmed, the ſaid goods ſhall be lodged in the cuſtom-houſe, under two different keys; one kept by the receiver-general of our cuſtoms, the other by whomſoever the merchants ſhall propoſe, at their own expence. As for the wines of Anjou, and other products of the river Loire, bound to Guinea, they ſhall be under the ſame reſtrictions as thoſe bound to the French American iſlands, according to the arret of council 23 September, 1710. And, with reſpect to the wines of Bourdeaux, we will and ordain, that they are regulated, as if ſhipped for the American iſlands, on taking a bill of loading there of the ſaid wines, and giving them the uſual ſecurity.

7. We grant to the ſaid merchants leave to lodge, in the ports of Rouen, Rochelle, Bourdeaux, and Nantes, the goods called cowries, ſtriped blue and white India cottons, printed linens, grain cryſtal, ſmall Dutch looking-glaſſes, Dutch tobacco-pipes, and others from the north, coming only by ſea for the Guinea trade: we grant likewiſe the ſame room in our cuſtom-houſe for two years and no longer, from the date of theſe preſents, for Dutch knives, kettles, and other ſort of copper utenſils. Provided the aforeſaid foreign goods ſhall be ſpecified to the commiſſioner of the cuſtoms upon their arrival, and afterwards depoſited in the king's warehouſe for that purpoſe, locked with two keys,

keys, one to remain in the hands of the commiſſioner, the other with whom the merchant ſhall name, all at their own expence.

8. The commiſſioner of the cuſtoms in each of the aforeſaid ports ſhall keep a regiſter, which ſhall be lettered and marked by the director of the cuſtoms, in which the aforeſaid commiſſioner ſhall regiſter in parcels the goods ſpecified in the two foregoing articles, as ſoon as they ſhall be depoſited in the warehouſe. The aforeſaid commiſſioner is forbid to give a certificate for their clearance, upon the ſecurity that was taken at the firſt office, until the proof, the regiſter, and the unloading of them, ſhall be examined into in the aforeſaid ſtaple warehouſe, from whence they ſhall not be taken until they are to be put on board the ſhips bound to the coaſt of Guinea. And, at the loading of the aforeſaid goods, both foreign and French, for the coaſt of Guinea: our will is, that there be mentioned in the margin of the regiſter, &c. the name of the ſhip they were put on board, and ſigned by the commiſſioner, the merchants they are conſigned to, and the captain who receives the goods on board, &c.

9. Nevertheleſs, we grant leave to the merchants and traders of the city of St. Malo to fit out and equip, in their ports, ſhips for the coaſt of Guinea, and for the French coaſts of America, and to make their returns to the aforeſaid ports on the foregoing clauſes, articles, and exemptions, already mentioned,

pay

paying us for the goods which ſhall come from the coaſt of Guinea, and the French iſles of America, the ſettled duties, according to the uſual cuſtom in the aforeſaid port of St. Malo, for the profit of our moſt dear and truly-beloved uncle Louis Alexander de Bourbon, count of Thoulouſe, duke of Penthievre, admiral of France, and governor of Bretagne, &c.

So ſoon after, as the 27th of September, 1720, there paſſed an arret of the council of ſtate, granting and re-uniting perpetually to the French Eaſt India company, the excluſive privilege of the trade of the coaſt of Guinea, &c.—The preamble to which, as contained in the regiſters of the council of ſtate, is as follows, and well deſerves the attention of this kingdom—It runs as follows, viz.

THE king's letters patent of January, 1716, being repreſented to the king in council, whereby his majeſty permitted all the merchants of his kingdom, to carry on freely the commerce of negroes, gold duſt, and all other the merchandiſes trafficked in on the coaſt of Africa, from the river Searraleone, incluſively, to the Cape of Good Hope; and his majeſty being informed, *that inſtead of the advantages that were expected from this general freedom allowed in that commerce, there reſulted three great inconveniences: viz.* (1) *the concourſe of numerous different traders, who came on this coaſt, and their endeavours to haſten their cargoes, to avoid the expence of demurrage,* *cauſing*

causing the natives of the country to fall the price of French commodities so excessively, and so greatly enhancing the price of Negroes upon the French; and also that of gold dust, and all other the merchandises of the African coast, that the whole trade became ruinous and impracticable to be carried on: his majesty has resolved to accept of the offers of the East India company, to send annually to the number of 3000 negroes at least, to the French islands in America, instead of the number of one thousand carried thither by letters patents in the year 1685; and his majesty is pleased to establish in favour of the said East India company, an *exclusive right* of trade to the said coast of Guinea, which will be easier for the said company, and more advantageous to the state, than the said company can otherwise afford to do; and can thereby be enabled to make such establishment, by which their ships that they send to the coast, will always find cargoes of slaves and merchandises ready for their return, and whereby they will not only be capable of supplying the French colonies in America, with negroes at a very reasonable price, that shall be necessary not only for the cultivation of their lands, but to carry thither a considerable quantity of gold and gold dust, and other sorts of merchandises fit for that traffic: his majesty upon this occasion desiring to make his intentions public, and being in council, with advice of the duke of Orleans ordains, &c.

1. His

1. His majeſty revokes the liberty of a free trade granted by his letters patent of January, 1716, on the coaſt of Guinea, and grants and unites the trade to the Eaſt India company for ever in negroes, gold, and other the merchandiſes, brought off the coaſt of Africa, from the river Searralyonne, incluſively, to the Cape of Good-Hope, &c.

2. His majeſty expreſsly forbids all his ſubjects to carry on trade and navigation to thoſe countries under any pretence whatſoever, and under pain of confiſcation of the veſſel, arms, ammunition, and merchandiſes of the ſaid Eaſt India company.

3. We grant to the ſaid Eaſt India company, the full propriety of all the lands, which they ſhall poſſeſs within the extent of the preſent grant, to make ſuch eſtabliſhments as they ſhall think proper; to erect forts for their ſecurity, and to tranſport thither arms, and cannon, and ſettle commandants and the number of officers and ſoldiers that they ſhall judge requiſite to ſecure their commerce, as well againſt foreigners, as the natives of the country: to which end the ſaid company is permitted to make ſuch treaties with the Negroe-princes as they think neceſſary.

4. All prizes taken from thoſe who ſhall interfere with the company's excluſive trade, ſhall be judged according to his majeſty's ordonnances and regulations for that intent.

5. The

5. The ſaid company ſhall be exempt from all duties of export on their merchandiſe exported to thoſe places within the ſaid grant, and for the French iſlands and colonies in America.

6. In relation to all merchandiſes that the ſaid company ſhall cauſe to be brought for their account from the countries within the ſaid grant, they ſhall be free from one moiety of the duties belonging to his majeſty, or to the farmers of the revenue; and all ſuch farmers, and their commiſſioners, and all other are obliged to demand no more, on pain of reſtoring the ſame in a fourfold degree—His majeſty commands that all ſugars and other ſpecies of merchandiſes that the ſaid company ſhall bring from the French iſlands of America, ariſing from the ſale and barter of Negroes, ſhall be entitled to the ſame exemption, in proving by certificate of the ſuperintendant of the ſaid iſlands, or one of their appointed commiſſioners, or the commiſſioner of the weſtern domaine, that the ſaid merchandiſes embarked from the ſaid iſlands, ariſing from the ſale and truck of negroes that have been diſcharged there in the company's veſſels; which certificates ſhall mention the number of veſſels, and the number of negroes which ſhall have been imported into the ſaid iſlands, and remain in the office of his majeſty's farmers, whoſe receivers ſhall give the duplicate without expence to the captains of the ſaid ſhips, &c.

7. His

7. His majeſty in the like manner forbids all mayors, ſheriffs, conſuls, jurats, ſindicts, and inhabitants of the cities, to exact from the ſaid company any duties of octroy, of any kind whatſoever, upon the proviſions and merchandiſes that they ſhall tranſport to their magazines, and ſea-ports, to lade on board their veſſels; his majeſty exonerating the ſaid company from the ſaid imports notwithſtanding all arrets, and ordonnances to the contrary.

8. He diſcharges the ſaid company from the duty of twenty livres for every negroe, and of three livres per ton of portage of the ſaid veſſels by the 3d article of the aforeſaid letters patents of January, 1716, laid upon the merchants who ſhould traffic to the ſaid coaſt of Guinea, and gives and grants to them forever all the forts and factories erected and eſtabliſhed upon the ſaid coaſt; whereby his majeſty ſhall be freed from all neceſſary expence, for the future, with relation to the ſupport and maintenance of the ſaid forts and factories, and that of the garriſons, and the appointments of governors and all other officers therein employed.

9. In conſideration whereof, his majeſty orders that there ſhall be paid to the ſaid company out of the revenues of the weſtern domaine, 13 livres for every negroe, that they ſhall make appear to have imported into the ſaid iſlands and colonies of America, according to certificate from the intendant of the

iſlands,

iſlands, or governor in his abſence, and twenty livres for every mark of gold duſt, that they ſhall make appear to have brought into the kingdom by the certificates of the directors of the mint of Paris.

10. Beſides the rights, privileges and exemptions before mentioned, the ſaid company ſhall be entitled to for the benefit of it's commerce on the ſaid coaſt of Guinea, all thoſe which it has a right to enjoy for the benefit of their commerce to the province of Louiſiana, in conſequence of letters patents of the month of Auguſt, 1717, together with all thoſe which have been enjoyed, in conſequence of letters patents of the late king of the month of January, 1685, by the antient Guinea company eſtabliſhed in virtue of the ſaid letters patents, as fully as if they were by theſe preſents expreſsly declared again, &c.

Letters patents, containing regulations for merchandiſes, which traders of this kingdom import from Holland and the North, for the Guinea trade. Given at Fontainbleau, September 7, 1728.

Lewis, by the grace of God, king of France and Navarre: to all our friends and faithful counſellors, members of our court of parliament of Paris, greeting: it being repreſented unto us, that our letters patents of the month of January, 1716, for the liberty of commerce upon the coaſt of Africa; in the ſeventh

ſeventh article of which we have granted to all our merchants permiſſion to warehouſe in the ports therein mentioned, amoug other merchandiſes, white, blue, and ſtripped cottons, printed linens, which they ſhall import from Holland and the North, by ſea only, for the trade of Guinea: and being informed that, by the indulgence of this grant, they have introduced into our kingdom, to the prejudice of our eſtabliſhed manufactures, India cottons, of a finer quality than what need be ſent for that trade; we have provided againſt it by the arret of this day, given in our council of ſtate, we being there preſent; for the due execution of which, we have ordered all neceſſary letters to be diſpatched: for theſe, and other reaſons hereunto moving us, by the advice of our council, we have, by theſe preſents, ſigned with our own hand, ordained, and we do accordingly ordain, as follows:

1. We expreſsly forbid, and prohibit, all ſhips in the Guinea trade, or other kind of trade, to import from Holland, or any other country of the North, into our kingdom, to commence from the publication of theſe preſents, under the pretence of warehouſing, any white India linen, called caladaris, painted India linen, called chints, or ſtuffs of all ſilk, or half ſilk, upon pain of confiſcation of the ſaid goods, and a penalty of three thouſand livres.

2. We

2. We permit, neverthelefs, all merchants, and traders to import from Holland and the North all other forts of linen and ftuffs fit for the Guinea trade, except thofe comprifed in the foregoing article, on condition they firft acquaint the fecretary of the admiralty of the place of their abode, the fhip's name on board which they are laden, and the office of cuftoms, of the quantity and quality of the linens and ftuffs which they fhall require to be imported from the faid foreign countries.

3. The captain who, in confideration of the aforefaid declarations, fhall import merchandifes fit for the Guinea trade, and allowed by the above article, fhall be obliged to load them on board the fhip fitted out for that purpofe, and fend them, in fix months at fartheft, to the coaft of Guinea, upon pain of confifcation of the faid goods, and a thoufand livres penalty.

4. If, neverthelefs, the merchant-adventurers fhould be, by any unforefeen accident, obliged to alter the voyage of the fhip which was intended for the coaft of Guinea, he may, in the fpace of fix months, appoint another, on board of which he fhall be obliged to load the faid goods, and, that time being expired, counting from the time of their goods being landed, they fhall be confifcated, and the adventurers fhall be condemned in 1000 livres penalty.

5. The owner of the goods ordered from Holland, or other country of the north, ſhall be obliged to ſend, by his factor or ſupercargo, the bills of loading, of which the captain is the bearer, the invoice of the ſaid goods, mentioning the particulars of their qualities and quantities, the bails, cheſts, or caſks, &c. in which they are contained.

6. In caſe the aforeſaid invoices are not according to the declaration before-mentioned, we will and ordain that the merchandizes ſpecified in the invoice be ſeized and confiſcated, and the adventurers condemned in the penalty of 1000 livres.

7. We alſo forbid the adventurers to make any declarations, in ambiguous terms, of goods unknown, and the commiſſary to receive them, upon pain of confiſcation of the ſaid goods, and the commiſſary deprived of his place for receiving ſuch declarations.

8. We further will and ordain, that our foreſaid letters patents of the month of January, 1716, be executed, according to the form and tenor, wherein they deviate from theſe preſents. Thus we will and ordain.

The king's proclamation, concerning the commerce of GUINEA; ordering that three negro boys ſhould be paid for upon the footing of two negroes of maturity; and two negro girls for one negro. Given at Paris the 14th of December, 1716. Regiſtered in parliament.

LEWIS, by the grace of God, king of France and Navarre, to all whom theſe preſents may concern, ſends greeting: the late king, our moſt honoured lord and great-grandfather, having permitted from the month of November, 1713, to the traders of the kingdom to go, by virtue of paſſports, which were delivered to them, to contract for negroes at the coaſt of Guinea, and afterwards to export them to the American iſlands; on condition of paying, for each of thoſe as ſhall be ſent to St. Domingo, 30 livres, and 15 for thoſe which ſhall be carried to the Windward iſlands, according to which they are to ſubmit; we have judged it neceſſary, in the month of January of the preſent year, to grant, by our letters patents, the free liberty of commerce to that coaſt (of which the Guinea company had the excluſive right of trade) till the ſaid month of November, 1713. And, in conſequence whereof, we have granted permiſſion, by the ſaid letters patents, to the traders of our kingdom, to ſend their veſſels thither, to agree for the pur-

purchaſe of negroes, and afterwards to tranſport them to the ſaid iſlands; for every one whereof that ſhould be diſembarked, we ordain that they ſhould pay to the treaſurer-general of the navy 20 livres. We alſo ordain, by an arret of the 28th of the ſaid month of January this year, that the merchants who have taken paſſports ſince the month of November 1713, ſhall pay to the ſaid treaſurer-general the ſums ſpecified purſuant to their obligations: but, the merchants having repreſented to us that the ſame duties were required for boys and girls, as for men and women negroes, although three negro boys coſt no more in Guinea than the price of two negroes of maturity, and are only ſold in the like proportion at the iſlands; and the ſame for two negro girls, who are bought and ſold for no more than one negro; whereupon we have reſolved to explain our intentions: for theſe and other reaſons moving us thereunto, and according to the advice of our moſt dear and well-beloved uncle of Orleans, regent, of our moſt dear and well-beloved couſin the duke of Bourbon, &c. we have by theſe preſents ſigned with our hand, declared and ordained, and hereby we declare and ordain, That ſuch merchants who have ſent, or ſhall ſend their ſhips to the coaſt of Guinea, to contract for negroes, and afterwards tranſport them to the iſlands of America, ſhall not be obliged to pay for every negro boy of 12 years of age, or under, that

ſhall

ſhall be diſembarked at the ſaid iſlands by the paſſport ſhips of the late king, only the two thirds of the duties to which they are liable for each negro; and for every negro girl alſo, of 12 years of age, and under, the moiety or half part of the ſaid duties ſhall only be paid; and for every negro boy of the ſame age that ſhould have been, or ſhall be diſembarked at the ſaid iſlands, by virtue of the ſaid letters patents, the two thirds of the duties ſhall be paid that is for each negro; and for every negro girl of the ſame age the moiety of the ſaid duties, &c.

An arret of the king's council of ſtate, concerning the commerce of Guinea, of the 13th of September, 1729. Extracted from the regiſter of the council of ſtate.

THE arret of his council, of the 7th of September, 1728, being laid before the king, and his letters patents diſpatched upon it the ſame day, containing regulations for merchandiſe imported from Holland and the North, for the Guinea trade; by the ſecond article of which, his majeſty has permitted to all merchants and traders to cauſe to be imported from Holland and the North all ſorts of linen or ſtuffs, excepting thoſe compriſed in the foregoing article; provided they firſt acquaint the ſecretary of the admiralty with the place of their abode, and the ſhips they are put

put on board of. His majeſty being informed, from the complaints of ſome merchants, that the officers of the admiralty retarded their voyages, by refuſing to receive their declarations, upon the terms of the ſaid ſecond article, by reaſon the ſaid letters patents were not addreſſed to the admiral of France, nor regiſtered: all which we being willing to remedy, the king being in council, and attending to the report of Sieur le Pelatier, counſellor of ſtate in ordinary, and comptroller-general of the finances, hath ordered, and accordingly orders, that the ſaid letters patents of the 7th of September, 1728, be executed, according to their form and tenor, to the intent that they may be regiſtered at the admiralty-board, eſtabliſhed in the ports, deſtined by the firſt article of his majeſty's letters patents, given the month of January, 1716, for the general freedom of commerce upon the coaſt of Africa: his majeſty commands and ordains Monſ. the count of Thoulouſe, admiral of France, to ſee the preſent arret put put in execution, which ſhall be regiſtered in the admiralty, eſtabliſhed in the ports deſtined for the general freedom of the commerce of Africa. Made at the king's council of ſtate, his majeſty being preſent, held at Verſailles, the 13th of September, 1729.

The

The king's ordinance, prohibiting captains of ſhips that ſhall bring negroes to the iſlands, from landing, or ſending their crews and cargoes thither, without permiſſion from the governors. Of the 3d of April, 1718. By the king.

HIS majeſty being informed that the captains of ſhips that bring negroes into the iſlands of America, have communication with the inhabitants of the ſaid colonies, and ſuffer their crews, their negroes, and other parts of their cargoes, to be landed, although the negroes that they bring, and other parts of their cargoes, are infected with the plague, which it is of high importance to prevent. To the end that from the frequency of theſe practices the ſaid contagious diſtempers may not infect the inhabitants of the ſaid iſlands: his majeſty, by and with the advice of Monſ. the duke of Orleans, regent, forbids all captains of ſhips who ſhall import negroes into the ſaid iſlands, from coming on ſhore, or to ſuffer their crews or cargoes to be landed; and likewiſe to have no correſpondence with the inhabitants, either by themſelves, or by any of their ſhip's crew or cargoes, without permiſſion firſt had and obtained from the commanding officer of the place where they ſhall arrive; which permiſſion ſhall be allowed them, provided there is no infectious diſeaſe on ſhip-board; and, in caſe there is, a place ſhall be provided for them, where they

they might land the infected, in order to have them cured before they have the leaſt communication with the ſaid inhabitants. His majeſty orders and commands Monſ. the count of Thouloufe, admiral of France, and all governors and lieutenant-generals in South America, particular governors, and other officers, to pay due regard hereunto, &c.

An arret of the king's council of ſtate, for the payment of the bounty of 13 livres for each negro, and 20 livres for every mark of gold that the Senegal company from the African coaſt ſhall cauſe to be imported into France, coming from thoſe countries, granted to the ſaid company by the 24th article of his majeſty's letters patents of the month of March, 1696, during the eſtabliſhment of the ſaid company. Of the 22d of Auguſt, 1724. Extracted from the regiſters of the council of ſtate.

Upon a petition preſented to the king in council, by the old directors of the royal Senegal company of the coaſt of Africa, eſtabliſhed by his majeſty's letters patents of the month of March, 1696, regiſtered where needful; containing that, by the 24th article of the ſaid letters patents, his majeſty had granted to the ſaid company, by way of bounty, the ſum of 13 livres for every negro that the ſaid company ſhould import into the iſlands

iſlands and colonies of America, and which ſhould be paid to the ſaid company by his royal treaſurer, in conſequence of certificates granted by the intendant of the ſaid iſlands, or the governors in his abſence; and, by the 25th article, his majeſty likewiſe granted to the ſaid company the ſum of 20 livres for every mark of gold that ſhould be imported into France, coming from thoſe countries within the company's charter, which ſhould be paid by the royal treaſury, upon the certification of the director-general of the mint at Paris. For the execution of theſe two articles, his majeſty granted two ordinances to the ſaid company, the one of the 13th of June, 1717, of the ſum of 34,374 livres, 7 ſols, and 6 deniers, in conſideration of the importation into Cape François, on the coaſt of St. Domingo, 2635 negroes, from the 17th of April, 1714, to the 27th of Auguſt, 1716, purſuant to the atteſtations of the captains of thoſe ſhips by which they were imported, as well as of the directors of the ſaid company eſtabliſhed at St. Domingo, and the certificates annexed, of Sieur de Boiſmorant, chief ſecretary of the marine of the 15th and 16th of November, 1716, and what the ſaid company had imported, from the 6th of October, 1715, being five marks, ſeven ounces, ſix groſs, of gold duſt, which were ſent to the mint at Paris, purſuant to the director's certificate of the ſaid mint: the other ordinance, of of the 10th of June, 1718, the ſum of 14,963 livres, for 1151 negroes that the ſaid company imported to the ſaid Cape François, from the 2d of February, 1717, to the 22d of February, 1718, according to five certificates for that purpoſe; two of which are from the ſaid Sieur de Boiſmorant, one from Sieur Mithon, commiſſary-general of the marine, and two from Sieur Chaſtenoye, major and commander of the iſland of the ſaid Cape François, bearing date 2 February, 26 March, and 30 November, 1717, and 22 February, 1718; all theſe certificates being dated and atteſted in the ſaid two ordinances: but, as the ſaid company are not able to produce theſe certificates to the Sieurs Gruyn and Turmenyes, they having been depoſited in the office of marine, where they were repreſented; that it is impoſſible to obtain duplicates, as well by reaſon of the death as of the exchange of officers who ſigned them; and moreover, becauſe it would be a great difficulty upon the ſaid company, under pretence that the ſaid certificates have not been given by the Sieurs intendants, governors of the ſaid iſlands, purſuant to the terms of the ſaid letters patents, but only by the principal officers, who were then on the ſpot: the company hope that his majeſty will be pleaſed to order the payment of the ſaid ſums of 34,374 livres, 7 ſols, and 6 deniers, on the one part, and of 14,963 livres on the other, in producing only, to the ſaid Sieurs Gruyn

Gruyn and de Turmenyes, the ſaid two ordinances, with the acquittances of the caſhier, atteſted by two of the directors, without being obliged to produce the ſaid certificates, which cannot be obtained, &c.

In conſequence of which petition of the company, the following patent paſſed the royal council; which ſhews how inviolably thoſe acts, in regard to trade, are obſerved:

Lewis, by the grace of God, king of France and Navarre, &c. The old directors of the royal company of Senegal, and of the coaſt of Africa, eſtabliſhed by our letters patents of March, 1696, regiſtered, where it was neceſſary, have repreſented to us, that, by the 24th article of our ſaid letters patents, we have granted to the ſaid company, by way of bounty, the ſum of 13 livres for each negro that ſhall be imported into our iſles and colonies of America; which ſhould be paid to the ſaid company by our treaſurer, on the certificate of our intendant of the ſaid iſles, or our governors in his abſence. And, by the 25th article, we have likewiſe granted to the ſaid company the ſum of 20 livres for each mark of gold that they ſhall cauſe to be imported into France, coming from places within the limits of the company's charter, which ſhould likewiſe be paid by our treaſurer, upon the certificate of our director-general of our mint in Paris: that, in due perfor-

mance

mance of theſe two articles, we had granted two orders to the ſaid company, the one of the 13th of June, 1717, of 34,374 livres, 7 ſols, 6 deniers, in conſideration that they had ſent, from thoſe parts of Africa to Cape François on the coaſt of St. Domingo, 2635 negroes, from the 17th of April, 1714, to the 27th of Auguſt, 1716, according to the copies of the declarations of the captains of the ſhips who brought them, and the directors of the ſaid company, ſettled at the ſaid St. Domingo, and the certificates of the Sieur Boiſmorant, principal ſecretary of our marine, commiſſary of the port of Cape François, of the 15th and 16th of November, 1716, and that the ſaid company had cauſed to come from Africa, the 6th of October, 1715, five marks, ſeven ounces, ſix grains, of gold duſt, that they had remitted to the officer of our bank of Paris, according to the certificate of our director of the bank. The other order of the 10th of June, 1718, of the ſum of 14,963 livres, for 1151 negroes, which the ſaid company had cauſed to be brought from Africa to the ſaid Cape François, according to five certificates, two of which were of the aforeſaid Sieur Boiſmorant, one of the Sieur Mithon, commiſſary-general of our marine, governor of the ſaid countries, and two of the Sieur Chaſtenoye, major of the iſland, our commandant of the ſaid Cape François, dated the 2d of February, the 26th of March, and the 30th of November,

vember, 1717, and the 22d of February, 1718; all which certificates were examined and dated in our two ſaid orders; but as the ſaid company could not ſend them to the Sieurs Gruyn and Turmenyes, our royal treaſurers (as mentioned in the preceding petition) being ſent to the office of our marine, where they were exhibited and depoſited, it was not poſſible to bring duplicates of them, on account of the death of the officers that had ſigned them, and likewiſe would occaſion the company ſome difficulty, upon pretence that the certificates were not ſigned by our governors and intendants of our iſlands, in the terms of our letters patents, but only by our principal officers that were there; the ſaid company petitioned that we would have ordered the payment of the ſaid ſum of 34,374 livres, 7 ſols, 6 deniers, for the one, and 14,963 livres for the other, producing only, to the ſaid Sieurs Gruyn and de Turmenyes our ſaid two orders, with the receipts of the caſhier, examined by the two directors of the ſame, without being obliged to produce the ſaid certificates, which they ſhould have done, if they had had them, &c. Upon which our orders were granted, which were ſufficient warrant and authority, to our treaſurer: whereupon we have, by our arret of council of the 22d of Auguſt laſt, provided in favour of the petitioners, and ordered all neceſſary letters to be diſpatched for the execution

cution of the ſame; which the petitioners have moſt humbly accepted: for which reaſons, and by the advice of our council who have ſeen the arret, made the ſaid 22d of Auguſt laſt, an extract of which is hung to the ſeal of our chancery, we have, by theſe preſents, ſigned with our hand, conformably to the arret ordered, and we do order, that the Sieur Rolland Pierre Gruyn, our treaſurer, and commiſſary in the office of his late father, Pierre Gruyn, ſhall pay unto the ſaid company, upon the caſhier's receipt, the ſum of 34,374 livres, 7 ſols, 6 deniers, expreſſed in our order of the 13th of June, 1717; and that Le Sieur Turmenyes de Nointel, alſo our treaſurer, pay the ſum of 149,63 livres, mentioned in our order of the 10th of June, upon the receipts of the ſaid caſhier; which ſums ſhall be allowed in the accounts of ſaid Sieurs Gruyn and Turmenyes, by virtue of the ſaid receipts, examined by the two directors of the ſaid company only, without being obliged to produce the certificates upon which our ſaid two orders were granted, which we have diſpenſed with, and to diſpenſe with the manner in which it was done, nevertheleſs not to be made a precedent, &c. This is our pleaſure. Given at Verſailles, the 2d of December, 1724, and the 10th of our reign.

The

The king's declaration concerning negro ſlaves of the colonies. Given at Verſailles, 15 December, 1738. Regiſtered in the parliament of Paris.

LEWIS, by the grace of God, king of France and Navarre, &c. to all that ſhall ſee theſe letters, greeting: the account we ordered to be laid before us, at our coming to the crown, touching the ſtate of our colonies, has made us ſenſible of the reaſonableneſs and neceſſity of thoſe orders, contained in the letters patents, in form of an edict, of the month of March 1685, relating to negro ſlaves. We ordered them to be put in execution, by the firſt article of our edict of the month of October 1716, and it being repreſented unto us, at the ſame time, that many of the inhabitants of our iſlands of America were deſirous to ſend into France ſome of their ſlaves, to be inſtructed in the principles of religion, and learn ſome art or trade, but were fearful leſt ſuch ſlaves, upon their arrival in France, ſhould pretend they were free, and not ſlaves; we have explained our intentions upon this ſubject by the articles of our edict, and have laid down regulations, which we have thought proper to be obſerved by maſters, who ſhall bring or ſend over ſlaves to France: We have been informed, that, ſince that time, there have been great numbers ſent over from thence,

thence, ſo that the inhabitants who have choſe to leave the colonies, and are come to ſettle in the kingdom, keep their ſlaves with them, contrary to the meaning of the 15th article of the ſame edict, whereby many of the negroes there have contracted bad habits, and entertain notions of independency, which may be of dangerous conſequence; and beſides, their maſters have neglected to have them taught ſome uſeful trade; inſomuch that, among the numbers that are brought to France, there are but few that have been ſent back to the colonies, and thoſe that have, were of little ſervice, and of very dangerous principles. The care we have always had, to the ſupport and increaſe of our colonies, would not ſuffer us to let ſuch abuſes continue, which are ſo contrary to both; in order to put a ſtop to which, we have reſolved to make ſome alterations in our edict of the month of October 1716, and to add others, that ſeem to us neceſſary: for theſe and other reaſons of our own knowledge, full power and royal authority we have declared and ordained, and by theſe preſents ſigned with our hand, we do declare and ordain, as follows:

ARTICLE I.

THE inhabitants and officers of our colonies, who ſhall ſend over negro ſlaves into France, of either ſex, for their improvement in the principles of religion, and inſtruction

ſtruction in ſome trade or employment, proper for the colonies, ſhall be obliged to have permiſſion for ſo doing, of the governor, general, or commanding officers of the iſland, where they ſhall be; which permiſſion ſhall expreſs the owner's name who ſends ſuch ſlaves, or the name of him to whoſe care they ſhall be committed; the names of the ſlaves, with their age and marks; and the owners of the ſaid ſlaves, and thoſe who ſhall be charged with their conduct, ſhall be obliged to regiſter the ſaid permiſſion, as well at the office of the place of their reſidence before their departure, as at the place of their embarkation, in eight days after their arrival, in the manner as is expreſſed in the 2d, 3d, and 4th articles of our edict of October, 1716.

2. In the regiſters that ſhall be made of the ſaid permiſſion, in the admiralty of the ports of France, there ſhall be mention made of the day of the arrival of the ſlaves in the harbours.

3. The ſaid permiſſion ſhall be regiſtered again, at the marble table of the palais at Paris, deſigned for ſlaves that ſhall be brought into our ſaid city, or at the regiſter of the places where they ſhall be brought to reſide; and it ſhall ſpecify, in the ſaid regiſter, the trade which the ſaid ſlaves ſhall learn, and the maſters who ſhall inſtruct them.

4. The ſlaves, of either ſex, who ſhall be brought to France by their maſter, or by

whom-

whomſoever ſent, ſhall not pretend they have their liberty, becauſe they are come into this kingdom; but ſhall be obliged to return into our colonies, whenever their maſters ſhall think proper: but, if the maſter does not obſerve the forms preſcribed in the foregoing articles, the ſaid ſlaves ſhall be confiſcated to our uſe, and ſent back to our colonies, and employed as we think fit.

5. The officers employed, by our authority in the colonies, ſhall have leave to come to France, and thoſe who ſhall have brought ſlaves to ſerve as domeſtics, ſhall not keep them longer than the times limited for their ſtay; but, at the expiration, ſhall ſend them back to the colonies, upon failure of which, they ſhall be confiſcated, and employed there, to our ſervice, as we ſhall think proper.

6. The inhabitants, who ſhall bring or ſend ſlaves to France, to learn ſome trade, ſhall not retain them there longer than three years, reckoning from the day of their arrival in the port; ſuch ſlaves as are not ſent back, as aforeſaid, ſhall be confiſcated to our uſe, and employed in the colonies, in our works.

7. The inhabitants of our colonies, that are willing to ſettle in our kingdom, cannot there keep, in their houſes, ſlaves of either ſex, when they have not diſpoſed of their habitations, in the colonies; and the ſlaves which ſhall remain, ſhall be confiſcated, to be employed in the colonies for our uſe.

They

They may, neverthelefs, fend them to France, obferving the rules above prefcribed, leaving the colonies to learn fome employment, in order to make them more ufeful, at their return to the faid colonies; and, in this cafe, they conform to the regulations prefcribed in the foregoing articles, under penalty of being carried there again.

8. All who fhall carry or fend negro flaves into France, and fhall not fend them back, according as prefcribed in the three foregoing articles, fhall be obliged, befides the lofs of their flaves, to pay for each flave not fent back, the fum of a thoufand livres, into the hand of the commiffioner-general of the treafury of the marine at the colonies, to be employed in the public works; and the licence which they might otherwife have obtained, from the governor-general, and the commanding officers, fhall not be granted until they have given fecurity into the hands of the aforefaid treafurer of the marine, for the payment of the faid fum, which fecurity fhall be mentioned in the faid licence.

9. All thofe who have negro flaves in France, of either fex, fhall be obliged, in three months, reckoning from the day of the publifhing thefe prefents, to make a declaration of them to the board of admiralty neareft their habitation, and give fecurity to fend back, in a year from the date hereof, the faid negroes into the faid colonies: upon failure of which, or not giving the aforefaid fecu-

ſecurity, the ſaid ſlaves ſhall be confiſcated, and employed in the colonies for our ſervice.

10. The negro ſlaves who ſhall be brought to France ſhall not marry there, without conſent of their maſters, notwithſtanding what is mentioned in the 7th article of our edict of October 1716.

11. Maſters that ſhall have brought ſlaves of either ſex, into France, ſhall not make them free, under any pretence whatſoever, only by will; and ſuch freedom thus given, ſhall not be of force, unleſs the teſtator dies before the expiration of the time, in which ſlaves, brought into France, ought to be ſent back to the colonies.

12. All ſlaves brought into France to learn trades, as aforeſaid, their maſters who are to inſtruct them therein, ſhall take care that they are brought up in the catholic religion.

13. Our edict of October, 1716 ſhall be in full force, where it does not derogate from theſe preſents.

Thus we give in command, to our friends and faithful counſellors, members of our court of parliament at Aix, ordering theſe regulations to be read, publiſhed, and regiſtered, and their contents kept, obſerved and executed, according to their form and tenor, notwithſtanding all edicts, ordinances, declarations, arrets, regulations, and uſages

to

to the contrary, wherein they differ from this. This is our pleaſure.

An arret of the king's council of ſtate, which prohibits GUM * from the river Senegal being exported out of the kingdom for one year, under pain of confiſcation, and three hundred livres penalty, 2d November, 1751. Extracted from the regiſters of the council of ſtate.

THE king in council being informed, the great quantity of gum from Senegal, that was exported to foreign countries, would occaſion a ſcarcity of the ſaid drug in his own kingdom, which his majeſty willing to prevent: the king being in council, and hearing the report, hath ordered, and does, by theſe preſents, order, that, reckoning from this preſent arret to the 1ſt of November, 1752, no gum Senegal ſhall be exported out of the kingdom to foreigners, on pain of confiſcation, and three hundred livres penalty. Therefore, his majeſty commands and enjoins the intendants and commiſſaries, in the ſeveral provinces of his kingdom, to

* This gum is an exceeding uſeful material in the ſilk manufacture of France; and, therefore, the French have engroſſed almoſt the whole gum trade of the coaſt of Africa, and even prohibited the exportation of the gum Senegal, leſt they themſelves ſhould have a ſcarcity, or rather other nations the benefit of the ſame in their manufactures.

have due regard that this arret of council be ſtrictly put in execution; which ſhall be read, publiſhed, and fixed up, wherever it ſhall be requiſite, and that none may plead ignorance thereof. Done in the king's council of ſtate, his majeſty there preſent, held with regard to the finances, at Fontainbleau, 2d November, 1751.

So well calculated for the advance of the French trade of Africa, as well as of their ſugar iſlands in America, do theſe meaſures appear, that the rapid increaſe of thoſe trades in that kingdom is not at all to be admired; and eſpecially ſo, ſince, from the treaty of Utrecht, they have had no competitors in thoſe trades, who have been able to do them any injury. Such has been the ſinking and almoſt bankrupt ſtate of our late African company, from this æra; and ſuch the jarring intereſt between them and our ſeparate traders, that France has taken the advantage of both; for they have ſome years ſince abſolutely excluded our ſeparate traders, as well as the company, from the whole trade of the Gum Coaſt; and, from the impotent condition of the company to ſupport their dignity and authority, purſuant to their charter, in Africa, this nation has, by means of the great French company of the Indies, traded uninterruptedly under the noſe of our Britiſh forts and ſettlements, while our traders have not

not been ſuffered to approach theirs with impunity.

CAN we wonder, then, that the French ſhould ſo well ſtock their ſugar colonies with negro labourers, as to be able, not only amply to ſupply their own European dominions with ſugars, which they formerly took from us and the Portugueſe, but to engroſs ſo conſiderable a ſhare of the ſugar trade out of our hands in foreign markets?

BEFORE the peace of Utrecht, the French had the Aſſiento for ſupplying the Spaniſh Weſt-Indies with negroes; which proved the means of introducing immenſe quantities of the French manufactures into Spaniſh America; and, therefore, as the Aſſiento trade was carried on by France, it was extremely beneficial to that kingdom. But, when they had greatly enriched themſelves, and thereby greatly impoveriſhed the whole Spaniſh Indies, as we have ſhewn in the preceding diſcourſe, and had ſo overdone that trade, as to render it good for little to any ſucceſſor, they very wiſely parted with it; and, by the treaty of Utrecht, transferred the Aſſiento to the Engliſh South-Sea company; and, what advantages they have made by it, is too well known to need explanation.

BY the French getting rid of the Aſſiento, at a time when they had made it worth nothing to any body elſe, they received this advan-

advantage by giving it up; they had greater plenty of negroes wherewith to ſtock their own colonies, and they came cheaper to them; whereas our acceptance of the Aſſiento, at that time of day, rendered them dearer to the Britiſh plantations, and they have continued ſo ever ſince: and yet the French have preſerved a very lucrative ſhare of the Spaniſh Weſt-India trade from that time to this.

Before I quit this point of French policy in relation to the African trade and the Aſſiento, there occur ſome obſervations that well deſerve our attention, viz.

1. The French Aſſiento with Spain was carried into execution by their Guinea company, while they enjoyed the excluſive privilege of that trade, and having no competition in that trade from the French ſeparate traders, the company purchaſed not only their negroes for the Aſſiento at a very cheap rate, but all other the merchandizes which the coaſt of Africa affords, and they alſo ſupplied their own colonies cheaply with negroes.

2. Such was the ſtate of our late Royal African company at this time, that they were in no condition to ſupport a competition in this trade with the French.

3. When England accepted of the Aſſiento by the treaty of Utrecht, when the French, as has been obſerved, had made the moſt of it, England carried this contract with the

the court of Spain into execution by the South-Sea company, inſtead of the late Royal African company, endowed with due powers, pivileges, and immunities, together with a large joint capital ſtock, which plain reaſon and national policy then dictated. For what was the conſequence of giving the Aſſiento to the South-Sea company? Did not this create ſuch a rivalſhip in the negro trade between the South-Sea company and the late Royal African company, as proved highly detrimental to both, by raiſing the price of negroes to an exorbitant price? Is it any wonder, therefore, that France made great advantages by this trade, while we made none? while we, indeed, ruined both our companies, as trading companies? But ſtill to encreaſe our diſadvantage in the African trade, with relation to the Royal Aſſiento with the court of Spain, England laid the whole African trade open to all the ſeparate traders; which not only compleated the ruin of the late African company, but of our South-Sea Aſſientiſts; for after this, there was not only a rivalſhip in the negro trade between our two companies, but there commenced a rivalſhip between all our ſeparate traders themſelves, and between them and both theſe companies.——This ſtill more and more enhanced the price of negroes from four or five pounds a head, as they formerly were, to that of thirty and forty, to the unſpeakable injury of our colonies; and

indeed

indeed to the unſpeakable injury of the whole African commerce of England.—But what was the conduct of France during this time? why truly they, in the year 1716, after they had vouchſafed to transfer the Aſſiento to our South-Sea company, laid their African trade open too, as we had before done.

BUT when France came to experience the effects hereof they changed their meaſures, as we find from the tenour of their royal ordonnances, which ſay, *that his majeſty being informed, that instead of the advantages that were expected from this general freedom allowed in that commerce, there reſulted three great inconveniences: viz. the concourſe of numerous different traders, who came on this coaſt, and their endeavours to haſten their cargoes, to avoid the expence of demurrage, cauſing the natives of the country to fall the price of French commodities ſo exceſſively, and ſo greatly enhanceing the price of negroes upon the French; and alſo that of gold duſt, and all other the merchandiſes of the African coaſt, that the whole trade became ruinous and impracticable to be carried on:* his majeſty grants the excluſive privilege of this trade to their preſent great Eaſt India company, &c—

HERE we find that the French did not try the experiment of laying this commerce open to all the ſubjects of France but four years, by finding the ſame deſtructive of the whole trade, as is expreſsly declared by the above ordon-

ordonnance: and, however great a friend I am to the free liberty of trade, and an enemy to monopolies in general; yet I can't help ſignifying upon this occaſion, that it ſeems to remain a matter of doubt with me, whether the French method of carrying on their African commerce hath not been preferable to ours? For, if the French experienced that trade to be ruinous and impracticable to be carried on, when it was laid open to all the ſubjects of France, by reaſon of the great and conſtant rivalſhip in that trade among the ſeparate traders, which raiſed the price exceſſively of negroes, and all the other merchandiſes, on the African coaſt: if this proved an undoubted truth to the French, how then can we be ſurpriſed, that the late royal African company that exiſted at that time, and the South-ſea-Aſſiento company alſo, who were rivals in that trade, could poſſibly proſper; and eſpecially ſo, ſince theſe two companies likewiſe, were not only rivals to each other, but had all the ſeparate traders of England to rival them both, and theſe to rival each other likewiſe? Is it to be admired therefore that our two companies became bankrupts, while this trade of France has proved extremely lucrative? And, by their management, under the wiſe regulations, which we have ſhewn has ſo ſurpriſingly enriched the French ſugar iſlands? Can we be ſurpriſed, that the French ſhould ſo greatly

greatly ſupplant this nation in the Sugar trade of Europe, when they have in the general ſupplied their ſugar planters with negroes, at leſs than one third of the price that we have done, for above theſe forty years paſt ?

HERE then ſeems to appear, (what has never been thought of, perhaps, or, at leaſt, has never been duly repreſented to the public) the true cauſe of ſuch a general loſs in our whole European ſugar trade; for, if our planters in the general have, by our method of carrying on the African trade, been obliged to pay two thirds more for their negroes than the French have done; how was it poſſible for them to maintain a competition in that trade with the French? So that although the ſeparate traders, who have been concerned in our African trade, ſince it has been laid open, may have been greatly enriched; yet does it not well deſerve conſideration, whether their peculiar proſperity has not occaſioned that loſs which our whole ſugar trade has ſuſtained ſince that period of time? I mention this only by way of quere, and as a matter of doubt. For, although the negro trade may have encreaſed, ſince it has been laid open, yet, as that freedom of trade, has, from the peculiar nature of it's rivalſhip, ſo highly enhanced the price of negroes to the Britiſh planter beyond what the French have paid, is not this

this cauſe alone ſufficient to account for the decay of our whole ſugar trade, whether we have recourſe to any other? If the African traders have gained what the ſugar planters, and the nation, in other reſpects, have loſt, does it not ſtill ſhew that our foreign competitors have raiſed their ſugar trade upon the ruins of ours? Although other cauſes may have concurred to the loſs of this trade; yet whether this cauſe itſelf, has been adequate to the effect, we ſubmit to future national enquiry; ſuggeſting theſe things, with a view only, to be reconſidered: and, if there is a poſſibility of regulating our African commerce upon a footing more nationally intereſting, and upon a footing that will the better enable us to compete therein, with the French; let it be thought of, and let it be accompliſhed. And the reader having now before him, the methods whereby the French have regulated their African, and their ſugar colony trade, he may impartially compare them together, and judge for himſelf, and for his country, which ought to have the preference in point of national policy, the great rudder whereby I ſhall endeavour to ſteer all my labours.

MUCH I could chearfully add, as is humbly conceived, that might tend to the happy reſtoration of this eſtimable branch of trade; but having no view, by detecting paſt miſtakes

takes to give the dangerous enemy advantage over the kingdom, I ſhall ſay no more publicly; but when I ſhall be properly called upon to give my judgment hereupon in private, I ſhall always be ready to do it to the beſt of my abilities, the moſt to the intereſt and the honour of the kingdom.

DISSERTATION XXII.

Another view of the French *management of their* African trade, *and the foundation they have laid to obtain the whole dominion in this commerce.*

BEFORE the French ſugar colonies flouriſhed, England ſupplied France with a great part of the ſugars for their home-conſumption.

SINCE the French ſugar colonies have been in a flouriſhing ſtate, the French have not only ſupplied themſelves with ſugars, but have greatly ſupplanted the Engliſh in the ſale of ſugars at moſt foreign markets.

THE trade of the French ſugar colonies depends on the following diſtinct branches of trade, (1) the trade carried on from Old France to Africa, by means of the great French Eaſt India company. (2) From Africa to the Weſt Indies to ſupply their ſugar-iſlands with negroes. (3) From the Weſt Indies to Old France to ſupply their home-conſumption for ſugars. (4) From the

the French ſugar iſlands to and from their colonies on the continent of America. (5) From the French ſugar-iſlands to and from the divers parts of Europe which the French now ſupply with ſugars.

FROM theſe various branches of trade, ariſing ſolely from the SUGAR-ISLANDS, the French have ſince the peace of Utrecht encreaſed their commerce, their ſhipping and their ſeamen beyond imagination: and the produce and trade of their ſugar-iſlands daily encreaſing in divers other productions beſides ſugars, muſt daily ſtrengthen the power of that rival kingdom.

THIS encreaſe of the trade and naval power of France has been greatly owing to their African trade, which we have ſeen is ſo regulated and encouraged as to ſupply them cheaply and plentifully with negroe-ſlaves, for their making of ſugars, indigo, cocao, cotton, and all other the eſtimable productions of their Weſt India plantations.

BEFORE the French got poſſeſſion of the forts upon the coaſt of Africa, in the river Sanaga, or Senegal, and on the iſland of Arguin and Gorée, the Engliſh traded freely and openly to all places on the ſaid coaſt. Since the French have been in poſſeſſion of the above-mentioned forts, they have not only taken upon themſelves to exclude the Britiſh nation from thoſe parts, and have many years, in times of profound peace, taken and confiſcated all ſuch Britiſh ſhips as venture tured to go thither, but they have come uninterruptedly, though unjuſtifiably, to traffick within the Britiſh rights and privileges, and daringly traded even under the noſe of the Britiſh forts and caſtles in Africa.

THAT part of the coaſt from whence the French have abſolutely excluded the Britiſh nation from trading, is called the *Gum coaſt*, which extends from Cape Blanco, to the river Gambia, which is above five hundred miles.

So beneficial is the gum trade in general of this coaſt, that we have a recent inſtance of two merchants of the city of London (viz. Meſſ. J—and F—)who gained above 10,000l. ſterling by a loading of Gum Senega, which they obtained on this coaſt in ſpite of the French, the firſt coſt of which, on the outſet, did not amount to 1000 l. ſterling.

THE gum, which the French monopolize on this coaſt, is called the Gum Sanagal, which is had chiefly in the river Sanagal. This gum is of ſuch important value to the French, that it appears from their regiſters of the council of ſtate before cited, there paſſed an arret of the French king's council of ſtate of November 2, in the year 1751, which prohibits all gum from the ſaid river Sanagal being exported out of the kingdom for one year, under pain of conſiſcation, and 300 livres penalty.

THE reaſon of ſuch prohibition was, that this gum is an exceeding uſeful material in divers

divers of the capital manufactures of France; such as the silk and other fabrics, which require a glossy beauty and lustre to recommend them to foreign nations. They prohibited the exportation of this commodity, not from any scarcity, but merely to prevent the English and others from rivalling them in such manufactures, wherein this gum would be necessary.

THE other particular places on the African coast, where the French have many years encroached on the British rights and privileges of commerce, are at Anamaboe, situate on the Gold Coast, within sight of Cape-Coast Castle; the principal fort in Africa belonging to the English African company: and from this place called Anamaboe the French have for many years carried prodigious numbers of the choicest negroes to be had in Africa, to improve their sugar colonies. But it is to be hoped, from the wisdom of the parliament in allowing 6000l. to rebuild the fort at Anamaboe, and from such other measures as shall be taken at this crisis, that our wrongs and injuries received in Africa will be redressed, as well as those in America. Another place whereat the French have of late years usurped a right of trade, is at *Whydah*, where the English have the fort called *William's Fort*, by virtue whereof the English enjoyed the sole right of trade.

IN the river *Sierraleone* the French have lately pretended to a right of trade, where they

they have no fort, and where the English have *Bence-Island:* and to such an unjustifiable degree has this nation carried their encroachments in this river, that they have fired upon British ships that have the sole right of trade here, and have thereby endeavoured to exclude the English as much from the commerce of this river, which may be rendered highly more beneficial than ever it has been, as they have from that of the Gum-Coast, from *Cape Blanco* to the *River Gambia.*

THE French likewise have lately attempted to settle themselves in the river Sherbro, on the coast of Africa, where the English had a fort at *York-Island,* in the said river; but at present have none, the old fort being demolished, or become quite useless, in regard to a defensible and commercial intent and purpose. The motive to settle themselves in this river, is by reason that slaves, gold, ivory, bees-wax, and divers excellent woods for dying, especially that valuable wood called *Cam-wood,* are here to be had cheaply and plentifully; and because here are also a good river, a secure harbour for shipping, and great plenty of good provisions. Nor should it be forgot that the *Cam-wood* above-mentioned, which is extremely useful in the dying of our woollen manufactures of various fashionable colours, is to be had no where else in any quantities; which renders this a commodity no less valuable than the logwood for the dying of blues and blacks.

To

To ſecure this important river to themſelves effectually, the French likewiſe attempted before the preſent war broke out, to ſettle at the Bannanas-Iſlands, near the mouth of the river Sherbro; which, as it is a very wholeſome ſituation, is certainly well judged to anſwer their intended purpoſe.

Nor do the projected encroachments of the French in this part of the world end here. For they have attempted even to ſettle themſelves at the *Cape de Verd Iſlands*, though they belong to the Portugueſe. This they did laſt year, and it ſeems the Portugueſe ſent a ſhip of ſome force to prevent their intended ſettlement; which ſhews that this nation are upon their guard to obſtruct ſuch encroachment at their firſt appearance. But,

This intended ſettlement of the French at the *Cape de Verd Iſlands* at this conjuncture, is hardly done with a view to give umbrage to the Portugueſe; it appears to be done rather with a view to have it more in their power to annoy the Engliſh; becauſe their men of war occaſionally, and their Eaſt-India ſhips conſtantly, touch at the Cape de Verd Iſlands for water, &c.

By virtue of *James-Fort*, belonging to the Engliſh in the river Gambia, the Engliſh nation long poſſeſſed the ſole and uninterrupted right to the trade of this river: but within theſe few years the French have ſo intruded on our rights of commerce here, that

that, by means of their *Fort Al Breda*, erected towards the north-side of the river, they have shared a great part of the trade of this river with us. And moreover, as a branch of the *Sanagal river*, possessed by the French, comes into the *Gambia*, the French, by means of this communication, and their Fort-Joseph in the said river Sanagal, cut off a great part of the English trade from the river, and thereby render the English settlement of James-Fort proportionably useless.

By means of the African trade, the French have reaped the following benefits and advantages.

1. They have, by dint of negro labour, brought their sugar-islands to that degree of prosperity and splendor wherein we at present behold them.

2. They have been enabled by this trade to settle the *neutral islands* of St. Lucia, St. Vincent, Dominica, Tobago, &c, by supplying them with a number of negroes to cultivate the West-India productions, and a proportionable number of whites to supervise and controul them, and discipline them for defence.

3. They have, by means of this trade, established and upheld the credit of their great *East-India company*, which enjoys the exclusive right and privilege of the whole *African trade*, and is the principal support of their *East-India trade*.

4. By means of this trade, and their before-observed encroachments upon the English rights and privileges of commerce, the French have raised the price of negroes upon many parts of the coast from 5 l. per head to 20 l. and 30 l. per head and upwards: and although the rise in the price greatly affects the English, yet it does not affect the French trade and planters, by reason of the extraordinary bounties, privileges and immunities which the French government allow for the encouragement of their African trade; which considered together with our too long disregard of the before-mentioned encroachments, have enabled our rivals so greatly to supplant us in this important branch of commerce, as well as in the whole sugar trade of Europe.

Although I have, in the arrets and ordonnances of the French relating to their affairs, given a general account of the beneficial privileges and immunities which they give for the support of their African trade; yet, as few will be capable of forming a just idea of those things, we shall explain them more specifically. They consist of,

1. An exemption from all local and provincial duties, of any kind, upon their goods and merchandizes in France, as also from all duties for merchandizes exported to Africa, wherewith to purchase negroes, &c. which, considering the number of ships the French employ in this trade, cannot be computed

at

at near ſo ſmall a ſum as 150,000 l. ſterling per annum; nor the whole exemption of duties at ſo ſmall a rate as 3 per cent. thereon:

	l.
Say, however, that the whole ſhall be computed at no more than - -	3000

2. An exemption from half the cuſtoms on all ſugars and other merchandizes imported from the French ſugar colonies in America, being the produce of the ſale of negroes there; the amount of which may be judged of by the following very moderate computation, viz.

Suppoſe 15000 negroes (whereas good judges reckon them at leaſt 40000) are imported into the French ſugar iſlands annually; and that 10000 of that number only ſhould be ſold for ſugars to be returned to France, at the rate of 40 hundred weight of ſugar only per head.

The duty on importation on ſugar into France is 3 per cent. on about two thirds of the value; which is at the rate of 2 per cent.. There is alſo an inland duty of 3 livres, or 2 s. 9 d. ſterling per hundred weight.

Suppoſe the price of ſugars is computed at no more than 25 s. per hundred on an average; this, upon 10,000 negroes, makes 400,000

weight

	l.
Brought over - -	3000
weight of ſugar: and this, at 1 per cent. being one half of the duty upon importation, amounts to -	5000
Then 400,000 hundred weight of ſugar at 1 s. 4 d. ½ per hundred weight, being one half of the above inland duty of 3 livres, or 2 s. 9 d. ſterling per hundred weight, is -	27500
3. A bounty of 10 livres, or 9 s. 2 d, ſterling, to be paid out of the king's revenue, for every negro carried to the French ſugar-iſlands and colonies in America; which, upon the ſaid 15000 negroes only, amounts to - - - - - -	6857
4. A bounty of 9 s. 2 d. for every ounce of gold duſt that ſhall be imported from Africa into France. Suppoſe only that 5000 ounces of gold was imported from Africa into France, which is quite trifling and inconſiderable, when we are aſſured how rich their ſhips in the Guinea trade are in gold, as appeared by ſome captures made in the laſt war, is no more than - - - - - -	2296
The total is per annum	44671

N. B. The exemption of duties on what the other 5000 negroes produce in coffee, indigo,

digo, cotton, cocao, &c. is left out in this account, that no exaggeration may be made. And indeed ſo moderate is the computation made in every article, that there is reaſon to believe if the total was eſtimated at double the ſum, it would not be over rated. And if to thoſe encouragements we add that of the excluſive powers and privileges given to their great Eaſt India company in this trade, it muſt give the French a great weight of influence and authority in this branch of commerce, and impower them to make ſuch intruſion on the Engliſh rights, as before repreſented.

YET their encouragements to the African trade do not terminate here only: there is one ſingle article alone, that may not be inferior in it's good conſequences to all the reſt; which is, the policy in that court of giving their moſt induſtrious planters credit out of the king's treaſury for negroes, and other materials, neceſſary to the proſperity of the plantations, the management of which lies between the comptroller-general of the finances, and the Eaſt India company, that theſe bounties may be allowed only to perſons of known probity and induſtry. To ſuch alſo the French king grants lands in his American plantations gratis, and lends money to the planters, in caſe of hurricanes, which deſtroy their plantations, and other unavoidable misfortunes.

5. By means of this management of the African, and American trades, the French have

have been enabled, not only to ſupply themſelves cheaply with ſugars, but have ſupplanted the Engliſh in this great article, at moſt of the foreign markets in Europe.

6. By means of their African trade, the French do in a great meaſure, reap the benefits of an *Aſſiento Contract* with the court of Spain, although there is no ſuch *treaty*, at preſent, ſubſiſting between the two crowns. For, by the preceding methods of encroachment on the commerce of Africa, and alſo the great encouragements we have ſeen that are given to their African trade, the French are enabled to ſupply the Spaniards, by the way of St. Domingo, with negroe ſlaves, to work their mines in Spaniſh America; whereby they pour in immenſe quantities of the French manufactures into New Spain, under the cover of this trade, whereby the lawful Britiſh commerce, by the way of Old Spain to New, is proportionably injured: and yet ſo it has long been, that this illicit trade from the French colonies to the Spaniſh Indies is never complained of by the court of Spain, although every traffic of that kind, ſuppoſed only to have been carried on by the Engliſh, or the Dutch, is always magnified by the Spaniards.

How dependant the French themſelves have long ſince judged their ſugar-colonies to be upon their African trade, appears from a memorial preſented by the deputies of the council of trade in France, to the royal council of ſtate,

ſtate, ſo long ago as in the year 1701; from which æra we may date the proſperity of the French ſugar-colonies, and all other branches of their trade dependent on that of Africa.

Le commerce de Guinée, ſays the memorialiſt, eſt ſi relatif à celui des Iſles Françoiſes de l'Amerique, que *l'un ne ſçauroit ſubſiſter ſans l'autre*: par ſes commerces nous avons retranché à nos concurrens les grands profits qu'ils faiſoient ſur nous, & nous pouvons nous mettre en eſtat d'en faire à nôtre tour ſur eux à leur imitation, & ſur tout *des Anglois*. Nous pouvons les augmenter conſiderablement; puiſque cette nation dans les iſles, avec moins d'avantage que nous, dans un terrain moins eſtendu, & dans beaucoup moins de temps, a trouvé le moyen d'occuper toutes les années plus de 500 vaiſſeaux, pendant que nous avons beaucoup de peine d'en occuper une centaine.

Tout le monde connoit l'utilité de la marine, & que le tranquilité, & la gloire d'un eſtat en depend trés ſouvent; on ſçait que le commerce ne peut ſubſiſter que par elle: La fortunes de negociants y eſt toûjours attachée, elle fait vivre un trés grand nombre de ſujets, matelots & artiſans. Perſonne n'ignore, *que la navigation de la France ne doive au commerce de ſes iſles tout ſon eclat, qu'elle ne peut ſe ſoûtenir, & s'augmenter que par lui.*

Ce commerce eſt ſans doute, de tous les commerces de long cours que les François font, le plus utile à l'état; parcequ' il ſe fait ſans

ſans tranſport d'argent, ſans ſecours des denrées & des manufactures etrangeres, & qu'il n'y a que les ſujets du roy & du royaume qui en profitent.

THIS was the ſenſe of the moſt experienced and judicious traders in France, in the year, 1701 ; and have we not too well experienced all that they preſaged of this trade?

SINCE then it is apparent, that not only the whole dependance of the French but of the Britiſh ſugar, and other colonies is on the African trade; ought not our African affairs to have been one of the principal objects of the care of every adminiſtration? How comes it to paſs that we have for ſo long time ſuffered the French to make thoſe encroachments upon this commerce, which is the great and fundamental ſupport and preſervation of our whole American trade? Has not the great care of the French, in regard to this trade, proved, according to their own acknowledgment, one principal cauſe of their extenſive trade and dominion in America; and has not our neglect and diſregard hereof proved one eſſential cauſe of the decay of our trade and dominion in this part of the world; and, in conſequence hereof, may we not reaſonably enough preſume, that France has been excited to turn their thoughts upon invading us both in America, and in Africa, at the ſame time?

HAVE

HAVE we not ſeen, from the before-cited French memorial, that our enemies allow the commerce and navigation of their ſugar-iſlands has proved one of the chief nurſeries of their naval power? And has not their African trade proved the only ſupport of this great maritime nurſery? What then can any man of common ſenſe and impartiality ſay, to thoſe meaſures, that have ſuffered for ſeveral years paſt thoſe encroachments of the enemy upon our African trade, that has ſo greatly tended to render their maritime power ſo formidable to us, as we now experience? And has not our want of due regard and attention to the encroachment of the French in North America encouraged them to inſult us there alſo, and provoke us to the preſent war? It is above ſeven years, ſince I have, with all becoming decency, and moderation, endeavoured to point out theſe, and numerous other great national evils, that ſeem to have concurred to bring the affairs of this nation into their preſent deplorable ſituation.—But we hope that things will ſoon take a different turn. To which end, however, it is neceſſary; it is of the higheſt concernment to this kingdom, that every ſore ſhould be laid open, and probed to the bottom; and that not by harangue, and declamation, or perſonal rancour, and acrimony, but from *facts*, and a plain deduction of candid reaſoning deducible therefrom, that carries it's own conviction with it.—This, we are willing to hope, hopė, will prove of no leſs public utility, in caſe of a peace, than if the war ſhould continue: for, if the former takes place, works of this kind will the better enable us to think of making a more laſting and honourable peace; and till wars ceaſe, they will ſhew were the greateſt ſtrength of the enemy lies, and where is our own greateſt weakneſs, in order to guard againſt injurious events.

DISSERTATION XXIII.

A ſummary view of the commerce of France in the Eaſt Indies, and by what practice and gradations they have encreaſed the ſame.

HENRY IV. of France was the firſt who attempted a ſhare in the trade of the Indies, which met with but bad ſucceſs, till that illuſtrious *commercial miniſter of ſtate*, Monſ. Colbert, ſo deſervedly honoured, by Lewis XIV, undertook that concern. This miniſter conceived the deſign of reviving the French Eaſt India company, notwithſtanding all the misfortunes it had met with, and which had over and over, baffled the ſkill of all his predeceſſors.

BEFORE he diſcovered his intentions, he was indefatigable to become perfectly well inſtructed in the affair he had reſolved to carry into execution. This he did by drawing to his acquaintance and careſſing ſuch merchants, ſeamen, and others, who were reputed to be the beſt acquainted with the ſubject.

ALTHOUGH this company had ſtood in need of no encouragement from the crown, yet,

yet, upon an enquiry into the ſtate of the company's affairs in the year, 1684, it appeared, that they had run out to the amount of above 300,000 l. ſterling, which was not leſs than one half of their original capital ſtock. Theſe, and the ſubſequent misfortunes of the company, occaſioned ſuch general clamours, that induced a univerſal opinion that it was even impoſſible for the French to carry on a trade with advantage to the Indies. But theſe vexatious circumſtances were little in compariſon to the loſs of their able and generous protector Monſ. Colbert, who ever exerted his influence in their favour, and would have brought the company much ſooner than it was into a proſperous ſtate, had he not been cut of, before there was time to accompliſh it.

MONS. Pontchartrain, his ſucceſſor, who neither wanted abilities, or probity, but whoſe notions with reſpect to commerce were either crude, or undigeſted, or, which was worſe, narrow, and obſcure, could effect little. Nor, from the commencement of his adminiſtration was he any friend to the company, he countenancing every attempt to their injury, and diſcouraging whatever might tend to their eſtabliſhment.

AFTER a tedious ſeries of difficulties and diſcouragements; there ſtill aroſe a new ſpirit in France of ſtill further diſtreſſing this almoſt bankrupt corporation, under colour of augmenting the royal revenues, and protecting

tecting their own manufactures, which afforded bread to the people.—Under this pretext, the company were restrained from selling chints, and other piece-goods, to foreigners; which proved not only a great loss to the company, but the nation, among whom the profits of that trade would have circulated: whereas, by the prohibition, so much money was kept out of France, and not more of their own manufactures vended in foreign countries.—They suffered divers other obstructions to their prosperity too tedious to enumerate.—And while they were envied and persecuted at home, from selfish views, they were no less maltreated and distressed abroad.

In the year 1682, they were reduced to such an ebb, as to be obliged to enter into a scheme for the permission of private trade, upon certain conditions.—Nor did they submit to this only, but were even under the necessity of resigning the whole trade to separate traders, upon easy terms. From this expedient they found some relief, which induced to the extension of their scheme; and for the preservation of their servants in the Indies, who were above ten millions in debt, they fairly sacrificed themselves. For, in the year 1712, they entered into a treaty with some private merchants of St. Malo, by which they yielded up to them all their privileges as a company, on the best terms they could obtain, with a view to furnish

niſh ſuch as were employed by them in the Indies with ſums ſufficient to keep under the intereſt of their debts, and thereby prevent all things from running into confuſion. On the expiration of their privileges, they ſollicited a renewal thereof, not from hopes of reviving their trade, but to renew their agreement with the merchants of St. Malo, merely for the preſervation of their ſettlements, and prevention of the ruin of their ſervants in the Indies.

THUS the private traders enjoyed all the advantagious trade derived from the company's ſettlements, without contributing to their original expence, or even to that by which they were ſupported.

THE duke of Orleans, who eſtabliſhed a new kind of government in France, ſuſtained his authority by ſchemes that never attended all the victories of Lewis the Great.—He affected to act on motives diametrically oppoſite to thoſe of his predeceſſors; he declared that the great end of government was the good of the people.—That it was impoſſible this ſhould be promoted by wars.—That peace was an univerſal bleſſing to France, as well as other nations.—That commerce was the effect of tranquillity.—That the conſequence of an extenſive trade were more certain reſources of power than conqueſt.—This gave the company great expectations; all which ended in the famous Miſſiſſippi ſcheme, to pay the public debts of France without money; which proved, as all ſuch deteſtable deſigns do, a ſuperlative bubble, like to that of our South-Sea company project, which took place almoſt immediately afterwards: ſo infatuated has this nation been to adopt every bad ſcheme, and reject the numberleſs wiſe and judicious, as we have ſeen through theſe papers!

THIS ſtate of public affairs occaſioned an union between the weſtern company and this; the former whereof had ſwallowed up ſome other companies.—The edict of union extinguiſhed the title of both theſe companies no leſs than thoſe others therein compriſed, and gave to the whole the name of the Company of the Indies, which it bears to this day.

To this new company was granted an excluſive privilege of trading from the Cape of Good-Hope to the extent of the Eaſt-Indies, as alſo to the iſlands of Madagaſcar, of Bourbon, and of France, and coaſt of Soffola in Africa, the Red-Sea, Perſia, and dominions of the Mogul, of the king of Siam, and of the emperors of China and Japan, as alſo to the South-Seas, from the Straits of Magellan, or La Maire, to the Eaſt-Indies that way, forbidding all the reſt of his ſubjects, and their ſeveral traders to be concerned therein, under pain of the confiſcation of their veſſels and effects.

To this company alſo was given the poſſeſſions and effects of the other companies, charging

charging them with their debts.—The better to discharge which, the edict creates in their favour 25,000,000 of new actions, to be purchased for ready money.—They have also full licence to import all sorts of manufactures of silk, silk and cotton, gold and silver stuffs, dyed cottons, as well as painted and striped, *on condition that none of these shall be vended in the French dominions, but sold to foreign nations, &c.*

THIS edict had more effect than the government expected from it; such an eagerness appeared of subscribing, that, instead of 25, the subscription amounted to 50 millions, which caused other regulations; the principal of which was, that they should take off four times of old actions, in order to be entitled to the new; so that, in order to purchase 5000 livres of the new actions, the subscribers were obliged to take 20000 of the old.

The great end proposed by all this was, to find means *of suppressing that immense quantity of paper money, which was so heavy a burden on the state.* To which end, annuities, to the value of 25 millions, were created; which not answering that intention, the new company of the Indies offered their assistance, and undertook to discharge them at the rate of 50 millions in one month; so that *the whole load of this paper money, amounting to near sixty millions of our sterling money,*

money, was to be extinguiſhed by the end of July, 1721.

In conſideration of the zeal manifeſted by the company in this propoſal, the king, by his arret, dated July 1720, changed the terms on which the company held their privileges, and declared them PERPETUAL, reſtraining himſelf and his ſucceſſors from ever treating them as other companies had been, in order to their eſtabliſhment—Thus this company acquired the title in France of the PERPETUAL COMPANY OF THE INDIES, with all the privileges of the other four companies that exiſted prior to this, confirmed to them for ever.

In two years time it was declared, that, in conſequence of the annuities granted and aſſigned to the company from the crown, they ſhould be able to aſſign annually the ſum of 10 per cent. which ſhould be paid duly and punctually for ever: in conſequence whereof, the directors were to be at full liberty to export and import what they thought proper, without being accountable annually to their conſtituents, becauſe the dividend was to be certain and regular; and they were to manage things ſo, as that the deficiencies of one year might be made good by the profits of another.

Though this courſe of management had one great convenience, by aſcertaining the intereſt to the proprietors, yet the circumſtance of not accounting for the profits proved

proved of ſuch ill conſequence, notwithſtanding the regular payment of the dividend, that the proprietors could never be cured of a ſuſpicion, that the Eaſt-India merce had been carried on rather for the benefit of the crown than the company; and this contributed to keep their actions low, though they had ſuch extraordinary intereſt paid them with great regularity.

The grounds of this ſuſpicion lying in the annuities paid by the crown to the company, which were ſufficient for ſecuring ſuch a dividend, without the leaſt aſſiſtance from the profits of their trade, made the thing not incredible; eſpecially when the dividends remained certain for 20 years together, though the commerce of the company had been greatly encreaſing.

To underſtand this matter rightly, as well as the true ſtate of the company's affairs in general, and how they came to have a fund capable of diſcharging regularly ſo high an intereſt for ſuch a number of years, it will be requiſite to give a ſuccinct relation of the riſe and progreſs of the other companies that have been incorporated with this, by the before-mentioned edict, and of the Weſt-India company in particular, wherein abundance of curious particulars will occur, that may be uſeful.

The China company in France was originally ſet on foot in the year 1660, but was ſoon after abſorbed by that of the Eaſt-India company,

company, which had the ſanction of royal authority in 1664.—When this company declined, the old company was revived, by the crown granting their licence, which was renewed to one Monſieur Jourdan, an opulent merchant, who fitted out a very large ſhip for that voyage, which ſailed in march 1698, and returned ſafely the 3d of Auguſt, 1700, very richly laden.

THIS ſucceſs encouraged Monſ. Jourdan, and others intereſted with him, to fit out the ſame ſhip again, which they accordingly did in the following ſpring, and returned again in September, 1705, with no leſs advantage to the adventurers than before. One would have thought ſuch ſucceſs ſufficient to have eſtabliſhed this new company; but the general war wherein France was then engaged, rendered it impracticable: thus the company lay dormant, though poſſeſſed of its rights, which extended to the coaſt of China, Tonquin, Cochin-China, and the iſles adjacent, till it was, for the reaſons of ſtate ſhewn, united to the weſtern company.

THE company of Senegal, though under another denomination, was one of the earlieſt in France, being carried on by a ſociety of merchants at Dieppe; yet without the ſanction of royal authority. This company made a little ſettlement in an iſland at the mouth of the river Sanegal in Africa, and carried on no inconſiderable trade thither. Afterwards this

com-

commerce fell into the hands of the merchants of Rouen, who, in the month of November, 1664, yielded up the ſame to the Weſt-India company.

WHEN that company was diſſolved, about 10 years after, the old Senegal company was revived, and three opulent merchants undertook that commerce; which they carried on with extraordinary advantage to themſelves, till the year, 1681; when the miniſter, Monſ. Colbert, conceiving intentions to enlarge this traffic, prevailed on thoſe merchants to accept of a valuable conſideration for their privileges, and to admit of it's paſſing into the hands of a larger number of perſons, with new privileges, which they poſſeſſed for many years. But it appearing, that their excluſive rights were too extenſive for their capital ſtock, it was judged for the public benefit, to divide this company; and hence ſprung the Guinea company of France, to whom the greateſt part of their privileges was aſſigned, and the reſt remained to the old Senegal company, which ſtill continued in a proſperous condition.

YET, from variety of accidents this company came to be ſo reduced, that they were obliged to give up their privileges to ſome rich merchants of Rouen, who carried on this trade with tolerable ſucceſs, when it became united, as we have ſeen, to the company of the Indies.

THE

The Guinea company alſo had it's ebbs and flows, till the acceſſion of Philip V. to the crown of Spain, who, in the year, 1701, granted them the liberty of the Aſſiento for negroes, under which it continued to flouriſh, to the enriching of France, and the great impoveriſhment of the Spaniſh Indies, as we have ſhewn in our preceding diſcourſes.—At the treaty of Utrecht this company loſt it's exiſtence; and yet ſo the French managed it, that they made this loſs, as England miſtakingly thought it, turn greatly to their gain by vaſtly improving their ſugar-colonies, as we have ſhewn.—But, when France had rendered the Spaniſh Aſſiento worth no nation's acceptance upon the footing that we took the ſame, it was very graciouſly conferred upon our South Sea company; and France took care to make the exerciſe of this contract a handle for heartburnings, between Spain and England; which gave riſe to the Spaniſh depredations, and, that at length, with other pretences of illicit commerce carried on by the Engliſh, occaſioned the late war, which ruined our Aſſiento company, and that trade has been largely carried on by France ever ſince, from Hiſpaniola to Spaniſh America, without any formal Aſſiento granted them by the court of Spain; which commerce, however illicit, has been connived at by Spain, though highly complained of if any thing of this kind is carried on our parts from Jamaica, &c.

At this conjuncture the Miſſiſſippi ſcheme took place in France, the conſequence of the pre-

pretenſions of that crown to Louiſiana. At this time the regent of France had under his conſideration, Mr. Law's projects, which was firſt to reduce all the public debts in France into one form. For which purpoſe it became neceſſary to erect, under ſpecious appearances, a new company, with ſuch privileges as might create hopes of moſt extravagant gains to the proprietors.—Hereby a conſiderable part of the whole commerce of France was thrown into the hands of this great French company of the Indies; and the royal bank of France was united hereto to give the greater colour and ſanction to this mighty Miſſiſſippi ſcheme; which proved at once the moſt iniquitous contrivance that ever entered into the heart of man; and unhappily for this nation, England did, in a great meaſure, follow this infamous example, by adopting of the South Sea ſcheme, which proved no leſs ignominious to this nation than the Miſſiſſippi project did to France.—Nor has this South Sea affair of ours ever yet been rightly laid before the public; but, I may one day, perhaps, open all the anecdotes belonging to this moſt deteſtible ſcene of iniquity.—To proceed.

THE company of the Indies at this time of day, was conſidered as the center of the whole French commerce; it monopoliſing ſo conſiderable a proportion thereof; and truly the riſe and fall of that company's ſtock might be then looked upon as a political,

or

or commercial barometer, which exhibited the ſtate of the French trade and the public credit.—To paſs over the Miſſiſſippi ſcheme, and ſtick to the progreſs of the company, as before obſerved.

THE regular dividend, made by this company had a double effect; they contributed greatly to uphold the public credit, and that of the company.—The former was neceſſary to prevent theſe confuſions as long as they could, which happened on the ruin of the regent's ſyſtem; which was near ruining the whole nation.—But the ſame regular payment of dividends was of unſpeakable ſervice to the company in their trading capacity, without which they could not have poſſibly ſubſiſted; this policy keeping the proprietors from either enquiring, or receiving any *general accounts of their dealings*.—This was one of the great ſecrets of the French councils, and the deſign of reſtoring the affairs of the company; and is what of all other that France has conducted with the greateſt addreſs; for, by this means they gained time for the company; and, by affording them money in ſeaſon, they revived their Eaſt India trade, put all the company's debts into a train of payment, replaced all her factories; and, if the laſt war had not broke out, would have ſoon placed her, as a trading company, in as good a condition in that capacity, as ſhe was as a corporation of public creditors.—And ſuch is the policy of France, that they have now con-

conquered all things, in regard to this company, and rendered the ſame as ſubſtantial to their general commerce, as to their public credit.

THE effectual eſtabliſhment of this great company was owing to the peaceable adminiſtration of the late cardinal Fleury; but this was no otherwiſe due to him, than as he continued the direction of theſe affairs in the hands of Monſ. Orry, who, perhaps, did more ſervice to this nation, than all the ſtateſmen, and generals, that were employed in this reign.—Though his management was ſomewhat thwarted, and thrown into diſorder a few years ſince, yet he overcame the greateſt difficulty, in regard to this company, and put her concerns into ſuch a channel, as will, perhaps, render their company formidable in compariſon to any other in Europe.

THE capital of the preſent company, as before obſerved, was compoſed of the original capital of the weſtern company, and of 25 millions added thereunto, upon the incorporation of the Eaſt India company therewith; but after the ruin of Law's ſyſtem, and all things were in confuſion, it was found requiſite, that the king ſhould make a reviſion of the actions poſſeſſed by proprietors, in order to diſtinguiſh between ſuch as had acquired their property fairly, and ſuch as had thruſt themſelves into the company's books, to ſerve the purpoſes of mere ſtockjobbing.

IN

In consequence of this revision, the king fixed the actions of this company to 56,000, and which formed a capital of 112 millions; for their dividend upon which, they had a yearly revenue assigned them of eight millions four hundred thousand livres.—By another arret in 1725, 5000 of these actions were cancelled, and burnt; so that the capital of the company, by this means, was reduced to 51,000 ACTIONS, and their DIVIDENDS secured by the annual payment of eight millions from the farmers-general of the farm of tobacco, the exclusive, perpetual, and irrevocable privilege of vending which, was granted to the company in 1723, and confirmed to them in 1725, together with the profits arising from the furrs imported from Canada; so that the fund for the payment of their annual dividends was as effectually settled, and secured, as it was possible a matter of that nature could be in France.

Yet the affairs of this company went on in a very precarious way for about fourteen years.—But, in the year, 1737, Monf. Orry being at the head of the finances of France, the company fell under his care.—He saw that great supplies were necessary to extricate them from the difficulties under which they laboured, and, therefore, having made a strict scrutiny into their affairs, he furnished them with

with ſuch ſums as were neceſſary for augmenting their commerce; ſo that in the ſhort ſpace of two years he doubled their returns, and, in three years more, brought them to thrice as much as they had formerly been.

By the management of this able miniſter, the company's ſales at Port l'Orient became regular and conſiderable, encreaſing in ſuch a manner, that the public ſale in the year, 1742, produced 'about a million ſterling; beſides which, they reſerved in their magazines goods, to the value of four millions of livres more; and the firſt ſhips that arrived in 1743, brought home ſtill a richer and more valuable cargo.—This ſudden and extraordinary change in the company's affairs alarmed all Europe, but more eſpecially the maritime powers, who ſaw, with unſpeakable concern, a company, that but a few years before was looked upon as annihilated as to it's commerce, now riſing into as high credit as any in Europe; which animated the northern powers to proſecute ſchemes of falling into the Eaſt-India trade likewiſe.

But what was ſtill more extraordinary than all he reſt, upon the firſt breaking out of the laſt war, the company did not ſeem to be affected ſo much as might have been expected, their dividends being ſtill regularly paid; and which kept up their credit to ſuch a degree, that, at Chriſtmas, 1744, their actions were at 2000.—But the war with Great Britain

Britain encreaſing the expences of France on the one hand, and leſſening her income on the other, the ſecret at laſt came out ; that Monſ. Orry was obliged to acquaint the directors of the company, that the king's affairs were ſo circumſtanced, as not to permit him longer to ſupply the company in the manner he had hitherto done ; ſo that now they were to ſtand upon their own bottom, and carry on their trade for the future as well as they could.—This unexpected ſtroke reduced the actions to 800.—And, during the time of the late war, their affairs were in a lamentable condition ; for that occaſioned ſo high a demand for money in France, that it brought on a ſuſpenſion of their dividends, and thereby gave a ſevere ſtroke to their public credit ; and the blow ſtruck by commodore Barnet in the Indies, and the loſs of their ſhips we took at Cape Breton, went ſo far towards the ruin of their commerce abroad,' that another ſuch ſtroke, from Great Britain, would, probably, have abſolutely annihilated the company as a trading corporation, for one 20 or 30 years at leaſt.—But, ſince the peace, the company has ſurpriſingly recovered itſelf *.

THAT

* Here then is a fact, with regard to the French Eaſt-India company ; that by the late war it was reduced to ſo low an ebb, that the continuance of the war for another ſeaſon would certainly have abſolutely ruined this great company, and have ſtruck ſuch a blow to the whole public credit

THAT ſome tolerable judgment may be made of the progreſs of this company, the following

credit of France, that we might not have been obliged to have given up Cape Breton—for the ſake of peace.—But how their great India might have been much ſooner ruined would be very eaſy to ſhew, if I was ſo deſired.—But

The weight of the laſt war, as to the enemy's part, muſt have been ſupported by one or both of the kingdoms engaged as principals, though it was reported that Spain was to have been the largeſt ſhare; but how either of them were to have got money, when we had ſo greatly the advantage of them by ſea, was the queſtion. France, that is the richeſt country, ſeemed pretty well exhauſted, at leaſt was more ways than one vaſtly on the decline, both on account of the failure of her commerce, and the large drains upon her from abroad, not only of money, but of men, to the prejudice of her manufactures. The crown of Spain, it is well known, never hoard up treaſures; their whole dependence is upon their American returns, which, at the time we are ſpeaking of, were ſo backward, that the court was greatly diſtreſſed for their own neceſſary ſupplies; therefore could, at this time, lend France no other aid than their credit on the future return of the galleons; which, though not to be deſpiſed, was very far from anſwering the like purpoſe as their having caſh of their own.

The armies of both crowns in Italy were extremely expenſive, as they were generally lodged in dear and expenſive countries; and as meeting many impediments by ſea, they were moſt generally obliged to ſupply their army by land-carriage, and often through very rough and difficult roads.—The French army in Flanders drew conſiderable ſums out of the conquered provinces; but as money levied that way is uſually told to the government over a gridiron, as the old phraſe has it, and if they had it all, it would not have maintained a fourth part of their army, there was an abſolute neceſſity for it that way, as well as in Italy; and that the finances fell very ſhort, is well known. In a word, the expence of France in the laſt war was not ſhort of fourteen millions ſterling yearly, which no nation in Europe can afford, without conſtant ſupply by trade; the principal branches of which are the Eaſt India, Weſt-India, North-America, following account of the number of ſhips returning annually from Pondicherry, and the value of their cargoes, may be uſeful.

America, and Great Britain.—And all theſe we know were greatly diſtreſſed.—And the Spaniſh treaſure not coming in aid, nor, as matters ſtood, could they have much credit abroad, as we got moſt of the caſh which foreigners had to ſpare, and their old friend Genoa then in a bad ſtate, it is very difficult to conceive how France could have ſubſiſted her troops another ſeaſon.—While the trade was open, France could not want reſources infinite, more eſpecially if allied with Spain, and the treaſures of America find their way home freely; but when neither of theſe were the caſe, the notion at that time of the reſources of France, ſeems to be very ill grounded. And therefore we appear to have been very unfortunate in making a peace with ſuch an enemy ſo circumſtanced, ſince it does not ſeem very eaſy to reduce them to the like ſtate again.—Yet there are ways to do it, and to a much worſe.

Of

Of the commerce of the French company of the Indies, ſhewing the number of ſhips returning annually from Pondicherry, and the value of their cargoes*, from 1727 to 1742 incluſive.

		Ships.	Pagoda's.
In 1727	October		
1728	January	3	248,265
	September		
1729	January	3	20,032
	September		
1730	January	3	248,083
	October		
1731	January	4	600,711
	October		
1732	January	4	302,006
	September		
1733	January	4	260,640
	September		
1734	January	4	392,987
	September		
1735	January	4	375,341
	September		
1736	January	3	223,484
	October		
1737	January	5	351,691
	October		
1738	January	5	522,315
	October		
1739	January	5	586,156
	October		
1740	January	4	485,732
	October		
1741	January	4	555,643
	October		
1742	January	7	954,376

* The reader is deſired to obſerve, that the ſame number of ſhips were ſent annually from Bengal as from Pondicherry, and

FROM what has been ſaid, it is apparent that the French have ſpared no expence, nor left untried any point of policy, to uphold the company of the Indies; and, notwithſtanding what it ſuffered in the late war, we find they are ſtill in a flouriſhing condition. Nor can it be otherwiſe; for this company is eſtabliſhed on ſo broad a bottom, that if one branch of trade proves temporarily bad, their other branches generally make them ſome compenſation: as the intereſt of this corporation is ſo intimately interwoven with that of the ſtate, we find, upon all critical emergencies, it ſtands in need of no aids which the ſtate can afford it.

ONE of the greateſt advantages that this company has been to France, ſeems to be the encouragement which has been given, by means thereof, to the French ſugar-iſlands and colonies in America; for the French Senegal company (which was the African company of that nation) being united to the India company; and this company having granted them ſuch bounties, exemptions, privileges, and encouragements, as amount to above 40,000 l. ſterling per ann.

---

and conſequently the numbers of this liſt are to be doubled. He is deſired to take notice alſo, that the ſums ſet down are the prime coſt of the goods in India —And, laſtly, that the value of a pagoda is about 9 French livres, or 7 s. 6d. ſterling; by the help of which directions, this table will be found to comprehend a ſhort hiſtory of the progreſs of this company.

in

in order to enable them to carry on their African commerce to the greater advantage of the company, as well as of their ſugar colonies; it is not to be admired, that the French ſhould make ſo rapid a progreſs in the trade of America, as we experienced they had done in the late war.

But what gives the French ſtill a greater weight of intereſt in Africa than the benefit of theſe encouragements, is the company's ſole privilege of this trade, excluſive of all the other ſubjects of France. For, by virtue of theſe powers and immunities, the French have ſupplied their colonies with 10,000 of the choiceſt and moſt robuſt negroes from the coaſt of Africa, to 1000 that have been carried by all the Britiſh traders to our own plantations.

By virtue of this great French company, inveſted with all thoſe extraordinary privileges, that we have amply repreſented in our diſſertations on the French police regarding their African and American commerce; we cannot be as little ſurpriſed, that our rival nation ſhould make ſuch extraordinary advances in their American and their African trade, as they have done in that of the Eaſt Indies. For, however, injurious in the general monopolies certainly are to commerce, yet this French monopoly is ſo politically tempered, ſo wiſely modelled, and conſtituted, that it's monopoliſing detrimental

tal edge is quite blunted; whereby this corporation has proved no leſs beneficial to the trade of France, than ſome others, have been hurtful and deſtructive, when not regulated by the like rational maxims and principles: which, to lay them before the reader in the light they appear to me, will fall under the following particulars, viz.

1. That the French have made their Eaſt-India company inſtrumental to the preſervation and encreaſe of their African commerce; wherein they have become more conſiderable upon the coaſt of Africa, than any other nation.

2. The French African commerce as it has been conducted by this company has proved the great nurſery of all the French ſugar-iſlands and colonies, by ſupplying them cheaply and plentifully with negroes, as we have ſeen, for the cultivation of their ſugars, cotton, cocao, indigo, and all other the valuable productions of thoſe colonies.

3. The French American commerce has enabled them to ſupplant the Engliſh in the ſugar trade of Europe; and to encreaſe in ſeamen, and mercantile ſhipping in a tenfold degree to what they were before the peace of Utrecht.

4. The French India company has maintained a competition in trade with the Engliſh in Aſia; and been thereby inſtrumental

to encreaſe the French ſeamen and naval power no leſs than our Eaſt-India company has done that of this kingdom. From hence we may eaſily diſcern, how powerful the motives have been to induce the French to ſupport and uphold this company at all events. For, we have ſeen from the French royal edicts and ordonnances, that after the Aſſiento with Spain was given to our South-Sea company, the French laid the African trade quite open to all their ſubjects, whereby not only their whole African trade was likely to have been ruined, but that alſo of their ſugar, and other colonies, which depended thereon: and, therefore, to ſave thoſe ineſtimable branches of their trade from abſolute ruin, the French declare, in their royal edicts, that they were obliged to grant the excluſive privileges in their African trade to their India company, with all thoſe immunities thereto annexed, which we have enumerated in our preceding diſcourſes. So that the advantages ariſing to the trade and navigation of France from granting the excluſive privilege therein to their India company, is thought by far to overbalance all the diſadvantages that might be preſumed to ariſe from ſuch a kind of monopoly: and, certainly, as this French company is modelled, at preſent, the French have not herein miſtaken their true commercial intereſts; reaſon no leſs than experience having

having evinced the rectitude of their policy in this respect. Thus we have seen how conducive to the flourishing state of the French commerce in general, this rival nation has rendered even a monopoly! We shall now touch the progress of this French company in Asia, and view what a figure they are likely one day to make in that part of the world, if they should not be somehow checked in their career.

THE original seat of government of this company in the Indies was at Madagascar; but, after the first Dutch war, they removed to Surat, and, after that, to Pondicherry.—This was in the year, 1674; and as the company, at that time, had an extraordinary demand for piece-goods, they could not have settled in a better place.—This place they immediately well-fortified, by order of the court; so that, in the year, 1710, this place was become one of the most considerable in the Indies; and, if their affairs in Europe had kept pace with their improvements made in the Indies, the French company would soon have been upon a level with those of their neighbours the English and the Dutch.

THE settlement of Pondicherry becoming the capital residence of the French East India company, is well situated for this commerce. The town lies in the province of Gingy, on the coast of Coromandel, and distant not above 100 yards from the sea-shore.—The magazines of the company, and of private persons,

perſons, are numerous and magnificent; a ſpacious and beautiful market-place, ſix fine gates, 11 baſtions, for the defence of their walls, a regular citadel well fortified; upwards of 400 cannon upon their works, beſides an excellent train of field-pieces, bombs, mortars, and all ſorts of military ſtores in their arſenal. — The governor lives with great ſplendor and dignity, and has, beſides his own palace, another grand one, adjoining to a moſt beautiful garden, ſuperbly furniſhed for the reception of the foreign princes and ambaſſadors of thoſe parts, who, whenever they reſort thither, are treated with infinite reſpect, and all their expences defrayed by the company; which has been found, by experience, of far greater conſequence to the intereſt of their commerce, than the expence it occaſions. No ſettlements in India are better regulated, or more wiſely governed, than this, and it is become extremely populous by Mahommedans and gentiles, as well as chriſtians.

THERE cannot be a place better ſeated for trade than this, being in the midſt of the European ſettlements on the coaſt of Coromandel, and having all the bay of Bengal open before them; ſo that here the company's magazines are full of all the commodities and manufactures, not only of the coaſt of Coromandel, but of other parts of the Indies, ſuch as Bengal, Surat, and the coaſt of Malabar, as alſo of ſuch as are imported

ported from Persia, and the coast of the Red-Sea.——Here likewise are warehouses for all sorts of European commodities, which are conveniently transported from thence, as occasion requires, to all the markets in the Indies.

THE staple trade of the place is piece-goods, of which the finest are in Golconda, and the best painted here; they have likewise great quantities of silk, raw and manufactured, gold and silver brocades, perfumes, spices, and diamonds; in which last branch of trade they have made a great progress of late, and for which it is certain they are very conveniently situated, as being at a small distance from the finest mines in the Indies; and by having persons amongst them as well skilled in jewels as any in the world, they reap no less advantages in this respect than any other Europeans settled here.—And certain it is, that the India trade of France has laid an extraordinary foundation for the encrease of their European trade in general.

DISSERTATION XXIV.

Of the policy of England with regard to her management of the African trade; with considerations how the same might have been better conducted, and far more extended for the general interest of the nation; with a further comparison between our management and that of France, respecting the same: and by what means our East-India company may be rendered instrumental to the security and advancement of this commerce.

FROM our last discourses, the measures taken by France to establish their African trade, which has proved the great instrument of advancing their whole American commerce, will be fresh in the reader's memory; and, therefore, by way of contrast, it may be proper next more fully to consider our own policy, in relation to the manner of carrying on this commerce.

I SHALL not enter here into a detail of the rise and progress of our late Royal African company, that being done in my Dictionary

tionary of Commerce; I ſhall at preſent only touch ſuch eſſentials relating to this trade as, is humbly conceived, may tend to its better eſtabliſhment, and more extenſive advancement.

FOR above theſe 250 years paſt, it has been the conſtant practice of all ſuch European nations as have made new diſcoveries in foreign parts, and gained any eſtabliſhed power and authority in remote and barbarous countries, to build and maintain forts and caſtles; and, by virtue of ſuch poſſeſſion, to claim a right to whole kingdoms, and to exclude all other nations from trading in, to, or from them. Thus the Portugueſe long enjoyed the whole trade to Africa and the Eaſt-Indies;—the Spaniards for many years claimed and engroſſed to themſelves almoſt the whole continent of America, and moſt of the adjacent iſlands;—the Hollanders have rendered themſelves maſters of the Spice-Iſlands in the Eaſt, and from them ſupply the whole world with thoſe univerſal commodities by ſuch quantities, and at ſuch prices as they think fit.—By the like practice the Dutch, for ſome time before and after the year 1660, attempted to gain the abſolute poſſeſſion of the moſt valuable parts of the coaſt of Africa, and to exclude this nation from any ſhare in that commerce, and thereby brought on themſelves a war with this kingdom in 1664.

BEFORE

BEFORE our late Royal African company had built a ſufficient number of forts and caſtles on the gold-coaſt, the Dutch interrupted our trade, and ſeized and confiſcated our ſhips on this coaſt, and within its dependencies.—After our company built and maintained forts and caſtles on the Gold-coaſt, the ſaid company, and other Britiſh traders, carried on a free and uninterrupted commerce here.

BEFORE the French got poſſeſſion of their forts in the river Senegal, and on the iſlands of Arguin and Gorée, on the north coaſt, the Engliſh traded to all places on the ſaid coaſt without moleſtation.—Since the French have poſſeſſed the before-mentioned forts, they have not only excluded the Britiſh nation from thoſe parts, but have, in times of peace, taken and confiſcated all ſuch Britiſh ſhips and veſſels as have ventured to go thither in time of peace; yet ſuch care has been taken of this branch of our trade, that we have ſuffered the French to trade uninterruptedly within our ſole rights of trade, and under the very noſe of our forts and caſtles.—In thoſe places where we have forts, we carry on trade with the natives;—where other nations have forts, and we have none, we are excluded the right of trade.—This proves the neceſſity of ſupporting our forts and ſettlements on the coaſt of Africa, and of ſo ſupporting them, that we may uphold our abſolute right, our weight and

dignity

dignity of trade here; or how can we expect to maintain the ſame? How can we expect to ſupply our colonies with negro labourers? How can we expect to enjoy the benefits of our ſugar-iſlands? and how can we expect to uphold a rivalſhip in trade with our powerful and deſtructive competitors the French in all thoſe eſſential branches?

WE have ſeen that France has upheld her African commerce by the weight and influence of an opulent company, a perpetuated company, ſupported and upheld by the crown of France by mighty privileges and immunities; by a company endowed with extenſive privileges for ever; by a company conſtituted upon ſo firm and ſolid a baſis, as renders it the grand ſupport of the whole American and Eaſt-India trade of France no leſs than that of Africa. And have we not ſeen, from the royal edicts of that nation, that, if they had ſuffered this trade to have continued open to all the ſeparate traders of France, not only this important branch of trade muſt have been abſolutely ruined, but likewiſe their whole American commerce that depended thereon? It is, therefore, they did not ſuffer this trade to remain open above four years.

AND what have the French declared by their royal edicts to have been the great cauſe that this trade was going to abſolute ruin, while it remained free and open to all his majeſty's ſubjects? Was it not that general

com-

competitorſhip therein that ſeparate traders maintained? Did not this raiſe the price of negroes to ſuch an exorbitant degree, that the French planters muſt have been ruined in the purchaſe of them? Did not this enhance the price of all African commodities as well as negroes, and depreciate thoſe of France? Does not the carrying on the trade in this manner evince this to be the inevitable conſequence thereof? And did not this compel the French to give the ſame to their great Eaſt-India company, together with all the privileges of their four former companies thereunto annexed? Has not this given the French ſuch influence in Africa, as to encourage them to drive the Engliſh out of the whole trade of the Gum-coaſt? Has not this encouraged them to rob us many years of our moſt valuable negroes from Anamaboe? Has not this excited them to interfere with us at Whydah, and made them inſult us in the river Sherbro, and Serralione; and, in a word, to take all thoſe advantages of us on the coaſt that I have before particularized in my former diſcourſes? And how could we expect otherwiſe, when we fairly draw the parallel between French and Britiſh meaſures, in regard to the management of this trade? Let any impartial man faithfully compare our meaſures with thoſe of France; let him put them in fair contraſt with each other, and let him ſay, if his reaſon will ſuffer it, that thoſe of France have been calculated for the

the ruin and deſtruction of this trade, and thoſe of England for its preſervation and proſperity, in the honeſt national light: no man can maintain this, though he ſhould aſſert it, according to my humble judgment.

WAS our African trade ever put on ſo good a foundation as the French is? Had our late royal African company ever any effectual encouragement to ſupport this trade, as the French have? Every one that is acquainted with it's hiſtory, knows the contrary. Did not the proprietors run out their fortunes to build forts, and eſtabliſh ſettlements for the benefit of the public? But what advantages did they ever gain in trade to make them compenſation? None. Where they not great ſufferers by our wars with the Dutch and the French? And what recompence did the nations make them? Had this company ever a beneficial Aſſiento with Spain as the French Senegal company had before the peace of Utrecht? After they had exhauſted their capital in building forts, making ſettlements, and engaging the negroe-princes in this nation's intereſt, without receiving any commercial benefit equivalent thereto, what public encouragement did they obtain to enable them to ſupport the trade? Why, truly, in 1697, the parliament laid the trade open to all the ſubjects of England for 13 years, and impoſed a duty of 10 per cent, *ad valorem*, on all goods and merchandiſes exported to Africa,

Africa, during that term, for the maintenance of their forts, and castles; the whole of which duties amounted to no more than 73,785 l. 10 s. 6 ½ d., and their expence in support of their forts did not stand them in less, at a medium, than 20,000 l. per Annum, for 14 years, from 1697, which amounted to 250,000 l. in the whole.—And when the said act was expired, did not all the subjects of Great Britain enjoy the benefit of this trade; and yet the sole expence of the forts was left to the company till the year, 1730? Did not this necessarily decrease our weight and influence in Africa all this time? For the company had no power to resist the shameful encroachments of the French on the Gum coast, and elsewhere; and the nation all this time never interfered, to maintain it's dignity and honour in opposition to the French intrusion.

THE court of England by the treaty of Utrecht, accepted of the Assiento contract, when, as I have observed elsewhere, it was not worth our acceptance, under the terms we received it, France having greatly overdone that commerce beforehand. But what tendency had this Assiento to promote the African trade, upon a national footing? From this time we had two African companies, as it were, subsisting; the one the late royal African company; the other, the Assiento company. Did not this create a competition

in

in trade between theſe two companies for a time? Did this benefit either, by raiſing the price of negroes on both? I am not inſenſible that there was an agreement between theſe two companies for a time, but that was ſo wiſely managed, as to anſwer the end of neither, and much leſs that of the nation: ſo that our Aſſiento had no tendency to advantage the African trade, nor to render negroes cheaper to our own Britiſh planters. This trade being open alſo to all his Majeſty's ſubjects; and a conſtant rivalſhip therein ſubſiſting between all thoſe ſeparate traders, as well as between the two before-mentioned companies, what became the caſe of the Britiſh planters all this time with reſpect to negroes? Did not this great competition in the whole trade encreaſe the price of negroes above 300 per cent.?

WHEN the French enjoyed the Aſſiento, and made conſiderable advantages thereby, they had only one African company; and theſe French Aſſientiſts poſſeſſed the ſole excluſive privilege of that trade; they had neither any other company to compete with them to raiſe the price of negroes, nor other African merchandiſe, much leſs had they the whole body of French ſeparate traders to rival them therein, as our late Britiſh Aſſientiſts and the royal African company both had. How can we wonder then that the French ſhould make ſuch extraordinary advantages thereof, while our South-Sea company made none?

none? Can we, therefore, at all admire, that while the French had the Aſſiento, they were capable of affording negroes cheaply and plentifully to the Spaniards, and by favour thereof to throw into all Spaniſh America ſuch immenſe quantities of their other merchandiſe, as we have ſeen they did, and ſo greatly to enrich France, and, at length, ſo highly to glutt New Spain therewith, as to make it not worth our acceptance at the treaty of Utrecht to take that negroe-contract from Spain? It certainly was not, unleſs it had been modelled upon quite other conditions than it was.

I SHALL not touch upon any other conditions of an Aſſiento at preſent that might be apprehended to have proved more beneficial to ourſelves, and have given leſs umbrage to the court of Spain in the exerciſe of that contract: I ſhall only here obſerve, that had our South-Sea company, as Aſſientiſts, been poſſeſſed of all our African forts and ſettlements, and carried that commerce on from the coaſt of Africa at the firſt hand, as the French had done before them; had this been the caſe under our Aſſiento company, ſo regulated, in relation to our African commerce, as not to have interfered with the rights of our ſeparate traders, in ſupplying the Britiſh colonies with negroes: had this been done, even under the injudicious terms and conditions of our Aſſiento, the South-Sea company, as Aſſientiſts, might have

have greatly advantaged themſelves and the nation by this commerce: our South-Sea Aſſientiſts, conſidered as a well-regulated company, in reſpect to the African trade, might have been able to have become the powerful protectors of our whole African commerce, as well that branch which reſpected our ſeparate traders, as that which related ſolely to the ſupply of the Spaniards with negroes.—A company, like our South-Sea company, backed with an ample capital trading ſtock, and ſupported with due powers from the crown of England, would have kept the French in due ſubjection on the coaſt of Africa.—Such a company would have effectually maintained our beneficial right of trade on the Gum-coaſt for 500 miles, which the French have inſolently excluded us from.—This company would have effectually excluded the French from trading for immenſe numbers of negroes at Anamaboe, under the noſe of our beſt Britiſh forts.—They would have prevented the French from encroaching on our trade at Whydah, Gambia, Serraleone, and Sherbro.—Such an Aſſiento company would have maintained, not only all the rights and privileges of the Britiſh commerce in Africa for their own benefit, for the benefit of our ſeparate traders, and for that of the nation in general: they would, we ſay, have not only ſupported the dignity and honour of the Britiſh empire in this eſtimable branch of our

our trade, but they might and would have been enabled ſo to have extended their commerce into the bowels of Africa, as might and would have unſpeakably advantaged the trade, the wealth, and the power of the whole kingdom, and have prevented all inſults and encroachments by our rivals.—All this might have been done; and no leſs than this ought to have been done; and if thoſe who formed our Aſſiento had underſtood this commerce as they ought to have done all this, and more, might have been done for the honour and intereſt of the nation in general, and no leſs for the advantage of our ſeparate traders, than that of our South-Sea company.—Theſe meaſures might and would have prevented the fatal effects of our never-to-be-forgotten South-Sea enthuſiaſm.

LET not our ſeparate traders be ſo partial to themſelves as to imagine that ſuch a company, properly and wiſely regulated, could have injured their private intereſt. On the contrary, it would be no great difficulty, perhaps, to ſhew how, and by what means the intereſt of ſuch a regulated company might have co-operated with our ſeparate traders to have kept the French in due ſubjection in Africa, to the mutual benefit of them both, for the common intereſt of our plantations, and the general intereſt of the kingdom. Theſe things might be eaſily ſhewn.—But,

In this place, it may be neceſſary for me only to take notice, that if all the negroes that the French have, in barefaced violation of our rights of trade, taken from the coaſt of Africa ſince the treaty of Utrecht, had been left to our South-Sea Aſſientiſts, and our traders of London, Briſtol, and Liverpool, they would have had at their ſervice three to one more than they have had to ſupply the occaſions of them both; — and, by proper ſtipulations, regulated by parliament, between our Aſſientiſts and our ſeparate traders, they might have purchaſed whatever negoes they both wanted, for at leaſt one-ſixth part of the price which they both were obliged to give; becauſe, on the caſe ſuppoſed, the attentive reader will pleaſe to obſerve, that our Aſſientiſts, nor our ſeparate traders would, in ſuch caſe, have had the competition of our old Royal African company of England to have combated, nor the competition of the French, which has proved infinitely more diſadvantageous: in fine, our Royal Aſſientiſts and our ſeparate traders might eaſily have went hand in hand, and have kept the French ſo effectually under, as would have put it out of their power to have advanced their ſugar and other colonies in America, by means of their African trade, as I have elſewhere ſhewed they have done; and conſequently the French could neither have ſupplanted us in the ſugar-trade throughout Europe, nor have become ſo formidable

to

to us in all America, as we, at present, experience them to be: In a word, I must beg leave to declare, from my attention to the measures of France, in regard to the advancement of their commerce, and their naval power, I cannot help ascribing the same, in a great measure, to our constant *ill management of our African commerce, and the wise management of the French with relation thereunto.* For I desire it may be remembered, as I have observed on another occasion, that although our African traders have prospered, yet our national loss of the sugar-trade throughout Europe, and our loss of the Assiento by our ill-regulation of that branch of our African trade, greatly over-balance all those gains.—And the power gained by France as well in Africa as in America hereby; the whole loss of the commerce of the Gum-coast, and the weight of the power of France in Africa, if they have dispossessed us of our forts and settlements in Africa, as we are informed they have, must demonstrate to every impartial man, that our African affairs have not been rightly conducted.

I AM too well apprized of the jealousies of our African traders to imagine, that they will easily be brought to think that they could have carried on the African trade so much to their private advantage as they have done, in conjunction with any opulent and powerful company to support that trade in concert with them,

them, though ſuch company had been ever ſo wiſely regulated for that purpoſe: but, with great deference to the judgment and experience of thoſe gentlemen, I cannot help differing from ſuch who may be of this ſentiment. For I humbly conceive, that they might have reaped much greater advantages than they have done, provided all our rights, privileges, and immunities in the African commerce had been inviolably preſerved, by the means of a weighty company; for had this been the caſe, would they not have been great gainers, as merchants, in the general ſugar-trade of Europe, that France has, by our ſhameful neglect of this trade, ſupplanted us in? And, if the Britiſh planters had had the cultivation of double the quantity of ſugar in conſequence thereof, would not this have proportionably encreaſed their demand for negroes? And if the French had not been ſuffered, ſince the peace of Utrecht, to have taken a negro from any part of the coaſt within the Britiſh rights, would not there have been at leaſt above double the quantity of negroes to have been purchaſed? And when the rivalſhip of the French had been abſolutely deſtroyed, within only our own limits of that trade, might not our ſeparate African traders have purchaſed two or three negroes for the ſame price they have done one? For certainly it would have proved no leſs for the intereſt of the regulated company to have kept the price of negroes low to have ſupplied

plied their Aſſiento, than for the intereſt of our ſeparate traders to have acted in concert with them for that purpoſe. Nay, might not ſuch an agreement have been made between the company and our ſeparate traders, that the former might always have had their magazines duly ſupplied with negroes, as well for the uſe of the ſeparate traders, as of themſelves? And might not this have been done alſo at certain fixed and ſtated prices? whereby might not our ſeparate traders have ſaved all theſe loſſes they have ſuſtained by demurrage, and from ſtrolling from one part of the coaſt to another to make up their cargo, at a great expence? That this was practicable might eaſily be ſhewn, was I diſpoſed to deſcend to particulars; and this might all have been done at the expence of France, not at that of the company, or the private traders.

Moreover, would not a great and a powerful company be capable of doing that in Africa that never can be accompliſhed by ſeparate traders in their disjointed capacity? Would not ſuch a company be able to extend the commerce of Africa into the very heart of that great empire; which can never be done by ſeparate traders? What ſhare we have hitherto enjoyed of this trade, is no more than a little of the coaſting part; we being ſcarce acquainted with the internal trade for above 200 miles, and in the whole of that we have but very little experience.—

The

The trade of Africa in general we look upon even yet to be only in its infancy, in comparison to the great extent of this part of the world. Have we ever enjoyed any thing more of this commerce than the mere skimming of the coasting trade, and that under difficulties and discouragements enough, arising, as well from the interruption of the Dutch as the French?

HAVE we not all reason to believe, that Africa will admit of a very extensive and lucrative commerce, if we can propagate the same into the very heart and center of these extensive territories? We know little of that infinite variety of vegetable, mineral, and animal production, that we may presume abound in this part of the world, and which might afford an infinite variety of trafficable objects. But do we not know, from our little coasting traffic, that these countries abound with commodities of inestimable value, though we have participated of but a small share of them? Do we not know that their vegetables afford us fine woods, as well for dying as workmanship; and may we not suppose that here are as fine drugs as any in other parts of the world, if we took proper measures to obtain a knowledge of them? We know with what a valuable commodity their elephants furnish us; and what numberless other animals this country may abound, that would afford matter for traffic, we are but very little acquainted with. Certain we are also,

alſo, that this country does no leſs abound in gold than in delicate vegetables, gums and ivory; and why not in diamonds and other precious ſtones, as well as innumerable foſſils and minerals of ineſtimable worth? Certain likewiſe it is, that there are ſcarce any productions in all our Britiſh American iſlands but might be cultivated on the continent of Africa, and that perhaps within few miles of the ſea-coaſts: and if ever we ſhould be unhappy enough to be diſpoſſeſſed of our ſugar-colonies, our trade in this part of the world might contribute to make us compenſation: at all events, however, it is wiſe and prudent to make every advantage in our power that this trade will admit of; for we know not what occaſion we may have to make the moſt of every thing we have the leaſt claim to.

In tracing mankind as near as we can to their origin, we find them in the general to have been no better civilized, than the Africans. What has ſo much tended to civilize the human ſpecies as commerce? This being the parent of treaſure, ſplendor, and magnificence, have not theſe prevailing motives been conducive to the general propagation of all the commercial arts? And where-ever they have been duly introduced, they have ſcarce ever failed to poliſh and humanize the moſt brutiſh ſavages. And why not the Africans? However ſome countries may abound with what we Europeans are pleaſed

to

to denominate humane barbarians; yet, we well know, that nature is one and the ſame in all parts of the world, ſuitable to it's climate and it's ſituation; and the colour, and ſtature in men is as little to be deſpiſed as the ſoil where they inhabit, and the productions of the earth: and ſoils of all kinds, and in all climes are improveable; and why not the human nature? Are not the rational faculties of the negroe people in the general equal to thoſe of any other of the human ſpecies? And experience has ſhewn that they are no leſs capable of the mechanical and manufactural arts and trades, than the bulk of the Europeans. I ſhall enter no further into the philoſophy of human nature.

For my own part, I cannot help expreſſing my diſlike to the ſlave-trade, and wiſh an end could be put to it; and I am inclined to believe that practicable without injury to our plantations. At preſent, however, we ſhall take things as they are, and reaſon from them in their preſent ſtate, and not from that wherein we could hope them to be. Certain it is that wherever the commercial Europeans have humanely cultivated a trade with the moſt ſavage people, they have always reaped advantages ſufficient to induce to purſue the practice. The Dutch afford us an eminent example of this in their Eaſt India ſettlements. Have they not by dint of trade civilized innumerable of the natives, and thereby brought them to the European way of cloathing,

cloathing, and imbibed moſt of their peculiar cuſtoms and habits? Why then may not numberleſs of the Africans be brought to do the ſame? If their country affords productions valuable enough to pay for our manufactures, why ſhould we neglect to induce them to a general wear of them? If they poſſeſs wherewith to give an advantageous barter for any of our productions of arts, why ſhould not effectual policy be uſed with them to induce them to a general liking thereof? That they have eſtimable commodities that will turn to profit to give in exchange for ours, is certain; and that it is practicable to bring them to a general uſe of multitudes of our commodities, is not leſs ſo, from what little we have experienced of their diſpoſition. If we could ſo exert our commercial policy amongſt theſe people, as to bring a few hundred thouſands of them to cloath with our commodities, and to erect buildings to deck with our furniture, and to live ſomething in the European way, would not ſuch traffic prove far more lucrative than the ſlave-trade only, or the dealing with them only for thoſe ſmall quantities of gold, and other commodities which we do?

If once we could propagate and eſtabliſh our faſhions amongſt them; if they could be brought to pride themſelves in living in our manner, and that it was thought diſgraceful not to cloathe and live in ſuch certain manner; would not this naturally rouſe their paſſion

ſion to obtain thoſe productions of their country, to give in return for our commodities? Would not this animate and inſpire them to ſearch their countries for every thing valuable both above ground, and below, to maintain a traffic, that once became generally faſhionable amongſt them? And as they have innumerable things in the ſeveral kingdoms of nature, whoſe uſes, and whoſe virtues they cannot be ſo well acquainted with, they would lay in time all nature's work at our feet; they would clear their lands; take to the cultivation of thoſe things, we have found valuable amongſt them, breed thoſe animals we eſteemed, and ſearch, at our inſtigation, to the very center of the earth for all her invaluable treaſures. May we not very reaſonably judge that this would prove the natural conſequence of cultivating ſuch a commercial correſpondence with theſe people? And when our people came to obtain a free and friendly trading intercourſe with the natives, may we not preſage that great muſt be the conſequence? For our cuſtoms and faſhions would ſpread from nation to nation; from country to country; till by travel and commerce, we became as familiarly acquainted with this rich and extenſive country as with any in Europe.

And what infinite advantages might ariſe to theſe kingdoms, if we ſhould prove the firſt who cut out ſuch new tracts of commerce? For the firſt eſtabliſhers will always obtain

obtain the greateſt advantages; and may ſo fix ourſelves in the favour and friendſhip of thoſe ſavage nations, as not eaſily to be ſupplanted by any rival traders.

By ſuch like meaſures, have not all branches of traffic with foreign countries been obtained? And what reaſon have we to deſpair of extending the commerce of this part of the world to a degree equal to that of any other belonging to the whole Britiſh empire? With a commerce that muſt prove of ſuch a nature and extent; and ſo beneficial to theſe kingdoms, what compariſon will the mere ſlave-trade bear, and that ſmall quantity of African commodities wherein we, at preſent, deal?

Are not theſe motives ſufficient to induce us to the preſervation of that footing we have obtained in Africa? But how theſe great things may be accompliſhed is the next point that falls under our conſideration.

As our African trade is, at preſent, carried on, we can never hope for any of thoſe advantages; and, therefore, other kind of meaſures muſt be thought of than what we have hitherto fallen upon. And what theſe meaſures are, muſt, from what has been urged in the preceding papers, be obvious to every one, who has attended to the matter.

But before I open myſelf explicitly upon this occaſion, I crave leave to premiſe the following particulars, viz.

1. That

1. That while no other means can be found to supply our colonies with white people sufficient to perform the laborious business requisite in our sugar-colonies; or, if experience should prove that whites like blacks cannot sustain the heat, and the fatigue necessary; or, if we cannot carry on our sugar-plantations to such advantage, by the means of whites, as our rivals in this trade, may do by blacks; we cannot think of giving up the slave-trade, notwithstanding my good wishes that it could be done.

2. That what I am about to suggest is not intended to interfere with such a share and degree of the African slave-trade, and the connections this gives with the West-India trade, as our British separate traders, at present, enjoy, though it grows worse and worse upon their hands; and will at length, perhaps, become quite impracticable to be carried on at all in the manner it is, by reason of the greater and greater dearness of slaves upon the coast; unless this trade shall be established upon a better foundation than it at present is.

3. From what has been said, it appears, that the French African trade, and all the advantages they have thereby received in regard to their sugar, and other American colonies, have been owing to this trade being effectually protected, supported, and enlarged by their great East-India company; and it also appears, from the French royal edicts, that

that this nation apprehended, their African commerce could not be duly ſupported for the benefit of their colonies, by the means of a free and open trade; and, therefore, they aſſert that they were under the neceſſity of granting the ſame to a company with excluſive privileges.—Theſe things premiſed, I ſhall now deſire permiſſion to obſerve what I would ſubmit to public conſideration, for the better ſecurity and advancement of this traffic; which is as follows; viz.

1. That though I would not adopt the meaſures of France wholly, in regard to the regulation of this trade; yet neither can I judge it eligible inviolably to adhere wholly to the preſent meaſures that we have taken for this purpoſe.

2. That, therefore, I would propoſe to adopt both; I mean that of a great and a powerful company, with excluſive privileges and immunities to propagate and eſtabliſh the *inland commerce* only of Africa to the utmoſt: and I would propoſe alſo, that the whole ſlave-trade, and the connection that has with our Weſt-India commerce, may be left, as it at preſent is, ſolely to our Britiſh ſeparate traders.

3. That every branch of the trade to Africa, excepting that which is commonly called the ſlave-trade, ſhall be given to the Eaſt-India company *by act of parliament*, with an excluſive privilege for ——— years, with liberty, to erect ſuch inland forts, and factories,

ries, as they think proper, and ſhall be inveſted with ſuch other immunities, as to the wiſdom of the legiſlature ſhall ſeem meet.

4. That the forts and caſtles in Africa, and every thing thereunto appertaining be veſted in the Eaſt-India company, and the 10,000 l. per Annum, which is now allowed by parliament to the preſent African company, ſhall be granted to the ſaid Eaſt-India company, in order the better to enable them to ſupport and maintain theſe forts and caſtles already erected in Africa.

5. That certain parts and proportions of theſe ſeveral forts, which are already erected ſhall be allotted by the ſaid act of parliament, to the ſole and uninterrupted uſe of the ſeparate Britiſh African traders, the better to enable them to carry on their ſlave-trade.

6. That in the carrying on the ſaid ſlave-trade, the ſeparate Britiſh traders ſhall have full and unreſtrained liberty to traffic with the negroes for ſlaves in the ſame manner they, at preſent do; and ſhall not on any account, be debarred and moleſted by the ſaid company, in trading with the negroes for ſuch gold duſt, or gold, or ivory, &c. as they at preſent do; but that this dealing ſhall be limited and reſtrained to a certain degree, according to the number of ſlaves, which theſe traders ſhall purchaſe on the coaſt: and that the company ſhall on no account interfere in the ſlave-trade with the ſeparate traders.

7. That

7. That in order to render the trade the more beneficial to the ſeparate traders, as well as the country, an agreement ſhall be ſettled between the company, and the ſeparate traders; which agreement ſhall be regulated by the act of parliament, aforeſaid, that the ſeparate traders ſhall not give more than things of ſuch a certain value for the goods they ſhall deal in beſides ſlaves; and that the company ſhall be reſtrained to the ſame value in their barters; whereby the price of theſe commodities may not be enhanced by rivalſhip in trade between the company and the ſeparate traders.

8. That the company ſhall always be obliged to protect the ſaid private traders in their traffic, as much as they ſhall their own agents; and ſhall prevent all foreign interlopers attempting to trade anywhere on the coaſt of Africa, within the limits of the charter of the late royal African company.

9. That every other branch of the inland African trade ſhall be ſolely under the controul, direction and management of the Eaſt-India company; and the ſeparate traders ſhall not interfere therein, further than they have been wont to do, in regard to the uſual cuſtom of carrying on the trade.

10. That the Eaſt-India company, when poſſeſſed, by act of parliament, of the additional powers and privileges, ſhall be diſtinguiſhed by the name and title of theRoyal Eaſt-India and African company, or by ſuch other appel-

appellation as the wiſdom of parliament ſhall judge eligible.

11. That one half of the commodities *ad valorem* to be vended in Africa, ſhall be of Britiſh produce and manufacture, and the other half of the produce and manufactures of the Eaſt-Indies, according to invoice, and all after-charges, &c.

12. That the ſaid royal Eaſt-India and African company ſhall be obliged to erect all ſuch inland forts and factories at their own expence, as may be neceſſary to facilitate all trade between the interior parts of Africa and the Sea-coaſt; and ſhall be at the ſole expence of making treaties and alliances with the negroe-chiefs and princes for the greater ſecurity and enlargement of their commerce.

THESE are the general heads that I would preſume to ſketch out, leaving them to be amended by thoſe who are better judges. If the whole African trade, except that part commonly called the ſlave-trade, was abſolutely veſted in the Eaſt-India company, upon ſome reaſonable terms and conditions, there is no doubt to be made, but that trade would, by means of ſo powerful and wealthy a company, be carried on to the very center of that great extended and populous country: and, what immenſe quantities of our own, as well as of the Eaſt-India commodities, might be vended among theſe people, is not eaſy to ſay; eſpecially, if the natives could be gradually

dually civilized, and brought generally to wear, and otherwiſe conſume the European and Indian commodities. But it can never be expected, without the erection of interior forts and factories; and thoſe duly maintained and upheld by a powerful company, with a large trading ſtock, that this commerce will ever be encreaſed to the degree it is capable of. And, as it would be the intereſt of this company to cultivate the inland commerce to the utmoſt extent, as having no manner of concern with the ſlave-trade, there is all reaſon to believe, that, where we now export twenty ſhillings worth of commodities to Africa, we ſhould then export one hundred pounds worth. There are conſiderable quantities of the Eaſt-India goods, at preſent, ſent to Africa; but, if that company were ſo ſettled there, as to encreaſe the commerce in that part of the world, to the degree it is capable of, the conſumption of thoſe would certainly, as well as that of Britiſh commodities, in general, encreaſe beyond imagination. And we very well know, that thoſe people have the valuable commodities of ivory, gums, dyeing woods, gold, &c. &c. to give in exchange; and doubtleſs, when the trade came to be extended to the degree it will admit of, there would be diſcovered an infinite variety of trafficable particulars, with which the Europeans at preſent are totally unacquainted.

So well conſtituted a company, ſupported for half a century only, with ſuch powers and privileges as before intimated, or with ſuch others as ſhall make it for the intereſt of the company to drive the inland trade to it's utmoſt height, would be inſtrumental, we may reaſonably believe, to make Britons as well acquainted with the interior territories of that extended country, as they at preſent are with the coaſt only. So that if the wiſdom of the nation ſhould, at any time hereafter, judge it for the public intereſts to deprive this company of it's excluſive privilege, and lay the trade quite open; would not the ſeparate traders and the public in general, reap unſpeakably greater advantage thereby, than they ever poſſibly can do, if ſome powerful company does not undertake the eſtabliſhment of this very extenſive and gainful branch of commerce?

Nor do we apprehend that ſeparate traders can have the leaſt reaſon to complain, or object againſt the eſtabliſhment of ſuch an extended commerce into the heart of Africa, as may eaſily be effectuated by virtue of a company, properly conſtituted and regulated for the purpoſe, and perhaps, by no other meaſures whatſoever.

Having endeavoured, to inform myſelf in regard to what has been urged againſt every kind of trading company that has exiſted in this nation; I am not unapprized of what may be be objected againſt my own propoſition, and particularly what may be offered from the conſideration of the miſcarriage of the late royal African company: from which ſome probably may pleaſe to argue, that it is impoſſible for any kind of African company long to ſubſiſt, without annihilation of their trading capital.

BUT, with all deference to the judgment of thoſe who are pleaſed to think ſo, I would beg leave to remind the reader of what has been before noticed: viz.—With reſpect to this late company, it muſt be obſerved, that they were never bottomed upon a parliamentary conſtitution; that they were ever in the precarious ſituation of depending only upon the royal prerogative, without any parliamentary ſanction. It is no wonder, therefore, that they could never raiſe above the capital ſtock of a hundred thouſand pounds; the bulk of which was ſoon ſunk in the purchaſe, repairs, and erection of forts and caſtles; and the profits of their trade ſunk by the wars we had with the Dutch and the French in Africa; in conſequence of which, they had ſo trifling a ſtock left wherewith to trade, that it was not poſſible, under all theſe diſadvantages and diſcouragements, they ſhould ever make a tolerable progreſs in this commerce, any way proportionate to the apparent extent it would admit of. Where is the admiration, therefore,

fore, that a company, erected upon ſo ſandy a foundation, ſhould never be able to ſupport it's head, and at length ſink?

As this trade has yet never had a fair trial, by means of a company founded upon parliamentary authority, no man can preſume to ſay, that what has never been tried will miſcarry.

DISSERTATION XXV.

Farther conſiderations on the African trade, and our Eaſt-India company; ſhewing wherein the latter may prove conducive, by having the trade to Africa annexed to it, as propoſed in the preceding diſſertation, to enable Great Britain the better to maintain the balance of trade and power againſt France in Africa, America, and the Eaſt-Indies.

FROM what has been already urged, no one can avoid diſcerning that the commerce of France, as it has been carried on in Africa, with relation to its important connection with the French ſugar and other colonies, has proved the eſſential cauſe of all the proſperity and dominion of the French in America, and has greatly contributed to render their Eaſt-India company ſo opulent and formidable in Aſia.

ON the other hand, we have ſeen, that England having carried on her African trade on principles diametrically oppoſite to thoſe

of

of France, it has, from time to time, greatly injured, and now almoſt totally ruined that trade as ſuch, and the French maintain the ſuperior dominion on that coaſt. It has alſo enhanced the price of negroes to ſuch a degree to our Britiſh planters, that it has proved the principal cauſe of the loſs of our ſugar trade throughout Europe, and occaſioned ſugars to come ſo exceſſively dear to us for domeſtic conſumption; this has alſo prevented the breaking up of more land in our iſland colonies, for the greater cultivation of ſugars, by reaſon of the extravagant price of negro labourers neceſſary for that purpoſe. Theſe things have done unſpeakable injury to our planters in general, ruined numbers of them, and raiſed the price, and obſtructed the production of all our other American commodities: and theſe have proved no leſs diſadvantageous to all our Weſt-India traders in general, than to the nation; for if we had prevented theſe evils by the right management of our African commerce, thoſe traders would have been far greater gainers thereby than they have been, and we ſhould have maintained ſuch a ſuperiority in our African, and conſequently in our whole American commerce, as would have hindered the preſent height of the French power in America, and elſewhere, that we now experience it has roſe to.

Since, therefore, it may be juſtly ſaid, that the preſervation of our whole commercial intereſt in America, and therefore, in

a great

a great meaſure, in Europe alſo, depends upon the proper regulation of our African trade, I hope I ſhall be excuſed if I urge all that appears to me needful to the permanent and proſperous eſtabliſhment of this ſo valuable a branch of the Britiſh traffic.

HAVING in the foregoing diſcourſe, given my thoughts how I apprehend this commerce may be carried on and extended by the means of ſuch an important joint-ſtock company as our Eaſt-India company at preſent is, in conjunction with our ſeparate traders ; it will be neceſſary to conſider ſuch objections as may be urged againſt this company ; more particularly ſo, ſince I have taken the liberty, unrequeſted, and perhaps unthanked, to ſuggeſt the propriety of giving additional powers and immunities to this company ; which, in the eye of many, is already looked upon as a detrimental and deſtructive monopoly ; and what I have propoſed further in their favour, may give a greater handle for clamour and calumny againſt them : and, therefore, as I have ſpontaneouſly undertaken the cauſe of this corporation, and to ſuggeſt the reaſonableneſs of extending its privileges to the African commerce ; I am obliged in juſtice to endeavour to vindicate this company againſt what, in the general, has been, and what may, on account of what I have now ſaid in its favour, be urged againſt them.

PREVIOUSLY to what I ſhall take the liberty to ſay in behalf of this trading company, I muſt deſire the reader's favour to recollect the ſubſtance of what has been already ſaid throughout the courſe of theſe diſſertations; for the prevalence of truth has obliged me to maintain a connection, and I hope a conſiſtency, throughout the whole. What I would, upon the preſent occaſion, require the reader chiefly to call to his mind is, how greatly we have ſuffered in the commerce of Africa, by laying that trade abſolutely open, without the exiſtence even of any joint-ſtock company to uphold our commercial dignity, weight, and influence in this part of the world; while the French, by following the contrary meaſures, have aggrandized themſelves at our expence.—We have laid before the reader likewiſe that ſyſtem of wiſe laws and regulations whereby our great rivals govern their African and American trade in a manner conſiſtent with the proſperity of both.—Whereas we ſeem to have paid no regard, by our regulations of theſe trades, to that eſſential and mutual dependency that ſubſiſts between them. We have ſeen alſo the difference of the conſtitution of our ſeveral colonies in North-America; and how, in conſequence thereof, the ſecurity of the whole have been endangered; —whereas the French colonies have all one uniform conſtitution, and every part cooperates for the general ſafety and preſervation

tion of the whole.—We have ſeen alſo how we have neglected to regulate our Indian affairs, and have thereby loſt the alliance and attachment of thoſe people;—whereas, on the contrary, we have ſeen by what means the French have gained the friendſhip of thoſe people, and made them ſubſervient to their miſchievous machinations againſt our dominions.—Theſe and many other are the principles of policy, the reader will recollect, that are placed in contraſt in this work, to ſhew wherein the French have outdone us in the cabinet, as if it were an indignity to us to counter-act them in their own way.—But does not every one ſee the egregious abſurdity thereof?

If the French can raiſe 100 ſail of men of war at preſent, will any one ſay it is not neceſſary for us to have more than 100 ſail?—May we not with equal wiſdom ſay, that although the French make uſe of arms and ammunition in combat, that we ſhould raſhly fight them unarmed? Every one ſees the folly of all this. Well then, if common ſenſe inſtructs us to put ourſelves upon an equality with an enemy in military concerns, why not in commercial ones? We do not ſay, that we are to follow France in all their points of government: that the judicious reader will diſcern is going beyond the ſtandard of policy we would come to: no; our free conſtitution, and our religion will not, without deſtroying our invaluable rights and liberties,

liberties, admit of any thing unconſtitutional: but our conſtitution will, with all ſafety, admit of our counter-acting France, or any other power, in our commercial ſyſtem, by the ſame policy by which they would ſupplant or over-reach us.—Are not theſe principles the baſis of all treaties of peace and friendſhip, and more particularly of thoſe of commerce?

EVERY true friend to his country will deſire that the due ſpirit of liberty may be ever cheriſhed amongſt us. I ſhall ever think it my duty to contribute thereto. But as our fondneſs for the words liberty and freedom ſometimes lead to licentiouſneſs, and even anarchy in government; ſo may not a too great eagerneſs for an univerſal freedom and liberty of trade carry us ſuch lengths, that we may, at length loſe all the trade we have? Though peculiar monopolies have certainly proved injurious to trade; yet is it not notorious that we owe all our trade originally to monopolies? In the ſtriking out new and unbeaten tracts of commerce, what private people will hazard their properties therein?

As the primary motive to the grant of monopolies was to cut out, by dint of joint-ſtocks, new channels of traffic; ſo the motives to their continuance ſhould be the preſervation of ſuch trades only, as we cannot preſerve without them. When the French laid their African trade abſolutely open to all the ſubjects of France, have not their royal

ordonnances

ordonnances explicitly declared, that not only that trade, but their whole American trade would have been ruined, if they had not taken other meaſures? And we preſume, that we have ſhewn the reaſon of the thing ſpeaks loudly for itſelf. Now, if at the time the French lately commenced the carrying on this commerce by their great extenſive India company, England had carried her trade on by a great extenſive company too, in conjunction, as has been obſerved, with an open ſlave-trade to our ſeparate traders; we may ſafely affirm that we ſhould have preſerved all the ſugar and plantation trade we have loſt, and prevented the growing power of the French upon the declenſion of our own. The reaſon of this has been before amply ſhewn.

If then we have abſolutely loſt all our European ſugar, and a great part of our other plantation trade, by the dread of a well-regulated monopoly to ſupport, protect, and extend the ſame in Africa, whereon it depends; if the French have raiſed their commerce and naval power in general, by the means of a joint-ſtock company, and have greatly reduced and almoſt ruined ours by the means of ſuch a company, are we to be frightened by the ſcarecrow ſound of a monopoly out of all our trade, when ſuch means are abſolutely neceſſary for its general protection? As we have loſt our ſugar and other parts of our planta-

tion

tion trade for want of a powerful company in Africa, who will undertake to inſure us that we ſhould not loſe the whole commerce of Aſia, if we were to annihilate our excluſive Eaſt-India company?

If it could be fairly demonſtrated that the Eaſt-India trade is really a loſing trade to this nation, as it is now carried on, we might be indifferent about the exiſtence of our India company. But this has never yet been done to my knowledge; when the circle of this traffic has been impartially taken into conſideration. Some, indeed, have inſinuated that the whole commerce of the Eaſt-Indies is a loſing trade to all the European potentates intereſted therein. Muſt we not with difficulty credit this? Is it not ſomething extraordinary that all the great ſtates who are engaged in it ſhould be ſo blind to their advantage? If this be the caſe, is it not ſtill more to be admired that ſuch a loſing and detrimental trade ſhould draw new ſtates into its circle? And that they all too ſhould chuſe to carry the ſame on by joint-ſtock companies, endowed with excluſive privileges? The preſumption certainly is, that all the ſtates engaged therein have found from experience that they are gainers by this trade and all its conſequences in the general: and that the ſeveral companies, in the general, have been gainers thereby is as little to be doubted. If they were extraordinary loſers, it could not be long concealed; and therefore we may

rea-

reaſonably enough preſume, that the credit of their general account of profit and loſs exceeds their debit.

BUT if the ſeveral companies therein concerned were no extraordinary gainers; yet, if the reſpective nations wherein they are eſtabliſhed experience, upon the whole, that they are gainers, would it not be impolitic to lay them aſide? On the contrary, would it not be wiſdom to ſupport them?

IF it be needful to maintain a balance of power in Europe, why not in Aſia among the European powers eſtabliſhed there? Will not the riſe or decline of their trade and power in the Indies effect that of their particular ſtates in Europe? Though the companies ſhould be loſers, yet does not theſe trades increaſe the naval powers of other various European ſtates, and thereby render them more or leſs reſpectable in the European balance of power? If ſo, then it is needful for England to maintain a balance of power in the Eaſt-Indies, that contributing to its maintenance in Europe.

BUT who will ſecure the nation that the balance of trade and power could be upheld by England in Aſia, if that trade was laid abſolutely open to all the traders of Great Britain? As the French, by laying their African trade abſolutely open, experienced how negroes and other commodities were greatly enhanced there; and how their own commodities were depreciated by a general rivalſhip among

among the ſeparate trade; ſo can we ſuppoſe that the French will ever try the like experiment in the Eaſt-India commerce? For would not a general competition amongſt their ſeparate traders in Aſia have the ſame effect it has in Africa? Would they not have reaſon to dread the ruin of this whole trade, as they had like to have experienced in regard to that of Africa?

In the encreaſe of the Eaſt-Indies, as well as in all other branches of foreign commerce, we muſt have an eye to the policy of our neighbours, and more particularly to that of a rival nation. And while all other nations make uſe of rich and powerful joint-ſtock companies, and thoſe poſſeſſed with ſuch immunities and encouragements given them by their reſpective nations, does it ſeem politic in any of the reſt to affect ſingularity in this matter, and carry the trade on in a manner different from all the reſt?

If we ſhould make any change in the manner of carrying on this commerce, while other nations carried the ſame on by the means of great joint-ſtock companies with excluſive privileges, all the change that we could with any ſafety, perhaps, make, would be by a regulated company without a joint-ſtock; and this might prove a dangerous experiment, if we may appeal to the touchſtone of experience. For, if in Africa, which is at home, in compariſon to the diſtance of the Eaſt-Indies, we have not been able to maintain

tain the balance of trade and power, and much lefs to extend the former there; if in Africa, we have loft all our weight and power among the negroe-chiefs and princes, for want of a powerful joint-ftock company to uphold our intereft; we have no great reafon to expect, that a regulated company without a joint-ftock could maintain our fhare in the balance of trade and power in the Eaft-Indies. Have we not reafon, on the contrary to fear too, that the trade would indeed foon prove quite ruinous to this nation, and that the whole of our proportion of that commerce would fall into the hands of our rivals? and if once we loft our fettlements and our commercial connections in that part of the world, we fhould have no fhare in the ballance of trade or power arifing therefrom.

If hereafter it fhould be judged eligible to make any alteration in our manner of carrying on the Eaft-India trade; it is fubmitted; whether private traders might not, under certain regulations, be admitted into fome certain proportion of this trade, in conjunction with the prefent joint-ftock company, without injuring either the one, or the other, and making both, by acting in concert, become more fubfervient to the general intereft of the nation? If they could be both made to harmonize and play into each other's hands for the common intereft, and to give us a more exclufive and beneficial trade there than we, we, at preſent, have, and add more to our weight and influence there, in oppoſition to foreign competitors: If, we ſay, the exiſtence of ſuch a company, and private traders too, could be made perfectly compatible, upon fair national principles, it would certainly prove the beſt way to carry on this commerce.

AND whether it is practicable for a good underſtanding to be maintained between ſuch a company and private traders, (the experiment being duly tried in our African commerce) would prove a good touchſtone afterwards to try ſomething ſimilar thereto in the Aſiatic traffic; for the regulation muſt be well adapted to the peculiar circumſtances of both thoſe trades: and although the general principles upon which the regulation ſhall be made in both trades may be the ſame; yet there may be ſome exception, to theſe general principles in the one caſe that may not be requiſite in the other.

ALTHOUGH the government ſhould be at the expence of ſupporting and maintaining forts and caſtles in the Indies, or impoſe a duty for that purpoſe, on the exports, or imports, *ad valorem*, &c.; yet, it is to be greatly feared, that ſuch meaſures would not uphold our weight and influence to ſuch a degree as our rivals do theirs by different conduct. This having proved our caſe in Africa, we muſt dread it from that experience.

MORE-

Moreover, ſuch is the nature of traffic, that a mere military force, capable only of ſupporting forts and garriſons, might, from the peculiarity of the conduct of ſuch uncommercial gentlemen, be more liable to deſtroy, than cultivate commercial friendſhips, upon a footing equal with thoſe who conſtitute a trading intereſt at the head of their military.

A regulated company, duly ſupported by a Britiſh government, might poſſibly be deviſed for the temporary ſupport of a general freedom of trade: but, that the nation could permanently preſerve ſuch a diſtant commerce, any thing like what the meaneſt of our rivals therein do, I have never ſeen ſatisfactorily proved; and until I do, I muſt, from national principles be an advocate for the continuance of our Eaſt-India company. Nor do I diſcern the diſadvantages that could ariſe to theſe kingdoms, if our Eaſt-India company were no leſs powerful in Aſia, than that of the Dutch; which is attended with unſpeakable commercial emolument to the Hollanders.

It has been frequently ſaid, that our Eaſt-India company does not trade to the extent of their charter; but that from an unreſtrained liberty of trade, it would be drove to the full extremity; that thereby no part of the Indies would remain untraded to: I am afraid, indeed, that this trade would ſoon be carried to ſuch an extremity that it would not be worth

worth carrying on at all, and that many would ſoon be ruined who engaged in it. But what ſhould induce the company to ſuffer any beneficial trade to remain uncultivated? It does not proceed from a deficiency of capital, or credit; and why ſhould we apprehend them neglectful of their intereſt? A company cannot, indeed, trade at ſo ſmall an expence, and therefore, cannot afford to trade at ſo ſmall profit as private traders: This is allowed in general: but the previous queſtion is; whether we ſhould long enjoy any ſhare in this trade at all without ſuch a company?

Certainly the excluſive correſpondence and high credit of the company in the Indies, enable them to traffic every where within their charter, where they can be gainers; and to do ſo where they could not, would ſhew no regard to their proprietors. But private traders will gain where they cannot. Is not this begging the queſtion? When our company dropt the trade, can we ſuppoſe that the chaſm of trade, which they had left, would not be inſtantly filled up by the other great trading company? If our traders did pick up a little paultry trade, by their ſtrolling coaſting; or, if the Indians brought trade down to the national forts and caſtles, whither our traders ſhould reſort, would not this general competition amongſt them raiſe the price of India commodities, and depreciate that of our European? Has not the experience of the African trade proved the truth

truth of this beyond doubt? But the African traders, ſince that commerce has been laid open, have been greatly enriched, and why might not the private Eaſt-India traders? This does not follow. The caſe is not parallel in it's eſſentials. If the African traders loſe by their direct trade to Africa, they gain by the Weſt-India trade, and the re-exportation of Weſt-India commodities: But has it not been ſhown, that although our African traders have become enriched, it has been at the expence of our planters; at the expence of the loſs of our whole European ſugar, and other parts of our plantation trade? &c.

If I am rightly informed, the point, in regard to the India trade lies here. Such branches of that trade, by which the company cannot gain, or are not ſo gainful as others they prefer, are carried on by private Britiſh merchants, trading under the company's licence. It is allowed there is a wide difference between granting licences to carry on a coaſting trade in India, and a free liberty to carry on the trade from Europe to India: but theſe free merchants, who obtain the company's licence, and traffic only in ſuch of our commodities as the company export, amply ſupply moſt places with our goods where there is any tolerable profit to be got. But, it is ſaid, private traders would ſupply them cheaper than licenced merchants do at ſecond hand. This is to be proved. I doubt it: private traders, perhaps, could not buy ſo cheap

cheap at home as the company does: nor could private traders ſell to ſuch advantage as licenced merchants do under the company's ſanction, and protection; for their general rivalſhip would induce the Indians to treat them as they pleaſed.

It is of the laſt conſequence to a nation that carries on a trade to the Indies, to have, from time to time, a diſtinct account of it's ſtate and condition. But how could this be done by ſeparate traders, who in ſuch diſtant countries are preſumed to have no inland correſpondence with the Indian artiſt and manufacturers, &c.—Should it be ſaid, that we might have Britiſh factories there, as in Spain, and Portugal. We might ſo; and what what would the conſequence be? If the goods were left in ſuch diſtant countries to be ſold; our traders might leave millions of money there, perhaps, to be annihilated. But if factors make their returns by barter from voyage to voyage, will not their commiſſion greatly diminiſh the profits of the trade? Beſides, muſt there not be the expence of ſupercargoes likewiſe?

Whoever conſiders how merchandiſes are to be diſtributed in India, and affairs in general conducted there; what a connection and dependency there is between the commerce of the ſeveral countries included within the company's charter, will eaſily diſcern, that if the whole trade was in the hands of a diſ-

jointed

jointed body of traders, and not under the direction of a company thoroughly experienced herein, it would certainly be difficult, if not impoſſible to carry the ſame on to advantage.

PROVIDED the forts and ſettlements were lodged in the crown, and the management of the trade only in the hands of a regulated company, it could not but be attended with great inconveniencies, as experience ſhewed, in Charles II. time, when Bombay came to the crown by his marriage with the Infanta of Portugal; and, therefore, both that iſland, and the iſland of St. Helena, have been granted the company for the ſake of public conveniency.

FROM the diſorder of the company's affairs in that reign, as well as in that of king James, we may diſcover that it is greatly detrimental to this commerce, that the company ſhould be under the power of the crown, to ſtand indebted to that for all encouragement, and to have no other reſource in caſe of grievance; for, does not this, on the one hand, render the trade precarious, and on the other hand, intereſt a great body of people in ſupport of the prerogative, a conſequence injurious to the conſtitution.

HAS not experience effectually ſhewn the miſchiefs which flowed from the ſubſiſtance of two Eaſt-India companies at the ſame time? Were they not convinced that nothing but their union of intereſts could afford a proper remedy? If this trade was laid open, would not this, as it were, multiply companies, all acting upon separate interests? would not this create eternal clashing of interests, and give the powerful united companies of other nations opportunity to destroy them all? Some have been so sanguine as to conceive, that by our laying this trade open, we should be able to ruin all the established companies in Asia. Let such remember the viper and the file.

UPON supposition that private traders could make it appear, that they could vend much larger quantities of our commodities in India than the company do, and that without importing larger quantities of India commodities: and supposing that proportion of India commerce neglected by the company, can be proposed to be carried on by private traders to the interest of the nation, and not detrimental to the company, why do not private traders apply to parliament with such proposition? And pray leave to carry on such neglected trade under the sanction of the company, on making them reasonable allowance for such licence?

IF on examination it should be found practicable for the company to open a direct trade, as has been suggested, in order to take off a greater quantity of our commodities, either by the Cape of Good Hope, or by the streights of Magellan, or with other parts of the Southern continent, it is right to recommend these things to the company.—And, if found ſound unexceptionably practicable, and profitable by competent and impartial judges, how can we ſuppoſe that the company would neglect ſuch advantages? But, if the company, from private views, incompatible with thoſe of the public, refuſed thus to exert themſelves in their own, and the public intereſt; upon fair proof hereof made in the face of the legiſlature; and becoming application to the ſame on the part of the petitioners, I make no doubt but the parliament would indulge them to undertake theſe trades that the company ſhould reject. For this, and all other companies are but ſo many corporations endowed with powers in truſt for the public, to whom they are always accountable; and by whom they are always liable to be over-ruled, and controuled, when they act repugnant to thoſe reaſons of ſtate whereon their charters are founded.

The objections that have been judged by ſome to have been of the moſt weight againſt this company are as follow: The firſt is grounded on the exportation of bullion, which is ſtated thus: the common meaſure of all things in a commercial way, is ſilver, and conſequently the great criterion of the wealth of the nation, is her extracting this common meaſure from other nations, by virtue of bringing the balance of trade in our favour; but the Eaſt-India trade is carried on by exporting this real, this intrinſic wealth, as it is called by ſome, and which never re-

turns,

turns, but is employed in the importation of India commodities, that are not neceſſary, but only mere inſtruments of luxury.

BEFORE we proceed to anſwer this objection, it may be requiſite to obſerve previouſly, that the neceſſaries of life are produced in every country, at leaſt in every habitable country: and it is to what ſome call luxury, that all trade whatever is owing: ſo that if nations are to deal in nothing but their own productions, here ſeems to be an end to all commercial intercourſe between foreign ſtates: if we admit this principle, we ſhould not only drink ſage inſtead of green tea, but make uſe of honey inſtead of ſugar, and water or beer at all times inſtead of wine; we ſhould, in ſhort, endeavour only to cultivate and improve the produce of our own country, ſubſiſt upon it, and leave all the reſt of the world to ſhift for itſelf.

How conſiſtent a maxim this would be, for people who inhabit an iſland, and how reaſonable it is for thoſe who derive moſt of the bleſſings we enjoy from trade and maritime power, to argue in this manner, we leave the reader to judge. But, if we ſet this objection ſo far aſide, as to allow that commerce between nations giving bread to myriads of the human ſpecies, and make the country wherein the ſame flouriſhes rich, happy, and powerful, the particular trade of the Eaſt-India company becomes as defenſible

ſible as any other; for if ſuch exportation of bullion does not injure the nation, then there is no weight in the objection: that it does not under the circumſtances of the preſent company, we have great reaſon to believe. For,

WHEN the firſt charter was granted them, leſt this ſhould prove an evil, it was properly guarded againſt by a proviſo, that the company ſhould be obliged to bring in as large a quantity of bullion as they carried out, in the interval between the voyages, made at the riſque of the company. Nor has it ever been made demonſtably appear, that the ſilver this company has carried out, has tended to the impoveriſhment of the kingdom; for if all that ſilver that has been in this kingdom remained in circulation; if we had neither exported any, nor had any converted into wrought plate, would not the price of all commodities have been conſiderably raiſed, eſpecially when added to that quantity of paper circulation that of late years has exiſted amongſt us?

BUT, inſtead of impoveriſhing the nation, as this commerce has encreaſed, it ſhould ſeem to have encreaſed the wealth of the nation in general, by bringing in, on the one hand, large quantities of ſilver for our Indian merchandizes re-exported, and detaining here, on the other, thoſe ſums of money which muſt otherwiſe have been exported for foreign produce and manufactures; which would have been

worn

worn here, if we had not long been better and cheaper ſupplied from India.

It has been formerly objected, that the wearing of India-piece goods prejudiced our own woollen manufactures; but this has, in a great meaſure, been cured by the laws paſſed for that purpoſe. It may not, however, be amiſs to obſerve, that thoſe manufactures are chiefly to be encouraged, which contribute to exportation; ſince it is certain, that the cheaper people can be cloathed here, let that cloathing come from where it will, the cheaper they can afford to work upon their own manufactures; and it is the general cheapneſs of labour and of our native commodities, that is the eſſential point to be ſtudied in a trading nation; for if we can underwork other countries, we ſhall infallibly undermine their trade, and extend our own; for though private people may be enriched by our home conſumption, yet the public may be no gainer thereby; which conſideration will enable the intelligent to diſcern how clamours may be raiſed againſt ſuch trades as are highly beneficial: and this, from confounding the intereſt of private men, or great bodies, with that of the public. If the India trade, therefore, has in its conſequences been inſtrumental, upon the whole, to bring in a greater balance of money than it has carried out, it has proved nationally gainful, and therefore ſhould be ſupported.

MONEY, as a medium, is neceſſary to the carrying on trade; for where that fails, the commercial negociations ſtagnate; for credit, which ſupplies that defect, is the expectation or aſſurance of money, when demanded.—Nevertheleſs it is a miſtake, perhaps, though a common one, to think that money is the cauſe of a good or bad trade; ſince it is not money that ſo much influences trade, as it is trade that diſcovers the money; which is the medium whereby trade is the more conveniently managed, but not the ſource from whence it ariſes: thus, when the trade is quick and briſk, then money, the medium, comes more into view than when it is otherwiſe; and then, by changing hands oftener, an hundred pounds makes as great an appearance in commerce as a much larger ſum.

No private trader, or company, ſends money or bullion into other countries, but with a view to gain the more by it. It was a maxim of the wiſe prince Ferdinand the firſt, great duke of Tuſcany, who raiſed the commerce of his ſubjects to an incredible height, to lend them money, and permit them to ſend the ſame out of his dominions in the way of traffic. Mr. Mun, a very ſkilful and eminent Engliſh merchant, tells us, that he himſelf experienced the duke's liberality upon the like occaſion, who lent him 40,000 crowns gratis, although he knew that he ſhould ſend the whole away in

ſpecie

ſpecie to Turkey, to purchaſe merchandizes; the duke being well aſſured, ſays he, that, in the courſe of that trade, the ſame would return again, according to the Italian proverb, with a duck in the mouth. This judicious gentleman further informs us, that, by this policy, the duke encouraged trade to ſuch a degree, that, of his own knowledge, Leghorn, which was only a poor little mean town, became a great and opulent city; being in his time become the moſt famous place of commerce in all Chriſtendom.

THERE has not been any point of trade more generally miſunderſtood, perhaps, than what relates to gold and ſilver, or bullion, which ſome would have not to be reckoned a commodity, or merchandize; and therefore not permitted to go out, when once brought into the kingdom. But thoſe who ſeem to have judged the beſt of the matter, have been of a different ſentiment, and contended for its free exportation no leſs than its importation.

THOSE nations that bring in gold or ſilver by means of their exports of variety of merchandize, are upon an equal footing with thoſe countries that have mines in their poſſeſſion, and barter their gold and ſilver for commodities; and, in ſuch trading ſtates, that have no gold or ſilver mines, gold and ſilver become a ſpecies of merchandize, as well as any other; a merchandize that may be turned in trade with advantage, and therefore more valuable in ſuch a country, than where they were firſt dug from the mines. Induſtry, and ſkill to improve trade, and the apt ſituation of a country for it, afford more real treaſure to a people than even the poſſeſſion of gold and ſilver mines: nor can any quantity thereof, that may be dug out of the mines, bear a proportion with what may be made to ariſe from the whole labour of a trading, induſtrious, and populous nation. For the national ſtock, though ſmall at firſt, is by ſuch means, ever increaſing, and that increaſe ſtill accumulating more and more; ſo that the augmentation ariſing from ſuch accumulating increaſe, and the gold and ſilver gained from other nations in trade for commodities, makes a perpetual addition: which being permanent, ſuch nation has no bounds to its wealth; while other countries that poſſeſs mines, and rely on their produce, generally work them chiefly for the induſtrious of other countries, and may become beggars, notwithſtanding their firſt property of all the gold and ſilver in the world.

THE firſt prohibition in Spain againſt exporting gold and ſilver, was an early obſtruction to their commercial induſtry, and rendered that treaſure in a great meaſure uſeleſs to the bulk of the people. But if, on the contrary, gold and ſilver had been allowed commodities, it would of courſe have put them upon methods of turning them to more advantage: whereas, while their hands have been

been bound up by their own laws, the gold and ſilver brought from thence have been the tools wherewith other nations have wrought, and gained their riches. Had not this miſtaken policy diverted their thoughts from an *active* commerce, they would certainly have been, at this day, a different nation to what they are. At preſent, indeed, they ſeem to be ſenſible of their *faux pas*, and *England*, as well as other countries, is likely ſoon to experience the effects of a different policy, unleſs the former in particular takes wiſe meaſures to prevent it, before it is too late.

SHOULD it be objected to this reaſoning, that as we have a great trade for our product and manufactures, and thereby bring in a general balance of gold and ſilver, beſides other returns in commodities for our expence; we ought only to carry out commodities in trade, and let the gold and ſilver remain among ourſelves, and by our laws prevent the exportation thereof; which is carrying out that treaſure again which comes to us by the balance of our trade.

To this it has been anſwered, that gold and ſilver are no otherwiſe of intrinſic value in themſelves than as they are a *ſettled* and *conſtant meaſure*, whereby to value commodities of all kinds; which ſeems manifeſt from hence, that in ſuch countries, as in *Africa*, &c. where they are not the *ſettled* and *conſtant meaſure for commodities*, they are of no more uſe than any other trafficable com-

commodity; and as particular ſpecies of merchandizes in demand throughout the world, are to be had ſome at one place, and ſome at another; ſo gold and ſilver are commodities wherein moſt nations agree that the difference in the barter of all other commodities is anſwered and made up, and thereby of general uſe almoſt every where; which being thus ſubſervient to trade, it is highly injurious, nay, it is its very deſtruction, to take it from that uſe: but as to the imagination of retaining the ſame in the nation, without circulating out of it, this muſt be a national loſs; for that is keeping ſuch a dead ſtock to that value, which affords no manner of increaſe, and is of no more uſe, while it ſo continues, to the increaſe of the public capital (however ſhifted in private hands) than the like value of ſtatues, paintings, buildings, &c.: the uſe of it among us ſerves to no other end than the convenient tranſacting of payments with one another, in our domeſtic negociations; and, when that end is anſwered, the plenty of gold and ſilver will be rather a national loſs (beſides its lying dead) as it will naturally enhance the price of our own merchandizes to ourſelves, and thereby leſſen the demand for them by foreign nations; and conſequently, in time, ruin the trade, and impoveriſh the people, by enabling them to purſue only a *paſſive*, inſtead of an *active* general commerce, as has been hitherto the caſe of countries

tries that have depended on their mines, and the miſtaken policy of not eſteeming gold and ſilver commodities.

BUT ſhould it be granted convenient for us to keep within ourſelves all the bullion we can acquire, yet long experience has ſhewn the impracticability of keeping it by any laws; that could only be effectuated by the good management and regulation of our trade. Though the Spaniards make the exportation thereof death, nevertheleſs, in the way of trade, it is exported at noon-day; the balance they pay for the manufactures of other countries, neceſſarily carries away their money, notwithſtanding the rigour and ſeverity of all their penal laws to prevent it *. It is, therefore, taking due care that the exportation of our native commodities ſhall always over-balance the importation of foreign commodities, which muſt keep our money at home, and that only can do it. For if, upon the balance of the exports and imports of our other commodities, we are gainers, and thereby payments are made to us in gold and ſilver, by other countries (for the balance can be paid us in nothing elſe at laſt) that gold and ſilver being ſuffered to be made a commodity to fetch goods from ſome other countries, whence we cannot

* This, alſo, ſhews the miſtaken policy of the *Portugueſe*, in regard to the treatment our merchants lately received at *Liſbon*.

have

have them for any thing elſe, the re-exportation thereof to other countries would become a beneficial article in our commerce, and return a great balance in its own kind, (our trade otherwiſe, in products and manufactures, ſtill over-balancing as before) and would add greatly to the national ſtock; and, without ſuch a freedom in trade, a ſuperfluous plenty of bullion, or money, would be rather injurious than otherwiſe.

If, by the wiſe regulation of our trade with foreign nations, the balance is on our ſide, and we are gainers by ſending out our money to purchaſe ſuch goods, that may be ſold again to other countries, we muſt, by ſuch an encreaſe of treaſure as this will give us, always be maſters of the exchange all over the world; which is ſuch an advantage in trade with any nation, that although it may only be a trifle in our favour, it has a national tendency ariſing from itſelf, to augment that balance ſtill more and more to our emolument.

From what has been ſaid, it ſeems pretty evident, that gold, and ſilver, or bullion, in any ſhape, ought to be reckoned a commodity, and is to be made uſe of to advantage in trade, as well as other commodities are; and therefore ought to have a free exportation, as conducive to the increaſe of the capital ſtock of the kingdom. It muſt, however, be allowed in the general, that, if we carry on ſuch a trade as importing conſumable

able commodities to be ſpent among us, more than our own commodities will anſwer in the balance, which thereby muſt be paid in gold and ſilver, this will certainly be to our detriment, by draining us, without any returns, to ſuch an exceſs of our bullion and our ſpecie, that we ſhall not have a competent quantity wherewith to circulate our trade, and be attended with a decay in our manufactures: but, if this ſhould be our caſe, it is not to be remedied by any laws againſt the exportation of our gold and ſilver, but by the due regulation of our trade, by retrenching our conſumption of foreign merchandizes; by eſtabliſhing new trades, new arts and manufactures in the nation: in a word, by purchaſing leſs merchandizes of other countries, and ſelling more of our own; for the exportation of our gold and ſilver could not be the cauſe of ſuch our loſs, but the effect of ſuch our ill-managed commerce.

THERE would be little difficulty ſtill further to corroborate this reaſoning with a train of weighty arguments, and to confirm the ſame from the concurring ſentiments of the ableſt ſtateſmen; but I think there is little occaſion.

HOWEVER, ſince we have great reaſon to believe, that neither the conſtitution of our Eaſt-India company, nor the manner of carrying on that traffic from the firſt to the laſt, are or can be ſo detrimental to the nation

tion as ſome have been wont to think; we ought to conſider how, and by what means this company may be conſtitutionally improved; and eſpecially ſo, if it is not ſo well adapted to the national intereſts as could be wiſhed.—But till we had endeavoured to remove the ordinary prejudices that may have been conceived againſt this company, I judged it would be to little purpoſe to attempt to ſuggeſt a word in regard to the encreaſe of its powers and privileges with relation to our African commerce.

We have ſeen the neceſſity of ſupporting and carrying on our African trade in a manner different from what we have ever hitherto done; and we know that no meaſures can extend the inland commerce into the heart and center of Africa but a great trading company: and the Eaſt-India company being greatly experienced in commerce, and their preſent trade having a connection with that of Africa, they ſeem a company the moſt ſuitably adapted for this great purpoſe.—And if they ſhould be endowed with the excluſive privilege of the inland African commerce, may they not hereby be made inſtrumental to bring both ſilver and gold in great quantities into the kingdom, by means of extending the inland African commerce? For the moſt authentic writers inform us, that there are ſilver as well as gold mines in thoſe parts. And why not diamond ones

alſo?

alſo? And what great variety of other articles of traffic this part of the world might produce, no one can ſay: but this we can ſay, with truth, that as yet we know very little of what great things this commerce will admit.

Its ſituation for commerce is certainly beyond either of the other quarters of the world. It ſtands, as it were, in the center between the other three, and has thereby a much nearer communication with Europe, Aſia, and America, than any other quarter has with the reſt. For, 1. It is oppoſite to Europe in the Mediterranean, for almoſt 1000 miles in a line eaſt and weſt, from beyond Tripoli to cape Spartel at the Streight's mouth; the diſtance ſeldom 100 miles, no where 100 leagues, and often not 20 leagues. 2. It is oppoſite to Aſia for all the length of the Red-Sea north and ſouth; the diſtance ſometimes being not above 5 leagues, ſeldom 50; and it fronts all the ſouthern coaſt of Aſia, viz. the coaſt of Cilicia; and that of India, though at a greater diſtance, yet much nearer than any other country. It is wonderfully accommodated for commerce, by the interpoſition of iſlands from Madagaſcar to Malabar; and more particularly by means of the alternate trade-winds, which render the navigation ſafe, eaſy, and conſtant. 3. It alſo lies oppoſite to America, or about the diſtance of 500 to 700 leagues, including the iſlands, for a coaſt of above 2000 miles: whereas

whereas America no where joins Europe, except where it may be a terra incognita, under a diſtance of 1000 leagues, and not Aſia under that of 2500.

It is furniſhed with the greateſt and moſt convenient navigable rivers, and, perhaps, with as many of them as any other of the chief parts of the world: ſuch are the Nile and Nubia on the north ſhore, running into the Mediterranean-ſea; the Niger, or Rio Grand, running into the Atlantic ocean, on the weſt-ſide of Africa; the Congo, the Zairi, and the Loango, three rivers of prodigious extent, ſouth of the line, which enter themſelves into the Ethiopic ocean on the ſame weſt-ſide, but beyond the Gold-coaſt: alſo the Natal, the Prio St. Eſprit, the Melinda, and the Mozambo, all rivers of a very great length and breadth, which enter themſelves into the Indian ocean to the eaſt-ſide of Africa.

These are all rivers of the firſt magnitude; beſides which, there are innumerable others, which, though not equal to the former, are yet very noble ſtreams, fitted for navigation and commerce, and which, by their long courſes, penetrate far inland: and was this country bleſſed with a people qualified for trade and buſineſs, they might become the medium of an endleſs commercial correſpondence.

The country is populous beyond credibility, the ſoil fruitful, the ſeaſon, for the greateſt part

part, mild and clement, and the air ſalubrious: and, if once a turn for induſtry and the arts was introduced among them, a greater quantity of the European produce and manufactures might be exported thither, than to any other country in the whole world. And, as the natives in general ſtand in great need of European commodities, ſo they have the moſt valuable returns to make for them. This the Europeans experience, from the ſhare of traffic they carry on with them at preſent.

To what a great degree this country abounds in gold, we have not only the teſtimony of the Portugueſe, the Dutch, and the French, as well as Engliſh, who have ſettlements on the coaſt of Africa, but the vouchers of the moſt authentic hiſtorians.

THERE is no country in the world, ſays the hiſtorian Leo Africanus, richer in gold and ſilver than the kingdoms in Africa; as thoſe of Mandingo, Ethiopia, Congo, Angola, Butua, Quiticui, Monomotopa, Caſati, and Mehenemugi. By means of ſettlements of ſtrength on the continent of Africa, adds he, the Europeans might, by the exchange of their commodities, draw into their hands all the gold of thoſe countries. And here is a prodigious number of elephants, which would not only facilitate the inland intercourſes of commerce, but alſo afford a very beneficial branch of traffic, in the teeth of theſe notable animals. In the ſame hiſtorian are

num-

numberlefs paffages relating to thofe rich mines, and fhewing how eafy it would be for the Europeans to carry on a very extenfive traffic with that part of the globe.

THIS account of the great treafures of Africa is confirmed likewife by the *Nubian geographer*, who fomewhere fays, that the king of Guinea, the greateft city in all the countries of Negroland, has a mafs of gold of 30 pounds weight, as it was naturally produced in the mines; which is completely pure, tough, and malleable, without having been fmelted by the ordinary arts of refining that metal from its native ore. Father Labat, a modern French author, has defcended to a very minute fpecification of great variety of rich mines, which he fays are very fhamefully worked by the Negroes, by reafon of their being totally ignorant of the nature of mining: nor have they ever yet come to the main vein of any of their mines.

THE copper is the next valuable ore found in this part of the world. The quantity of this metal is not fully fearched into, though there is great reafon to believe it is exceeding great: fo great, that it is commonly faid amongft them, that the mountains, which we call Atlas, are all copper. Thus much, however, is certain, that the quantity is extraordinary great, that is difcovered in feveral countries diftant and remote from each other; as in Fez, Tunis, Abyffinia, or Ethiopia; and

and it is allowed to be the fineſt copper in the whole world.

On the northern coaſts they have ſuch plenty of corn, that their fields, though but very meanly cultivated for want of a knowledge in agriculture, yield them an hundred-fold encreaſe. Gums, ivory, wax, civet, oſtrich-feathers, are in ſuch quantities, that any expence of them can ſcarce ever be miſſed.

And, in theſe warm climates, the country, beſides what nature has of herſelf diſſeminated, is, and muſt be, capable of improvement, in all the niceſt and moſt eſtimable productions, which the well-cultivated world ſupplies us with, from other places in the ſame latitude.

It cannot be doubted, but the fruitful rich lands, every-where to be found upon the coaſts, and within the country, upon the banks of the rivers near the gold-coaſt, and the ſlave-coaſt, would produce all the richeſt articles of the Eaſt- and Weſt-India commerce. Doubtleſs the ſpices of Banda, Ternate, and Amboyna, might be produced on the rich and fruitful ſhores of Melinda, on the eaſt ſide, or, of the ſlave-coaſt on the weſt-ſide, of Africa; and that as eaſily, and to as great advantage, as where they are now produced; the latitude being the ſame, and the ſoil not unlike.

The cinnamon of Ceylon, the tea of China and Japan, and the coffee of Mocha would

would all there be produced, on the ſame coaſt, from the Rio de St. Eſprit, and ſouthward to the river Natale; a temperate, fertile, healthy, and manageable ſoil.

UPON the foundation of theſe facts, nothing ſeems wanting to render Africa equal by nature, if not in many reſpects ſuperior, to any of the three parts of the world. For although the middle of it, lying between the tropics in the torrid zone, and under the line, is exceeding hot; yet even in the hotteſt part it is habitable, and inhabited; and the people who dwell in theſe extreme hot climates, do abound in plenty, have cattle, corn, cooling-fruits, ſhades, rivers, &c. and live very agreeably and healthy; as in the iſland of St. Thomas, under the very line, alſo on the gold-coaſt, and in the kingdom of Benin, and Angola on the weſt ſhore; and in Ethiopia, Melinda, the coaſt of Zanguebar, and ſeveral of the more intemperate places on the eaſtern ſhore.

BUT, making allowance for ſome of the inland countries remote from the ſea, which we are told are without water, and therefore deſert, yet they are not equal to the uninhabited waſtes either of Europe, Aſia, or America. Notwithſtanding this, Africa, in one reſpect, has greater advantage than the other parts of the world, for it feels no cold, the moſt northerly latitude being about 37, and the moſt ſoutherly about 35 degrees, ſo that infinitely

infinitely the larger part enjoys the fineſt and moſt temperate climate.

It is melancholy to obſerve that a country, which has near 10,000 miles ſea-coaſt, and noble, large, deep rivers, ſhould yet have no navigation; ſtreams penetrating into the very center of the country, but of no benefit to it; innumerable people, without knowledge of each other, correſpondence, or commerce.

At the entrance of theſe rivers into the ſea are the moſt excellent harbours, prodigious in number, deep, ſafe, and calm, covered from the wind, and capable of being made ſecure by fortifications; but no ſhipping, no trade, no merchants, even where there is plenty of merchandiſes. In ſhort, Africa, though a full quarter of the globe, ſtored with an inexhauſtible treaſure, and capable, under proper improvements, of producing ſo many things delightful, as well as convenient within itſelf, ſeems utterly neglected by thoſe who are civilized themſelves, and it's own inhabitants quite unſollicitous of reaping the benefits which nature has provided for them. What it affords in it's preſent rude, unimproved ſtate, is ſolely given up to the gain of others, as if not the people only were to be ſold for ſlaves to their fellow-creatures, but the whole country was captive, and produced it's treaſures, merely for the uſe and benefit of the reſt of the world, and not at all for their own.

WHETHER, inſtead of making ſlaves of theſe people, it would not rather become ſuch nations that aſſume to themſelves the name and character of Chriſtians, to give them a reliſh for the bleſſings of life, by extending traffic into their country in the largeſt degree it will admit of, and introducing among them the more civilized arts and cuſtoms, may be ſubmitted to conſideration.

THE Dutch, by recommending their dreſs, and introducing their cuſtoms among the natives, have prodigiouſly improved the commerce of the ſpice iſlands, and wonderfully humanized the inhabitants, who were as ſavage in their manners as the negroes.

BUT it is to be feared that, while the ſlaving trade with theſe people continues to be the great object of the Europeans, it will ever ſpirit up wars and hoſtilities among the negro-princes and chiefs, for the ſake of making captives of each other for ſale. This, therefore, will ever obſtruct the civilizing of theſe people, and extending of the trade into the bowels of Africa, which, by the contrary means, might be eaſily practicable.

THE obtaining a competent number of ſervants to work, as the negroes at preſent do, in the colonies belonging to the ſeveral European potentates, who have ſettlements in America, does not ſeem at all impracticable. Europe in general affords numberleſs poor and diſtreſſed objects for that purpoſe; and, if theſe were not over-worked, as the negroes

negroes particularly are in Martinico, and in other the French colonies, the Europeans would make as good ſervants for the American planters as the blacks do: and, if alſo all the Europeans were upon a level in regard to the price of labour in their colonies, we cannot but think they would all find their account in laying abſolutely aſide the ſlave-trade, and cultivating a fair, friendly, humane, and civilized commerce with the Africans.

TILL this is done, it does not ſeem poſſible that the inland trade of this country ſhould ever be extended to the degree it is capable of; for, while the ſpirit of butchery and making ſlaves of each other is promoted by the Europeans among theſe people, they will never be able, perhaps, to travel with ſafety into the heart of Africa, or to cement ſuch commercial friendſhips and alliances with them as will effectually introduce our arts and manufactures amongſt them.

WE muſt, however, at preſent, take the ſtate of the trade as it ſtands, and men as they now are: theſe hints may poſſibly ſome time or other rouſe ſome noble and benevolent Chriſtian ſpirit to think of changing the whole ſyſtem of the African trade, which, as things are now circumſtanced, may not be ſo eaſily brought about.

THIS trade, in it's preſent ſtate, is of as great advantage as any we carry on, and is, as it were, all profit, the firſt coſt being ſome things of our own manufactures, and others generally

generally purchaſed with them, for which we have, in return, gold, teeth, wax, and negroes; the laſt whereof is a very beneficial traffic to the kingdom, as it occaſionally gives ſo prodigious an employment to our people both by ſea and land. Theſe are the hands whereby our plantations are at preſent improved; and it is by their labours that ſuch quantities of ſugar, tobacco, cotton, ginger, fuſtic, and indigo are raiſed, which employ a great quantity of ſhipping for tranſporting them hither; and the greater number of ſhips employs the greater number of handicraft trades at home, ſpends more of our produce and manufactures, and breeds more ſailors, who are maintained by a ſeparate employment; for, if every one raiſed the proviſions he eat, or made the manufactures he wore, traffic would ceaſe; which is promoted by a variety of employments men have engaged in, which conſtitutes a mutual dependence, without invading each other's province. Thus the huſbandman raiſes corn, the miller grinds it, the baker makes it into bread, and the citizen eats it; thus the grazier fats cattle, and the butcher kills them for the market: thus the ſhepherd ſheers his ſheep, the ſpiniſter turns the wool into yarn, the weaver makes it into cloth, and the merchant exports it; and every one lives by each other: thus the country ſupplies the city with proviſions, and that the country with neceſſaries.

On the whole, the African trade, both for exports and imports, and alſo as it ſupplies our Britiſh plantations with labourers, and advances navigation, is certainly very beneficial to this kingdom: but that the laying this trade abſolutely open, while our rivals carry the ſame on, by the means of great trading companies with joint-ſtocks, will prove the moſt effectual means to promote our ſhare therein, is greatly to be doubted.

Certain it is, that this way of carrying the trade on can never tend to it's advancement into the interior parts of Africa. And why ſhould we not attempt this? Will not whatever encreaſe we make herein prove a new acquiſition of trade to the kingdom? And if our private traders cannot accompliſh this, why ſhould we not eſtabliſh a rich and powerful company that can? What motive can private traders have to deny, or envy that trade to a company, which they can never obtain themſelves? But, if once this inland trade ſhall be thoroughly ſettled, and the nation ſhall think fit to lay the ſame again open to all his Majeſty's ſubjects, then our private traders will be gainers, by virtue of the foundation which ſuch company ſhall have laid. Was not the foundation of all our preſent trade laid, in the reign of Queen Elizabeth, by joint-ſtock companies with excluſive privileges? Why ſhould not the ſame reaſon rule now for the propagation of any new trades that will not be undertaken by private traders, becauſe of the hazard that attends it? Why then ſhould not the Eaſt-India company have annexed to it the excluſive privilege in all the inland trade of Africa, if they ſhould think proper to accept of it? Would not a meaſure of this kind, uphold our balance of trade and power in Africa, in a manner equivalent to the weight of the great French India company? And whatever tended to add to the wealth and the power of our India company in Africa, would not this ſpread it's happy effects into Aſia, and enable the company the better to maintain our national balance of trade and power in India, alſo in oppoſition to our formidable rivals? And our American trade greatly depending upon our African; by theſe means it ſhould ſeem that this our India company might be capable of ſuſtaining our commercial weight and dignity in America, Aſia, and Africa, as does the French Eaſt-India company; and by their timely watching, and timely checking for the future, all inſults and encroachment in thoſe trades under their peculiar care, might they not become greatly inſtrumental to the prevention of future wars, and thereby ſave an immenſe expence to the nation? Or, if it ſhould be judged, that ſuch an additional power would be too much to be given to the Eaſt-India company, why ſhould not a new company be eſtabliſhed to carry on the inland commerce of Africa to the utmoſt extent it will admit of? But for the reaſons before given

our

our Eaſt-India company being well experienced in commerce; and the India trade being connected with that of Africa, they would be reciprocally beneficial: and, if our India company brought us ſilver as well as gold from Africa, this would help their India commerce, and take off that odium under which they labour for exporting our ſilver in the preſent way of their traffic.

DISSERTATION XXVI.

The encreaſe of the naval power of France and Spain by means of their fiſheries, and of the neceſſity of England's balancing that degree of naval power, by the carrying of her fiſheries to the full extent they will admit of.

IN queen Anne's wars, when the French king was importuned by his people to admit the Dutch and Engliſh fiſhing boats into Dieppe, Dunkirk, St. Vallery, and other ports, with their herrings, the king anſwered, NO! BY NO MEANS; IF MY PEOPLE WILL HAVE HERRINGS, WHY DO THEY NOT CATCH THEM, AS THE ENGLISH AND DUTCH DO? Upon which, the merchants of thoſe parts immediately fitted out veſſels, and took herrings ſufficient for all the country.

FROM this time the French have taken every meaſure to improve their fiſheries; in which capital article of commerce, they have been encreaſing ever ſince the treaty of Utrecht, and have become our moſt dangerous rivals

rivals herein. The French have a considerable whale-fishery, and the French fishermen of St. John de Luze, Bayonne, and other ports in that part of the bay of Biscay, are become the most expert harpooners in the world, without excepting the Dutch, and the Hamburghers.

But the French have not only encreased in the whale-fishery, but, which is of far more consequence to Great-Britain, they have exceedingly encreased their fishery to Newfoundland, as well on the coast as on the great bank. The consequence of this encrease of their fishery we have, to our sorrow, too sensibly felt. Nor do they fish only on the great bank of Newfoundland for such fish which are cured without drying, as the Dutch do in their white herring fishery in the open sea, but have had the address to obtain that the island of Cape Breton should be yielded up to them, to fortify, and do what they please with ; where there may, and doubtless will, make a second Dunkirk, as I have observed upon another occasion, and where they may carry on their dry fishery, as well as at Placentia. But, as if this was not privilege enough for them, they have obtained that, in the fishing-season, they may resort to the very island of Newfoundland itself, and erect stages, &c, to cure and dry their fish at *.

* Ought not this to be guarded against in making a peace with France ?

BUT this is not all; the world is well amended with the French ſince the time that they paid a tribute for the liberty of curing and drying fiſh at Newfoundland, which was granted them by king Charles I. in the 10th year of his reign. At this time the French are not only exempt from tribute, but, by their neighbourhood at Cape Breton, will oblige us to keep large garriſons as well at Nova Scotia, as Newfoundland, if we will prevent our being ſurprized; where at Newfoundland they have the liberty of the fiſhing ſeaſon equally with us, from Cape Bonaviſta northward to the northern point of the ſaid iſland, &c. by which ſituation they are alſo become our rivals in another branch of our fiſhery; that of ſalmon: for, at the harbour of Bonaviſta, which is to the northward of the Cape, and therefore within their limits, is an extraordinary good fiſhery of ſalmon.

HAD the late king William granted the Dutch any one of the iſlands of the Orkneys, in propriety to fortify, or a liberty of reſorting to, or erecting drying-houſes neceſſary to cure red herrings in any ſuch iſland, or in England, or Scotland, it would have been remembered, with good reaſon, a thouſand and a thouſand times over. But the French have had the cunning to procure for their fiſhery ſuch liberties and privileges as can ſcarcely be conſiſtent with our ſafety, or intereſt; and, therefore, the world may be left to judge who are our GREATEST and MOST

DAN-

DANGEROUS rivals in the FISHERY. They are now become ſo much our rivals in this trade, and are encreaſed to ſuch a prodigious degree, that they employ yearly above 500 ſail of ſhipping from St. Malo, Granville, Rochelle, St. Martins, Iſle of Rea, Bayonne, St. Jean de Luze, Sibour, &c. to carry on their fiſheries on the great bank of Newfoundland, and on the coaſt of that iſland; that is, in their wet and dry fiſh: nor do they now only ſupply themſelves with the fiſh they formerly had from us, but furniſh many parts of Spain and Italy therewith, to our prodigious loſs.

THEY have the propereſt ſalt of their own, which renders their voyages much ſhorter than ours; for, we have been obliged to go from hence to Rochelle, Olleron, St. Martin, &c. to fetch that commodity, which they have at their own doors; and thereby we have moſt frequently ſpent a month or ſix weeks more in our voyage than they do.

THE French are ſo ſenſible of the prodigious advantage of this fiſhery, and ſo very intent upon purſuing it, that, from their firſt attempts to make themſelves conſiderable at ſea, they have had it perpetually in view.— They firſt obtained leave to fiſh at Newfoundland, upon paying a duty of 5 per cent. afterwards they got that acknowledgment relinquiſhed: but, at the treaty of Utrecht, they went far greater lengths; for thereby they procured a ceſſion to be made to them of Cape Breton, a maiden fiſhery, that had ſcarce ever been touched; whereas Newfoundland was greatly exhauſted, and alſo ſeveral iſlands in the gulph of St. Lawrence. Not content with that, they further obtained a liberty of curing and drying their fiſh, ſetting up ſtages, and reſorting to OUR iſland of Newfoundland, during all the time that it is of any uſe to reſort thither; which is during the fiſhing-ſeaſon.

THEY, indeed, delivered up to us the poſſeſſion of Placentia, and ſome other places in Newfoundland; but then they took care to have a much better place for their fiſhery yielded to them, in lieu thereof; with this extraordinary favour to them, more than to us, that they have the liberty granted them to frequent OUR iſland of Newfoundland, and erect ſtages, &c. thereon, for curing and drying their fiſh; but we have not the privilege allowed us of doing the ſame on any of their iſlands, or on the iſland of Cape Breton, while they have expreſs permiſſion granted them to fortify as they pleaſe.

THUS the French are become our rivals in the FISHERY by our own conſent; which is the more wonderful, in that it is owing to this fiſhery, that they dared to contend for the maſtery at ſea with the maritime ſtrength of England and Holland united.

IT is true, the Engliſh and Dutch are moſt frequently called the maritime powers; but we we think it a jeſt, at this time of day, to appropriate the name of maritime powers to Great Britain and Holland, excluſive of France, when we conſider what a figure that nation made at ſea before the battle of La Hogue in 1692, and what a figure they are able to make at preſent from the daily encreaſe of their marine, ſince the late treaty of Aix la Chapelle.

THE hiſtory both of France and England will ſhew us, that ſince the former procured leave to fiſh at Newfoundland, and their ſettlement and fiſhery at Cape Breton, they have grown very formidable at ſea, and that their royal navy has augmented in proportion to the number of ſhips employed in theſe fiſheries.—What have we not to expect then, ſince they have obtained a right to a better place for their fiſhery, in the opinion, even of the French themſelves, as the reader will ſoon ſee by the incloſed letter, written by a miniſter of ſtate in France, to the duke de Gramond at Bayonne ? The occaſion of it was, that the people of St. Jean de Luze and Sibour (two places in the county of Sibour) being under apprehenſions that their fiſhery at Newfoundland was to be delivered up wholly to Great Britain, the duke wrote a letter to Paris to be rightly informed, and received the following anſwer.

Copy

Copy of a letter written by Monſieur de Pontchartrain, to Monſ. the duke de Gramond, from Fontainebleau, 19 September, 1713.

"I have received, Sir, the letter you did me the honour to write me the third of this month, with two letters that were directed to you by the inhabitants of St. Jean de Luze and Sibour, upon the ſubject of their fiſhery of dry fiſh. From the account I have given the king of their demand, his majeſty directed me to write, by his order, to Monſ. the duke d'Aumont, his ambaſſador extraordinary at London, to aſk of the queen of Great Britain a permiſſion for them to go the next year to Placentia, and the liberty to continue their fiſhing in ALL the ports and harbours upon the coaſt of Newfoundland. I ſhall do myſelf the honour to acquaint you with Monſ. the duke d'Aumont's anſwer.

I agree with you, Sir, that the country of La Bour will ſuffer much, ſhould they be deprived of their liberty of carrying on their fiſhery of dry fiſh; and you will be perſuaded of the attention I have to procure to the merchants that drive this commerce, the means to continue them in it, when I have informed you, that the king ſent from Rochford, in the month of May laſt, one frigate, to go and lay the firſt foundation of an eſtabliſhment in the iſland of CAPE BRETON, where

fiſh

fiſh is MUCH MORE ABUNDANT than at the iſland of Newfoundland, and where one may make the fiſh, and manage the drying thereof eaſily. This frigate arrived June 26 at Placentia, from whence ſhe was to continue her courſe for Cape Breton, to which place I have cauſed to be tranſported 100 men, to begin the ſettlement. His majeſty will ſend, in the beginning of the year, three ſhips, to tranſport thither the garriſon of Placentia, and the inhabitants of the iſland of Newfoundland, and to put the laſt hand to the eſtabliſhment of that port. The merchants of this kingdom may then ſend all ſuch ſhips as they ſhall think fit to order, for the fiſhing of dry fiſh, and for the oils that are made from the fiſh on the ſaid iſland. This favour ought to animate the merchants that drive this commerce, to carry it on with vigour, from the advantage they will draw from it. This is all I have been able to do in their favour. I deſire you to be perſuaded of the great ſincerity wherewith I have the honour to be ———".

FROM this letter it is plain the French never intended to quit the fiſhery of dry cod, and that they have, from this period, very much rivalled us therein, to our great detriment, and their unſpeakable emolument.— And, with regard to their herring-fiſhery, have we not frequent accounts of many hundreds of their buſſes being upon our coaſts in the ſeaſon? which may one day prove highly dangerous

dangerous to this kingdom upon other occasions, as well as injurious to our own fisheries of that kind.

THE present commercial system of Spain being grounded on that so zealously recommended by that great Spanish patriot and statesman Don Geronymo Utzaritz, we shall shew his sentiments in regard to the fisheries which he exhorts his countrymen to strike into.—After having shewn the advantage which the Dutch, the French, and the English have reaped from their fisheries, he takes no little pains to animate the Spanish nation to pursue the like policy; and he even asserts, that the Spaniards have a right to fish at Newfoundland: so that we are one day likely to have rival upon rival in this branch of our trade.

"IT ought to be a principal concern of the government, says this politic Spaniard, to prevent foreigners from enervating the the kingdom so much as they do, by the importation of salt-fish, and the great consumption it meets with in Spain, that of bacalao in particular, which is known to be so considerable a part of the food of all its provinces in general.

IN order to calculate the consumption, it is to be observed, that, in the provinces of the crown of Castille, the fast-days amount to a hundred and twenty in a year, and that they exceed a hundred and sixty in those of the crown of Arragon, and in Navarre, where flesh

fleſh is prohibited on Saturdays, which is not the caſe in Caſtille. The computation may be a little over or under, on account of ſome variation there is in the devotional faſts. But, if we rate the number to be a hundred and thirty in the year, one kingdom with another, throughout Spain, upon a moderate ſuppoſition that every family, one with another, ſhall expend four ounces of bacalao every faſt-day (which is not an ounce to one perſon) there will be conſumed, in a million and a half of families, ſix millions of ounces, which amount to 3750 quintals per day; and for the hundred and thirty faſt-days in a year, 487,500 quintals; which, at the rate of five dollars, the current price, a little more or leſs, when foreigners ſell it to us, amount to 2,437,500 dollars. And, if we add the great quantity of cured ſalmon, herrings, pilchards, and other fiſh from abroad, which is alſo expended in theſe kingdoms, one may reaſonably imagine, that the money they annually drain from us, by this article, is above three millions of dollars: and it is one of the principal cauſes of our unhappy ſituation.

I AM aware there is no ſmall number of perſons who, for want of health, are diſpenſed with eating fiſh upon days of abſtinence; but there are alſo many convents of men and women, ſome of which live upon fiſh every day in the year, others the greateſt part of it; ſo that what theſe ſocieties exceed the hundred

hundred and thirty days of abſtinence, may be a balance for ſuch as eat fleſh on thoſe days.

This general calculation I have thought proper to give, in order to have it more clearly ſeen how much of our ſubſtance other nations drain from us by the ſale of cured fiſh; though I do it with ſome reluctance, becauſe I am to draw preciſe concluſions from principles doubtful, and incapable of being aſcertained. But, ſhould any one think I run far wide of the truth in my eſtimate, either exceeding or falling ſhort of it, every one will be at liberty to correct them, and form others more exact from better information, and clearer notions of this matter.

I am alſo very ſenſible, that bacalao is a diet of great relief to thoſe parts where freſh fiſh is ſcarce; but we ſhould not, on that account, throw off all thoughts of repairing the great injury they do us by the ſale of this and other ſalt fiſh, and neglect to avail ourſelves of ſuch meaſures as prudence ſhall dictate, in particular the advantages which our own Seas afford, and ſome other prudent conſiderations invite us to, and flatter us with an eaſy way to ſupply our wants, if not wholly, at leaſt in a great meaſure; ſince it is well known what plenty of fiſh there is on the coaſt of Spain, eſpecially that of Gallicia; as is alſo certain, that, on the coaſt of the Andaluſia's, there is abundance of tunnies, ſturgeon, lampreys, cuttle-fiſh, chevins,

chevins, and ſeveral other ſorts of wholeſome fiſh, ſome of which ſalted, and others dried, are kept whole years, not only for a ſupply to thoſe provinces, where there is a great conſumption, but alſo to furniſh us in the inland parts; and the only thing we want is to encourage a fiſhery, both on our own coaſts, and in other ſeas; and in this ſort of commerce by his majeſty's ſubjects, I ſhall, therefore, proceed to point out ſuch meaſures as ſeem to me moſt prudent, and likely to take effect.

In chapters 73 and 74, I recommend the ſtationing of guarda coſta's, and ſhew that, among other great advantages, they would be a means to enlarge our fiſheries on the coaſt of Spain and elſewhere. To their contents I refer for what concerns the encouragement and ſecurity of thoſe fiſheries, and intend only to add, that I eſteem it a very prudent ſtep to lay as heavy duties, as treaties of peace and commerce ſhall allow, upon the importation of bacalao, and other ſalt-fiſh into Spain, without any abatement or indulgence whatever, not excepting the voluntary and accidental allowances which of late years have been made to fiſh, and ſome other things in the cuſtomhouſes of Catalonia, on their importation, beſides their not being charged in that principality, or the kingdom of Valencia, with the duty of the millon, which moſt part of the ſalt-fiſh pays in the ports of Caſtille.

It

It will alſo be proper for ſalt-fiſh to pay intire the duties of the alcavala and ciento's, in all places where it ſhould be ſold, or the ſale repealed, guarding it with neceſſary precautions, whether the towns be under compoſition or adminiſtration. This is to be underſtood of the provinces where thoſe duties are eſtabliſhed.

In chapter 23, giving examples from the French, I ſet forth ſome of the immunities which his Moſt Chriſtian Majeſty, in the year 1713, granted to bacalao, and oils proceeding from the fiſhery of his ſubjects; and alſo obſerve, that they were allowed to export ſtores, arms, ammunition, utenſils, and proviſions for the ſhips, or veſſels, intended for the ſaid fiſhery, and even the ſalt that ſhould be wanted to cure the fiſh. To this I may add, that in ſeveral articles under tit. 15, of the ordinance of 1680, in reſpect to the ſettling of the gabel, or revenue of ſalt in that kingdom, are alſo found many indulgences, and other encouragements granted for curing of bacalo, ſalmon, herrings, pilchards, and other ſorts of fiſh; in particular the abatement of the price of it, and alſo the rules and precautions neceſſary to prevent frauds, ſet forth at large.

The 24th chapter contains a prohibition, that was made in France, againſt the importation of pilchards from foreign countries, in order to favour their own fiſhery, and the trade

trade of his majeſty's ſubjects in this commodity.

IN chapter 28, where I produce ſome examples taken from the Engliſh, it is obſerved, that the duty upon ſalt uſed in curing white herrings was taken off in that kingdom in the year 1722, as alſo what was charged upon the exportation of the ſame herrings.

IN chapter 36, which treats of the meaſures employed by the Dutch, mention is alſo made of ſome indulgences, and other encouragements, in favour of their fiſheries.

UPON the foundation of theſe examples, taken from three nations that beſt underſtand commerce, and moſt proſper in it, and what one's own reaſon ſuggeſts as proper to be done, I am of opinion we ſhould give leave to all his majeſty's ſubjects that go to the fiſhery in their own veſſels, whether on the coaſts of Spain, or in the Mediterranean, to carry out, free of all duty, at leaſt biſcuit, all ſorts of pulſe, dried or green, and ſalt-fiſh caught in the Spaniſh fiſheries, and even a certain quantity of oil, vinegar, and brandy, in proportion to the number of hands and days, a few over and under, that they ſhall be employed in the fiſhery, being fully convinced that the ſubjects of other powers, upon no pretence whatever, can fairly claim an equal privilege in this caſe with his majeſty's people. For all conventions, or treaties of commerce, even though they ſhould be ſtrictly obſerved, were made for very different purpoſes.

purpoſes. Nor ſhall I ſtay to explain this matter, as the motives, caſes, and other circumſtances that diſtinguiſh the two things, are invariable and manifeſt. But it is further obſervable, that, for theſe indulgences to the fiſhery, and his majeſty's ſubjects, there will be no reaſon to make an allowance to the farmers of the revenue, both on account of their trifling value, and becauſe they muſt experience, from the great improvement made by this means in the fiſhery, and trade of the towns, where the revenues are farmed, a conſiderable encreaſe of them other ways, as has been already ſhewn in the caſe of manufacturies. And, to take away from the farmers all pretence for it, there ſhould be an excluſive article to this effect in their contracts for the kingdoms of Mercia, Granada, Seville, Gallicia, the Aſturias, and the four towns; for in the provinces upon the coaſt, the provincial revenues are never farmed, nor the cuſtoms any where elſe.

The navigation and commerce (ſays the ſame eminent Spaniſh writer) of theſe provinces [meaning Biſcay and Guipuſcoa] by ſea, have been much impaired by loſing ſeveral ſhips in the expeditions of the late war: for they have not yet been able to replace them, and build others, as they have had very bad harveſts, and are not yet paid the whole of what was due to them for freights and other things: ſo that it will be very reaſonable and expedient to order the balance

of

of their accounts to be paid immediately, that they may be enabled to build and fit out other veſſels, and thus revive and improve their fiſhery and commerce by ſea.

As it is alſo certain that money is now very ſcarce in Guipuſcoa, where the principal diſburſements were uſually made for building ſhips, and other neceſſary and chargeable preparations for a fiſhery that is any ways conſiderable, I ſhould apprehend it a very good piece of policy to make them a tender, out of the king's revenue, of 25 or 30,000 doublons, without intereſt, for their firſt expences, which uſually run high, upon condition of their repaying it in ſix years. My intention is, that in the two firſt years they be not obliged to return any part of it; but, in the four following, to do it in equal payments, till the whole be diſcharged; and, for a ſecurity that the loan be repaid in the form and manner that ſhall be ſtipulated, let the province of Guipuſcoa ſtand engaged for it, beſides the joint bonds given by the private perſons who are to receive the money. That the diſtribution of the money, the execution of the bonds, the ſecurities, and other points, may be well conducted, and with all the precaution that is requiſite on ſuch an occaſion, let there be choſen out of that province, or ſent from the court, a miniſter of known abilities and public ſpirit, charged with this commiſſion; and, to diſpoſe their minds to it, encourage aſſociations, and every thing that

that ſhould tend to enlarge the fiſhery of bacalao, on the banks of Newfoundland, as alſo the fiſheries for whales, herrings, &c. in thoſe parts where found to be in plenty.

SHOULD the Engliſh, in oppoſition to all the reaſons above-mentioned, ſtill perſiſt in diſturbing his majeſty's ſubjects in this fiſhery, and it be not proper to employ force in order to take ſatisfaction, and maintain their juſt rights, till we have firſt tried all the gentler methods which prudence dictates; in my opinion, they ſhould alſo be given to underſtand, that his majeſty, among other expedients, may avail himſelf of the ſovereign right he poſſeſſes to prohibit the conſumption of bacalao in all his dominions. This too is a meaſure very practicable, and may be done without any great inconvenience to the common people, whenever the fiſhery of his majeſty's ſubjects, both on *our own coaſts*, and in *other ſeas*, ſhall be encouraged and enlarged in the way I propoſe, and alſo ſupported by the proviſions I before recommended on the ſubject of guarda coſtas. For as the fiſhery of bacalao was not begun, or even diſcovered, in Newfoundland, but ſince the year 1500, and Spain, though much more populous, was able to ſupport herſelf for above a thouſand years without this commodity, and all the time obſerve the vigils and days of abſtinence in the Catholic religion; it ſhould, methinks, be no extraordinary or difficult thing to maintain ourſelves without it, and ſo well as to find

find no want of it. But I ſhould not adviſe this ſtep till the other, which I have pointed out as a means likely enough to relieve, in a great meaſure, the misfortune we ſuſtain from the large conſumption of ſalt-fiſh from abroad, prove to be inſufficient for the purpoſe.

IN chapter 29, which treats of the conduct and practice of the Engliſh, and the vaſt ſums of money they drain from us by the ſale of bacalao *, and other ſalt-fiſh, I introduced a few remarks and obſervations upon this calamity, and the means which might be employed to prevent it in a great meaſure, and which I was led into by the reflections of an Engliſh writer, well affected to the crowns of Spain and France, in his treatiſe, under the title of *The intereſt of England ill underſtood in the war of queen Anne.* And as we ſhould never loſe ſight of the principal of thoſe obſervations and reflections, which are the foundation of the particular proviſions in ſupport of the fiſheries, I have thought proper to repeat ſome part of them in this place.

THIS miniſter invites the biſhops to allow, throughout the year, the uſe of certain kinds of food prohibited upon particular days, and means,

* If the Spaniards ſhould attempt to lay any prohibition, or higher duties on our fiſh, than what are now laid by ſubſiſting treaties, they may ſoon be convinced that the crown of Great Britain has it in her power to retaliate upon them, by proper meaſures to be taken in regard to the regulation of our own commerce.

no

no doubt, eggs, cheeſe, milk, and butter, which ſome religious foundations are reſtrained from many days in the year. In all probability he would alſo inſinuate, that the prohibition of fleſh might be moderated, as it is in the provinces of the crown of Caſtile, in reſpect to Saturdays, and may be extended to the town of Arragon. In all theſe meaſures he apprehends the pope will readily concur, for the reaſons he there gives, and others hinted at; and, without daring to ſpeak out, was, in my opinion, willing to tell us, that if by ſuch means we would reduce the conſumption of bacalao, and other cured fiſh, which they bring us from the north and Newfoundland, we might take away this great advantage from the Engliſh, and other powers, who, by the ſale of them, drain us of millions of crowns, increaſe their own ſtrength, and ruin us. Theſe great diſadvantages ſo very much intereſt our conſcience, as well as all good policy, that they deſerve the particular attention of all Catholic princes, and eſpecially the pope. From the pious zeal of this holy father we have reaſon to flatter ourſelves, that as ſoon as he ſhall be informed of theſe inconveniencies, he will allow, and even encourage, the meaſures that tend towards a remedy, even though it be neceſſary to ſubſtitute, in the place of numerous faſt-days, another *ſpecies of abſtinence and reſtraint, that equally adminiſters to the mortification of our ſouls, and does not turn out ſo much to the advantage of the rivals of the*

crowns

crowns and the Catholic church, as those frequent fast-days do, by opening a way for the importation aud consumption of their salt-fish, which is a main branch of their commerce, and a great foundation of their riches and strength.

THOUGH I have some reluctance at the thought of giving my sentiments as to the generality of these points, that are of so delicate a nature, methinks I may, without any scruple, decide in one particular. It is to sollicit the permission of his holiness to allow of flesh in the kingdoms of the crown of Arragon, and in Navarre, upon those Saturdays that happen not to be particular vigils, under the restraints, and as it is practised, in the provinces of Castile. This I propose, both on the strength of the solid and well-known motives already given, and because it would be no more than what has been established for many ages, and is now practised in most parts of the kingdom of Spain, &c.

As to the measures insinuated in the reflections of this writer, which regard the taking off in part the prohibition of flesh on some other days in the year, and permitting religious houses certain sorts of food, which they are restrained from, besides flesh, during the whole, or most part of the year, I judge it a point of greater moment, and to require more deliberation. The utmost I shall have courage to offer is, that there be laid before his holiness the reasons already given, and others that will occur, in particular the increase

creaſe of ſtrength, and other advantages, which ſeveral nations, by means of the great conſumption of ſalt-fiſh in Spain, acquire and employ againſt the Catholic church itſelf; that, in his wiſdom, he may vouchſafe to determine upon, and eſtabliſh thoſe proviſions, which he ſhall judge moſt effectual, and proper for a remedy; ſo far at leaſt as to take off part of the inconveniencies that have been deſcribed. For never ſhall we be able to find a more ſure way to ſucceed in redreſſing either the grievance itſelf, or its accidental circumſtances, than by referring it entirely to the great piety, holy zeal, and infallibility of his holineſs." Vide *The theory and practice of commerce and maritime affairs*, written in Spaniſh, by the late Don Geronymo de Uztariz, member of his Catholic Majeſty's privy council, of the royal board of trade and the mint, and his majeſty's ſecretary in the council and chamber of the Indies.

THUS have we given an idea of the nature and importance of the fiſheries to Holland and France, as alſo of the meaſures that are likely to be taken in Spain in relation to to the ſame branch of commerce. What ſeems to confirm this to be the real intention of the court of Spain, is their apparent endeavours to increaſe their royal navy, by enticing away numbers of our ſhip-builders for that purpoſe: and, if they are determined to increaſe the number of their men of war, and likewiſe to eſtabliſh fiſheries in

order

order effectually to man them, is it not time that we ſhould be upon our guard, as well with reſpect to Spain as France? There are, it ſeems, alſo other powers that are attempting fiſheries, and aiming at the acquiſition of ſome ſhare in maritime commerce.

THESE are facts, not groundleſs conjectures. In regard to the pretended claim of the Spaniards to fiſh upon our coaſts of Newfoundland, it may not be uſeleſs to obſerve, that there was no more care taken of that fiſhery in the Utrecht treaty than before; for they went ſo far, that they ſent one Gillingham, at this time an Iriſh papiſt, to our court, to get the liberty of fiſhing at Newfoundland. That this Gillingham was far from being ſnubbed by the then miniſtry, for coming about ſuch an impudent buſineſs, is well enough known. Nay, the lord Lexington, who had not refuſed the embaſſy to Spain, when that monarchy and the Weſt-Indies were about to be raviſhed from the houſe of Auſtria, and given to the duke of Anjou, thought this Iriſh papiſt was ſo welcome to the miniſtry, that, in his letter to the lord Dartmouth, then one of the ſecretaries of ſtate, he frequently excuſes himſelf for not writing upon that ſubject, becauſe they had full accounts of the matter from Gillingham. Nay, the queen's plenipotentiaries, the earl of Strafford and Dr. Robinſon biſhop of Briſtol, went ſo far, as to ſuffer a clauſe to be inſerted at the end of the

15th

15th article of the peace with Spain; whereby, to uſe the words of the ſecret committee, they gave a pretence to the Spaniards to claim a right to fiſh at NEWFOUNDLAND, contrary to the 7th and 8th articles of the treaty made with that crown by Sir William Godolphin.

THE board of trade being conſulted upon this occaſion, made the following anſwer to the lord Dartmouth, dated January 13, 1712-13:—"We have conſidered the extract of a memorial from the marquis de Monteleone, relating to a claim of the inhabitants of Guipuſcoa to fiſh on the coaſt of Newfoundland, and thereupon take leave to inform your lordſhip, that we have diſcourſed with ſuch perſons as are able to give us information in that matter, and we find that ſome Spaniards are come hither with paſſes from her majeſty, and others may have fiſhed there privately; but never any, that we can learn, did do it as of right belonging to them."

WE ſee by this, that, even before the concluſion of that French peace, the queen's paſſes had been given to the Spaniards, to take the benefit of the moſt profitable branch of the Engliſh commerce; but the Spaniards have not carried their point in it; and, by the 4th article of the treaty which Mr. Dodington made in December 1713, ſome of the ground loſt to them by the Utrecht peace was recovered, and all innovations made

in

in trade were to be aboliſhed; the moſt ſcandalous of which was their fiſhing at Newfoundland.

THE policy of other neighbouring nations who have long eſtabliſhed fiſheries, and others who are daily attempting the ſame, at the expence of Great Britain, ſhould effectually rouze and alarm us, not only to preſerve that ſhare in the fiſheries we already have, but to excite and animate us to make the utmoſt advancement in this invaluable branch of traffic that we are capable of; more eſpecially ſo, ſince we have it in our power, by a natural right, to fiſh upon our own coaſts, and perhaps have an equal right to hinder and prevent all other nations from doing ſo.

I SHALL not here, however, enter into the ſole right of Great Britain to the ſovereignty of the Britiſh ſeas, though a great fund of argument might be urged on that head. What I ſhall obſerve at preſent is, that, although it may not be adviſable, at this conjuncture, to attempt to put an abſolute ſtop to all other nations from fiſhing upon our own coaſts; yet it is to be hoped, that this indulgence to others is not to prevent ourſelves from making the beſt advantages that God and nature has given us, by ſtoring our coaſts with ſuch immenſe plenty of fiſh.

NOR can we ſee reaſon for indulging any other power to make free with our coaſt-fiſhing except our ancient and natural allies the Dutch; but, if they will not act vigorouſly

ously in concert with us against the common enemy; if they will allow themselves to be so far influenced by France as to suffer their own state as well as ours to be ruined and undone; if our old friends and allies will turn our enemies, and suffer the whole protestant cause to sink together with themselves, and England; how can the Dutch reasonably expect, that we can cordially grant them any indulgence in trade that is in our power to deprive them of? On the contrary, if the Dutch will at present remain refractory, and deaf to all the remonstrances of the court of London, touching the preservation of the whole protestant interest; will it not, at the proper time, become the wisdom of the court of England to change her system with regard to the Dutch, and grant them no favour whatsoever that is in her power to deprive them of? And how England may be enabled to do this, and that with advantage rather than any injury to herself might be here shown, if it was prudent: but that I leave others to think of, whose duty it more particularly is.

For my own part, I have for many years past endeavoured to show, the necessity, the indispensable necessity of a stricter union between Great Britain and Holland than ever yet was; and I am willing to believe, that when I have the honour to submit my private memorials to the consideration of such who will make the right use of them; the ways and means will

will appear no leſs practicable then rational, and perfectly compatible with the intereſt of the two ſtates, and preſervative of the proteſtant cauſe in general.

So greatly have the principles which I have endeavoured to propagate upon this point affected the court of France, that they have employed, it ſeems, one or more of their ableſt writers * to blunt the edge of all that I have urged, in regard to a topic of ſuch weight and importance.

We have now taken a view of the meaſures, which the court of Spain is about to purſue, with reſpect to the advancement of fiſheries; and we have alſo ſeen how the French have actually encreaſed theirs, and in conſequence thereof their whole maritime power. Let theſe facts be weighed, with their united effects, and no friend to the liberties of Chriſtendom, will ſay, that it can be for the intereſt of Great Britain and Holland to be divided, or become lukewarm to each others intereſts, either about the fiſheries, or any other point of commerce. But, it is well known, where machinations have been eternally hatching to diſtract both England and Holland at home, and divide them from each other, in regard to their intereſt abroad, by groundleſs jealouſies. Is it, however,

* L'obſervateur Hollandois—Said to be wrote by the abbée de la Ville, late miniſter from the court of France to the States General of the United Provinces.

ever, leſs impolitic in Holland to liſten to ſuch deſtructive ſuggeſtions with relation to our fiſheries, than it would be in England, till ſufficiently provoked to deprive the Dutch of the privilege of fiſhing on our coaſts?

If the Dutch are ſo unhappily circumſtanced as to be divided and unſteady in their councils, dwindling in their marine, and in danger of loſing for ever their barrier: if Holland ſhall loſe all her weight and influence in Europe, as a proteſtant potentate, it is neceſſary, it is wiſe and politic in Great Britain to encreaſe in her power, her weight and influence, as Holland ſhall decline: it will be no leſs for the intereſt of Holland than Great Britain that the latter ſhould encreaſe in her fiſheries, and every branch of commerce, if ſhe alone is to ſupport the proteſtant cauſe, and Holland among the reſt. While Holland ſhall depend upon England for her ſecurity, ſhe can have no cauſe to complain, if England was to deprive her of ſuch branches of her trade, as ſhe has no right to: but this is not her caſe, with regard to her own coaſt fiſheries: and, if ſhe indulges Holland therein upon the ſame conditions as ſhe does her own ſubjects, as being a natural and ancient ally, and always expecting her friendſhip; Holland can have no ſufficient grounds for reſentment againſt England on this occaſion; and, therefore, ought ſhe not to deſpiſe all inſinuations on the part of the common enemy to divide us on this account?

If

If these intrigues to divide us are not seen through in Holland, it becomes the more necessary, that this kingdom, for her own safety as well as that of the Dutch, should see for them, and improve their own coast, and other fisheries to the utmost. And, if Holland is displeased at this, do they not act upon the same principles that the enemies to us both do? For, they know the consequence of improving our fisheries, is improving the British maritime power; and, if the Dutch suffer their royal marine to dwindle, England should be on her guard to advance hers at least in the like degree; and, especially so, since that of the common enemy is daily encreasing. While this is the case, the common enemy well know that they will with difficulty enslave the republic, while Britain shall maintain and duly exercise a superiority of naval dominion.

If the Dutch will neglect their safety, is there not a greater necessity for us to take care of our own? And gain in trade and power what the Dutch shall lose? And have we not the most natural right to it, who are obliged, though for our own safety, to protect them, while we are able? Had Britain neglected her marine as the Dutch have done; had she been regardless and inactive with respect to France as the Dutch have been, must it not have proved fatal to them both before this time? As it seems inexcusable in the states of Holland to suffer that, so it would be be inexcusable, from that motive only, in Britain to neglect the most extensive improvement of her fisheries, that thereby she might be capable of advancing her marine, as the Dutch shall disregard theirs: and in this light, let every patriot Dutchman look upon our endeavours to improve this amongst other branches of our commerce: but whoever looks upon this in a light to divide us and the DUTCH, can be no friend to either, nor to the liberties of Christendom.

WHEN the Dutch were at war with England, and they wanted to mann twenty or thirty sail of men of war, it was only having recourse to their fisheries, and in a few days, they were in a condition to give us battle, the seamen being only transferred from a smaller to a larger vessel on the same element. It is to be hoped, therefore, that since Great Britain has undertaken the protection of the British herring-fishery, she will never suffer it to drop, although the Dutch should resent it; which, from what has been said, it does not appear to be their interest, notwithstanding their apprehensions to the contrary.

AND here it may not be improper to observe, that there are, in the humble judgment of the writer of these papers, ways and means to remove all umbrage from the Dutch on this, and some other occasions, that has prevented their acting in concert with us: but these I durst not publicly declare, lest the

the common enemy ſhould take advantage of it.

THE benefits ariſing from our herring-fiſheries are extraordinary, if we conſider the number of people therein employed; as ſeamen, fiſhermen, ſhip and houſe-carpenters, ſmiths, ſawyers, coopers, caulkers, butchers, bakers, brewers, carmen, boatmen, ſail-makers, net-makers, block-makers, trinel-makers, rope-makers, pump makers, compaſs-makers, baſket-makers, hook-makers, packers, dreſſers, ſorters, labourers, tanners, and ſpinners of net-work, and ſails.—Several of which trades are effected by children, the lame, the blind, and the aged.

" WITHOUT primary encouragements, (ſays a judicious writer in the year 1680, who intitled his work Britannia Languens, &c.), and ſuperintendance of the government, it will be hard to nouriſh up any new branch of trade, &c.

Amongſt the exportations, the fiſhing-trade ought not to be forgotten, ſince according to modern calculations *, the mere fiſhing-trade for HERRINGS AND COD, on the coaſt of England, and Scotland, employs above 8000 Dutch ſhips, or veſſels, 200,000 of their ſeamen, and fiſhers; and the her-

* See Mr. Smith of improvements, &c. page 268-9-70, who computes the whole profits of this fiſhery to be, in his time, ten millions ſterling per annum, and in a manner all gained by other nations.

rings and cod ſold by the Dutch in foreign countries, do bring an annual profit of 5,000,000 l. ſterling to that nation: beſides which, it is accounted that there are at leaſt, 25,000 people more employed and maintained at home about this particular navigation, as in making of fiſhing-nets, and the curing, ordering, and preparing of the fiſh, &c. beſides the Iceland, Newfoundland, and Greenland-fiſhings, of very great advantage."

Are not theſe conſiderations motive ſufficient to animate us never to ſuffer this fiſhery to ſink? While our common enemies are raiſing their maritime power by means of their fiſheries, ſhall not we uphold ours to the utmoſt? Will not this greatly contribute to enable us to maintain the balance of maritime dominion, on which our ſecurity chiefly depends?

DISSERTATION XXVII.

Of the European commerce of France.

HAVING taken a view of the commerce of France in America, Aſia, and Africa, and of the wiſdom and policy of that nation in carrying on the ſame; and having ſhewn likewiſe, by way of compariſon, wherein the meaſures taken for their proſperity therein, ſeem to be in many reſpects preferable to ours; it may prove no leſs uſeful to take a ſuccinct ſurvey of the commerce of this kingdom, as it ſtands connected with the chief ſtates of Europe: my intention being to ſhew what an extenſive foundation they have laid for commercial dominion; and, in conſequence thereof to convince us, that we can never expect to withſtand the power of France, unleſs we put bounds to her trade and navigation. And, however well many may apprehend they are thoroughly acquainted with the commerce of France and England, from a general idea only thereof; yet to make a preciſe judgment, they will

will find it neceſſary to enter into the details, and to penetrate into that police that has raiſed each to the pitch we find it. For, by ſo doing, we ſhall eaſily diſcern their miſtakes or our own, and be the better able to rectify them in our own ſyſtem.

THE French European trade being cloſely connected with thoſe of Africa, America, and India, it was previouſly requiſite to conſider theſe latter, as being a great foundation of the former. We ſhall now enter upon their commerce in Europe, and begin firſt with that between Great Britain and France. And, if we take a retroſpect hereof from the peace of Utrecht, we ſhall find that we have been great ſufferers hereby.

FROM this period, France has taken from England coals, and allum, copperas, and vitriol, tobacco, ſome lead, and tin, flannels, and corn in time of ſcarcity; but all theſe articles have of late years greatly decreaſed. Yet we have imported from France, ſince the ſame time, wines, brandies, linen, fine laces, fine canbricks, cambrick-lawn, to a prodigious value, brocades, velvets, and many other rich ſilk manufactures, which have either been run in upon England, or come by the way of Holland.

WE have before repreſented the deteſtable ſcene of ſmuggling French commodities that has long been, and ſtill continues barefacedly to be carried on at the iſland of Man; from whence it has ſpread itſelf all over the North of of England, and to Scotland, and Ireland. And is it not notorious enough that the ſmuggling of wool from Ireland is not the leaſt branch of the French trade that has been carried on with Ireland? Nor has the trade carried on between our continent colonies and the French ſugar-iſlands proved of little diſadvantage to us in the general balance of our trade with France. Such, in a word, has been our taſte for French products, French manufactures, and French faſhions, that we have been frenchified out of more, at an average, than half a million per Annum, in our balance of trade with France, ſince the Utrecht peace; which amounts to above 20 millions ſterling, gained from Great Britain and Ireland by France. Nor do we hear of any ſmuggling of Britiſh commodities and manufactures into France, to compenſate for theſe outgoings to that kingdom.

So bewitching is our French taſte, that the Britiſh, and Iriſh money, ſpent in travel there can hardly be ſo little one year with another as 200,000 l. ſterling per annum, balance againſt us in this article; the French ſpending little here, in compariſon to what our gentry do in France.

The commerce of France with Holland is prodigiouſly to the advantage of the former, the Dutch paying to France in the balance very conſiderable ſums; the reaſon whereof is, that the Dutch take off immenſe quantities of wine and brandy from the French,

French, as also of silk manufactures, wrought glass, and very great variety of other commodities of that nation; which they carry for sale to most parts of the trading world, either for Dutch account wholly, or for Dutch and French account in company, according to the merchants usage, the Dutch sailing cheaper than the French. They have done great business for French account wholly: on the other hand the Dutch carry little of their own to France, except fish, train-oil, whale fins, pantiles, and spices; all which excepting the latter, are greatly diminished, since the peace of Utrecht.

THE Dutch likewise trade in large quantities of French manufactures to Spanish America from Curaçoa, Surinam, Barbice, &c. And the great inducement to give their manufactures the preference proceeds from the two following causes. (1) The greater cheapness of French commodities in general than English. And (2) their greater variety of fashions that take of late years more with the Spaniards than ours do; wherein the French are always beforehand with us. The Hollanders too take no inconsiderable quantity of French manufactures for their East-India trade.

THE trade of France with old Spain we have all reason to fear has been greatly encreased of late years, to the disadvantage of that of England. Has England at present near the number of British merchant's houses of trade

at

at Cadiz, or any other of the chief trading ports of Spain, that ſhe had thirty years ago? If I have been rightly informed, the French have conſiderably more than we, though we uſed to have above ten to their one. And we well know that French factories will not vend Britiſh commodities, while they can be well ſupplied from their own country.

LET the value of the foreign merchandizes not only conſumed in old Spain, but ſent from thence in Spaniſh bottoms to new Spain, be eſtimated, and we ſhall know whether the trade of France has not been more favoured by the Spaniſh nation than that of England; we ſhall then know who are moſt intereſted in the galleons and flota, the French or the Engliſh. Though England may have a right by treaty to be no leſs favoured by Spain in trade than France; yet, by certain ſecret encouragements given to the trade of the one, in oppoſition to that of the other, treaties of commerce may be evaded, and rendered uſeleſs. If the commerce from France to Spain has encreaſed to the advantage of the former, and that of England has declined, it muſt be owing either to certain mercantile machinations, under ſecret influence, or to the greater cheapneſs and delicacy of the commodities of the one, which gives them the preference to the other. If the latter is the caſe, we know the remedy; if the former, we muſt uſe the ſame arts that our rivals do to uphold our trading influence.

WITH

WITH regard to the commerce of the Spaniſh Indies, it is well enough known what a ſcene of trade the French have carried on there from their Miſſiſſippi ſettlements over the gulph of Mexico, though the Spaniards have been very complaiſantly ſilent upon that occaſion. Nor is it leſs certain that the French have long exerciſed a beneficial trade from St. Domingo to the Spaniſh main; and yet we have heard of no umbrage taken at thoſe practices. We do not hear but the Spaniards have a plentiful ſupply of negroes for the working of their mines in America; and from whence do the bulk of them go, but from St. Domingo? And, under the cover of this negoce, we can hardly ſuppoſe but other is carried on. Thus may the French enjoy all the advantages of an Aſſiento, without any treaty for the purpoſe, though we had little benefit with one. So it is, that we never hear of any complaint by the Spaniards of illicit trade on the ſide of France, though great clamours are made againſt the Engliſh about a little logwood, which they have a right to cut too.

THUS, though England may flatter herſelf that ſhe is as equally favoured in her commerce by Spain as any other nation; yet, by management, treaties may be evaded; and, inſtead of being upon a level in trade with nations the moſt highly favoured, we may be the moſt disfavoured: and I wiſh this may not be our caſe. To ſave appear-

ances,

ances, treaties may ſubſiſt: but we have ſeen how they may be rendered a dead letter. Spain is certainly a great gainer by the commerce of Great Britain; her loſs by the French trade is very conſiderable. The French are no leſs rivals to Spain than to England. And is not Spain at preſent bent upon the eſtabliſhment of manufactures of her own? If they ſhall ſoon be able to ſupply themſelves with one part of their manufactures, and the French ſhall be artfully ſuffered to ſupply them with the other part of their wants, what will our treaties with Spain avail us? Is not Spain likewiſe ſtriking into an active commerce? Nothing, therefore, can ſave our trade from ruin, as well with Spain as other ſtates, but the ability to ſell as good a commodity for as little money as our rivals do.

We are dazled with the ſplendid appearance of Portugal gold, as well as Spaniſh pieces of eight, and are apt to think that we are mighty gainers hereby. Our trade with Portugal has heretofore been very lucrative; but this, like that of Spain, is greatly upon the decline; the French having wormed us out, and themſelves into a conſiderable part of this trade which we enjoyed. The French now ſend to Portugal fine woollen cloths, various kinds of ſtuffs, particularly a ſort of black goods called DRUGGETS, of which they ſell immenſe quantities for the habits of the clergy (having thereby deſtroyed the Engliſh

crapes,

crapes, once a very important article of our trade) wrought ſilk, a great quantity of linens and cambricks, dreſſed CALVE-SKINS (another loſt article of the Engliſh commerce) alſo HATS, SILK STOCKINGS (both which articles they are getting from us every day) all ſorts of toys, furniture, ribbands, and moſt of the ornamental parts of the female dreſs; grain of all kinds, when the French have it to ſpare, and ſometimes in immenſe quantities; claret, champagne, and brandy, though prohibited, are ſmuggled into Portugal in great quantities; as are flowered and figured ſilks, gold and ſilver lace, India goods, and other contraband commodities: they likewiſe import from France printed books, ſome ordinary ſorts of cutlery ware, and abundance of ſmaller articles, too tedious to enumerate. By the help of wool ſmuggled from England and Ireland, the French have made attempts to rival us in Portugal in our very great article of the trade in LONG BAYS; but hitherto without ſucceſs: but it is to be feared that their vigilance and policy, aided by our inattention, may bring this deſign to bear; and thus we ſhall imperceptibly loſe the Portugal trade too.

THE Italians import into Portugal immenſe quantities of wheat, a great deal of barley, and alſo a good deal of Levant rice, vermecelli, and oil. They likewiſe import prodigious quantities of writing-paper, abundance

dance of wrought ſilks and velvets, coral, and many expenſive curioſities, toys, and other inferior articles, not to particularize religious traffic, which is very great and public.

THE Italians alſo export from Portugal, hides, a conſiderable quantity of ſugars and tobacco's, cocoa-nuts, pepper, ordinary ſpices, elephants-teeth, braſil-wood, ſome drugs, and an immenſe quantity of bullion. Inſomuch that of late years, while gold has bore a high price in England, it has been a drug all over Italy: a circumſtance that has been well worthy of Britiſh attention. And our balance of ſome trades in Italy being thus paid us in Portugal gold, we have flattered ourſelves that all the gold of that country has been owing to our direct commerce with Portugal, when the fact has been otherwiſe; and if our Italian trade declines from the loſs of Minorca, or from any other cauſe, we ſhall ſoon experience a ſcarcity of Portugal gold.

How well the port of Marſeilles is ſituated for the whole Italian, the Turkey and Levant trade, and what a conſiderable ſhare they have obtained therein, is well enough known in the general.

FRANCE was the firſt nation that made treaties of commerce with the Porte: they were the firſt likewiſe that eſtabliſhed a court of juſtice, under the title of that of conſulſhip, to maintain a good harmony between their own ſubjects and the Turks, and obtained

tained the whole trade, as it were, to themſelves for many years, and other nations traded under their banner.

SUCH an aſcendancy have theſe rivals got in the Turkey trade, that they have reduced our ſales of above 30,000 woollen cloths a year to about 7000; whilſt the French cloths have encreaſed from a ſale of 2000 a year to above 50,000: and the advance the French has made in the Italian trade in general, is too well experienced by our merchants who are concerned therein. That the meaſures we have taken to reſtore this trade will effect the end aimed at, a little time will ſhew. The meaſures we depend upon for ſucceſs herein, are laying the trade open, thinking that a competition amongſt our traders is the ſovereign remedy to make our commodities cheaper, and to ſupplant our foreign rivals; but I am afraid that our advancement in the Turkey trade will rather depend upon abilities to ſell our commodities in general as cheap as France can afford to do, and not upon our traders underſelling each other: the only maxim, it ſeems, we depend upon for outdoing our rivals; a maxim that will prove no leſs ruinous to the trade, I fear, than a monopoly.

So greatly have the French encreaſed their trade ſince the peace of Utrecht, that they now carry their wines and their brandies in their own ſhipping into the Baltic, where, before the Dutch ſent them in Hollands bottoms;

toms; and they bring their naval ſtores from Peterſburg and Livonia in their own veſſels, where before that treaty, no French ſhip had ſcarce ever been ſeen. Nor have the Hanſe-towns any ſhare like what they had in furniſhing France with iron and copper, or timber, pitch and tar, as they heretofore had.

THEY alſo carry on a beneficial trade with Dantzic, and have greatly increaſed their commerce in Muſcovy, as well as Denmark. Their trade is likewiſe greatly extended through many parts of Germany within theſe twenty years.

WE have now before us a general view of the trade of France, as connected with the chief ſtates of Europe; and it would be no great difficulty to ſhew that the particular balance is conſiderably in favour of France with moſt, if not all of them; and the general being great, it is no wonder that they figure it as they do, and find themſelves as capable as diſpoſed to yoke Europe.

IF the efforts of this nation to encreaſe their commerce and navigation, were deſigned to promote the happineſs inſtead of the miſery of other ſtates, I could rejoice at their ſucceſs, and would endeavour to promote rather than obſtruct it. But the caſe is otherwiſe, they make the benefits of their trade and navigation a ſtalking horſe to enſlave mankind. It is certainly, a virtue in a ſtate to promote induſtry, encourage arts, multiply traders, and extend commerce, provided

vided it be done to make the people happy. But if we examine the politics of the French, we ſhall find theſe beneficent motives, the leaſt of their regards. No, the vain-glory of their monarch, acquired by cutting throats, and raviſhing the territories of their neighbours from them, whilſt even their own lie uncultivated, and neglected, are the motives which induce them to favour arts, and promote commerce: commerce is to ſupport conqueſt, and conqueſt is to extend commerce, but pride and vain-glory are the *primum mobile*, not the happineſs of ſociety, and the good of mankind; though the French moſt blaſphemouſly rob and plunder their neighbours under thoſe pretences.—Commerce brings them in the treaſures of all the Indies; and theſe are employed in raiſing armies, and in making the world their own: and I am apt to think there is but one way to prevent it; and this very way will make France infinitely more happy and more opulent than it is; for I would conquer the enemy by theſe arts rather than by deſtructive meaſures; providence having afforded treaſures to mankind infinitely beyond their wants: and, if it pleaſe God to prolong my life for the purpoſe, I ſhall have little difficulty to convince them of the truth of the aſſertion.

However ſevere many may think my writings ſometimes appear againſt the French; yet the wiſe will not conſtrue them as a conceived antipathy againſt that nation: on the

con-

contrary, I profeſs myſelf a great admirer of the wiſdom and policy of that nation. If they were no leſs faithful in their treaties, than they are artful in violating them, their ſtateſmen would not be leſs admired for their honour than their nation is for it's profound ſagacity and politeneſs. But it is time to tie the hands of their perfidious miniſters, in order to ſpread general felicity over the whole French nation: and this may be eaſier done, than is imagined.

DIS-

DISSERTATION XXVIII.

Of navigation, and fisheries, as they contribute to give the balance of commerce and power.

HITHERTO we have seen how agriculture maintains and employs men; and how the ingenious arts multiply their conveniencies, by forming and working up the productions of nature, and introducing into a body politic, a double encrease of the means of occupying it's members: so that those two branches are mutually dependant on each other, and their connections cannot be broke through without hurting the perfection of both; nor consequently without depriving society of a great part of their utility. That perfection cannot exist without the help of the greatest foreign consumption possible. A communication between the several parts of earth surrounded or divided by seas, supposes navigation, or the art of crossing those seas.

WE will consider that art at present, so far only as it establishes a lucrative communication

tion between different people; because the benefits resulting therefrom sufficiently prove the necessity of a national communication not subject to precariousness.

We say a lucrative communication; for a navigation undertaken in order to import foreign commodities only, cannot be justified but by absolute necessity, or so far, as it may be the cause of a greater exportation.

In this sense it is plain, that the object of navigation is to transport the superfluities of a nation to others, and to bring back proper and necessary commodities in exchange.

Before we consider the principles that emane from the object of navigation, it is proper to know the various effects that result from it's operation.

The operation of navigation should be considered in two lights. The art of sailing furnishes employment for a class of men called seamen, or sailors: the building of the ships in which those men cross the seas, is properly a manufactory. As such it is subject to the laws and principles of manufacturies: it has the same effects, for it affords employment to builders, carpenters, caulkers, sail-makers, rope-makers, weavers, smiths, and an infinity of other men; if the earth produces iron, hemp, wood, pitch, and tar, those materials being used in the building of ships, their value is thereby increased: in short, that manufactory is carried to perfection by the

the ſame means that others are, and deſerves the ſame encouragements.

NAVIGATION, conſidered in theſe two joint lights, affords a great multitude of men, the means of conſuming the fruits of the earth, and of procuring the conveniencies invented by uſeful and ingenious arts. The wages of the men, and the price of the materials employed in navigation, either as an art or a manufactory, is neceſſarily paid by the conſumer of the goods exported. For the charges are always a part of the value of a commodity: nay, the charges of freight are more ſure to be paid, than the firſt value of the goods. For example; if a merchant ſends goods to a foreign market, he is ſure that the freight or hire of the ſhip and ſailors who carry them, will be paid in full, though he is not ſure that the goods he ſends will produce, when ſold, ſo much as that freight amounts to: that has been the caſe in ſome ſudden revolutions of trade; and we ſee every day inſtances of goods bearing a lower price abroad than their intrinſic value at home; the freight, however, is paid at all events, without abatement or delay.

THE profits of navigation are, therefore, as clear, as thoſe of agriculture, and manufactories. Conſequently navigation encreaſes the real and relative ſtrength of a body politic.

Every nation that lets another carry on a navigation which ſhe might do herſelf, diminiſhes in proportion her real and relative ſtrength in favour of her rivals.

The intent, or object of navigation affords two principles, from which many conſequences may be drawn.

First, a nation that has no ſuperfluities to export, would have no navigation, unleſs ſhe were to carry for others.

Secondly, ſuperfluities would be of no value to a nation that did not cultivate the art of navigation; or, if ſuperfluities had a value, that value would abſolutely depend on people who are navigators.

From the firſt principle it muſt be inferred, that agriculture and induſtry are the baſis, or motive of a ſolid navigation. Whatever hurts the true principles of the two former, is deſtructive of navigation, and deprives ſociety of it's real and relative effects.

The motives of navigation cannot poſſibly be encreaſed without navigation's being ſo too, if no inward defect prevents it's progreſs.

If the motives of navigation have ſuffered no change, it's decline is a moſt certain ſign, of the diminution of foreign conſumptions of the productions of art, or nature, of the ſubject's being leſs employed, and conſequently leſs able to live comfortably.

If the motives of navigation are changed, that is to ſay, if one commodity ceaſes to be exported at the ſame time that another now commodity is exported; or, if one exchange in return, is ſubſtituted in the room of another; the balance of trade in money may have encreaſed, though at the ſame time, neither more ſhips, nor more ſailors, are employed: and, on the other hand, navigation may be encreaſed, though the balance in money be not; that will depend on the diverſity of bulks and intrinſic value.

CONSEQUENTLY, the number of tons of ſhipping employed by a nation, cannot be a general rule, whereby to judge whether the balance of it's trade was more in it's favour at one time than another. For the ſame reaſon we cannot judge by that compariſon of the real riches of the trade of two nations.

SUPPOSING all things in other reſpects equally advantageous between two nations for ſome navigations; we may determine by the number of ſhips each employs, whether the one makes a better uſe of it's advantages than the other.

FOR, if the one drew from it's colonies, maſts, wood, pitch, tar, rice, and tobacco, and the other neglected thoſe branches of navigation; it is certain, that the former would have a ſuperiority of trade, and of relative ſtrength.

LASTLY, if the combination of the exchanges a nation makes in the whole extent of it's commerce, be very complicated; it may, by the encreaſe of it's luxury, have exported more ſpecie than productions either of it's it's lands, or induſtry. Conſequently, the encreaſe of it's navigation cannot be a real and certain indication of the advantage or diſadvantage of the balance of it's trade, as Sir Joſiah Child, and other writers, have ſaid. That uncertainty would be ſtill greater, and of longer duration, if, by meaſures taken at home to ſupport the public credit, the nation was prevented from perceiving eaſily the diminution of it's maſs of treaſure.

THE ſecond principle is, that a nation's ſuperfluities would have no value without navigation: or, if they had a value, it would depend abſolutely on people who are navigators.

WHENCE it follows, that, if agriculture and manufactures are the baſis and motive of navigation, they are not leſs mutually intereſted in it's preſervation and progreſs.

IF a nation navigates for another, or monopolizes it's commodities, which is the ſame thing, the agriculture and manufactures of the latter will be checked or encouraged, according as it ſuits the intereſts of the former; that is to ſay, the labour of the people, and conſequently, the populouſneſs and reſources of the ſtate that ſells, will be in the power of the ſtate that navigates. By the ſame reaſon, if the dependant nation wants foreign commodities, it will receive only that quantity of them, which it ſuits the other to furniſh, or, at what price that other ſhall think proper to put on them.

The profit of the navigating nation will be the amount of the difference between what the goods coſt, and what they are ſold for; and that profit will be ſo much loſt by the dependant nation.

Under thoſe circumſtances, than which worſe cannot be imagined, the political intereſts of the dependant nation muſt, by it's wants, be ſubordinate to the political intereſts of the navigating nation.

As it is a maxim in practical trade, that they who have the greateſt capitals trade with moſt advantage, and have the preference; ſo it is evident, that the longer a nation has been dependant on another for the exportation of it's ſuperfluities, the more difficult it will be to ſhake off that yoke; unleſs the navigating nation loſes it's advantage by it's own fault.

Though a nation ſhould not be quite deſtitute of navigation, yet, if that nation does not extend it's navigation to the utmoſt of it's power, it will ſtill labour under the difficulties we have been ſpeaking of, in proportion to it's degree of neglect. Whence it may be inferred that the welfare and preſervation of a ſtate require, that ſtrangers be never permitted to rival our own navigation in the exportation of our own productions, or the importation of neceſſary commodities.

Such is the intent of our excellent act of navigation in England, to which we owe all our trade and maritime ſtrength. But all circum-

circumſtances do not admit of an equal application of the ſame maxims. If every nation with which England traded, had made at that time ſuch an act with regard to her, ſhe would have loſt ſeveral profitable branches of her trade; ſuch as that to the Levant and Eaſt-Indies. And ſome branches did ſuffer till ſhe got a ſufficient number of ſhips, though her docks were then very numerous.

ALL nations are now too intent on their commercial intereſts, for any one of them to venture on ſo bold a ſtep: it would no longer be prudent to lay duties on foreign ſhips, nor to raiſe thoſe that are paid on what is exported, or imported, by thoſe ſhips. But another more gentle and more certain method might be taken.

I SAY nothing of the juſt prohibition againſt making uſe of foreign ſhips to carry national commodities from port to port, and along the coaſts of a ſtate, becauſe that is indiſpenſable, and cannot be complained of in any ſhape: beſides, the like treatment in return would not be dangerous, if one were forced to put a ſtop to the progreſs of that toleration. The only effectual way to avoid the ſuperiority of foreign navigators, is to promote the greateſt rivalſhip poſſibly in our own navigation.

THAT rivalſhip regards two ſorts of perſons: navigators, and thoſe who employ them. The rivalſhip of thoſe who employ them, that

that is to ſay, the merchants, depends on ſeveral circumſtances.

The number of good harbours in a country, is one of the greateſt encouragements to navigation: for the eaſier an undertaking is, the more it will be attempted: conſequently, ſuppoſing things equal in other reſpects, that country which has the greateſt number of harbours has it in its power to carry on the greateſt foreign trade.

From this inconteſtable maxim follows the neceſſity of ſupplying as much as poſſible by art, what nature has been deficient in; of keeping up thoſe harbours, and eſpecially of not laying the navigation of any one of them under the leaſt reſtraint or difficulty. That would be depriving ourſelves of our own natural advantages, of the rivalſhip of capitals in trade, of the benefits of fitting out ſhips, of ſeamen; and, in ſhort, it would be ſtripping the poor of one of their kinds of occupation, the moſt abſolutely neceſſary.

This general rule can admit of only one exception: that is, when a ſtate has inſtituted *free ports*, in order not to be deprived of the advantages accruing from the re-exportation of foreign commodities, not permitted to be uſed within that ſtate. If the navigation of thoſe free ports be not laid under ſome reſtrictions, they will not fail to leave their re-exporting trade for other more profitable branches; and all the uſe they will make of their

their privileges will be to ruin other rival ports by the ſale of the commodities of which the have the monopoly. The intent, therefore, of the ſtate will not be anſwered; and the equilibrium ſo neceſſary between the ſubjects occupations, and the ſeveral counties of the ſtate, will be deſtroyed.

ACCORDINGLY, in order not to reſtrain any part of navigation, ſome nations have thought it better to let goods be depoſited in their ports, than to grant thoſe immunities in favour of any in particular. If that manner of depoſiting them facilitates commerce, and renders it more general, it muſt likewiſe be granted that the preſervation of ſome branches of re-exportation becomes more difficult thereby, or that they are leſs eaſily made to agree with the laws of home trade.

REASONS which require the deepeſt combination, ſeem to contend for preference: we will at preſent take notice only of the exception which reſults from the principle in favour, even of its preſervation.

THE rivalſhip of merchants depends particularly upon the perſonal advantages they find in that profeſſion. Few would embrace it in a country where they ſhould not have room to hope to be diſtinguiſhed, in proportion to the ſervices they render; where the retailer and mechanic ſhould be put on a level with him that ſupports them. In ſhort, where that profeſſion could not be ſafely or peaceably exerciſed, either on account of enquiries

quiries into their gains, or the instability of the laws. The profession of a merchant must likewise be in general lucrative, because gain is the motive as well as the reward of his labour. It cannot be lucrative, if the interest of money be much higher than what is paid by merchants in other countries; if the law subjects navigation to expences unknown elsewhere; if inland duties, or duties on exportation, prevent the sale of a commodity at foreign markets; if the formalities to be observed at customhouses are multiplied without cause, or depend on the pleasure of a clerk, whom it is not thought worth while to bribe: in such cases it is necessary to call to mind Cassiodorus's reflection, 7. cap. varia. 9. *Avara manus portus claudit; et cum digitos contrahit, navium simul vela concludit: meritò enim illa mercatores cuncti refugiunt quæ sibi dispendia esse cognoscunt.* "A covetous hand shuts up ports, and furls the sails of the shipping: for merchants always justly shun what they know to be attended with expence."

These general observations naturally lead to this maxim; that navigation, like all other parts of trade, cannot be safely guided without the help of calculation. Every operation that promotes the advantage of other nations in point of rivalship, is destructive of the riches of the subject, and of the state; every operation whereby their advantage is promoted,

moted, is, to the body politic, a ſource of new proſperity. It is in conſequence of this principle that ſkilful nations leſſen, in favour of what is exported by their own ſhips, a duty, generally more hurtful than advantageous to a ſtate; and likewiſe favour them in licit importations in proportion to the want of the things imported. It is, however, ſtill more injudicious to ſuppreſs entirely all duties on the exportation of national productions, and to let the duties already laid on importations ſubſiſt in full; but moſt of all, to grant our own national ſhips a reward or bounty of ſo much per ton, in order to enable them to compete with foreigners in ſuch branches as it is our national intereſt to encourage and ſupport. By that means a nation may form in a ſhort time a great maritime ſtrength, without being expoſed to the reſentment of other ſtates, and without ſuſpending the courſe of its ſales. It is by riſking large ſums that merchants grow rich: ſtates muſt ſubmit to the laws of trade, if they would reap the advantages of it.

A COMPARISON of the methods practiſed by two nations cannot be otherwiſe inſtructive than by comparing their effects; for their principle may be the ſame, tho' their practice be different: the beſt is that which moſt fully anſwers the intent and object of the principle. We muſt, however, agree with that excellent writer, that the cuſtom of claſſing

claſſing ſeamen affords greater reſources for the public ſervice, and that it is moſt reaſonable to acquaint men with the duties of their ſtation. In all caſes, the leſs the duty incumbent on a profeſſion is burdenſome, the more eaſy it will be to eſtabliſh and maintain an idea of equality of treatment among thoſe who follow it, and the more men will be ready to embrace it.

THERE is, among ſuch ſeamen as are claſſed, a rank of men deſtined to govern and command the reſt, diſtinguiſhed by their views, fortune, birth, and education: it is equally juſt and important to make a difference between them and common ſailors, as we cannot, without danger to the public welfare, confound the farmer with the plowman, the manufacturer with the workman, or the merchant, who fits out a ſhip, with the carpenter that builds it. It is not riches that entitles them to ſuch diſtinction, though ſome regard ought to be paid to that; for if the rich man does not enjoy his eaſe in his own country, he will carry his fortune to another, where he can. But it is the degree of general uſefulneſs that the ſtate receives from the talents or qualifications of its ſubjects that ought to make them be conſidered and reſpected in proportion. The experience of all ages, and of all countries, ſhews, that numbers of the beſt hands are not always ſufficient to replace one good head.

If the profeſſion of ſeamen, deſtined to be captains of trading ſhips, was to be depreciated or ſlighted without very ſtrong perſonal reaſons, no man of middling birth would follow it. That would be deſtroying the ſeminary, in which numbers of great and brave men have been formed: by leſſening their ideas of honour, their views and undertakings would be more circumſcribed; there would be fewer privateers in time of war, and the enemies of the ſtate would be leſs moleſted in their trade; in peace, fewer would be ready to undertake thoſe great voyages which require ſtrength of genius and knowledge ſuperior to what is found in him who is generally called a good ſailor; the ſubordination, ſo neceſſary, and ſo uncommon in merchants ſhips, would degenerate into licentiouſneſs, and the common men would always be ready to mutiny againſt their officers; in ſhort, the children of ſeamen being diſcouraged from following their father's profeſſion by the prejudice againſt it, their ſituation would certainly be leſs favourable, and the principle of their emulation viciated. The profeſſion of ſea-officers in the merchants ſervice is honourable in itſelf, on account of the dangers to which they are expoſed, and lucrative without requiring any great ſtock of money. Far from encouraging any prejudices againſt thoſe people, the ſkill of the legiſlator conſiſts in taking advantage

of

of their foible, and in guiding men towards what ought to be their end, by the very means by which they are led aſtray.

IT muſt have been after repeated experiments, by which men grow by degrees more familiar with the ſea, that they ventured to croſs that element: the firſt rules of that art probably aroſe from fiſhery. That precious branch of employment ſtill maintains its rights over navigation, by being always the nurſery and beſt ſchool of ſeamen. We have made no diſtinction between them, in order to conform ourſelves the more to the generally received ideas, and not to interrupt the chain of our arguments.

IT is evident, from the hiſtory of trade, and that of all maritime powers, not one excepted, that great fiſheries have always been the epocha of a great trading navigation, and of a great marine. The example of Holland is too well known to require our entering into a detail about it: their herring-fiſhery alone is valued at about three millions three hundred thouſand pounds ſterling a year.

BESIDES the advantage which a ſtate receives from its fiſhery, conſidered as a branch of the art of navigating, and of the manufactory of ſhip-building, it likewiſe encreaſes the value of ſalt-pans in countries that have any. It produces every where a conſiderable value, which before did not exiſt, in return for an inconſiderable exchange: for the ſeven eights

eights at leaſt of the value of a fiſhery centers in the hire of men and money. Whence it follows, that a nation that ſells abroad the produce of its fiſhery, gains as clear a profit as if that nation ſold wine or corn of its own growth; with this difference only, that, value for value, the fiſhery will have employed moſt men of different claſſes; that the lands of a ſtate are limited, and can employ but a part of the inhabitants; whereas the fiſhery has no bounds, but every man may be a ſharer in the profit in proportion to his money. In a word, we need not ſcruple to ſay, that fiſhermen are in navigation as uſeful and neceſſary as huſbandmen in the culture of the lands, and that they deſerve, in their way, to be as much regarded and encouraged.

The home and foreign conſumption of fiſh, dry and ſalted, is the meaſure of the decline or increaſe of a nation's fiſhery.

The home conſumption depends on the degree of eaſe of the common people, by whom the greateſt quantities of plain and ordinary things are conſumed; and likewiſe on the duties, which the commodity pays before they have it. In a country where dry and ſalt fiſh ſhould be found to have paid half the amount of its value between the ſea and inland parts of that country, it is probable that, by reducing thoſe duties to only a quarter part of the value, which is ſtill too much, double the quantity would be conſumed, the revenue would be the ſame, and the number

ber of fiſhermen would be as many again. The home conſumption would likewiſe be encreaſed, in proportion to the means taken to prevent the importation of foreign fiſh. The more a ſtate is deficient in its marine, the more ſtrict it ought to be in ſo ſure and advantageous a way to encreaſe it.

FOREIGN conſumption depends on cheapneſs: ſince the ſeven-eighths of the value of a fiſhery centers in, or is to be imputed to, the hire of men and money, it is plain that the rate of the intereſt of money muſt have a great influence on the price. So that ſuppoſing things equal in all other reſpects between two nations, rivals in their fiſheries, that which pays the higheſt intereſt will have the diſadvantage in its ſales; or rather its traders will ſpeculate no farther than the home conſumption, and employ the reſt of their money in more lucrative branches. Bounties only make up for that difference; for the ſea produces for all alike: the beſt methods for fiſhing, and curing fiſh, can never remain a ſecret long, and they are practicable by all nations who have any ſhare of navigation.

RIVALSHIP of merchants is likewiſe an effectual way to equal other nations, and to ſave in a ſhort time rewards or bounties on exportation. That rivalſhip will be promoted by the motives already ſpoken of, and in proportion to the degree of home conſumption, which is always

always a preſent inducement to ſpecula-tion.

An ineſtimable advantage to nations, who know how to procure wherewith to form a great navigation, is, without doubt, to have within themſelves, or in their colonies, materials fit for building and fitting out ſhips. This is a ſelf-evident truth; and the adminiſtration of affairs both at home and abroad, equally concurs to eſtabliſh this maxim, that a people never is ſtronger than when it leaſt depends on others for it's wants. Agriculture, therefore, again comes in here to the aid of navigation, and in her turn receives her reward from it. The advantage of the lowneſs of the intereſt of money is of to both, is again evident on this occaſion. If, for example, we ſuppoſe a country where the intereſt of money is at five per cent, a thouſand pounds put out for 40 years, and intereſt upon intereſt added, the capital ſum will produce 6,810 l. If a thouſand pounds in wood, are not likely to produce their owner the ſame encreaſe in the ſame ſpace of time, every one will chuſe to put his money out at intereſt rather than to have the trouble and run the riſk of planting: very few will let their woods grow till they are fit to cut.

Since the eſtabliſhment of European colonies in the Eaſt- and Weſt-Indies, the navigation of the countries, by which they were founded has been conſiderably encreaſed. It's object has from that time been extended farther, it's effects have been multiplied, and the application of it's principles has become more important, as we have obſerved, in regard to colonies. Mother countries, who underſtand their intereſts, have thought it a point of prudence to include, even their colonies in their reſtrictions relating to navigation: their conduct in that reſpect is founded on ſound policy.

Even, though a nation could be neither traders, nor conquerors, it would be difficult to conceive how it could ſupport itſelf without a ſea force againſt the ambition of it's neighbours, if they had any: now, it is certain that a ſtate which has neither fiſhery, nor foreign trade, can have no maritime force. But if that nation has colonies, or fiſheries; if it has a great ſuperfluity of productions to export, either of it's own growth, or ariſing from the labour and ingenuity of it's inhabitants; the preſervation of thoſe concerns bemes a chief part of it's political intereſts. All that it gains on that ſide is a diminution of the real and relative power of it's rivals; who conſequently gain on the other hand whatever the other loſes. Theſe reſpective intereſts oblige ſtates to keep up fleets and a naval ſtrength at a great expence, that they may be able at the ſame time to protect their own labour and induſtry, the ſole ſupport of that ſtrength; and to moleſt, or even ruin the induſtry

duſtry the ſole ſupport of that ſtrength; and to moleſt, or even ruin the induſtry of their enemies. Commerce is what on thoſe occaſions gives life and motion to thoſe forces by the number of ſeamen, which it brings up and forms during the time of peace.

SUPERIORITY of naval ſtrength ought naturally to decide the conteſt. But it is very proper to obſerve, that the ſuperiority of naval ſtrength between two nations does not abſolutely conſiſt in number and ſtrength of ſhips, if other circumſtances are not equal.

THE proportion between the marine of two ſtates compared together, is a political problem not eaſily ſolved; the combination does not, however, ſeem impoſſible. This is not a proper place to attempt it; wherefore, we ſhall only obſerve, that in order to determine the proportion it is neceſſary to know the uſes that may be made of the reſpective naval forces of each, the neceſſity, or occaſion for thoſe uſes; how far a leſs ſtrength may be able to reduce a greater to an inability of acting, by the advantages of it's ſituation and proper diſtribution of it's forces.

THAT proportion being once ſettled with regard to any ſuppoſed numbers, may eaſily be applied afterwards to any other numbers.

IF the proportion be always exact between the marine of two ſtates, the ſuperiority of the one over the other will depend on the diſpatch and ſecreſy, with which they arm; on on the capacity of their commanders, and the experience, courage, and intrepidity, both of their officers, and ſailors; on their manner of fighting; on the ſuperior degree of care taken in victualling and providing proper ſtores for their fleets, ſquadrons, and arſenals; and on the beſt combination of their reciprocal expeditions.

DISSERTATION XXIX.

Of ſtationing convoys and cruizers for the ſecurity and protection of our own trade and navigation, and for the annoying thoſe of the enemy.

UNDER the article ASSURANCE, in my univerſal dictionary of trade and commerce, I have very fully ſtated the practical nature of inſuring ſhips and merchandize, to which I refer the reader, who would thoroughly underſtand this ſubject.

BY the tables therein repreſented, the difference between an high and a low inſurance will very plainly appear, and conſequently the advantage the Britiſh nation may reap from the ſuperiority of her naval force, in time of war, by a wiſe regulation of our convoys, and cruizers, in order to protect our own commerce in the firſt place, and then to annoy that of the enemy; as the one will lower the inſurance on our trade, in proportion to the care that ſhall be taken of it's preſervation; and the other will raiſe the inſurance

ſurance on our enemy's trade, in proportion to the force that ſhall be properly ſtationed to annoy the ſame. From whence it appears of what prodigious conſequence the proper or improper direction of our naval force is in the article of inſurance only;—not to mention the national gain by captures, the property, lives, and liberties of multitudes of his Majeſty's ſubjects that may be thereby ſaved as well as a great proportion of the public revenue, beſides the reducing our enemies to great diſtreſs.—That an idea of the high concernment hereof may appear, it may be proper to obſerve, how, in time of war now with France, a few ſhips of war may be employed to anſwer thoſe purpoſes.

SUPPOSE a convoy ſhould go from England every four or ſix months, for Africa, America, and then home to Great Britain, beſides the convoys that ſhall go at proper times directly to America.

SUCH convoy may ſee all the trade that are ready to ſail to the ſouth-weſt at a proper diſtance, and, particularly, the trade to *Portugal*, as far as their reſpective ports; the *Streights* trade as far as Gibraltar, or Cape St. Vincent; and then to proceed to Africa, and relieve ſuch ſhips of war as ſhall be before ſtationed there; which relieved ſhips may proceed with the trade from *Africa to America*, and relieve ſuch ſhips of war as ſhall be ſtationed there; which relieved ſhips may convoy the trade that ſhall be ready to

ſail

ſail from their reſpective colonies for Europe and North America, as far as their reſpective tracts, or latitudes.

THE ſhips of war that may be thus appointed convoys, will ſail in ſuch tracts, as will give them frequent opportunities to annoy the enemy, and gain great advantages to themſelves, as they may be from four to ſix months cruiſing on the coaſts of *Africa*, and as long or longer in *America*.

THE ſhips bound from *Africa* to our weſtern ports may rendezvous at Plymouth, Falmouth, Cork, or Kingſale.

THE advantage of ſuch a rotation of convoys will be very great, with regard to eaſing freights and inſurance, two very ſenſible articles in trade in time of war; and the markets on all ſides will be more regularly ſupplied.

FREIGHTS, by the means of frequent and certain convoys, and quick voyages, will be lower, at leaſt, one quarter, as there will be great ſavings in ſeamen's wages, victualling, demurrage, and the preſervation of the ſhips, by means of quick diſpatch.

SINCE this rotation may, by means of thus exchanging ſtations, be performed in five or ſix months, it is apprehended that a few ſhips of war, over-and-above what are neceſſary to be ſtationed in *Africa* and *America*, will anſwer all theſe advantages: and, moreover, this will, in a great meaſure, prevent the decay

cay of his Majeſty's ſhips, by keeping them too long in *Africa* and *America*.

THE practice in queen Anne's war was to let the convoys to the trade to America go out one year, and return home the next, after being relieved by other convoys, whereby they uſually remained in *America* 14 months; but of late years, moſt of our ſhips of war have remained in *America*, and particularly in the *Weſt-Indies*, about three or four years: wherefore it is ſubmitted whether the method abovementioned, is not to be preferred to the other? Since his Majeſty's ſhips will then croſs the weſtern ocean oftner, which will afford much ſtronger, and more frequent, more certain and more regular convoys, and our trade would be much better protected, than it was in the late war with *France*, and that with the ſame number of ſhips as we employed in that ſervice; and the ſhips would be fitted for the ſea, with more expedition, and at leſs expence, after their arrival in England.

THE ſtrength of France may be depreſſed by keeping cruizing ſquadrons at Gibraltar, and on the coaſt of Portugal. And as our ſhips of war may be encreaſed, it will be proper to have a great many ſhips of ſmall force in fair weather, in a conſtant courſe of ſailing to ſuppreſs privateers, and ſeize our enemy's trading ſhips.—The commanders of ſuch ſmall ſhips ſhould be accountable for their time *.

* Why may they not be always at ſea for a certain fixed time, as well as other ſhips trading ſome where or other?

The

The accounts of their remaining in harbour, &c. may be tranſmitted to the government by it's civil officers. As large ſquadrons of men of war have not many opportunities of engaging with our enemy's ſhips of trade, thoſe ſmall ſhips will be highly ſerviceable: one ſquadron of thoſe cruizers, well made for expedition, and well appointed and regulated, carrying about 12 or 14 guns may be ſtationed about the iſlands of *Guernſey* and *Jerſey*, there being good harbouring; and they might be a very proper additional force to our cruizing ſquadrons of ſmall ſhips at Gibraltar, and on the coaſt of Portugal, and others may be ſteddily cruizing on the moſt convenient parts of our own coaſts, where we may intercept the enemy's ſhips.

DIS-

DISSERTATION XXX.

The ill policy of our inſuring the ſhips and merchandizes of the enemy in times of war: with conſiderations on neutral powers.

IT is to be feared that all our endeavours to encreaſe our maritime ſtrength, and to annoy the trade of the enemy, will little avail us, if the practice of our inſuring the ſhips and merchandizes of the enemy ſhall prevail, either directly or indirectly. We may as well, we apprehend, inſure all their royal navy, perhaps, as their mercantile commerce and navigation. A matter of this concernment in time of war, being cloſely connected with the ſcope of our intentions, it is conceived that this work would not be ſo uſeful as we are ambitious it may without it; and therefore ſhall give a ſummary of the argument with what brevity and perſpicuity we can.

THOUGH inſurances in general are both uſeful and neceſſary, we beg leave to ſay, that

that thoſe made for Britiſh account on the ſhipping and merchandiſes of enemies in times of war, ſeem to be attended with very bad conſequences. During the late war in 1747, the parliament of England, when they prohibited all commerce with France, took into conſideration, whether the inſurance of goods, imported into, or exported from France, and her colonies, ſhould not likewiſe be prohibited? Several magnified the advantages ariſing to the nation from this branch of inſurance: and ſeveral of our eminent inſurers very patriotly ſpeeched it in parliament upon this occaſion, as they had done before in the year 1741. But the ſubſtance of what was urged in favour of the eſſential point then under conſideration ſeems to be badly grounded. For all parties agreed that no aſſiſtance ſhould be given, or meaſures ought to be taken on our part, to enable the enemy to carry on the war to greater advantage than they could do without ſuch aſſiſtance and meaſures on our ſide. The inſurers, whoſe immediate intereſt it was to execute the orders for theſe inſurances for the enemy, inſiſted, with confidence, that they were attended with large profits to the nation, that is, to themſelves; and that the making ſuch profits on the enemy ought not to be neglected, and transferred to other countries, by a prohibition here. Several worthy members of parliament enquired ſtrictly into the true ſtate of this buſineſs, in order to diſcover whether the nation was ſo highly benefited by theſe foreign inſurances as was aſſerted; and many diſintereſted merchants impartially declared their opinions thereon to the following effect:

1. That the ſuppoſed profit of 3 per cent. on a premium of 30 per cent., ſaid in ſome of the above-mentioned ſpeeches, and calculations of profit to be made, is quite uncertain: that, in proportion as the number of the Britiſh ſhips of war and privateers encreaſe, much more may be loſt than ſuppoſed to be gained; and that when only 18 per cent. premium was paid for inſurance here, the inſurers, as well as others, actually know they were great loſers by ſuch riſks.

2. That no merchants, by their ſkill in computing of chances, can demonſtrate what the profits on any voyage will be; and all that can be known is, that thoſe alone have reaſon to promiſe themſelves advantage from inſurances who do or do not underwrite greater or leſſer ſums, in proportion as the premiums ſhall riſe or fall, and the circumſtances ſhall be more or leſs dangerous.

3. That we have more or leſs reaſon to expect profit or loſs from foreign inſurances, in proportion as there is a greater or leſs number of perſons who have ſufficient experience, and know how to make the proper choice.

4. That

4. THAT it is evident, if more clear money be paid for loſſes upon foreign inſurances, then the groſs ſums received for premiums and all charges amount to, the articles ſet forth by the advocates for the practice of commiſſion, brokerage, and deductions are by no means to be conſidered as indiſputable items of profit: for although they bring clear ſums into the pockets of the factors, or brokers, who negociate ſuch inſurances, the loſſes paid by inſurers may greatly exceed the whole foreign diſburſement, and conſequently the balance will be a national loſs.— This point, therefore, as mentioned above, is extremely difficult to aſcertain: but there is a plain and inconteſtable argument againſt foreign inſurances being made for an enemy, which will always ſubſiſt ſo long as Great Britain maintains the ſuperiority of naval power; which is, *That the great object of a maritime nation ſhould be, to take advantage of any rupture with another trading ſtate, to deſtroy and diſtreſs their ſhipping and commerce, and to cut off all reſources for naval armaments. But to permit ſuch inſurances is manifeſtly to defeat this end, and is contradictory to common ſenſe: for the government and private merchants are, on the one hand, fitting out veſſels at a great expence to make captures, and to annoy and diſtreſs the enemy; whilſt another ſet of merchants make good the loſſes, and furniſh means for the continuance of their commerce.*

5. WHEN

5. WHEN orders come for inſurances from places where the eager purſuit of premiums is as ſtrong as it is here in England, it ſhews that a high premium has been there inſiſted on: and as people on the ſpot can be better judges of the nature of the concern, the navigation, ſhips, commanders, &c. than thoſe at a diſtance, there can be little hopes of profit of inſurances which foreigners have rejected.

6. THAT as it is now cuſtomary to accept of eſtimations, in which the foreigner inſured, in caſe of a loſs, finds his account better than if the veſſels had not been loſt or taken; nay, it is agreed to pay ſuch a ſum inſured, whether on board the ſhip or not; it is evident that ſuch agreements have a bad tendency, as they give ſo much room for frauds.—That no perſon ever *had proved to a certainty, whether by inſurances on foreign trade, more, on the whole, had been gained than loſt.*—That it was contrary to ſound and good policy, to grant aſſiſtance to undertakings which were contrary to the general intereſt, and diametrically oppoſite to the intention of *prohibiting the trade with France*, the natural conſequence of which ſhould have been the prohibition of inſuring their ſhips and goods. This is to be underſtood only in times of war; for in thoſe of peace, ſuch inſurances ſhould be conſidered as a buſineſs that is to be left to the free will of the merchant.

FROM

FROM the ſuperiority of our maritime power in the laſt war with Spain, we might have gained far greater advantages over them than we did, had it not been for the practice of our inſuring their ſhips and merchandize; nay, we muſt have ſubdued them, and ſubdued them perhaps without a battle, and without the poſſibility of reſiſtance; for againſt ſuch an enemy as we then were, their courage or their diſcipline was of little uſe; they formed armies, indeed, which only ſtood on the ſhore, to defend what we had no intention of invading, and beheld thoſe ſhips ſeized wherein their pay was treaſured, or their proviſions ſtored.—Such was our natural ſuperiority over the Spaniards, a ſpecies of ſuperiority that muſt have inevitably prevailed, if it had not been defeated by our own folly; and certainly a more effectual method of defeating it the Spaniards themſelves could not have diſcovered, than that of inſuring their ſhips amongſt our merchants. When a ſhip thus inſured was taken, we examined her cargo, found it extremely valuable, and triumphed in our ſucceſs, by cavalcades of waggon-loads of money through our ſtreets; we not only counted the gain to ourſelves, but the loſs to our enemies, and determined that a ſmall number of ſuch captures would reduce them to offer us peace upon our own terms.

Such were the conclusions made, and made with reason, by men unacquainted with the secret practices, amongst ourselves, and who did not suspect us to be stupid enough to secure our enemies against ourselves; but it was frequently found, upon a close examination, that our ships of war had only plundered our own merchants, and that our privateers did indeed enrich themselves, but thereby impoverished their country: for it was discovered, that the loss of the Spaniards was to be repaid, and perhaps sometimes with interest, by our British insurers!

If it be urged, that we ought not to enact any laws which may obstruct the gain of our fellow-subjects, may it not be asked, why all trade with Spain in time of war with them is prohibited? May not the trade be equally gainful with the insurance; and may not the gain be more generally distributed, and therefore be more properly national? But the trade with Spain at such times is prohibited, because it was more necessary to our enemies than to ourselves; because the laws of war require, that a less evil should be suffered to inflict a greater: it is upon this principle that every battle is fought, and that we fire our own ships to consume the navies of our enemies. For this reason it appears to be evident beyond contradiction, that the insurance of Spanish ships ought to have been prohibited in time of war with that

that nation; we ſhould indeed have loſt the profit of the inſurance, but we ſhould have been reimburſed by the captures, which is an argument that cannot be produced for the prohibition of commerce in time of war.

It has been ſaid, and inſiſted on by ſome, though never made appear, that our enemies may inſure their ſhips in other countries; but this, if true, would lay them under the neceſſity of eſtabliſhing a new correſpondence for the purpoſe: and would not this prove at leaſt ſuch a temporary obſtruction of their trade, which, though of ſhort continuance, might lay them at our mercy during the interval of ſuch eſtabliſhment. But let us conſider the weakneſs of this argument.—They *muſt* be allowed to inſure here, becauſe they *may* inſure in other places.—Will it not be equally juſt to urge, that they *muſt* trade with us, becauſe they *may* trade with other nations? And may it not be anſwered, that, though we cannot wholly ſuſpend their commerce, it is yet our intereſt to obſtruct it, as far as we are able? May it not be farther affirmed, that, by inſuring in other nations, they may injure their allies by falling into our hands, but do not the leſs benefit us? That, if they do not grow weaker, we are, at leaſt, ſtrengthened; *but that, by inſuring among us, whatever ſteps ſhall be taken to put*

a ſpeedy

a ſpeedy end to the war, the equilibrium of it is ſtill preſerved the ſame?

We have introduced this topic among others, to ſhow how induſtriouſly we have laboured to ſtrengthen and enrich our enemy the better to enable them to humble us. —*Riſum teneatis!*

DIS-

DISSERTATION XXXI.

An enquiry how long France may be presumed to carry on the war from the present state of affairs.

WE have ſeen upon how extenſive a bottom the commerce of France ſtands, and how invincible ſhe muſt, at length, become by peace, if ſhe meet with no remora to her progreſs in commercial dominion. Let us penetrate her cabinet now in time of war.

SHE has not a grand alliance now to cope with. Her trade and navigation being at preſent carried on chiefly by neutral ſtates, it is not in our power to reduce her revenues; for what ſhe loſes in freight, ſhe in a great meaſure, ſaves by inſurance. Nay, the general commerce of France is more extenſive now than in time of peace; for their neutral carriers, as well for their own as for French account force the ſales of French commodities more than the French themſelves do in times of peace by their cheapneſs; for the Dutch themſelves cannot work ſo cheap as the French,

French, though they can and do ſail cheaper. For, as an ingenious gentleman has obſerved *, " Bread, in Holland, ſuch as our manufacturers in England eat, is commonly at 3 d. a pound ſterling; fleſh at 9 d. ſuch as is ſold in England at 3 d.; labour as high as in England: whereas, in France, in the provinces, bread is in common at one half penny ſterling per pound, or at leaſt at about half the price it is at in England; and fleſh in the ſame proportion. Labour in France, likewiſe, is but from 3 d. per day, of 14 hours, or from five to ſeven o' clock, in the cheapeſt countries, and at about 7 d. half penny in the deareſt: in manufactures, at but half the price as in England. Sailors wages a-board the French navy, but from about 8 to 12 s. per month; whereas in England, a ſailor has 20 s. per month a-board king's ſhips. Muſt not this render their commodities exceeding cheap in compariſon to ours at foreign markets?

AND here it may be obſerved, that this cheapneſs of labour, proviſions, and commodities, was, at firſt brought about by the ſole artifice of the enhancement of their money from 27 livres, to 50 livres the mark of eight ounces of ſilver troy weight; and this has been done ſince the beginning of the confederate war in 1702. It is true, this cauſed

* The progreſs of the French in their views of univerſal monarchy.

great

great convulſions in the kingdom at firſt, but in the iſſue, it has been the inſtrument by which they have ſapped the foundations of our trade; and, if a remedy be not applied, this artifice of the French will worm out Britiſh manufactures by gentle degrees in every market in the world: and that no leſs in time of war than peace, by virtue of neutral powers carrying on their trade for them; which they cannot do to ſuch advantage by Britiſh commodities, by reaſon of their greater dearneſs.

By this artifice they have rendered their labour ſo cheap, that they reap a plentiful harveſt in every country, *where they pay but the ſame cuſtoms as the Engliſh*, whilſt the Engliſh merchant is obliged to wait for the gleanings of the market, after the Frenchman has finiſhed his ſales.

The project of the enhancement of money, has given an undue preference in France to money, above land and commodities: but where lies the diſadvantage at preſent, if the gentleman receives but a hundred pound weight of ſilver for his lands, where he uſed to receive two hundred pound, if, at the ſame time, he can purchaſe as many commodities with a hundred pound, as before the enhancement he could with two? It is certain it would only affect his foreign conſumption. By this ſcheme the French have reſtrained the bulk of the people to the conſumption of their own manufactures, and commodities, and have prodigiouſly extended

their

their commerce, by underſelling all nations. This has enabled their iſlands to ſend home ſugars, indico, &c. ſo cheap, as to rival us in all the European markets, and in the Levant: and all this they do, though their manufacturers pay ſix times as much in taxes on the neceſſaries of life as they do in England.

DUTOT ſays, the price of bread, corn, and proviſions, is no greater now than in 1683; though in this laſt year the mark of ſilver was but 27 livres *, and now 50 are coined out of it. This circumſtance, as obſerved, has rendered their commodities ſo cheap, that they underſell us, and engroſs all the markets in the world from our merchants. It is likewiſe this enhancement of their coin, and the conſequent cheapneſs of their commodities, which has enabled our ſmugglers to carry on ſuch an advantageous trade with them. If but 20 l. 5 s. were now coined out of their mark of ſilver of eight ounces troy weight, which was the caſe in the year, 1660, the French would not be able to ſell a gallon of brandy under 5 s. ſterling, which now they can ſell for 2 s.; nor a pound of tea under 7 s. 6 d. ſterling, which they now ſell for 3 ſhillings; nor a yard of ſilk damaſk under 12 s. 6 d. which they now

* When the mark was at 20 livres about 1660, labour was dearer in France than in England.

ſell for 5 ſhillings; nor a yard of cloth under 15 s. which they now ſell for 6 ſhillings, abating only in the manufactures, the difference made in the price of thoſe manufactures, with regard to the raw-materials, which coſt both French and Engliſh men much the ſame, though the raw ſilk comes to them cheaper from their Turkey-traders; and their wool uſed in their fine woollen ſtuffs dearer from our ſmugglers than to us.

But, though they have got, by this, and the other ſchemes of policy, that we have repreſented throughout theſe papers, the greateſt part of the trade to Spain from us, the Turkey trade, the Italian trade, and great part of the Eaſt-India and African trades; the northern and cod-fiſhery and furr trades; yet they cannot be eaſy, but muſt attempt to rob us alſo of our colonies; our trade to which is the only valuable branch we have left, except that of Portugal, where we have ſeen they are ruining us by their black druggets and by every imaginable artifice.

The immediate deſign of the French in their encroachments upon our territories in North-America, and in their approaches towards our colonies, is to open to themſelves a communication through thoſe colonies to the Miſſiſſippi, and Canada.—They regret the advantages we have in the tobacco trade, and intend to eſtabliſh plantations for that

com-

commodity in the fertile plains between the river Miſſiſſippi, and our ſettlements in Virginia; though all theſe lands belong to us.

Is it, therefore, to be wondered that the commerce of France is ſo greatly advanced throughout the world, as we have ſhewn it really is? What can hinder that nation from obtaining the commercial dominion they ſo zealouſly aim at? Nothing can prevent this effectually but our capacity to ſell our commodities as cheap and as good in quality as this rival nation does. But how can this be ever accompliſhed, if we continue to encreaſe our public debts and taxes? Our conſtitution and public faith will not admit us to play ſuch tricks with our money as the French have done. What then ought we reſolve to do? The anſwer is now obvious. Let the meaſures be taken, that I have faithfully and impartially laboured to recommend in this and all my other writings for the public intereſt and happineſs, or ſuch other as ſhall be more eligible: Let ſuch a quantity of more land be taken into cultivation as will fairly render things as cheap in England, as in France: and let the whole, or a conſiderable part of the ſupplies to carry on the war be raiſed within the year, without perpetuated taxes ſtill further to enhance the price of our arts, and manufactures: and let the public debts be put into a certain way of redemption: let alſo England and Ireland be united;

and

and our plantations properly regulated: and let ſmuggling of every kind be extirpated, eſpecially, that to the iſle of Man, by annexing the ſame to the crown: let every wiſe domeſtic meaſure be taken that tend to the encouragement of the commercial arts: Let the ſociety for the advancement of arts, and trades, be incorporated and ſupported by parliamentary authority: and after all; let ſuch a ſyſtem of foreign affairs be adopted by the crown of England as will put it long out of the power of France to diſturb our tranquillity, or that of Europe: and let not this humble attempt be ſlighted and contemned, becauſe it comes from a private perſon, becauſe it is not impoſſible but a private ſpeculative man may happily fall upon that which may eſcape the moſt public active perſon of infinitely greater abilities, and only, becauſe he is too much abſorbed in public buſineſs.

FROM the death of Philip the fourth, king of Spain, to the league of Augſburg in 1683, Monſ. Colbert took care to encourage arts, diffuſe manufactures, promote fiſheries, and inland commerce, and all with a view to raiſe a powerful marine to rival the united forces of the Engliſh and Dutch. This was the principal part of the plan of conqueſt; and this the French ſucceeded in to their wiſhes; ſo that in a few years we ſaw France alone contend with the united ſquadrons of

the

the English and Dutch for the empire of the main.

HOT-HEADED Lewis would never have attained his end, had it not been for the prudent counsels of his minister Colbert, who addressed him in this manner when he was venting his spleen against the Dutch, who obstructed his conquest:

"THE advice I would presume to give your majesty is, to disband the greatest part of your forces, and save so many taxes to your people. Your very dominions make you too powerful to fear any insult from your neighbours. Turn your thoughts, Sir, I intreat you, from war, cultivate the arts of peace, the trade and manufacture of your subjects: this will make you the most powerful prince, and your people at the same time the richest of all nations.—There never will be wanting fools to purchase the manufactures of France; but France must be strictly prohibited to buy those of other countries. But above all, peace will ingratiate your majesty with the Spanish nation during the life of their crazy king; and, after his death, a few seasonable presents among his courtiers shall purchase the reversion of his crowns, with all the treasures of the Indies, and then the world is your own."

THUS commerce is to bring in riches, the treasures of the Indies; and these are to be employed in raising armies and navies, and

making

making the world their own. Here the end the French purſue in promoting commerce is avowed, viz. that they may be able to plunder their neighbours, and rob them of their territories, that they may recover the empire of Charlemagne, or all that lies between the Baltic and the Adriatic, and from thence to the Mediterranean and the Atlantic ocean, after which, *the world is to be made their own.*

CONQUEST is the deſign of the French; trade is only attended to as the inſtrument. The French raiſe armies, build ſhips, erect forts, and favour manufactures and commerce, not to make their people happy, but to be in a condition to take advantage of every conjuncture for extending their dominions, and robbing their neighbours. Colbert avows this, and that the dominions of the French king are too great, and make him too powerful to fear any inſult from *his neighbours.* And their other politicians ſay, one ſtate is weak, *another* divided, *another* ſlothful, and from thence encourage their princes to make a prey of all. And if the commerce is aided and aſſiſted by neutral potentates during a war, will not their revenues be kept in good plight, notwithſtanding we may take more of their ſhips than they ſhall do of ours; and eſpecially ſo if we inſure them?

WE have ſeen how their connections in trade with the Spaniards are managed; and

pro-

provided Spain ſhall join them againſt England, how ſhall we be able alone to withſtand their united power? Do we not experience that our royal navies have not hitherto been able to do them any ſignificant miſchief? Nay, they ſeem to deſpiſe our maritime power. And if the whole maritime power of Spain ſhould unite with that of France againſt us, what head can we expect to make againſt both, when we have done ſo little againſt France alone?

THE royal navy of Spain is ſaid to conſiſt at preſent of the following ſhips, viz. one of 114 guns, ſix of 80, thirty-ſeven of 70, four of 64, ſix of 60, one of 54, one of 50, five of 30, four of 26, four of 24, four of 22, five of 16, four packet-boats, mounting 16 guns each, thirteen xebeques of 24 guns, four bomb-ketches, each carrying 12 guns, and four fire-ſhips; in all *one hundred and three* ſail.

I WOULD be the laſt perſon in the kingdom who would ſpread falſe alarms; but I would be one of the firſt who would apprize my country of danger, in order to prevent it. And all I would intend by theſe repreſentations is, that we might prepare againſt the worſt; and I wiſh the king's miniſters would think of the moſt effectual meaſures to reduce the power of France within ſuch bounds that we may obtain an honourable and a laſting peace: but this does not appear

poſſible

poſſible, in my humble judgment, according to the faſhionable politics of the day.

For how can we expect to deal with France without any maritime allies, when they are ſuch greater gainers in their trade by neutral ſtates than we can poſſibly be, as our commerce is at preſent circumſtanced? The trade and navigation of France was never till now brought to the height it is; the foundation for commercial dominions was never ſo formidable as at preſent. If, when this nation was leſs powerful, and we millions leſs in debt, and formed the grand alliance for our ſecurity, we could not eaſily cope with them, what reaſon can we have to flatter ourſelves that we can ſo eaſily defeat all their deſigns at preſent?

Whilst France continues to enjoy ſo extraordinary advantages in her trade as we have ſeen ſhe does in every part of the world, ſhe will have great reſources to continue the war, while ours will every day diminiſh, by reaſon of the great activity of the neutral carriers in favour of the trade of France, and their inattention and diſregard to that of Great Britain; for this plain reaſon, that the dearneſs of our commodities renders them not worth their while to deal in them, while they are great gainers by trafficking with thoſe of France. Thus all the neutral powers contributing to the advancement of the commerce of France, while ours is more and

and more loaded with tax-incumbrances, it does not ſeem poſſible for England, under ſuch circumſtances. to be able to reduce France to a laſting and an honouaable peace: for although his Pruſſian majeſty ſhall attempt to make all the head he can againſt France; yet this will not help our trading intereſt: he will not be able to cut off all eſſential reſources, which enable France to carry on the war. We ſee by what intereſting ties, the ties of a commercial neutrality, that the Dutch have reaſon to be attached rather to France than England.

TILL, therefore, we can ſo change the ſyſtem of Europe, as to raiſe ſuch powerful allies to act vigorouſly and faithfully againſt the power of France, and thoſe allies which ſhe may further draw into her meaſures, what reaſon can we have to amuſe ourſelves with a peace that is likely to be either honourable or permanent? I wiſh this could be ſatisfactorily demonſtrated to the public. But I am very doubtful that it cannot, without ſome eſſential alteration is made in our foreign ſyſtem; and this alteration, we humbly judge, not impracticable: we apprehend, on the contrary, that ſuch a change might be effectuated with far leſs difficulty than the old ſyſtem can be ſupported to check ſufficiently the career of France.

BUT

BUT till ſomething of a new foreign ſyſtem ſhall be happily adopted, we humbly recommend theſe diſſertations to the conſideration of the public: if they are right in the general, they will live; and if they are wrong, it is to be hoped that the intention will attone for miſtakes.

DISSERTATION XXXII.

Some general maxims regarding the advancement of the national commerce, as founded on experience, and the opinion of the most knowing and judicious.

THE history and nature of commerce furnishes us with three important reflections:

1. PEOPLE have been seen to make up, by dint of industry, for what was wanting in the productions of their own country, and thereby possess more of what men have agreed to call riches, than those who were proprietors of natural riches. But that industry always consisted in supplying one country with the natural riches of another, of which it stood in need: and on the other hand, without industry, no people ever possessed any plenty of gold and silver, which are what men have agreed to call riches.

2. A NATION loses its commerce insensibly, when it does not carry on so great a trade as it is able to do. Every branch of trade supposes a want, either real or imaginary:

nary: the profits ariſing from them are a means of undertaking more; and nothing is ſo dangerous as to force other nations to ſupply their wants themſelves. The greateſt induſtry has ever been the effect of the greateſt neceſſity: the prodigious efforts it occaſions are like the flowing of an impetuous torrent, whoſe waters beat with violence againſt the banks that confine them, till at laſt they force them down.

3. A COUNTRY in which a great trade flouriſhes, a conſtant indication of which is its opulence, will always be moſt populous. It is certain that the conveniences of life are what moſt attract mankind. Let us ſuppoſe trading people ſurrounded by others not traders: the former will very ſoon bring over to them as many of the latter as can reap a profit by being employed in their trade.

THESE three reflections indicate the principle of commerce in a body politic in particular: agriculture and induſtry are the eſſence of it: their union is ſuch, that if the one prevails over the other, it deſtroys itſelf. Without induſtry the fruits of the earth can have no value: if agriculture be neglected, the fountain of trade is dried up.

THE intent of commerce in a ſtate is, by labour to maintain in eaſe and plenty as many men as poſſible. Agriculture and induſtry are the only means of ſubſiſtance: If both of them are advantageous to thoſe that

follow

follow them, inhabitants will never be wanting.

THE effect of commerce is, to give a body politic all the weight and ſtrength, influence and dignity it is capable of receiving. Theſe conſiſt in the number of inhabitants attracted by its political riches, which are at the ſame time both real and relative.

THE real riches of a ſtate are its ſuperior degree of *independence on other ſtates* for neceſſaries, and the greater quantity of ſuperfluities it has to export. Its relative riches depend on the quantity its trade procures of what men have agreed to call riches, compared with the quantity of the ſame kind of riches brought into neighbouring ſtates by their trade. A combination of theſe real and relative riches is what conſtitutes the art and ſcience of the adminiſtration of *political commerce*.

EVERY operation in the commerce of a ſtate contrary to theſe principles, is deſtructive to commerce itſelf.

CONSEQUENTLY, all that can be ſaid on this head is founded on this fundamental maxim, that there is a beneficial national trade, and a national trade which is not ſo. To be convinced of that, it is neceſſary to diſtinguiſh between what the merchant gains and what the ſtate gains. If the merchant imports foreign goods, by which the conſumption of the national manufactures is hurt, it is certain that, though the merchant gains

gains by the ſale of thoſe goods, the ſtate loſes, firſt, the value of what they coſt abroad; ſecondly, the wages which would have been earned by divers workmen in fabricating thoſe goods at home; thirdly, the value of what the firſt materials would have produced to the planters of the country or colony where they grew; fourthly, the benefit of the circulation of all thoſe values; that is to ſay, the eaſe and convenience, the conſumption of them would have afforded to numbers of others; and fifthly, the aſſiſtance the prince has a right to expect from the affluence of his ſubjects.

If thoſe firſt materials are the produce of its colonies, the ſtate likewiſe loſes the benefits of navigation. If they are foreign materials, this laſt loſs ſtill takes place; and inſtead of immediately affecting the produce of the lands, will fall upon the national commodities, which would have been exported for thoſe firſt materials.

The gain of the ſtate is, therefore, exactly what we have juſt ſaid it muſt loſe on the foregoing ſuppoſition; the merchant's gain is only what he ſells his goods for more than what they coſt him.

On the other hand, the merchant may loſe when the ſtate gains. If a merchant ſends imprudently manufactures of his own country to another where they are not wanted, he may loſe by the ſale of them: but ſtill the ſtate will gain ſo much as they are ſold for abroad; the circulation of what ſhall have been paid the land for the price of the firſt materials, the wages of the workmen employed in manufacturing them, the value of the navigation, if they are exported by ſea, the benefit of circulation, and the tribute which the public wealth owes to the ſtate.

WHAT the merchant gains by his fellow-ſubjects is therefore abſolutely indifferent to the ſtate, which gains nothing by it; but that gain is not indifferent, when it increaſes the debt due by other nations, and is an encouragement to other undertakings lucrative and beneficial to ſociety.

BEFORE we examine by what means legiſlators fulfil the intent and effect of commerce, I ſhall obſerve that there are nine maxims, which our Engliſh commercial laws have adopted, whereby to judge of the advantage or diſadvantage of a trade.

1. THE exportation of ſuperfluities is the cleareſt profit a nation can make.

2. THE ſuperfluous produce of the land is exported to moſt advantage after it is worked up or manufactured.

3. The importation of foreign materials for manufacturing, unwrought inſtead of importing them ready manufactured, ſaves a great deal of money to the nation.

4. Ex-

4. EXCHANGE of merchandize for mer-merchandize is advantageous in general; but not in cases where it is contrary to the fore-going maxims.

5. THE importation of foreign commodities, whereby the consumption of national commodities is hurt, or the progress of a nation's manufactures and the culture of its lands prejudiced, must necessarily bring on the ruin of that nation.

6. THE importation of foreign commodities of mere luxury, in exchange for money, is a real loss to the state.

7. THE importation of things absolutely necessary, cannot be thought an evil; but the nation is not less impoverished by it.

8. THE importation of foreign goods, to be afterwards re-exported, leaves a real profit behind.

9. To hire out one's ships for freight to other nations is a beneficial commerce.

THE general operation of commerce ought to be directed by this plan.

WE have defined that operation to be the home circulation of the produce of a country, or its colonies, the exportation of its superfluities, and the importation of foreign commodities, either to be consumed at home, or re-exported.

THIS definition naturally divides trade into two parts, home and foreign. Their principles are widely different, and if not distinguished

guiſhed from each other, muſt occaſion great confuſion.

The home trade of a nation is that which the ſeveral members of a ſociety carry on among themſelves. It holds the firſt rank in trade in general, becauſe what is neceſſary is more eſteemed than what is ſuperfluous, which is not for that reaſon leſs in requeſt.

This home circulation conſiſts in the conſumption of the produce of the country, and of the induſtry of the inhabitants, of which that conſumption is the ſoul and ſupport. We have already obſerved, that the real riches of a nation are at their higheſt period when that nation has recourſe to no other to ſupply its wants. The rules eſtabliſhed in conſequence in different ſtates, vary according to the greater or leſs abundance of their natural riches; and the well-judged induſtry of many has compenſated for what nature has refuſed them.

The value of a home trade is exactly the ſum to which the private expence of every inhabitant amounts, for lodging, food, cloathing, and the conveniencies and ſuperfluities of life. But whatever is conſumed of foreign commodities muſt be deducted from that value, as a real loſs to the nation, ſo far as it is not compenſated by a foreign trade.

The populouſneſs of a ſtate is the ſoul of this home conſumption, the perfection of which conſiſts in a plenty of commodities of the

the national growth, adequate to the want and demand for them: its preſervation depends on the profit which thoſe commodities yield to the proprietor of them, and on the encouragement given them by the ſtate.

So long as the lands receive their greateſt and beſt culture that can poſſibly be given them, the uſe of articles of convenience and luxury cannot be too general, provided thoſe articles are of the growth of the country, or its colonies.

THEIR value increaſes the amount of private expences, and is divided among the ſeveral inhabitants employed therein.

IT is good for a ſtate not to want any of the ſweets and conveniencies of life, becauſe that people is more happy by poſſeſſing them than it would be otherwiſe. It would ceaſe to be ſo, if thoſe conveniencies exhauſted its riches: nay, it would ſoon be quite deprived of happineſs, becauſe real wants are impatient and tormenting creditors. But when thoſe articles of convenience and luxury are the produce of the country, the pleaſure they procure is attended with ſeveral advantages. They are an allurement to other nations, who are taken with them, and procure the ſtate that poſſeſſes them wherewithal to increaſe its exports. Let me be allowed to extend this maxim to the liberal arts and ſciences: they cannot be degraded by being conſidered in a new light of commercial utility. Men require inſtruction and amuſe-

ment:

ment: every nation that is obliged to have recourſe to another for thoſe inſtructions or amuſements, is ſo far impoveriſhed thereby, as the expence on that occaſion amounts to, which is ſo much clear gain to the nation by which they are furniſhed.

WHAT to the eye of reaſon might ſeem a moſt frivolous art, or a moſt trifling commodity, is a very eſſential object in *political commerce*. Philip II. though poſſeſſed of the mines of Potoſi, iſſued two edicts during his reign, only to forbid the importation of all foreign dolls, glaſs-ware, combs, and pins, eſpecially French.

ALLOWING faſhions, and the continual changes of them, to be the effect of the levity and fickleneſs of a people; yet it is certain that people could not act more wiſely for the benefit of its trade and circulation. Thoſe only are to blame who follow them when not able to afford it: the real ridicule conſiſts in complaining of faſhions or finery, and not in abſtaining from them.

IT is, however, far from being impoſſible, or even difficult, to carry luxury to too great a height; the conſequence of which would be, that the lands and moſt neceſſary arts would be much neglected, and other leſs uſeful arts and leſs neceſſary cultures applied to.

IT is always in the legiſlature's power to check that exceſs, by ſtriking at its cauſe: they will always be able to maintain a juſt equilibrium

equilibrium between the ſeveral occupations of the ſubject, to eaſe the part that ſuffers by granting privileges and immunities, and to make the taxes fall on the home conſumption of articles of luxury.

THAT part of trade falls properly under the cognizance of the particular laws of the body politic, in whoſe power it is to encourage, reſtrain, or abſolutely prohibit the uſe of commodities, either national or foreign, according as the welfare of the ſtate requires. For that reaſon it is that all colonies are under a ſtate of perpetual prohibition.

LASTLY, it muſt always be remembered, that the home-trade of a country, is what particularly keeps up the real riches of the ſtate.

FOREIGN trade is that which a political ſociety carries on with others: it tends to the ſame end that the home-trade does, but is more particularly calculated to procure relative riches. For, if we ſuppoſe a trading people abounding with commodities of which foreigners make but little uſe, the home-trade of that people will keep up the ſpirit of culture and induſtry by what is conſumed among themſelves; but the foreign trade will go no farther than barely to favour it, without ſacrificing to it any opportunity of encreaſing the relative riches of the ſtate, by the ſale of any other commodity more ſuitable to a foreign market. This part of trade is ſo cloſely

con-

connected with the political interests of a state, that it partakes of their nature.

PRINCES are always in a forced state when considered relatively to other princes; and those who would procure their subjects any considerable export of their commodities, are obliged to consider the circumstances, maxims and interests of other trading nations, as well as the taste and caprice of the consumer.

THE operation of foreign trade consists in supplying the wants of other nations, and drawing thence wherewith to answer one's own. The perfection of that trade consists in supplying others with as much as is possible, and in the most advantageous manner that can be: it's preservation depends on the manner in which it is carried on.

THE produce of the land and of industry is, as we have before said, the basis of all trade. Fruitful countries have consequently an advantage for exportation over barren ones: and the more a commodity is necessary and perfect, the more other nations must depend on it.

To be very populous is one of the advantages, by which a nation is enabled to supply to the utmost the wants of other nations: whilst on the other hand it's foreign trade employs all the hands which it's home-trade could not have maintained.

A NATION will be more or less populous according as it's inhabitants are more or less able

able to ſubſiſt by their labour, and as their property is more or leſs ſecure. If their labour does not afford them the means of ſubſiſtance, experience ſhews they will ſeek it in other countries. Accordingly, when by extraordinary circumſtances that is like to be the caſe, the legiſlature takes care to prevent the evil by finding employment for the ſubject. From the neceſſity of a country's being well peopled, it follows that idleneſs ought not to be ſuffered.

One country can not ſupply another with any commodity, which it does not ſell as cheap as it can be bought elſewhere: if cheaper, it will always be preferred at home. Four things are ſure to conſtitute that cheapneſs: rivalſhip in trade, oeconomy of men's labour, ſmall charges of exportation, and low intereſt of money.

Domestic rivalſhip in trade produces plenty; and plenty cheapneſs of proviſions, of the firſt materials, of labour and of money. Rivalſhip is one of the moſt important principles of trade, and a conſiderable part of it's liberty. Whatever cramps or hurts it in theſe four points is ruinous to the ſtate, and diametrically contrary to it's intent, which is the happineſs and comfortable ſubſiſtence of the greateſt number poſſible of men.

The oeconomy of men's labour conſiſts in ſubſtituting in it's ſtead that of animals and machines, when it can be done either with leſs expence, or more ſafety to the men.

Far

Far from preventing, it is a means of encreaſing the populouſneſs of a ſtate. The miſtaken notion of it's being a hindrance to the propagation of the human ſpecies prevailed longeſt in thoſe countries whoſe trade was confined within themſelves. And, indeed, it muſt be allowed that where there is but little foreign trade, the general intent would not be anſwered, if the home-trade did not employ as many men as poſſible. But, if foreign trade, that is to ſay, navigation, the colonies, and wants of other countries, is able to employ ſtill more men than are to be found, it is neceſſary to oeconomiſe their labour that it may anſwer all thoſe ends as far as it poſſibly can. Experience ſhews, that a nation loſes it's trade when it does not carry on ſo great a one as it is able to do. It is evident that the ſtrength of a body politic depends on employing in the beſt and moſt extenſive manner whatever men are invited thither by it's political riches. A conſideration it is neceſſary never to loſe ſight of. To oeconomiſe the labour of men cannot, therefore, hurt the encreaſe of the ſpecies, when the legiſlature only directs with prudence their labour from one object to another, which is properly the buſineſs of particular laws and regulations.

THE ſmallneſs of the expences of exportation is the third ſource of cheapneſs, and, conſequently of the vent of the productions of a country.

THOSE

THOSE expences are the charges of carriage and duties outwards. The carriage is either by land, or water. Land-carriage is known to be by much the dearest. For which reason, canals to supply the want of navigable rivers, the keeping up and rendering convenient rivers that are navigable, and an absolute freedom of inland navigation, are an essential part of the administration in a trading state.

DUTIES, either inland, or on exportation, laid on the produce of a country, are of all charges those which foreigners are most unwilling to pay. The merchant looks upon them as an enhancement of the real value of a commodity, and policy considers them as an encrease of relative riches.

WISE nations either suppress those duties when commodities or manufactures of their own produce are exported, or proportion them to the foreign demand for those commodities. Above all they take care to compare the price of their goods delivered at the market where they are to be disposed of, with the price of the same kind of goods sent thither by their rivals in trade. Such a comparison is of great importance. Though the quality and prime cost of a commodity be the same in each of two manufacturing nations, yet the duties outwards ought not to be equal, if the charges of carriage be not the same too. The smallest difference influences the market.

SOME-

SOMETIMES the legiſlature inſtead of laying a duty on the exportation of ſome goods encourages it by granting a bounty. The intent of that bounty is to add to the profit of the labourer, or workman, when that profit is not otherwiſe ſufficient to ſupport a uſeful induſtry, in oppoſition to other nations. If the bounty be ſuch as leſſens the price of the commodity, the preference foreigners will give it in a few years will be ſufficient to eſtabliſh that new branch of trade, which will afterwards be able to ſupport itſelf. The effect is certain; and the practical part cannot but be beneficial to a body politic. It is like the warmth which, in a human body, one member communicates to another when in need of it.

A NATION could not be ſaid to ſupply another with as much as poſſible, if it was to trade in nothing but commodities of it's own growth. Every one knows by experience that it is natural to go for what one wants to the ſhop that is beſt ſtocked, and that choice of goods often makes cuſtomers want what they did not think of before. The caſe is the ſame in trade in general. Trading nations go to other nations for what they want, in order to ſell them again to the conſumers. This kind of trade, generally called the carrying trade, may be very properly called *œconomical.* A prudent nation will foregoe no branch of trade; and though it's articles of luxury do run high, yet, if it has plenty of inhabi-

inhabitants, and ſtore of money at a low Intereſt, it is evident that nation will be able to carry them all on ſucceſsfully. I will go farther; the moment when it's merchants find their account, will be the moſt certain epocha of it's riches.

In order not to deprive a nation of the profit to be made by foreign goods, but on the contrary to encreaſe it's relative riches, ſome ſtates have opened ports in which the importation of whatever it is advantageous to re-export, is allowed free of duty: they are called *free ports.*

In other ſtates goods are only depoſited; and, in order to facilitate the general exportation of even permitted foreign commodities, either the whole or part of the duties of entry are repaid on exportation.

The foreign trade of a nation cannot have attained it's greateſt perfection, if it's ſuperfluities are not exported, and what it wants imported in the moſt advantageous manner poſſible.

Such exportations and importations are performed either by national ſhips, or foreign, and by traders either denizens, or aliens.

There is, therefore, an active, and a paſſive commerce. It is plain that a paſſive commerce leſſens the advantages of exportation and enhances the price of importation.

It is contrary to the intent of commerce in a ſtate, by depriving the ſubject of his labour and means of ſubſiſtance; and prevents it's it's effect by lessening the relative riches of that state.

A PASSIVE trade is productive of another disadvantage: the nation that engrosses the active trade of another, keeps that other in a state of dependance: whenever their union ceases, that which has only a passive trade, loses all it's vigour. It's Agriculture, industry, and colonies, are in a state of inaction; the number of it's inhabitants decreases, until it recovers an active trade; which it is never sure of doing, and must at all events be a work of time.

THE difference that results from the exports and imports during a certain time, compared, is called the *balance of trade*. That is always paid or received in money, because the exchange of commodities, or metals, by which they are represented, is indispensable when one has no other equivalent to give for them. States balance with each other just as private men do.

ACCORDINGLY, when the balance of trade is in favour of a nation, it's capital stock of conventional riches is encreased by so much as that balance amounts to: when that balance is against a nation, it's amount is a diminution of the capital stock.

THIS balance ought to be considered as particular, and general.

THE particular balance is that of the trade between two states; it is the object of the treaties they make with each other, in order

to

to eſtabliſh, as nearly, as poſſible, an equality of commerce. Thoſe treaties ſtipulate the kinds of commodities they are allowed to ſupply each other with; the mutual convenience and advantage of importing them; and the duties ſuch goods are to pay.

If two nations had only the ſame kinds of productions to communicate to each other, there would be no other treaty between them than what humanity dictates, to uſe each other well; becauſe that of the two which had the advantage over the other, would, at laſt, engroſs it's trade both home and foreign. The trade between two ſuch nations would then be reduced to that, which a third would give them room to carry on by the re-exportation, before mentioned.

Perfect equality of trade between two nations, implies equality of value, and of the number of men neceſſarily employed by each. It is hardly poſſible for ſuch a thing to be in reality; for which reaſon, equality of value is what is uſually calculated.

Though the numbers of men employed be not reckoned, one would incline to think it ought to be conſidered, according to the reciprocal neceſſity of the exchange. If the balance is not equal, the difference of the number of men mutually employed is not to be conſidered by the gainer; becauſe it is certain that the ſum received in money will increaſe the nation's home circulation, and conſe-

consequently procure a greater number of men the means of subsisting comfortably.

If a foreign country is in absolute want of a commodity, the success of the means by which it is intended to bring it near to an equality in trade, depends on the degree of competition in that article; for if other nations having an equal quantity of the same commodity, offer better terms, that which is less advantageous will be excluded the market. If that foreign country has nothing to offer in exchange but goods of the same kind and species with those we are in actual possession of, it is proper first to compare the product and advantages that may be made by the sale of our own commodity, with the loss that may result from the importation of foreign commodities; and in the next place, by what means to prevent their interfering at home. Circumstances, which now no longer subsist in Europe, might formerly require a different policy in the case we are speaking of: when one or two nations, exclusive of others, carried on the general trade, it was not always proper for them to refuse the commodities of a third, because that would have been laying that third under the necessity of encreasing its own correspondence and navigation.

The finishing of such a treaty of commerce requires also a thorough knowledge of the trade of the two contracting nations,

of

of their mutual resources, their populousness, the price and quality of the first materials, the price of provisions and labour, their kinds of industry, reciprocal wants, particular and general balances, their finances, and the proportion of the interest of money, which being too low with one, and high with another, makes the latter lose where the former gains.

IT may happen that the balance of trade with a country is disadvantageous, and yet that trade may be useful; that is to say, it may be the cause and necessary means of another trade, which more than compensates for that loss.

THE general balance of the trade of a nation is the profit or loss resulting from the particular balances compensated with each other.

THOUGH the amount of the general exportations should be lessened, if that of the importations be likewise lessened in proportion, the state cannot be said to have lost any part of its useful trade; because it is, generally speaking, a proof that a greater number of hands are employed in its home trade.

BY the same reason, though the general exportations be less, if the importations have lessened more than in proportion, it proves an encrease of useful trade.

IT is plain that of several nations, that whose general balance is always most in its favour,

favour, muſt become the moſt powerful. It will have moſt conventional riches; and thoſe riches, by circulating at home, will maintain comfortably a greater number of inhabitants. Such is the effect of trade, when carried to perfection in a body politic: to procure thoſe advantages is the aim and object of the government: and to ſucceed therein requires very ſuperior views, and the utmoſt vigilance in watching over the ſteps, regulations and motives of rival nations; together with a thorough knowledge and exact calculation of real and relative riches compared. Circumſtances vary continually, but the principles are ever the ſame. He who conſiders them in all their lights, will know how to apply them.

THE reſtrictions under which trade is laid for political reaſons, cannot be ſaid to cramp it. Freedom of trade, ſo much talked of, and ſo little underſtood, conſiſts only in carrying on with eaſe that trade which is conſiſtent with the real general intereſt of ſociety.

WHATEVER extends beyond that is a licentiouſneſs deſtructive of trade itſelf. I ſay, the real general intereſt, becauſe what ſeems an advantage does not always prove ſo.

DECEIT and fraud cannot be too ſeverely proſcribed: formalities are requiſite to enquire into them. All exceſs of them is deſtructive of liberty, and to neglect them entirely, introduces licentiouſneſs. Thoſe formalities

lities ought, therefore, not to be quite laid aside; but care should be taken to keep them within due bounds, and to provide for their being properly observed.

THERE is a necessity of domestic rivalship in commerce: it is the soul of freedom properly understood.

THAT is one of the nicest points in government: its principles will ever be a part of the plan by which a state obtains a general balance more advantageous than its neighbours.

WE have purposed examining trade as the occupation of a citizen. We will consider it in that light in relation to the body politic.

TRADE being the soul of that body, the profession of a trader is commendable, as is every profession useful to society. Every member of society ought to be distinguished in proportion to the services he renders; and trade cannot be encouraged in a country where such distinctions are not made.

A MAN may be personally concerned in trade three ways.

FIRST, by purchasing the productions of the land, and of the industry of its inhabitants, to sell them again in small quantities to his fellow-citizens. Dealers that way are called *retailers*.

THIS business, more convenient than necessary to society, promotes circulation at home.

SECONDLY, the induſtry of the citizen may be exerted in guiding and directing the labour of a number of other citizens, to prepare and form the firſt materials. Thoſe who apply to that branch are called *manufacturers*.

THIS kind of induſtry is very neceſſary, becauſe it increaſes the real and relative riches of a ſtate.

THE third kind of trade, in which a citizen may be engaged, is, the exportation of the productions of his country, to be exchanged abroad for other neceſſary productions, or for money. That trade, whether it be carried on by ſea or land, in Europe or to the extremities of the world, is diſtinguiſhed by the name of *wholeſale trade*, and the perſon that carries it on is called a *merchant*.

THIS profeſſion is very neceſſary, for it is the ſoul of navigation, and increaſes the relative riches of the ſtate.

THE ſtricteſt probity is a duty incumbent on, and gives life to theſe three ways of trading: their object is the ſame, gain: their effect different, as it contributes more or leſs to the general effect of trade in a body politic.

THIS effect is what the ſtate ought to diſtinguiſh them by, and eſteem each individual in proportion as he co-operates more or leſs.

Not that the immediate deſign of the legiſlator is to have merchants immenſely rich: he values them becauſe they have contributed greatly to the ſucceſs of his views; but it would be ſtill more uſeful, in caſe where trade is limited, to have many rich, rather than a few very rich. Twenty merchants with ten thouſand pounds each, do more buſineſs, and have among them greater amount of credit, than five with forty thouſand pounds a-piece. Beſides, fortunes divided among many are a much greater help to the circulation and real riches of a country. A great diſproportion of fortunes in trade is not, however, a burden to the ſtate, becauſe they generally circulate wholly to the advantage of uſeful arts; it were even to be wiſhed they were to remain in trade, becauſe they ſettle numbers of factors or agents abroad; thoſe factors increaſe the branches of trade of their nation, and likewiſe procure it the advantages they make in the trade of which the country where they reſide is ſuſceptible. Such fortunes would not be taken out of trade, if the condition of a merchant was as much reſpected as it ought to be. As to the great undertakings in trade for a government, its own credit is ſufficient; if the ſecurity be good, and a profit can be made, a ſufficient number of ſolid undertakers will ſoon be found.

To know how to trade, or how to direct trade, are two very different things. To direct it properly, requires a knowledge of how it ought to be done; a man may gain by trade, without knowing how it ought to be directed.. The merchant's science is in the detail of his particular business: the political science consists in the use that may be made of all those details. It is therefore necessary to know them; but that knowledge cannot be gathered but from merchants. One cannot converse with them too much in order to learn; but in deliberating, their advices are to be received with caution. We have already distinguished between the merchant's gains and the gains of the state;— and it is plain that the merchant, taken up with his own detail, seldom has an eye to what is general, unless he happens to have acquired that turn by travel, or an extensive experience on which he has meditated and reflected: such as are so qualified in that case may decide safely. The more there are of them, the more the profession of a merchant will be respected by the state, and deserves to be so. I may likewise add, that the several branches of general trade will increase thereby.

To send from one foreign country to another the goods that are wanted there, although those goods be prohibited by the society of which one is a member, cannot be deemed an act contrary to the love we ought

to

to have for our country. It is plain that ſince thoſe goods were neceſſary to gain what would have been gained by the country that produced them, had that country ſold them herſelf, is adding to the relative riches of one's own country.

DIS-

DISSERTATION XXXIII.

Of arts, and manufactories.

MANUFACTURE, or ingenious labour, is the art of working up the productions of nature. Desire of convenience and of a more comfortable being, gave birth to this art, and preserves, and promotes it: the productions of nature are the matter on which it is exercised: the elements, the animal creation, and, in short, all that exists, are the means by which it is exercised. We will, at present, consider ingenious labour only in regard to the effects it has in the body politic: we will afterwards endeavour to shew what are the principles, which most certainly conduce towards a society's enjoying the benefits of those effects.

OUR physical wants are so few that, strictly speaking, corn, (or even roots) fruit, water, milk, and the flesh and skins of beasts, are sufficient for the calls of nature. If, therefore, men could be content with what is absolutely necessary, they would desire no other productions from the earth, except it be what little

little iron is neceſſary to enable them to till it. Nor do I ſay, they would be leſs happy if their deſires extended no farther.

If we ſuppoſe for a moment all the inhabitants of the earth in that firſt ſtate of ſimplicity; and that ſome one nation ſhould ſet about to work up and fabricate the productions of the earth; the conſequence would be, 1ſt, that that nation would raiſe a greater quantity of productions on it's lands.

2dly, That the culture of thoſe productions would required a greater number of hands.

3dly, That the art of forming or fabricating thoſe natural productions, would be to the inhabitants of that nation, an encreaſe of occupations, or of means of ſubſiſting comfortably.

4thly, That when ever other nations ſhould become acquainted with the productions of that new art, the natural deſire of living comfortably would give birth to new deſires.

5thly, Thoſe deſires could not be ſatisfied, but by an exchange of commodities. Now, as art gives an additional value to the productions of nature, it follows, that the induſtrious nation would receive in exchange more than it would give. Such exchanges of commodities becoming troubleſome, and ſcarce metals being ſubſtituted as their common meaſure and equivalent, the ſame proportion would ſtill take place in favour of the induſtrious.

6thly,

6thly, The nation, in which that induſtry, or ingenious labour, is promoted, abounding moſt in natural commodities, or money, the meaſure and repreſentation of them, ſeveral members of other ſocieties would flock thither to have a ſhare in the conveniencies reſulting from ſuch labour.

7thly, The number of inhabitants encreaſing continually in that induſtrious ſociety, it would become ſtronger and more powerful than others.

THOUGH no civilized nation is now a ſtranger to ingenuity: it is not the leſs evident, that the real and relative effects of the foregoing hypotheſis muſt take place, in proportion to the greater or leſs progreſs of that ingenuity.

OF two nations the ſuperior progreſs of the one in ingenious labour, depends on it's ſuperior degree of conſumption, either home, or foreign.

THE principles of both are in ſome reſpects the ſame; in other reſpects each has it's diſtinct, but never contradictory principles. We will begin with the latter.

TWO things evidently concur to conſtitute a ſuperiority of home-conſumption between two ſocieties. To attain that ſuperiority it is neceſſary, 1ſt, that a ſociety ſhould have in proportion to it's populouſneſs and the extent of it's lands, a greater number of men able to conſume the productions of art, than another has: 2dly, that it conſume leſs than the

the other does of the produce of foreign ingenuity.

The first condition demonstrates, that if in a nation a multitude of men should require nothing beyond the absolute wants of nature, ingenious labour would fall short of it's perfection, in proportion to the number of those men. Now since, as we have seen, productions of the earth are the basis of ingenious labour, and as the use of those productions is multiplied by that labour, we may justly infer, that in such a nation agriculture would likewise fall equally short of perfection.

From the second condition it follows, that those manufactures, which serve for what is most generally wanted, are the most useful, and the first that ought to be established. The use of a thing is more common in proportion to the greater necessity for it, either real, customary, or imaginary, for the latter is looked upon as indispensably necessary by the generality of mankind. Even though the value of commodities should be but small the repeated consumption would make the aggregate value very great; and in the mean time a great number of hands will have been employed, and a great quantity of the natural productions of the country used; both which objects are the most essential a state can have in view. We may likewise add, that if a nation was to abandon it's more common arts, and apply to others of less general use, the riches of its trade would dwindle away

away imperceptibly ; juſt as that man would ſoon want, who ſhould turn into parterres, or groves, part of that field on the produce of which he ſubſiſts. To prevent that evil, the legiſlator reſtores a juſt equilibrium by various means. The moſt uſual is to raiſe the price of thoſe ſuperfluities, but, at the ſame time without hurting the nation's foreign trade; which it muſt be owned is a very nice and delicate point. The ſureſt way of all is to attack the ſource of the evil: for no remedy can be efficacious, which does not reach the cauſe.

In order to conſume as little as poſſible at home of the produce of foreign labour, every ſtate has enhanced the price of ſuch articles by duties of entry, or has abſolutely prohibited them.

A right of ſo doing cannot be diſputed in any free ſociety, unleſs the treaties of commerce, by which that ſociety has entered into engagements with other nations, ſtipulate the contrary.

But ſuch duties and prohibitions, though, lawful and often neceſſary, are not always what moſt ſuits the real intereſt of a ſtate. For, if it be natural for a nation to make as little uſe as poſſible of foreign manufactures, it is certain, that foreigners have a reciprocal right to lay the manufactures of that nation, under equal reſtrictions. Before ſuch a thing be put in practice, it is, therefore, proper to examine carefully, whether the amount of the importations intended to be forbid, ex-

ceeds

ceeds that of the exportations a nation ſhould, in conſequence thereof, be deprived of. National enmities have ſometimes carried thoſe duties and prohibitions to too great a height, when all either party has got by it has been to cramp it's trade, or make room for a third to ſhare it's profit.

It is undoubtedly fit to ſettle duties on both ſides, in order to encourage the ſubject's labour; but it might, perhaps, be very poſſible, in general, to fix reaſonable bounds to thoſe duties. A manufacture, even in it's infancy, ſeems not to have any reaſon to fear foreign competition, when the duties of entry are at 15 per cent; for the charges of carriage, commiſſion, and others, will come to four or five per cent. more. If 18 or 20 per cent, beſides the foreign manufacturer's profit, do not content the home manufacturer; one may readily conclude, either that ſuch home manufacturer wants to gain too much, or, that his undertaking is badly managed; or, in ſhort, that there are ſome obſtacles in the way at home, which muſt be removed before ſucceſs can be expected.

In all ſtates very profitable branches of trade have been loſt, or miſſed being eſtabliſhed, for the ſake of things, which never were compaſſed, or which might have equally well been brought about by more gentle methods. Such problems are always very intricate; but, with the help of good principles, and a competent knowledge of the particular details relative to the object proposed, the solution of them is far from being impossible.

It is, however, a generally received maxim, that each nation ought to endeavour as much as possible to do without the produce of the labour or ingenuity of others. The principle is very just, if this essential clause be added to it, *without forcing those other nations to do without one's own.* In that the skill consists; there are proper ways of doing it, of which we shall speak hereafter.

One only thing can secure to a nation a superiority over another in the foreign consumption of it's manufactures: that is, *the art of seducing, or pleasing to a higher degree the consumer of every kind.*

This principle is the same with that between one workman and another in matters relating to home-consumption; it becomes that of the state, with regard to foreign consumption. For, in this case the legislator is divested of his character, and becomes merchant. He may govern and direct his manufacturers as he pleases, and dictate to them what law he thinks proper: but, if he intends to sell his goods abroad, his counsels, directions, and laws must be agreeable to the taste and caprice of the independent consumer.

That taste changes with the climate, customs, and richness of the countries, where the goods are sold: each must, therefore, be

con-

conſulted. From theſe truths, ſo clear in themſelves, ſeveral important conſequences enſue.

1ſt, The ſame ſtuff ought to contain more or leſs matter, according to the climate of the country to which it is ſent, the oeconomy of the inhabitants of that country, and the particular uſe it is deſigned for. An intelligent buyer generally explains thoſe points in the orders he gives; and a judicious ſeller will not execute thoſe orders, till he knows perfectly well how to do it, for fear the goods ſhould remain for his account, or that his correſpondent ſhould apply to him no more.

2dly, It is not always adding to the perfection of a manufacture to ſell it's productions dearer, even though they be finer, or more laſting; becauſe it is not certain that thoſe who took them at one price, are either able, or willing to purchaſe them at a higher price.

3dly, There are in every country people as well of different abilities as of claſſes: to tempt and pleaſe them all, it is proper to offer them aſſortments of every kind proportioned to their different abilities in point of purchaſe. Beſides that general advantage, aſſortments of each particular kind of goods have likewiſe another in the operation of trade. The merchants, in the country where the goods are conſumed, chuſe always to buy what beſt ſuits the taſte of that country, and yields them the moſt profit. Aſſortments of different

different prices of the ſame ſtuff, are a very proper means of helping them to a reaſonable gain; and that motive is alone ſufficient to determine than to promote the conſumption of it.

4thly. A STUFF of the moſt inferior quality may be called perfect in its kind, as well as that of the moſt ſuperior quality, if both are equally worth their prices.

5thly. A wide difference ought to be made between the perfection of workmanſhip or labour; and the general perfection of the manufactures of a ſtate. The latter, without doubt, conſiſts in obtaining the preference of every claſs of conſumers.

A STATE attains a general perfection of its manufactures by two means. The greateſt variety poſſible in its kinds of works; and a great number of factories in foreign countries.

IT plainly reſults from the principles before laid down, that choice of various kinds of goods multiplies the deſires of other nations. Of the new inventions, which the active genius of workmen will produce, ſome will be of ſhort duration; that is, their buſineſs. Materials will ſtill have been uſed, men employed, and wages paid. The legiſlator is the guardian of ſociety in general; and if he ſometimes enters into particular concerns, it never can be attended with benefit, but ſo far as he protects or favours in

par-

particular ſuch eſtabliſhments as to him ſeem moſt conducive to the general intereſt.

FACTORIES in foreign countries are the ſureſt way of increaſing our own ſales by a natural chain of conſequences, and a more exact knowledge of the ſeveral taſtes of the conſumers. Settlements of this kind are of ſuch important ſervice to the trade of a nation, that they cannot be too much encouraged, nor too numerous.

BESIDES the particular riches ariſing from the taſte of conſumers in each foreign country, there are likewiſe ſeveral rules, calculated equally to facilitate the conſumption of goods in all countries; thoſe rules are likewiſe applicable to home conſumption.

WHAT ſtrikes the buyer's eye being always moſt apt to tempt him, it is neceſſary to ſtudy particularly how to make goods look well.

THE faith of a nation is moſt certainly concerned, in not ſuffering the buyers to be deceived by what his eye cannot diſcover; ſecurity and honour, in that reſpect, is a great help to conſumption. For which reaſon too great care cannot be taken to ſee that the ſtamps, or other marks affixed to goods, indicate no more than what is in reality to be found. As to viſible defects, they can never be called deceit: the buyer ought to be a judge, and the legiſlator would have too much to do, if obliged to lead every man by the hand from ſhop to ſhop. Theſe Platonic ideas,

ideas, in the general police of nations kept the arts a long time in a ſtate of thraldom.

CHEAPNESS is always a temptation to the buyer, and is conſequently one of the great advantages manufactures ought to have.

THE words *cheap* or *dear*, when applied to a commodity, relate to its kind, quality, and goodneſs of fabric; they likewiſe often ſignify the great or leſs value of a thing, abſtracted from all compariſon. To remove all doubt, we underſtand in general, in this work, by thoſe words, the higher or lower price of a commodity, compared with another of the ſame kind, quality, and perfection of workmanſhip. We muſt, however, add, that if it be impoſſible to afford a commodity equally well wrought, as ſubſtantial, or as fine as that of others, at a lower price than they do, the ſureſt way is to let the quality be rather inferior, in order to bring it to a lower price: the reaſon is plain. 1ſt. The generality of buyers are influenced and determined by the look of a thing, and its cheapneſs. 2dly. The purchaſe of a fine, ſolid, and well-finiſhed thing is, as I may ſay, a piece of oeconomy in rich people: conſequently few (in compariſon to the multitude of conſumers) are able to afford it. The intereſt of a ſociety is plainly to ſell to the greateſt number poſſible: a greater quantity of materials is uſed; more men are employed in working them up, in their carriage, and in their navigation.

tion. 3dly. The luxury of buyers in general is excited by lowneſs of price. The mechanic's wife will not buy a damaſk of fifteen ſhillings a yard; but will have one of eight or nine: ſhe does not trouble herſelf much about the quality of the ſilk; but is ſatisfied with making as fine a ſhew as a perſon of higher rank or fortune.

Many things contribute to the cheapneſs of goods; plenty of the firſt materials, rivalſhip of workmen, cheapneſs of proviſions and labour, and eaſy charges of carriage.

All that we obſerved to be conducive to the progreſs of agriculture, is productive of plenty of firſt materials. From their plenty enſues their cheapneſs; from their cheapneſs the progreſs of manufactures; and by that means the greateſt conſumption of the productions of the land.

The mutual dependance of all the branches of occupation among men on each other, and the active ſpirit and motion given them all by the ſame principles, is well worthy being attended to. It is a demonſtrable proof of the excellence of thoſe principles, and of the cloſeneſs of the ties and connections by which the welfare of each claſs of people is cemented with that of every other claſs.

From this obſervation it may be inferred, that it is not in reality a way to favour manufactures to prohibit the exportation of firſt materials, unleſs thoſe materials be the only ones of the kind, and the culture of them

elſe-

elſewhere is not attended with thoſe conditions which render the conſumption of them neceſſary.

FROM what has been ſaid in the preceding part, it is plain that agriculture cannot flouriſh, when not conſidered as an object of trade. If that maxim be true with regard to corn, it muſt conſequently be ſo in other productions of nature: and if firſt materials are the food of manufactures, as corn is that of men, it muſt be proper to employ the ſame methods to proportion the means of ſubſiſtance of the grower of thoſe materials, with the ſubſiſtance of the manufacturer.

IF, from a calculation of the prices of thoſe firſt materials on an avarage for ſeveral years, a certain price was fixed, under which the exportation ſhould be permitted, our manufacturers would always be ſupplied at a cheap rate; cheaper at leaſt than ſtrangers would, who are obliged to pay carriage, freight, commiſſion, and other charges. Some ſmall duty might, if thought proper, be laid on the exportation; provided always that the price of thoſe materials be ſuch, as that foreigners will find their account in preferring ours, and thereby enrich our huſbandmen. All that need be done in ſuch a caſe, would be to calculate the average price of the ſame materials in ſuch other countries as are rivals in thoſe branches, together with the charges there, and other conſiderations of trade, in order to compare them with the

the ſame circumſtances at home. The product of that compariſon will be the true medium by which it will be proper to regulate the duty on exportation, or ſuppreſs it. Profit is what animates culture, and every claſs of occupations among men; if any one of thoſe occupations be deprived of that hope, it muſt periſh. The loſs of it would be ſooner or later felt by every other; for the effect is ſure: and when agriculture is the part that ſuffers, or that gains the leaſt, it almoſt inſtantly affects all the reſt at once. Accordingly, if the medium prices, I am ſpeaking of, were fixed with regard to the exportation of firſt materials, it would be indiſpenſably neceſſary to raiſe them in proportion to the increaſe of the expences of cultivation, or as the gains of other profeſſions grow greater by the increaſe of conventional riches. If the prohibitions we are ſpeaking of have ſometimes ſucceeded, yet no conſequence ought to be drawn from thence againſt the principle here laid down, unleſs the kinds and circumſtances be particularly diſtinguiſhed; and, on a due examination of them, they will be found to coincide with what is advanced.

All countries do not produce all things; conſequently there are materials which ſome manufactures require being ſupplied with from abroad.

If the entry of them is attended with higher duties in one country than in another, it it is plain that, supposing all other things equal, what is made of those materials must be so much dearer in the former country, as the duties amount to more than in the latter: for which reason, wise trading states allow the importation of first materials, free of duty.

It is, however, proper to lay duties on the importation of foreign first materials in two cases. 1st. When we have reason to expect a sufficient quantity of them of one's own growth, and that nothing is wanting but to help the price a little to promote the cultivation of them: the duty ought then to be proportioned to the degree of want the manufactures are in, and to the encouragement wanting to assist the cultivation of those materials.

2dly. When a first material of any kind is imported, after having undergone some kind of dressing or preparation abroad, which might as well have been done by the nation that buys it, it is not just for it to be imported subject to no greater duty than if not wrought at all.

These remarks are a necessary consequence of the foregoing principles: manufactures ought to give the lands of a state to the highest value possible, and its men the greatest plenty of work possible.

Some nations have laid pretty high duties on the re-exportation of such foreign first materials; but that seems in reality to

be

be depriving manufactures of a more useful rivalſhip in favour of one leſs uſeful, which is thereby avoided. It is offering up an apparent ſacrifice to them, at the expence of navigation, and of which they in reality bear the loſs.

WHEN a nation is ſo happy as to procure foreign materials ſo much cheaper than others can, that rival nations find their account in purchaſing them from her, it is evident that not only her national manufactories will be well ſupplied, but likewiſe that the greater plenty of the commodity muſt make it bear a leſs price. For in that caſe, the rivalſhip of the buyers is ſeldom ſo great as that of the ſellers, who are always animated more and more by the profits they make. We have already obſerved, that what a nation fabricates with foreign firſt materials, muſt, ſuppoſing all other things equal, be dearer than if fabricated by that nation from whom thoſe materials were purchaſed. If that nation who procures ſuch firſt materials cheap enough to ſell them back to others, chances to meet with difficulties in that trade, it is clear that her ſhips will no longer bring any more than juſt what is neceſſary for conſumption. The rivalſhip in thoſe materials decreaſing, the price of them muſt increaſe; fewer ſhips will be employed, freight will conſequently be dearer, and the commodity muſt pay it. Nor is that the only diſadvantage: it may happen that the meaſure of ex-

changes

changes being no longer the ſame, the owners of the firſt materials will conſume leſs wrought goods than they did before, when their own ſales were more conſiderable.

TRADERS of other nations will likewiſe be forced to ſend their own ſhips to purchaſe thoſe materials at the firſt hand, and endeavour to introduce their own manufactures in exchange. The freight being then divided between what is imported and what is exported, they will be able both to buy and ſell cheaper.

THUS one ſingle ſtep would be the ruin of a uſeful branch of trade and navigation; manufactures would feel the diſadvantages of an increaſe of price in the firſt materials, and of a new rivalſhip in the ſale of their productions. Domeſtic rivalſhip among workmen is abſolutely neceſſary to make manufactures cheap and elegant. That rivalſhip will be eſtabliſhed firſt by the progreſs of the home conſumption of a commodity; next, by the rivalſhip or plenty of the firſt materials of that commodity; and laſtly, by the quantity of foreign conſumptions. So, on the other hand, it may be ſaid, that all theſe things will afterwards increaſe by the competition or rivalſhip of workmen.

BUT that rivalſhip of workmen will not take place, if their condition be not comfortable and happy, in proportion to the pains they take. To that end induſtry muſt be

ſafe,

ſafe, the whole of what it produces muſt belong to him that is poſſeſſed of it; that part excepted, which he ſhall of his own accord lay out for his neceſſary ſubſiſtence and convenience. Juſt as a fortune poſſeſſed by a man without the privity of others, ceaſes to be a fortune in their eye, ſo, the ſuperfluous expences of artiſans, and workmen, will always be in proportion to the eaſe and ſafety they enjoy. On the other hand, the price of the neceſſaries of life, is leſs conſidered by workmen, as a diminution of the progreſs of their induſtry, than as an indiſpenſable reaſon, why they ſhould exert that induſtry. And, accordingly, in thoſe two reſpects, a well judged regulation of the finances makes a country ample amends, by the ſmallneſs of what is demanded, and the care that is taken not to overburden the ſubject.

A MAN cannot be ſaid to enjoy a certain, nor a happy ſtate, if the profeſſion he embraces be cramped, or the profits attending it limited, when there is nothing in them contrary to ſtrict juſtice. As a farmer would be diſcouraged, if he was forced to ſow a field with hemp, which would produce him more if planted with hops.

RIVALSHIP of workmen, or mechanics, would be badly eſtabliſhed, if it coſt much money for liberty to apply to any kind of ingenious labour; becauſe moſt of thoſe, who do apply to working trades are poor. Conſequently, the eaſier workmen are introduced into a comfortable buſineſs of livelihood, the more they will encreaſe.

FROM the ſame conſideration of poverty we may conclude, that few men would betake themſelves to laborious trades, if they could not be bound apprentices, till paſt their youth. Parents who are poor, would be afraid of having children to bring up and keep ſo long: if any came, thoſe children, oppreſſed by want, would chuſe eaſier ways of ſubſiſting. Every uſeleſs way of living is unfortunately of that kind, and the number of them is terrible. Perhaps too, the children ſo abandoned might take to begging. I do not mention the reſource of huſbandry, becauſe though that be often left for other kinds of occupations, yet thoſe occupations are never left by any to turn plowman: a fatal experience, and well worthy the moſt ſerious attention!

IN ſhort, if the hands we are ſpeaking of were not loſt to uſeful labour, they muſt at leaſt have loſt a moſt valuable time: for it muſt be in their tender years, that men imbibe a real inclination to work, which afterwards ſtands them in lieu of pleaſure the reſt of their lives.

TO tolerate thoſe private regulations, by which the number of apprentices each maſter of a trade may take is limited, is another bar to the emulation, or rivalſhip of workmen.

men. It would, on the contrary, be of great ſervice, to oblige every maſter to have a certain fixed number of apprentices, within a limited number of years; and on failure to forfeit a ſum to be diſtributed among ſuch as ſhould have exceeded the number appointed by law. But to ſuppreſs apprenticeſhips, as burdenſome, would be the greateſt fault to the principle of rivalſhip: they are ſtill farther uſeful for two reaſons.

Firſt, the buſineſs of the mechanics is, in general, leſs laborious than that of the huſbandman; it is, therefore, proper, in order to put them on a level, that it ſhould be moſt eaſy to ſubſiſt by tilling the earth.

Secondly, It is of moment to the ſtate to have it's mechanics excel. Not that the legiſlator is obliged to enter into the particular details of each family, but, becauſe the reputation of a nation's artiſts and mechanics is neceſſary towards extending her trade; for, if her workmen are not ingenious and ſkilful, they will not be able to hit the taſte of foreign purchaſers; to tempt them with new inventions, or imitate thoſe of other nations; nor, in ſhort, to ſatisfy the various humours and caprices of conſumers. The workman, who does not fall in with this taſte, will not be able to ſell his goods; without doubt that is a puniſhment to him: but, if he be not intelligent enough to alter his method, and follow the advice that is given him, a whole family is deprived of work: the ſtate

ſhares

ſhares that puniſhment with him. If the workman be maſter of his buſineſs, every neglect of labour in him will be puniſhed, either by loſs of trade, or diminution of his profits; but the community will be no great ſufferer thereby, becauſe he will amend his faults.

APPRENTICESHIPS are, therefore, not ſo burdenſome as they are uſeful and neceſſary: the fault would be in making them too long, and in the manner of ſerving them. Though a ſeven years apprenticeſhip, as is cuſtomary with us in England, may be thought hard, yet it is, perhaps, not too long to learn a trade, or buſineſs in the leaſt complicated. If it be to the woollen branch, for example, that a man would apply; he ought, in the firſt place, to make himſelf a thorough judge of the qualities, properties, and effects of wool: to that end, a great deal muſt paſs through his hands, and he muſt likewiſe be aſſiſted by his maſters inſtructions. He muſt begin with cleanſing and beating the wool; after which he muſt learn how to comb or card it. Thoſe inſtructions will require ſome time, and he will thereby gain a more perfect knowledge of the qualities and properties of that material. From thence he muſt proceed to a knowledge of ſpinning, the various kinds of which will require freſh application. The knowledge of that is the true principle of fabricating well, and of the profit attending it. During this time the apprentice will have become acquainted with the ſeveral tools and inſtru-

inſtruments uſed in preparing the materials employed, the looms, and various parts of which they are compoſed; he will underſtand the working of them, their perfection, or defects. Without theſe preliminary requiſites, which are more or leſs rapid, in proportion to their difficulty and the learner's parts, a workman can never know how to mount his loom to the beſt advantage, make the moſt of his materials, or direct how to prepare them; much leſs will he be able to invent, or ſtrike out new roads for the improvement of his workmanſhip.

THE quantity of what is conſumed is ſo much greater in Holland, than the quantity of what the land produces, that agriculture is one of the moſt lucrative profeſſions there. For which reaſon the equilibrium naturally ſubſiſting in that republic between the cultivators of land, and the manufacturers, required no precautions to be taken on that head. The Dutch had no reaſon to invite men to embrace one profeſſion more than another.

MANUFACTURES were not invited into Holland nor did they ſpring up there, but fled there for ſhelter from every country, where workmen have been moleſted in their liberties, fortunes, or religion. Thoſe workmen could not be ſubjected to ſerve an apprenticeſhip to a trade, or art, which they brought with them, no more than the French could require it from an Engliſh workman, who

who carried over to them the art of calendring, or watering ſilks.

THE manufacturers, who were received in Holland, naturally inſtructed, as apprentices, their children, relations, friends, and fugitive countrymen: as their trade encreaſed, they were probably obliged to inſtruct and bring up others, who have all continued to work as they were taught, or have improved their art. It was of leſs importance to the ſtate to have the moſt famous and moſt excellent workmen, than to acquire new men, who brought into it's trade values, which before were in the trade of other nations: ſuch is ſtill and ever will be the policy and intereſt of Holland.

THE Dutch have, indeed, given a great proof of their wiſdom in not ſuffering any monopolies to be eſtabliſhed among them; I mean, in not allowing thoſe regulations of workmen, whereby the number of hands to be employed in a profeſſion, and even the quantity of work, is limited. But a maſterſhip, which cannot be refuſed any man capable of working, is attended with none of the inconveniencies of monopolies: and it may be of ſome moment to the public welfare, to know thoſe who have embraced each kind of profeſſion.

IT is plain that the ſo eſſential emulation amongſt workmen is incompatible with the excluſive privileges of which we ſhall ſpeak preſently. It is not leſs ſo with the immunities

nities granted to ſome towns and cities preferable to others. If it be once admitted that it is of advantage to a ſtate to have manufactories: it follows, that it muſt be ſo to multiply them in as many places as poſſible, in order to eſtabliſh a natural and indiſpenſable equality between all the children of the ſame father. The ſtate is always a gainer by multiplying emulation and rivalſhips, amongſt it's artiſans of every rank, becauſe it's foreign ſales are thereby encreaſed, as well as the ſubject's abilities to ſubſiſt comfortably.

THE emulation of capitals in trade, the natural effect of public credit, and the lowneſs of the intereſt of money, are two of the ſureſt ways to procure emulation amongſt workmen; but both thoſe objects deſerve to be conſidered ſeparately.

CHEAPNESS of workmanſhip is as much the effect of the emulation amongſt workmen, as of the lowneſs of the price of commodities of the firſt or moſt abſolute neceſſity towards ſubſiſtance: for ſuch emulation leſſens the profits, or improves the work, in order to preſerve the profit it does yield. It is, however, evident that ſuch lowneſs of price contributes greatly to it. In regard to the laying of taxes upon native commodities, if this policy ſhould be always judged requiſite, there are two general rules that ſeem neceſſary to be obſerved. The firſt is, to continue raiſing the duty in proportion as the commodity becomes leſs abſolutely neceſſary: the

the ſecond, to proportion, in every place the value of the duty on commodities of the firſt or moſt abſolute neceſſity, with the loweſt price of hire, or wages; for, by that means by only reckoning the number of day's work, the workman's clear profit is ſeen at once.

In order to enjoy the benefits of cheap living, manufactures ſtill ſtand farther in need of the rivalſhip of cultivators of land, and of cultivated lands: whilſt, on the other hand, both thoſe rivalſhips will be promoted by that of workmen grown rich. But a wide difference muſt be made between a commodity's being cheap, and its bearing no price at all; for, in the laſt caſe, the cultivation of it would be neglected, and manufactures conſequently hurt.

From the neceſſity of keeping the price of ſubſiſtance at a moderate rate, it may be inferred, that manufactories are never eſtabliſhed to advantage in capital cities, or great towns, unleſs they are inhabited by manufacturers only. Beſides its being impoſſible for things not to be dear in places where extraordinary quantities of them are conſumed, it is farther to be obſerved, that example never fails to introduce ſuperfluous wants, which ſoon become neceſſaries in the opinion of men; example too introduces diſſipation, and neglect of work, much more dangerous than expenſive living. If the manufactories thrive, notwithſtanding theſe inconveniencies,

niencies, yet a real disadvantage still results to the state: higher wages tempt workmen from places where they earned less: industry is absorbed by a few towns, instead of promoting a circulation in every part of the state: in short wages of all kinds, even in the country, rise; and if the natural equilibrium be properly maintained, the value of all commodities must rise too.

ANOTHER way to procure cheapness of labour is to encourage and reward all inventions tending to abridge or ease the labour of men. The skill and rivalship of artists naturally lead to it; and that is the utmost period of perfection of the manufactories of a state.

SUCH discoveries are not, as may be thought at first sight, contrary to the object and first intent of manufactories, which is to employ the greatest number of men possible. They will, on the contrary, be found, with very little reflection, to tend to that end, by multiplying works, and increasing the produce of the balance, which never ceases to increase home consumptions.

BEFORE principles are applied, it is proper to distinguish circumstances. A nation destitute of all foreign trade would be secured by a perpetual state of prohibition, and would find it advantageous to multiply all opportunities, even of superfluous labour, in order to preserve the greatest number of men possible. Accordingly it has been observed, that the prejudice against the means of abridging

ing labour ſubſiſted longeſt in thoſe countries, where trade is moſt recent, and in the minds of thoſe whoſe knowledge of that ſubject is leaſt clear.

But in a nation where men are wanting for ſeveral kinds of labour (and that muſt always happen where there is great variety of labour); where it appears plainly by the ſales rival nations make, that ſomewhat may ſtill be added to one's own, either by ruining their manufactures of the ſame kind by *underſelling them*, or by ſubſtituting the productions of our own labour in the room of other kinds poſſeſſed by them, but which we have not ourſelves: ſuch a nation need never fear having too many hands, if her police be good.

It is true, that changes of this kind, if conſiderable, require being managed with due circumſpection and prudence. The workman will certainly be alarmed, if told of them, becauſe it is not his buſineſs to calculate: it will even be impoſſible not to excuſe his fears proceeding from his ignorance and perſonal feeling. The blame and puniſhment ought, in ſuch a caſe, to fall on thoſe who foment thoſe fears out of ſordid views of intereſt: for it is proper always to remember, that rivalſhip, ſo favourable to the trade of a ſtate, leſſens the trader's profits.

But it is indifferent to the ſtate, whether a manufactory be in one town, or fifty miles

off

off in a village, which will become a town in its turn. Experiments are there made quietly, by a ſmall number of choſen workmen, and their example by degrees invites others thither. It is proper to obſerve, that theſe kinds of changes are always ſuppoſed to facilitate the art; otherwiſe there would not be ſuch clamour againſt them as there generally is. What is practiſed there may become general, without the leaſt prejudice to the order of things. A prudent police, likewiſe, takes care to have work ready, or at leaſt to have in the mean time a ſubſiſtance to offer ſuch as may chance to want it. We ſay ſuch as may chance to want it, becauſe that want can never proceed from any thing but a falſe terror or obſtinacy, when matters are properly prepared before hand for ſuch a change, and it is brought about by degrees.

We do not ſee any objection that can be made to the oeconomiſing of time, or facilitating the work of manufactories, which may not be equally well made to all inventions of new faſhions, or of new ſtuffs, by which the old are forgot. And yet ſuch changes do happen every day without the leaſt prejudice to ſociety; and I believe no man will ſay it is the intereſt of a nation to prohibit new manufactories, in order to favour the workmen employed in the old.

In ſhort, the prejudice we are ſpeaking of is incompatible with the preſervation of the

foreign

foreign trade of a ſtate; for the ſteps a ſtate takes muſt be guided by thoſe *which foreigners take*. Even ſuppoſing the exportation of manufactured goods not to be increaſed thereby, the home conſumption will at leaſt be more conſiderable.

If we could object againſt any of the machines made uſe of in fabricating, it would be thoſe that are uſed in the making of rich ſtuffs. I might aſk whether it be poſſible for them to equal with their hard motion (for if not hard it would not long be even) the ſuppleneſs, ſoftneſs, and pleaſing gloſs given by the hand of a ſkilful and careful workman? Would not thoſe machines be fitter for thread and woollen than for ſilk?

We muſt add one word more to clear this ſubject of all doubt. Care muſt be taken not to judge of the machines made uſe of in manufacturing, as one would of ſuch as might be invented to abridge the tillage of the earth.

Manufactories are at moſt but a precarious and accidental income to a ſtate: *the utmoſt induſtry, vigilance and care, are requiſite to keep them from foreigners.* When ſo rich a treaſure once paſſes into their hands, the men therein employed, and thereby maintained, ſoon follow. The legiſlator cannot, therefore, act more wiſely than to increaſe the number of home wants, or the quantity conſumed by the ſubject, in order to preſerve, at all events, the greateſt number poſſible of manufacturers. The home circulation

tion can never be better ſecured than by the increaſe of that claſs of men, who are the fund of the populouſneſs of a ſtate; I mean *the cultivators of its lands.* Every machine tending to diminiſh their employment would really be deſtructive of the ſtrength of ſociety, the maſs of men, and home conſumption.

WE have before obſerved concerning the quantity of men, which the effectual culture of the earth furniſhes every other kind of occupation with; it will be eaſily perceived, that the uſe of mechanics in manufactories tends to preſerve populouſneſs; and that there are, between theſe two objects, differences eſſential to their nature.

BUT to come to the fourth cauſe of cheapneſs of workmanſhip.

THE charges attending the carriage of a commodity are ſo much added to its intrinſic nature: conſequently the lowneſs of thoſe charges is of very great importance, with regard to the cheapneſs of manufactures, relatively to other nations, rivals in the ſame branches. The ſtate may provide for that, partly by laying no duties at all on the exportation of them; by the greateſt poſſible competition or rivalſhip of navigators; by keeping up properly or improving the roads and navigable rivers; and, in ſhort, *by all the encouragements that can be given to agriculture*, becauſe plenty of forage will keep that forage cheap, and plenty of carriages will increaſe the conſumption of it.

In judging of the ſuperiority of manufactures between two nations, it would be dangerous to loſe ſight of this maxim, that the ſeller is in a ſtate of dependance on the buyer: whence it follows, that the ſteps taken by a trading nation ought to be regulated by what is practiſed, not only in the country where the commodity is to be conſumed, as before obſerved, but likewiſe what is practiſed by its rivals. It is neceſſary to know what are with the latter the coſt of firſt materials, the expence of delivering them at the manufactory, the price or wages paid for the fabricating each branch, the price of commodities of abſolute neceſſity, as well as of ſuperfluous commodities, how much of either kind is generally conſumed, in what manner the materials are employed; and laſtly, the charges of carriage of the goods, when fabricated to the place where they are to be conſumed.

Nor is this the whole requiſite to be comprehended within our conſideration: the ſuperior degree of cheapneſs of work between different nations depends in a great meaſure on the better or worſe terms each of them may have been able to make by their *treaties of commerce* with other nations. The concluſion of ſuch treaties requires a deep combination, not only of the general and reciprocal intereſts of the two contracting parties, but likewiſe of thoſe of other rival nations. Nor is it enough to know thoſe general

ral intereſts: it is likewiſe neceſſary to be acquainted with the detail of the particular operations of the merchants concerned in each branch, in order to foreſee what uſe thoſe merchants may make of ſuch or ſuch a clauſe; wherein ſuch or ſuch conditions may be diſadvantageous to them; and in ſhort, the various revolutions which the circumſtances of things ſeem to promiſe in their commercial negociations. A good *treaty of commerce*, independent of the art of negociation, may be ſaid to be a maſterpiece of ſkill. That which England made with Portugal in 1703, and with Spain in 1667, are moſt excellent models.

WHAT we have hitherto ſaid of the means by which a nation may acquire a ſuperiority over another in point of perfection in workmanſhip, proves that manufactures cannot ſupport themſelves in a flouriſhing ſtate without ſome aſſiſtance. They are indebted for that ſtate, partly to the concourſe of ſeveral various cauſes, always collected in one point of view by the legiſlator, whoſe wiſdom and vigilance direct them equally towards the ſame end.

WHATEVER care the preſervation of ſo rich a mine requires, the greateſt difficulty of all lies in the firſt finding out and opening of it: the ſtrongeſt efforts are never too great then. Rude and ignorant men are to be inſtructed, and their hands taught to have more intelligence than their heads are ſuſceptible

tible of; and thoſe novices, are to be made not only to equal foreign rivals conſummate in their art, but even to influence and ſeduce thoſe who are to judge between them.

In times of ignorance, excluſive privileges were granted under pretence of rewarding undertakers of new manufactures, for the riſk of what they advanced, and to ſecure them a profit in return for their zeal. That was renouncing in favour of a few, all rivalſhip of firſt materials, workmen, capitals, and, in ſhort, the perfection of the art and cheapneſs of it's productions; which can be the fruit of thoſe rivalſhips only. The undertakers themſelves often felt the weight of thoſe chains, with which they intended to fetter commerce: miſunderſtanding, the uſual concomitant of bad ſucceſs, or bad management, ſtopt the progreſs of thoſe undertakings. The privilege, however, remained; and private workmen, blameable enough for having ſtolen or imitated our art, become uſeleſs, and were ſubject to fines and forfeitures, The misfortune was much greater, when thoſe manufactories were brought from other countries: for, in that caſe, if new workmen, often more ſkilful than the old, invited by their hopes of making more ſpeedy fortunes, offered; they were forced to carry elſewhere their labour, induſtry, conſumption, and good will. The loſs of one ſingle family often occaſioned that of many more, deterred from leaving their country by ſo fatal an example.

WHETHER

WHETHER matters turned out well, or ill, the intereſt of the undertakers being to gain time, the art was but little improved at the expiration of the patent, or privilege. Sometimes too, if matters did not ſucceed well for want of good management, thoſe to whom the miſcarriage was owing, blaſted the art ſo as never to be retrieved in that country.

THERE is, however, perhaps, a kind of mitigated patent, or excluſive privilege, with regard to manufactories, which would not deprive a ſtate of the advantages of rivalſhip. That is, when the patent is limited to a ſmall number of years, and to one, or at moſt two counties, or provinces, in order not to raiſe the price of either firſt materials or workmanſhip too much at once. And even then it is proper, that ſuch a favour ſhould be purchaſed by an encreaſe of population and induſtry; that is to ſay, the undertaker ought to be obliged to bring from abroad, and maintain, a certain number of foreign workmen, and likewiſe take a certain number of national apprentices.

THE means generally made uſe of in France to encourage the eſtabliſhment of manufactories, are to purchaſe at the *public expence* the particular ſecrets, either for preparing or dying materials, or the engines, whether new, or not known there before; and to grant rewards proportioned to the importance of ſuch new undertakings. Thoſe rewards, always judged neceſſary, are perſonal diſtinctions

tions and prerogatives granted to the directors of the undertaking; funds advanced; proper places allotted to save expence at first, till the profits became certain; the purchasing of what is manufactured, or wrought, at a fixed price during a certain time; a thing by no means to be slighted, and of which great advantage has been and may be made; or lastly, a bounty on the exportation of those productions, until they are able to compete with foreign productions of the same kind at their proper market.

The expence of maintaining skilful foreign workmen in all branches, is not less necessary towards the preserving of manufactories, than towards the establishing of them. Small causes will always be productive of great effects in that respect: for example, it is probable that the maintaining of a few women, good spinsters, in different parts of the country, which might be done at a small expence, would contribute infinitely to promote manufactories, by inculcating in the wives and daughters of husbandmen and other labourers, a spirit of industry, which would not interfere with any thing else they may have to do.

No part of the state, but the stockholders, can find fault with those expences; because they are the only men, who would not be repaid their disbursements with usurious interest. That remark alone sufficiently shews

that

that ſtates have not any more certain way to encreaſe their riches.

A LAST way to encourage manufactories, is to annex an idea of merit and diſtinction to the profeſſion of manufacturers, or of thoſe who by their extenſive correſpondences procure a vent for their productions abroad. That is but juſt; ſince thoſe men, the merchants, are the diſpenſers of employment and food to the induſtrious workman, and of the cultivator's reward. The ſtate is in a manner partner in the merchant's profits, without ſharing the hazard he runs, or the fatigues he undergoes; and, therefore, ought never to ſlight him, but cheriſh, careſs, and honour him. The productions of labour and ingenuity may, in general, be compared to a-piece of clockwork; the ſprings of which relax and ſpoil, when not taken care of, and which at length ſtop if not wound up in time. The men who keep thoſe ſprings in order, who compoſe, connect, and put them in motion, ought to be diſtinguiſhed by their country and by every citizen who is a friend to it.

DISSERTATION XXXIV.

An enquiry into the reasons for Holland changing her system of late years towards the court of England; being an abstract of a certain remarkable speech said to be made at a conference by the g——d P——r of Holland, in the year, 1742, before certain British lords, who were sent on an embassy to engage them in British measures: with remarks, shewing that Holland expects Great Britain should change her system towards that republic, before she can alter hers.

My Lords!

"AFTER so many solid reasons, (says the Dutch politician) heretofore assigned by the ministers of Holland, for not entering into any *offensive alliance*, it should seem unnecessary to add any thing on the subject: but since the uncommon eagerness with which such an alliance is still pressed, requires a clear and definite answer, it becomes incumbent on those in the direction of public affairs in this republic, not only to give such a final answer,

anſwer, but their reaſons at large for then diſinclination to their contracting any new engagements that might throw the States into meaſures of violence and expence, without any views of advancing either the immediate intereſt of their country, or that of thoſe who would provoke the ſame, from motives that are no way intereſting to Holland.

THE deference due to the auguſt princes from whom the overture comes, requires that our refuſal of the alliance in queſtion ſhould be ſo juſtified, as that not only the nations immediately concerned, but all Europe may perceive the rectitude of our conduct, from the force of our reaſons in ſupport of it.

BUT though the nature of my ſubject requires that I ſhould explain myſelf with freedom, I ſhall carefully avoid all perſonal reflection; a caution, which, I am ſorry to ſay, has not been obſerved with regard to the chief miniſters of Holland.

THOUGH, we Dutchmen, whether from diſcretion, or phlegm, hold or ſeem to hold a deaf ear to all tale-bearers; yet are not the leſs acquainted with the ſecret calumnies of them who make us openly the warmeſt profeſſion.—But, I hope to make it evident to the world, that no French gold, the dread of a ſtadholder, nor that of being ſtripped of power, have had any the leaſt influence on our conduct by not chiming in with the views of a neighbouring miniſtry.

IF

IF from what I ſhall ſay on the ſubject of the propoſed alliance, it ſhall appear to be deſtructive of the tranquillity, trade, and intereſt of the Republic, I hope diſapprobation will not be imputed to either the influence, or the gold of France. I will not take upon me to charge either the late or the preſent miniſters of L——n with being penſioners to that crown; but, I ſay, that they could not have ſerved her more efficaciouſly, had they taſted liberally of her bounties *, &c.

BUT the being penſioners to France is not the only charge induſtriouſly whiſpered againſt the miniſters of the Republic. The dread of a ſtadholder is imputed to them as the moſt heinous crime. How great has been the pains, how refined the addreſs, to inſure the people, on this head, with ſentiments injurious to the honour and probity of thoſe in the adminiſtration of our affairs †?

THE dread of being ſtripped of power, or rather the luſt of power, is the third charge privately ſuggeſted againſt the miniſters of the Republic. They little know how greatly the toil of office in this country exceeds the emoluments that accrue from it, who arraign Dutch miniſters of unfaithfulneſs to their

* I have here omitted more ſevere reflections on the Britiſh miniſters at the time, as tending not to anſwer my purpoſe of unanimity and concord in this nation ſo deſireable at preſent.

† I ſhall not repeat what was urged on this occaſion, it not being conſiſtent with my view.

country in order to continue their power. It is not here as with thoſe who artfully ſeek to diſcredit us with our fellow ſubjects. We have no immenſe public revenue to count over a gridiron; every town in each province having it's own diſtinct receivers; and the revenue of each applied under their own particular inſpection.

FROM this ſhort but faithful pourtraiture of the miniſterial function here, you may perceive the juſtice of the odium ſecretly endeavoured to be fixed upon thoſe in the adminiſtration of our affairs, for ſupporting the intereſt of the Republic.—It is an ungrateful taſk to rake into the miſconduct of others, particularly, of thoſe whom one is inclined, for intereſt, as well as choice, to think well of; but, ſince ſpeaking without diſguiſe is become of abſolute neceſſity, in order to juſtify the conduct on this ſide the water, I hope I ſhall ſtand excuſable for what the nature of my ſubject requires I ſhould conſider with plainneſs and freedom. Here, was I inclined to lay open old ſores, might I prove, from the ſeveral gradations of miſconduct in the cabinet of L——n ſince queen Anne's death, that the preſent power of France, the inability of this Republic, and that of B—n itſelf, the misfortunes of the heireſs of Auſtria, and the diſtractions of Europe, are not ſo much the effects of chance and French politics, as of B——h blunders, and corruption. Of the latter I am ſatisfied the miniſters

ſters of this Republic may be acquitted : but I am ſorry I cannot ſo juſtly acquit them of error in embracing too implicitly many of the falſe maxims of their neighbours.

THE late miniſters of the Republic, who alone are accountable for a miſtaken deference to the cabinet of L——n in the late reign, might be excuſable for ſuppoſing that a new family would take no ſtep to irritate or weaken the *only powers* they could depend upon, much leſs court and aggrandize thoſe whom they had moſt reaſon to dread and guard againſt.—Our late ſtateſmen might be deceived in concurring with a court where their intereſt was now become *the ſame with the republic's.* This was the foundation they built upon in acceding to the *quadruple alliance*, and the treaty of Hanover.—Here ariſe many other rancorous reflections upon the conduct of the court of England ; which, as I conceive they will anſwer no end to either nation at preſent, I have expunged only reaſon for hinting what has been urged in favour of the conduct of Holland is to ſhew, that the cabinet of Holland think that we have not acted upon a right footing of policy with them : and does not this ſeem to point out the neceſſity for the court of England *to change her ſyſtem towards the Dutch?* It certainly does : but how that ſyſtem may be happily changed, ſo to content the Dutch as to draw them abſolutely into the Britiſh ſcale of power, ſeems to be be the great political problem neceſſary to be inveſtigated, for the mutual ſecurity of both *. —*That Holland has changed her ſyſtem towards Great Britain is certain; and that if Great Britain would effectually induce Holland to fall in with her meaſures; there is a ſomething wanting, that neither court ſeems yet to have fallen upon. But, if Holland had hit upon the one thing needful; unleſs the court of England were ripe for it, Holland would never ſuggeſt it; the propoſition would never come firſt from the cabinet of Holland to that of Great Britain: no; the latter muſt take the lead; England muſt herſelf hit upon the grand arcanum of union between the two ſtates, and Holland will chearfully embrace it; if it is conducted with the addreſs requiſite on an occaſion ſo importantly intereſting to both potentates.*

But to continue the Dutchman's reaſons for change of conduct in the States General towards this nation, leaving out every thing acrimonious, that may irritate rather than conciliate.—' The Engliſh miniſtry, continues this ſtateſman, do not, or, perhaps, will not ſee that the unequal load [meaning their public debts and taxes] is, and always muſt be a drawback upon the credit, or influence of that country while ſhe continues to

* Here again ariſing further reflections contrary to my intentions, I paſs them over.

be burthened with them. *What nation*, ſays the Dutch miniſter, *in Europe can reckon on Britain's ſupporting a war againſt France with the neceſſary vigor, while ſhe groans under the weight of fifty millions ſterlings of debt?* Here let Engliſhmen ſeriouſly, reflect upon the Dutch miniſters reaſons.—As our public debts and taxes are in the road to be doubled the above ſum before the war is ended, ſhould not this rouſe and animate us to change our *domeſtic* as well as our *foreign ſyſtem?* From theſe motives, I laboured the laſt year, to ſhow the indiſpenſable neceſſity of raiſing the ſupplies within the year, in order to put a ſtop for ever to the encreaſe of the public debts, and taxes ‖; than which nothing will give greater weight, with Holland, and other powers, and induce them to liſten to what may be urged in favour of a new foreign ſyſtem.

"HOWEVER drained and impoveriſhed, continues the Dutch miniſter, France has been painted of late in *memorials* and *ſpeeches*, we, *in theſe provinces are too well acquainted with her natural and political ſtrength, not to dread that ſhe will, as in her late wars, when ſhe had all Europe for enemies, be able to wage a ten or twelve years war, if ever ſhe ſhould be forced into one, by either one or both the maritime powers. In ſuch caſe, what muſt become of Britain, that power which is expected*

‖ See my Great Britain's true ſyſtem.

will

will always bear the greater part of the expences of ſuch a war: what, I ſay, muſt be her condition then, if even now all Europe ſee her drop under the weight of her preſent debts, taxes, and the decay of her trade, and induſtry? In ſuch a ſituation, how feeble her efforts in the general cauſe of liberty; how miſtaken would they be, who ſhould reckon upon her being able to defray her proportion of the expence of a war, which the miſconduct of her cabinet had brought upon all Europe? Is it not more natural to ſuppoſe, that once mighty and powerful ſtate would become bankrupt in the courſe of ſo long and expenſive a war as that with France would neceſſarily be? Would not this be more likely, than that ſhe ſhould be able to maintain ſo vigorous a war with that crown as might induce her to ſue for peace with humility, as in the days of Anne? Should not theſe ſevere reflections excite us to form ſuch a ſyſtem of power as will enable England and her allies to cope effectually with this great leviathan?

"Upon recollection, ſays he, I don't know but I might have been guilty of a breach of charity in imputing to one man all the miſconduct of the cabinet, which he was ſuppoſed to direct. For, though it be criminal to concur in deſtructive meaſures, yet, as there are degrees of guilt, he who only concurs, cannot be deemed as highly criminal as he who lays the plan and directs. If, therefore,

fore, the great delinquent was under any controul, he may be looked upon as an accessary rather than a principal; and, though by the civil law there are no accessaries, in cases of homicide all are principals; it is not so in treason, either against a single magistrate, or the state. In these cases, the first mover is the most obnoxious.

If then the favourite was obliged to steer by the lights set up by his immediate predecessors in the administration; if he was compelled to walk in the paths chalked out for him, he was guilty, but not superlatively so. He was criminal for stooping to *address*, or shrinking at *frowns*; he was guilty for having soothed the *passions* of any man or men in violation of his allegiance to his country, or regard to the freedom of mankind, but still is less guilty than———

The successors to that great man's power may possibly, on the strength of his strain of reasoning, plead the same excuse in bar of any exceptions which may be taken to their conduct, since he has laid down. But their own *opposition* to the late ministers administration, *cuts away all ground of excuse for their shaping their conduct by his*, &c. [Here the Dutch statesman speaks out; he declares the necessity of a change of measures in the British court; that a change of men only can answer no end: but here seems to arise a difficulty; raw, fresh men, unexperienced in public business do not seem capable of changing

ing the Britiſh ſyſtem as they ſhould do: however good their hearts may be; and, however great weight and influence they may have in parliamentary debate; yet, when they attempt a new plan of government, and come to carry it into execution; they often find themſelves in a labyrinth, and incapable of forming ſuch new plan of power, that ſhall remedy the defects in the conduct of their predeceſſors; and, therefore, however public ſpirited and glorious their intentions may prove; yet, if they are found unequal to the forming of the proper plan or plans themſelves, requiſite to extricate the nation from thoſe difficulties under which it may labour, they are bound in duty as chearfully to give up the helm, as they were ready to embrace it: or, to endeavour at a hearty *union* with the more experienced ſtateſmen, and with an amiable and true patriot-condeſcention communicate to them their overſights, and join their hearts as well as their heads with the more experienced, to ſave their ſinking country: let theſe true friends of their country lay aſide all private reſentment, and let them call into their aid all who may prove any ways aſſiſting, in the divers branches of the miniſterial function. And, if they know the integrity of their own hearts; if they are ſenſible that their intentions are to rectify paſt miſtakes in the government, or to eradicate all malverſation; it is no leſs their duty to call into their aſſiſ-

tance

tance all perſons of any talents to be uſeful to the ſtate, than to aim at taking the lead? A miniſter may act with great abilities and dignity in a particular department, becauſe he may be more than equal to the ſame in all reſpects: but, when he graſps at being premier, and undertakes the whole miniſterial duty upon himſelf, and to direct and controul all ſubordinate to him, it is impolitic to reject and contemn ſervices that are tendered him, where they promiſe any thing conſiſtent with the public felicity: becauſe ſuch who are able to ſerve a wiſe and a faithful miniſter, may be provoked to do otherwiſe from motives of reſentment. Men of capacity, and of malignant ſpirit may, from revenge, lay ſchemes to clog the beſt and wiſeſt adminiſtration; and, although this is a deteſtable principle; yet it being too prevalent, the profound ſtateſman will guard againſt evils of this kind, and cheriſh, inſtead of deſpiſe merit, becauſe it muſt at length, bring ſcorn and contempt upon themſelves, and indicate that they are no thorough paced politicians.

But, if there is a neceſſity of alteration of meaſures, in regard either to our foreign or domeſtic concerns, why cannot the miniſters experienced in public buſineſs as well undertake the requiſite reforms, as thoſe who have never been tried? Do not all men acquire knowledge by experience? If the ſtateſman has once experienced that he has committed miſtakes, is there not more diſcredit to perſiſt in them, than rectify them? And how can they better be convinced of this, with reſpect to Holland, than to find it's cabinet ſo refractory to Britiſh influence?

To return again to the Dutch miniſter, waving all particulars conſiſtent with the then ſtate of public affairs.—"As for this Republic, urges he, though the late miniſter paid her not ſo open court, nor was ſo laviſh of his profeſſions to her, as the ſucceſſors; yet I muſt ſay in his behalf, that if he did not behave towards her with ſo great politeneſs, and ceremony, he was not leſs candid and ſincere. If ſhe found him no courtier, ſhe could not prove him a hypocrite.

But it is needleſs to deſcant more minutely on the ſituation of foreign affairs at the time when the miniſter laid down; there is none here can be ignorant of it! It is more to our purpoſe to take a view of affairs as they ſtand at preſent.

The new miniſtry were no leſs eſteemed abroad than at home. Their ability was not doubted, and their virtue not ſo much as ſuſpected. They had the hearts of their countrymen with them, and the wiſhes of all Europe, except the partiſans of France. So pleaſed were we in Holland with the change in London, that public rejoicing had been made on the occaſion by ſome, if our more moderate magiſtrates had not thought them indecent, as being obliquely reflecting on the judgment of one whoſe character they were tender of. Great men ſeldom make a

wrong

wrong choice; but, if they do, they ſoon rectify their error. Reſolution in ſome often degenerates to obſtinacy, and then ceaſes to be a virtue.

THE eyes of Europe were upon the ſucceſſors of the removed miniſter. France trembled that ſo powerful a neighbouring nation ſhould be wiſely *conducted* and become *united*, as there was ſcarce a doubt that they would by their new leaders. Spain began to repent that ſhe had formed any ſchemes on Italy; in ſhort, every prince, every ſtate that had been inveigled into the ſchemes of France was in dread that new ſalutary meaſures in the cabinet of L——n would be the certain conſequence of the late miniſters removal.

THE independant friends of univerſal freedom, on the other hand, expected *a change of meaſures in E——d*; but far from dreading any evil conſequence that could attend ſuch change, they doubted not that it would tend *to the cementing ſuch an alliance as muſt have a view to ſtopping the carreer of France, and ſecuring the liberties of Europe.*—But we of theſe provinces out-went all others, in hopes that we might now ſafely rely on the wiſdom, ſteadineſs, and integrity of a cabinet, which we could not reckon upon for upwards of twenty years before.—We ſaw France extending her power; and we ſaw the neceſſity of checking her ambition, *but could not with any hopes of ſucceſs enter into any meaſures for the purpoſe, whilſt the late miniſter*

minister presided over the councils of the only nation in Europe most capable of aiding in the glorious design.

But now the scene was changed: we saw a sett of men rise to power that had for many years professed to have *opposed* the late minister, solely on account of his misconduct at home, his subserviency to France, and his neglect of *all the natural allies of his country.* As from such men all that was great and glorious might have been expected, no wonder that we were as sanguine in our hopes of their conduct as all their own fellow subjects were. They might have influenced us here in Holland as easily as their own countrymen; and might have as readily brought us into alliance, as they commanded the treasure of their own nation: such was the high opinion conceived here, as well as at home, of their virtues and abilities.

But how delusive are hopes built upon probity of men! Scarce had we the pleasing news of the advancement of the late *opponents*, but we had advice that they *capitulated* before they were advanced; that they were not only to secure the retreat of the late minister, but embrace his maxims, and steer as he should direct from behind the curtain. Though this piece of intelligence came confirmed to us from those whose fidelity we had no reason to suspect; yet were we slow, and I the slowest of all my colleagues, in believing any thing so injurious to the characters

of

of the riſing ſtateſmen, &c.—I was, however, miſtaken. I too fondly ſuppoſed that ſenſible men would act as it became them to do.—Miſtaken notion, particularly with regard to a *neighbouring nation! To judge of them with any certainty, in their political capacity, the ſafeſt way is to ſuppoſe they will always act in direct oppoſition to the true intereſt of their country.*

If the cabinet of Holland has judged of the Britiſh miniſtry according to the undiſguiſed ſentiments of the Dutch ſtateſmen, it is no wonder that they do not draw with us; and that all harmony between us is deſtroyed: and that they do judge ſo in reality, their conſtant conduct has too long ſignificantly declared;—and this effectually accounts for their meaſures.—It ſeems then that the *miniſtry of England has not yet happily ſtruck upon the right ſyſtem to gain over the Dutch; and the latter, as we find, repreſent it as if they had been under the ſame French influence, with which many in England have ſuſpected the Dutch miniſtry to have been.*—For my own part, who have no reaſon to be partial towards either, I cannot help declaring, that I am rather inclined to think this general charge on either ſide to be groundleſs and defamatory: I rather attribute ſuſpicions of this kind to the difficulties that the men in power in both councils have found in falling upon thoſe meaſures that can produce and cement the deſired good underſtanding, union

and

and friendſhip between Great Britain and Holland; and the lucky policy of France in projecting ſuch as have tended to divide them.

THE ambition of France, continues our Dutch orator, and the diſtractions on the continent, required *domeſtic unanimity*, without ſeeing which confirmed, the ſtates of Europe could not ſafely rely on the alliance of B—n, &c. [This gives us the natural idea of the ſentiments which the Dutch entertain of our eternal miniſterial diſtractions; what high diſhonour do they not reflect upon the king's councils, and the glory of the nation. While things are ſo, is it to be wondered that we can neither influence the Dutch, or any other cabinet of Europe to good purpoſe? If the axe was once laid to the root of theſe evils, we might expect things to go better with us; and miniſters get more wealth (if that was their idol) as well as more laſting glory to themſelves and families.]

AFTER leaving out much of Mynheer's matter that was agreeable to the then circumſtances of affairs, and that bears extremely hard againſt our Engliſh miniſters, the gentleman proceeds thus:—" The late miniſter having been univerſally condemned for ſtooping to French influence, it was thought neceſſary that his ſucceſſors ſhould ſhew that they were men of high mettle, and more exalted virtue. But as nothing could more effectually remove all ſuſpicion of being held

in

in the late miniſter's leading-ſtrings, as taking, or at leaſt affecting to be inclined to take, young Lewis by the whiſkers, it was reſolved they ſhould aſſume a *ſtrutting* air, ſtamp the foot at the old cardinal, call him hard names, and tell him he muſt be civil, or —— what? Why that the ſimple Dutch would be forced, if they proved wiſe enough not to ſee the fallacy, to join againſt France in ſpite of their teeth: that the beſt troops of B—n would be tranſported to Flanders; with ſome reflections that I chooſe to omit, as thinking them unſeaſonable, as well as indecent, upon —— Here was the ſcheme, ſays the miniſterial Dutchman; and it muſt be owned it was ſpecious and artful.

WHO could imagine that there was no intention of a rupture with France, when ſo many engines ſhould appear at work for tearing her to pieces? Who could ſuſpect a *court* of having abſolutely determined to break with France, unleſs ſhe ſhould attempt an invaſion in favour of the p—r, who ſhould ſend one of the principal nobles to preſs and bully the States General into an offenſive alliance againſt that crown? With much more to the like purpoſe, turning our whole conduct into a frenchified farce.—

THEN he goes on again:—" The ſcheme was well concerted, and executed ſo ſpeciouſly, that all Europe began to think that a rupture would neceſſarily enſue; but, my l—ds, *we of the ſtate had quite another idea of the*

the warlike preparations of your country. We ſaw, as has been obſerved, a new miniſtry under an abſolute neceſſity of appearing to ſwerve from the meaſures of the former miniſter, become univerſally hated, more from his cringing ſubſerviency to the houſe of Bourbon, than even to his corruption, and profuſion of public money.—We ſoon diſcovered the drift of thoſe hoſtile preparations, which ſo much employed the thoughts of the politicians of Europe, and diverted thoſe of the ſubject at home from obſerving that the cabinet was ſtill influenced by the late miniſter, and that the new leaders *had ſervilely adopted all his maxims. We could perceive the new miniſters implicitly bowing to every deſire of the court for requiring power; but ſtill covering themſeves under the ſhelter of ſuccouring the queen of Hungary, and diſtreſſing France.* [Heavy charge, and betrays great diſguſt againſt England.]

We ſaw, my l—ds, your court, as moſt courts are, enamoured more with the power of doing harm than good. We ſaw her all along graſping at all that could make her dreaded at home, and ſlighting all that might acquire her the good confidence and affection of the people. This was the light we viewed your court in, when we heard of your embarkations for Flanders; nor did we alter our opinion when you urged us ſo eagerly to act jointly with you againſt France. Even now we ſee no reaſon for altering our ſentiments.—[He then proceeds to ſupport his

charge

charge againſt our Britiſh miniſters, by an induction of particulars, and endeavouring to make them act in diſguiſe, and from quite other motives than appeared to the people; and goes on as]—I have made a curſory mention of the motives, which, I think, induced the court of L--n to preſs us ſo earneſtly into an *offenſive alliance againſt France*; I ſhall now endeavour to point out our motives for declining to contract any engagements that ſeem to threaten the tranquillity of the republic.

"I HAVE taken ſome pains to trace out the conduct of the late miniſter, in order to ſhew that the republic could, with no ſafety imaginable, contract with, or rely on, the court of L--n, whilſt he was at the helm: and I have obſerved ſuccinctly on the conduct of the *new miniſtry*, and compared it with the late, that it might be ſeen whether or no the reaſons ſtill ſubſiſt, which induced the ſtates to harbour a diffidence of the virtue and wiſdom of their ancient allies. If the conduct be the ſame, as it ſeems to me evident that it is, the ſame reaſons ſtill ſubſiſt for our diſtruſting the court of L—n at preſent, as much as during the public influence of the late miniſter; and that the conduct of the late and preſent miniſtry is the ſame, appears, I think, manifeſtly from the conſequences.—[Here the Dutchman is again exceſſively ſevere againſt our miniſters, and then proceeds:] My l—ds, at the time

that

that we engaged with B—n against France there were no divisions, no discontent that could possibly obstruct a vigorous prosecution of that just and necessary war, &c. In those days your debts were not great, and your taxes were moderate; your trade was beneficial, your industry was quick, your luxury was a pigmy, if compared with what it is at present. Sure I need not shew how greatly the same is altered of late: I need not be at the pains of pointing out what every one knows; what all Europe knows.

WE cannot but see what all the world sees, that B—n has neither s—n to direct her councils, nor generals to fight her battles, except your l—ps. We cannot avoid seeing the *decrease of her trade, the weight of her taxes, her luxury, and her debts, which might have been paid off before now; and we must be infatuated not to perceive, that she is infinitely in a worse plight at this time than when we entered into an offensive alliance with queen Anne.*

IN those days we could rely on the wisdom of B—n, her steadiness and regard for the liberty of Europe, and the Protestant interest; but can we do so now, after so many repeated tests of her bad conduct? Can we shut our eyes to her conduct towards her natural allies, since the death of that excellent princess, who was the soul of the late general alliance? Have we not seen the late emperor, the princes of the empire, the king of Sardinia, and this republic, ſlighted always, often irritated, whilſt ſervile court was paid to France, &c.

"THE fatal conſequences of ſo miſtaken a conduct are too viſible to be overlooked. We ſee them with that ſincere concern which friendſhip dictates. We ſee a divided, diſcontented people, overburdened with taxes, groaning under the preſſure of debts, decay of trade, luxury, and penal laws.—We ſee this people not long ago the terror of tyranny, and the delight of the virtuous, now become the object of general ſcorn and deriſion, and

YOU may perceive, my l—ds, from what I have ſaid of the conduct of your cabinet, and the ſituation of your country, that I don't hold it prudent or ſafe for this republic to embrace the overtures you are pleaſed to make us. I obſerved that it may be neceſſary for the miniſtry *to ſeem to be inclined to a war with France*; *but that in reality they never intended it*. But ſuppoſing that the tongue had ſpoke the ſentiments of the heart, how unfaithful ſhould we be to our mother-country, ſhould we involve her in an unjuſt quarrel, to ſooth the preſent peeviſh humour of *thoſe* whoſe miſconduct has precipitated a daring, powerful, faithful nation into irreſolution, poverty, and perfidy? *Can we venture on your councils, or your efforts in the proſecution of a French war, when we ſee how you have miſapplied your force and your time in carrying on your preſent war with Spain? To embark*

embark the republic in an expenſive dangerous war, in conjunction with a divided, diſcontented, debilitated, burdened, ill-conducted nation, would be a weakneſs, removed but by a very ſlender partition from madneſs. Forbid it heaven! that the ſervants of the ſtate ſhould be enemies and betrayers of the republic. [May we not reaſonably believe, from the conduct of the Dutch, that theſe ſentiments, however falſe they may be in the opinion of ſome, ſtill prevail in the cabinet of Holland? And, if they are falſe, ſhould we not thoroughly convince the Dutch of their miſtake, by our manifeſt contrary conduct? for that only will have weight with them.—Then he proceeds again:]

IF Britain, who prides herſelf in being empreſs of the ocean, makes ſo miſerable a hand of a war on her favourite element, what a ſcurvy figure muſt ſhe make in a foreign land war, againſt the powerfulleſt nation in the world?—[Are not theſe powerful motives for the Dutch to act as they have long done, and ſtill continue to do?]

But, my l—ds, are you in earneſt when you tell us that France is reduced? What are her debts? I'll anſwer they do not amount to a fourth of what Britain owes. What are her taxes? Not half what is paid in England. The trade of France is viſibly increaſed; that of Britain is abſolutely decreaſed. The gaſconade of pulling down France, this eagerneſs to preſs the republic into

into an offenſive alliance againſt that crown, may ſerve the purpoſe of the B—ſh miniſtry; their meaſures may require ſuch props. But, my l—ds, the ſervants of this republic want no ſuch aids. They have no views, no intereſt ſeparate from the good of their dear country. They ſerve her to the beſt of their ſkill, and the utmoſt of their power. They have not, nor ever will, put their country to an immenſe or any expence, in order to ſhare of the ſpoil, or delude their countrymen. Had the ſervants of B—n obſerved this wiſe and patriot maxim, their country would be at this time as powerful as ſhe is otherwiſe, and France as impotent as ſhe is falſely painted to be.

TO put an end to the conference, which we hope will be the laſt on the preſent ſubject, I muſt freely declare, that the conduct of B—n all along has been ſuch as would deter us from entering into new contracts with her, ſuppoſing they thought her in earneſt. But as there is room for believing that all her late buſtle and outcry are calculated to ſome certain domeſtic purpoſes, we deſire to be excuſed from having any hand in countenancing miniſterial colluſion.—The neutrality of the Netherlands is ſo much our intereſt, 'tis much the intereſt of Europe, that we are reſolved to preſerve it at all hazards. Therefore, my l—ds, to convince you of our candour, we plainly tell you, that we ſhall look upon thoſe who commit hoſtilities in the Netherlands as enemies to the repub-

lic.

lic, and treat them as ſuch to the utmoſt of our power.—Your l—ps will be pleaſed to look upon this as the *final anſwer* to the propoſals you have made us from your court. I am now to beg your l—ps pardon for having taken up ſo much of your time, and particularly for my harſhneſs of expreſſion, to which the nature of the ſubject obliged me."—The end of the abſtract of the Dutch miniſter's ſpeech.

Other REMARKS.

WE find that the Dutch miniſter roundly charges the Britiſh miniſtry with being quite frenchified ever ſince the treaty of Utrecht.—That they have *pretended* only to go to war with France, but were never ſince in earneſt. —That they have increaſed the public debts and taxes, not to humble *France*, or right ourſelves with SPAIN, but to anſwer other domeſtic purpoſes, which the Dutch refuſed to countenance.—That it is the intereſt of the republic to adhere to their *neutrality.*— That it would prove ruinous to them, if they were to be influenced to follow the *offenſive meaſures* that may be neceſſary to the views of the Britiſh miniſtry.—That our wars by land and ſea have been ſo illy conducted, that they cannot ſafely ally with us againſt any enemy.—That though miniſters have been changed, there has been no change in our meaſures.—That our meaſures have been ſuch, that they have brought an indignity and

and contempt upon the Britiſh nation at all the courts in Europe. That our commerce has decayed, while that of France has increaſed.—That we grow poorer and poorer, and France richer and richer; and that while Britain purſues meaſures ſo deſtructive to her intereſt and her honour, the Dutchman bluntly tells our noble lords, that the cabinet of Holland will never be ſwayed by this nation to come vigorouſly into any war with us againſt France; and therefore, that if we are brought into any broils, we muſt get out of them ourſelves as well as we can, and not depend upon their aſſiſtance; for that they cannot depend upon our fidelity or ability.—That they think themſelves able to take care of themſelves, with what other allies they can obtain, whereon they can better depend than on Britain. This ſeems to be the ſubſtance of Mynheer's ſpeech; from which I have expunged ſuch matter, as I thought might tend, at preſent, rather to widen than heal our domeſtic breaches.—This I have done to ſhew my moderation at ſo critical a conjuncture; and yet have gone ſo far as may be requiſite to remind us of what may be neceſſary to be done, to wipe off thoſe reflections of the Dutch; and that not only from a motive to the re-eſtabliſhment of old friendſhips between Great Britain and her ancient and natural allies the Hollanders, but to diſſipate every evil impreſſion that may be made on other courts to the diſhonour of our

own;

own; for if we loſe all our weight and dignity with the States General, we cannot expect to maintain them in any other courts; becauſe the political contagion will inevitably ſpread itſelf throughout Europe; and what muſt prove the conſequence? Why truly we muſt exhauſt our vital treaſure, while we have a ſhilling left, to purchaſe the friendſhip of every court, that may have it in their power to do us the leaſt miſchief; becauſe, according to the Dutch miniſter's ſentiments, they look upon us with contempt, and as an ignominious milch-cow. Whereas, a nation that ſuſtains its honour and dignity with foreign ſtates, and is famed for the wiſdom of its councils, will do more with a nod, than the other can with her millions.—Let theſe reflections of the Dutch be true or falſe, they have done unſpeakable injury and diſhonour to theſe kingdoms, becauſe we know they have been induſtriouſly propagated by our enemies at all the courts in Europe. If the Dutch have been impoſed upon, why have they not been unanſwerably refuted? Why has not the whole republic been convinced of the falſhood of thoſe accuſations, and thoſe prejudices conceived in Holland againſt this nation eradicated? For they have done infinite miſchief to this kingdom in point of trade, as might be eaſily ſhewn.—But, on the contrary, if theſe charges are true, and will hold good againſt former miniſters only,

why

why is not our miſtaken conduct rectified? Why do we not inſtantly convince the Dutch, and all the world, that our miniſters are not a frenchified crew, as to pretend only to declare war againſt that nation, but with no intent to fight or hurt them, our views being ſolely, as the Dutch miniſter barefacedly aſſerts, to raiſe immenſe ſums of money for the ſake of domeſtic plunder, and to participate of French gold too! For a charge of this nature to be made againſt Britiſh miniſters, by our moſt ancient, our moſt natural, and our moſt important ally, muſt greatly concern, if not ſhock, every true friend to theſe kingdoms. And what can diſſipate theſe notions, at home or abroad, but a thorough change in the whole Britiſh ſyſtem? If thoſe who ſhall take the helm are not able to effect this, they ſhould not attempt it; for nothing elſe will retrieve the intereſt and the glory of the nation. But I hope the nation has thoſe who are not leſs able than willing to retrieve the honour and glory of theſe kingdoms, and every honeſt man will lend them their aid.— Such, and ſuch only, I ſhall be ambitious to ſerve as a private man.

To lay a foundation for the deſirable change that ſeems abſolutely neceſſary, has been the end of all my poor political labours; but the ſuperſtructure can never be erected by ſcribbling alone; that muſt be accompliſhed by other meaſures, deſigned to be communicated to ſuch only who are no leſs capable than willing to ſet about the great work in earneſt: and it is to be hoped that heaven will ſoon raiſe up in this kingdom miniſters of ſtate that will cordially and chearfully embrace the tender of my ſervice upon this and ſome other occaſions, that I humbly apprehend will be attended with conſequences importantly intereſting to the kingdom, and no leſs honourable to themſelves.—

LET me not be miſunderſtood here, that I mean only meaſures, whereby Holland alone muſt be convinced of the rectitude of our intentions, and her patriots in power influenced to acquieſce therein. No; we mean much more than that: for the whole power of Holland alone, as it ſtands at preſent, being united with that of Britain, would not anſwer the end of reducing France as ſhould be done, to procure a laſting and an honourable peace: we propoſe likewiſe ſuch an increaſe to the power of Holland, as will ſoon give that republic much greater weight both by ſea and land than thoſe out of the ſecret can conceive.—Nor is this all; we aim at nothing leſs than the bringing ſuch other allies into the Britiſh ſcale, as will anſwer the end aimed at: and, what will not eaſily be credited, I am ſenſible all that we humbly pretend to may be accompliſhed at one third part of thoſe continental expences that have only brought about rope-of-ſand confederacies,

deracies, and been productive of nought but temporary amuſements; nought but a peace liable to be broke, as it were, the ſucceeding year.

But if the Dutch, upon the ſyſtem intended, be deaf to their intereſt, it may be executed without them: ſo that the court of England would not depend upon the Dutch; ſhe would then have many ſtrings to her political bow, and Holland would be glad to make one amongſt the reſt, when that republic ſhall be convinced that ſhe could not act with ſecurity, but in concert with Great Britain, who then would fully have it in her power to diſcover infallibly which was the real frenchified court, either that of London or the Hague. But if the States General, in ſuch caſe, ſhould ſtill prefer a neutrality, that would no leſs determine her to be under French influence, than her throwing her whole weight into the French ſcale againſt Britain and her allies: and if ſhe did do ſo, ſhe would run the hazard of abſolute ruin, and that none but faithleſs miniſters would ſuffer, and they would certainly ſuffer for it, from the juſt reſentment and indignation of the people, who would be no leſs ſenſible than the wiſeſt patriot of the intereſt and glory of their ſtate, when the court of England ſhould undertake to render it more than ever the High and Mighty States of Holland: and this appears, to my humble judgment, to be

in

in the power of Great Britain to accompliſh, and that with as much intereſt and honour to herſelf, as to the States General of the United Provinces.—And I will preſume farther to declare, that all this may be done without any objection from the moſt ſanguine ante-ſtadtholderian.

I AM too well acquainted with the preſent ſtrength and power of France, to imagine ſhe is to be ſo eaſily reduced within the bounds needful for the ſecurity of Great Britain and Holland, and the liberties of all Chriſtendom; and I have too ſufficiently proved, in theſe diſcourſes, the commercial broad-bottom, that crown has eſtabliſhed, for the future augmentation of her trade and her maritime power, to think that we ſhall be ever able to reduce her within the requiſite preſervative bounds, unleſs we do it by the preſent war; apprehending that any peace we can expect to make with them now, muſt prove far more diſadvantageous and diſhonourable than the continuance of a war; eſpecially if it be not conducted upon other principles than it has ever yet been: and for not carrying on a war upon the principles hereby hinted at, I am certain that no miniſters in this kingdom have ever been blameable, becauſe I am too ſenſible that ſuch is the nature of the deſign, that it never ſo much as entered into their imagination; and, therefore, there could be no guilt where there was no knowledge; for we cannot put certain undiſcovered maxims of policy upon the footing of diſcovered and promulgated laws; for although *ignorantia juris non excuſat*; yet it is quite otherwiſe with regard to the meaſures we allude too; nor have they, I am confident, been leſs thought of by the Dutch miniſtry, than the Britiſh; if they had, we may preſume they might and would have found ways to have ſuggeſted them to our own; unleſs indeed they have had indubitable reaſons, in a long courſe of negociations with the king's miniſters, to know that they really are as hearty friends to the French as the Dutchman would have us believe they have been enemies to his country: but this cannot eaſily be known to others. However, if the ſtates of Holland have heretofore had reaſon to know, or even to imagine, that the court of England has uſed them ill, and been more in the intereſt of France than in that of their natural ally, we cannot blame the Dutch for acting the part they have done, and which they at preſent do: but it is to be hoped that we ſhall ſoon have a miniſtry at the head of the king's affairs, who will diſſipate all thoſe evil impreſſions in Holland, by convincing them that they are not of the frenchified ſtamp.— The nation expects to ſee a truly patriot miniſtry; ſuch a miniſtry as ſhall have well ſtudied, not only the eſſential political lines of

public

public businefs, as well with regard to foreign as domeftic concerns: a miniftry alfo thoroughly inftructed in all the various departments, and all the practical fubordinate dependencies and connections: a miniftry that will court and not defpife ufeful information from all quarters, and who are fo happily turned for the adminiftration of national affairs, as to be capable of fuperintending every department, and directing the rudder of the whole: a miniftry who will fcorn to fcreen themfelves by urging that this was not done within my department, this is out of my province, I am not anfwerable for it, &c.—We fay, it is to be hoped, that the king will make choice of fuch able minifters for the chief domeftic officers of ftate who have wife heads, as well as honeft hearts, to conduct public bufinefs with eafe to themfelves, general fatisfaction to the people, and joy to our aged fovereign, and dignity to the heir apparent to the crown. And as the ftate and management of our home and foreign affairs is clofely connected, it is likewife to be defired, that we may have a miniftry no lefs fkilled in foreign than domeftic concerns; a miniftry as well acquainted with the finances of other countries as of their own, and no lefs informed of the trade and the arts of other ftates and empire than of thofe of Great Britain.—A miniftry thus informed in the ftate of foreign nations, will always be able to treat with them to the advantage and ho-

nour

nour of their country, and to make ſuch treaties of commerce, friendſhip, and alliance, as will prove the mutual ſteady ſupport and proſperity of theſe kingdoms, and all with whom they ſhall ally.—This being the caſe, Great Britain will have no occaſion to expend *millions* in the purchaſe of alliances: on the contrary, every ſtate will court our friendſhip, and be lead by the wiſdom of Britiſh councils; becauſe ſuch councils will conſult the proſperity and happineſs of our natural allies, in conjunction with our own: for upon the baſis of reciprocal intereſt only can ſolid and permanent treaties ſubſiſt.

STRANGE it is that there ſhould be no obſervation more common amongſt our neighbours abroad than this, That the people of England, of all others, are the worſt reaſoners on foreign affairs; and this I fear is as juſt as it is general: for our ſituation, which deprives us of eaſy intercourſe, and happily ſaves us from any *immediate* connection with the people of the continent, renders the ſtudy of their intereſts and policies at once more difficult and leſs intereſting; while the few who have had the opportunities of being well informed in theſe things, inſtead of making the proper uſe thereof, have turned their thoughts to other kind of reflections: and, indeed, if the ground-work is not well laid before travel, it it is rare that any ſolid knowledge is gained by tour after tour; for the ſubſtantials of treaty-making are not to be acquired, we apprehend, by the mere converſe of the world, that ſcarce ever entering into its fundamentals, whereon it eſſentially depends.

DIS-

DISSERTATION XXXV.

Of the conduct of the court of Spain towards that of Great Britain ſince the peace of Utrecht; with conſiderations on the extraordinary friendſhip that we may reaſonably expect from that nation at preſent.

IT has been no uncommon thing for us to have from three to four, and even ſometimes five hundred veſſels, great and ſmall, of theſe nations in ſeveral ports of Spain at once; and ſeldom, throughout the whole year, leſs than two hundred at a time. It has been common to ſee a hundred, and often two hundred ſail of Britiſh and Iriſh ſhips in the Bay of Cadiz at a time. Two thirds of our Newfoundland and New England trade for *fiſh* depended on *Spain*; nor were we leſs obliged to that kingdom for the great advantage that accrued from our being their carriers of Europe, during times of peace with that nation.—We traded with the Spaniards, and for them, from Hamburgh, Holland, and from all the Eaſt and North ſeas; and

and to and from the extended coaſts of Italy, Turkey, Barbary, as well as from Great Britain and Ireland.—We ſhared in the Spaniſh Weſt-India trade as largely as any nation in Europe;—and the balance of trade between Great Britain and her other dominions, and the kingdom of Spain, was conſiderably in our favour, and it was well worth the while of this kingdom to maintain a ſtrict friendſhip with this nation, for the ſake of our commercial connections; when the old Spaniſh proverb we know was, *Paz con Angleterra con todos otos la guerra.* Peace with England and war with all the reſt of the world.

BUT ſo it is, the caſe is greatly altered of late years. Spain has greatly decreaſed in her imports of Britiſh manufactures, as well to *old* Spain as to *new*; and yet our imports from thence have been far from declining in the like proportion; the French have not only greatly ſupplanted us in the Spaniſh European trade, but have obtained by far the greateſt ſhare in the ſupply of the galleons and flota, they being of late years by far more highly favoured then Britain in their commerce to old Spain as well as new; their woollen manufactures are become now far more in vogue there than the Engliſh; and their linens, ſilks, and gold and ſilver manufactures are no leſs acceptable to the Spaniſh dons. The French alſo have cut us out in a conſiderable part of the ſupply of the

the Spaniards with fiſh.—And that our whole trade with Spain muſt daily decline no one can doubt, when he conſiders that the Spaniards, though long reproached for their commercial indolence and inactivity, having now ſtruck into an active commerce, are determined to become their own maritime carriers, are ſtriking into fiſheries, and are taking every wiſe meaſure to eſtabliſh nurſeries for ſeamen, in order to raiſe a formidable royal navy.

THEY have likewiſe ſettled manufactories of almoſt every kind; they have allured away our woollen and ſilken manufacturers, and even our ſhip-carpenters, who, it ſeems, have already inſtructed the Spaniards in thoſe our moſt ineſtimable arts, and they appear reſolved to raiſe themſelves into a great manufactural and commercial ſtate; the foundation of which was laid by the Dutchman the duke de Ripperda, who ſucceeded Alberoni as chief miniſter in Spain; and his ſcheme has ever ſince been gradually carrying into execution, as is manifeſt from the teſtimony of that patriot-Spaniard, Don Geronymo de Uztariz, whom I have frequently cited upon this occaſion.

IN Madrid, ſays he, has been ſet up a manufacture of tiſſues, luteſtrings, and other ſilks, no leſs curious in the workmanſhip, than in the colours and mixtures, in imitation of the fabrics of Lyons in France; and this

this manufacture has produced ſuch as the king himſelf was not aſhamed to wear.

THIS ſucceſsful eſtabliſhment in Spain has been owing to workmen, and a famous dyer from the city of Lyons, procured by his majeſty, at the charge of his own royal revenue; and to the encouragement of a houſe and ſupplies of money, which he ordered to be advanced in the infancy of the undertaking, giving alſo a monthly penſion of 15 doublons to the maſter-dyer, and 12 doublons to the head manufacturer.

WITHOUT the gates of Madrid has been raiſed alſo a fabric of prime tapeſtry, in imitation of thoſe of Flanders, by a maſter and workmen, whom his majeſty procured from that country, at the charge of the treaſury; and they continue in this important manufactory, working for his royal palaces, having the encouragement of houſes, workſhops, and indulgences, which his majeſty has granted them.

AND notwithſtanding there is not yet in either of the fabrics a competent number of maſters and workmen, for the conſiderable conſumption of this kingdom: yet the main difficulty has been ſurmounted, which is ſettling and bringing the manufactures to the perfection already mentioned; *for it is an eaſy thing to enlarge, or add to what we have begun, and already eſtabliſhed upon a good footing.*

' By this plain fact, says a celebrated Spanish author, IN THE VERY FACE OF THE COURT, many persons might be undeceived, who believe and propagate a notion (upon what grounds I know not) that in this kingdom we cannot arrive at the perfection we have seen in these and other manufactures, either on account of the delicacy of the work, *as if there was neither genius to invent, nor hands to execute in* Spain; or for colours, as if his majesty's provinces did not really supply the principal and best materials for them; or from our water, which they suppose not proper for them, even when both the declaration of foreign artificers, and experience, shews it to be very fit for dying all sorts of colours; and it is also certain, that, notwithstanding foreigners introduced these curious fabrics, *many* SPANIARDS *now join in them, and already make them in equal perfection* *.

THE grand fabric of fine cloths at Gadalaxara is wholly owing to the vigilance and protection of his majesty, though there has

* By these very measures the great Colbert laid the foundation for the present flourishing trade of France. And, by these and the like maxims of policy, Spain is likely to raise her trade and navigation to what pitch they desire. Do we not see that Spain is daily drawing away ingenious artificers from various parts of Europe, as well as Great Britain? Wherefore, is it not the interest of these kingdoms to give all fitting encouragement to ingenious artificers and mechanics, to keep them at home, to prevent their loss from impoverishing our own nation, and enriching our rivals, by their commerce and navigation?

not been yet, in the management of it, the good oeconomy, which is requisite, and has been directed by his majesty's orders. *But one great point has been obtained; that many of the good workmen employed in these manufactures are* SPANIARDS, *and some, who have been bred up in them, have dispersed into other parts of the kingdom, which is the principal advantage resulting from the arrival and introduction of foreign masters and workmen; therefore no scruple ought to be made of bearing the expence of their journey, and their first settlement.*" [BRITONS! permit me to do myself the honour earnestly to recommend to you to cherish and caress your ingenious ARTIFICERS, your MECHANICS, your MANUFACTURERS, that no inducements may prevail with these most useful subjects of the three kingdoms to abandon their native country, to enrich others, and ruin their own!]

" AND it well deserves our notice (continues this wise Spaniard) that it has been found by experience in Guadalaxara, and other parts of Spain, that the Spanish women, and even the very young girls, spin wool better and quicker than the mistresses of foreign families that instructed them, and were brought over for that purpose.

BY means of due supplies and encouragement from his majesty to Don Joseph de Aguada, knight of the order of Calatrava, for the fabric of cloths in Valdemero, the Spaniards have also gained the point of manu-

facturing

facturing them in that town, as fine as thoſe of ENGLAND, and of good colours and mixtures; as is manifeſt from the approbation they have received from his majeſty, who has worn them himſelf upon ſeveral occaſions *.

THIS is but a ſlight ſketch of what is doing in Spain, in regard to their trading intereſts. Hear what this noble Spaniard further urges, and which is now duly attended to at the court of Spain.—“ It is out of diſpute, ſays he, upon another occaſion, that the commerce, we have many years carried on with other nations, has been very injurious to the Spaniſh monarchy; and the cauſe, whence our damage has ariſen in the ſame commerce, has been pointed out. So that it will be eaſy to conceive, that, in order to promote our own intereſt, and poſſeſs the great and happy conſequences, which we aim at, and we are invited to, and enabled to obtain from the great plenty, and ſuperior quality, of our materials and fruits, we ought to labour, with zeal and addreſs, in all theſe meaſures, that can avail towards ſelling more commo-

* This again is following the example of Lewis the 14th of France, who, by the very ſame means enabled his ſubjects, firſt, to ſupply his own kingdom with the woollen manufacture, and afterwards encouraged them to ſupplant us at foreign markets. It is certain, from this policy of the court of Spain, that we muſt loſe the greateſt part of the trade of both *Old* and *New* Spain. Does not this merit the conſideration of the wiſdom of the nation?

dities and fruits to foreigners, than we buy of them, *for here lies all the ſecret, good conduct, and advantage of trade*, or, at leaſt, that we be upon a par in the barter of commodities, which might be even ſufficient for the conſtitution of this kingdom. For, by virtue of it, there would be detained, in Spain, the greateſt part of the wealth that comes from the Indies, and theſe kingdoms be conſtantly rich and powerful. Nor ought we ever to loſe ſight of this maxim, that the vaſt treaſures, which arrive at Cadiz from theſe parts, contribute nothing to our relief, or advantage, but will rather be turned againſt this monarchy, ſo long as they paſs, directly from the ſame port, to the rivals of the crown, &c."

I AM ſatisfied, ſays he again, that there are now in the kingdom of Valencia above 2000 looms of ſilk and wool; in the principality of Catalonia, above 500; and, in the kingdom of Granada, 1000, including both ſorts; and there are alſo in other provinces manufactures of ſilk, though not very conſiderable; and, in almoſt all of them, no contemptible number of looms for the ſeveral fabrics of wool, ſuch as the middling and coarſe cloths, bays, ſerges, camblets, druguets, &c. One may, I think, without raſhneſs, ſuppoſe the ſilken and woollen looms, that are now in Spain, to be 10,000. Now theſe, with the 60,000 new *ones that have been imagined to be ſet up*, would amount to 70,000; and one may reckon

reckon 14,000, or about one fifth part of them to be ſilk looms: and the remaining 56,000 of fine, middling, and coarſe wool, of which laſt there is no leſs conſumption.

I HAVE already remarked, that in every ſilk and woollen loom, taken together, there might be yearly manufactured to the value of 700 dollars, including the expence of materials, and dying goods. In this eſtimate I am moderate, as well to ſtand clear of every thing that might ſeem forced, either in the facts, or the reaſoning. But, as preciſeneſs is neceſſary in calculations, I ſhall here produce that made, a few years ago, by the preſident and inſpectors of the ſilk manufacture in the city of Seville, which is as follows:

THAT, in every loom of entire tiſſue, there is yearly wrought up 100 weight of ſilk, and 220 ounces of leaf ſilver, or gold, more or leſs. Theſe manufactures yield 150 yards, which, at the moderate price of 3 doublons, amount to 450 doublons.

IN each loom for middling tiſſue, 150 pounds of ſilk, and 150 ounces of metal yearly, and theſe wrought up yearly 190 yards, which, at the rate of 2 doublons a yard, amount to 380 doublons.

IN every loom for brocades, 200 pounds of ſilk, and between 70 and 80 ounces of metal, which are manufactured annually into 300 yards, and, at a doublon and a half per yard, make 450 doublons.

IN

In a loom of double taffeta, there is uſed 280 pounds of ſilk annually, which wrought up produce 1800 yards, and, at the rate of 10 reals de vellon, will amount to 300 doublons.

In every loom of ſingle taffeta, is expended 200 pounds of ſilk yearly, with ſmall difference, and they yield above 3000 yards, which, at the rate of 6 reals de vellon, are worth 300 doublons.

In every loom of plain or ſtriped ſattins, there is uſed yearly 200 pounds of ſilk; which woven yield 1200 yards, and at the rate of 16 reals a yard, one with another, the whole amount will be 300 doublons.

In every loom of damaſk, there is yearly expended 280 pounds, which wrought up produce 1200 yards, and at the rate of 29 reals, one with another, are worth 400 doublons.

Though ſome perſons, continues our writer, may be a little jealous of theſe calculations; and willing to reduce them even one ſixth, or one fifth, it muſt be acknowledged, that after this reduction, there will be manufactured annually in every loom, one with another, to the value of 1000 dollars, including the price of the materials. So that in the 14,000 looms appropriated to ſilk, out of the 70,300 for this commodity and wool, there would be manufactured to the amount of 14 millions of dollars; not forgetting that there is a fluctuation in the prices from year

to

to year, according to the quantity of ſilk and fruits, and from other accidents, that uſually raiſe and fall the markets.

From the information of people of experience, and to be relied upon, we find that in every woollen loom, one with another, allowing for the difference between fine, middling, and coarſe cloths, there can be yearly manufactured to the value of above 700 dollars, including the materials. Hence there would be annually wrought up in the above 56,oco woollen looms, to the amount of 39 millions, which, added to the 14 millions produced by the ſilk manufactures, would make 53 millions of dollars.

It may be obſerved, indeed, that all poſitions, founded on principles that are not quite determinate, are liable to ſome uncertainty: however, they do not fail of affording light, by their approaches to truth; eſpecially, when ſome of the principles whereon they are founded are certain.

From what I ſhall offer elſewhere upon the number of inhabitants in Spain, it will be found that it contains near 7,500,000 ſouls; and though there be many of theſe that yearly expend in manufactures of ſilk and wool, or of both ſorts, above 100 crowns, without any regard to linen, it is alſo known, that the greateſt part of the inhabitants of both ſexes are found to be dreſſed in middling and coarſe cloths, and that every ſuit laſts them about two years: and when we conſider

ſider that the country people, and mechanics, take up for a ſuit ſix yards of ordinary cloth (which is narrower than the fine) this, at 15 reals a yard, will amount to ſix dollars, and that two dollars more will be neceſſary for linings, the whole commodity will coſt eight dollars yearly: and, upon ſuppoſition a ſuit of cloath ſhall wear two years, there will be expended by every individual four dollars a year. But, as it is alſo certain that many of theſe wear a cloak, and a cap, the annual expence of every one of this claſs may be ſtated, in theſe commodities, at five dollars.

Nor ſhould it be unobſerved, that younger boys, and girls, of the lower claſs, will not expend, in cloaths, four dollars yearly; the ſame, alſo, will happen to a great number of women, excluſive alſo of linen; but, in conſideration there are many of both ſexes that yearly expend in commodities of ſilk and wool from 20 to 100 dollars, and more, I am perſuaded that, for every one of the 7,500,000, one with another, we may fairly calculate their annual expence, in both commodities, at four dollars and a half, which, for the whole, will amount to ſomething above 33,000,000 of dollars: and, if we deduct this ſum from the 53,000,000, the ſuppoſed value of the fabrics manufactured in the above 70,000 looms, there would remain to us, of both commodities, the value of 20,000,000. And, by means of this over-

overplus, one may, I think, furniſh his majeſty's Indies both with the ſilks they are in want of, and alſo the fine cloths that go thither from Europe, ſince they have no occaſion for ordinary cloths, by having them in plenty from their own fabrics. Nay, I am apt to believe, that, after the neceſſary ſupplies from Spain and the Indies, there will ſtill remain conſiderable quantities of the above ſilks and fine cloths, for exportation to ſeveral kingdoms and countries in Europe, eſpecially thoſe of the North, that yield no ſilk, and but very little of fine wool.

By this, and other wiſe proviſions, we ſhould accompliſh the grand point of ſelling others more commodities and fruits than we buy. For, even by the ſingle proviſion of ſetting up the 60,000 *looms abovementioned, there would be, after ſupplying the kingdom of* Spain, *and the* Indies, *ſo many goods left, as would ſuffice, and even be more than a balance for the ſpices, linens, bacalao, and other cured fiſh, we are obliged to have from foreign parts, for our faſt-days; though the laſt article from abroad might be conſiderably reduced, by taking ſuch ſteps as ſhall be propoſed in another place* *.

After the ſuppoſed exportation of our ſilks and woollen cloths, we ſhould ſtill have the benefit of our wines, brandies, oils, rai-

* Theſe we ſhall occaſionally ſhew, with humble expedients propoſed, to guard againſt any injury that this nation may ſuſtain thereby.

ſins,

ſins, and other fruits, that are more than we conſume ourſelves, and go abroad in conſiderable quantities, beſides a great many ſmall wares, that might be made of the excellent iron of Biſcay, and other provinces, both for home and foreign conſumption; and great quantities of cryſtal and ſoap, that might be manufactured in theſe kingdoms, by means of the ſoſa and barilla, which they abound with, and are acknowledged to be of ſuch ſuperior quality, that theſe two ingredients are eagerly deſired by all nations in Europe, and in preference to all other ſought after, and exported from Spain.

"Moreover, the quickſilver, copper, tin, and other profitable metals, which his majeſty's dominions yield in great plenty, merit our conſideration; as alſo, that in many parts the ſoil is peculiarly adapted to the growth of flax and hemp, materials very advantageous, and will furniſh us with rigging and ſail-cloth, both for *our own, and the ſupply of other countries.*

By theſe natural means, and which the conſtitution of theſe kingdoms renders very practicable, there would not only be prevented the extraction of many millions of gold and ſilver, but there might come in from foreign countries a conſiderable quantity of money.

But, ſhould we ſucceed no farther than to detain all, or a moiety of the treaſures that come

come from the Indies, and have hitherto gone directly to other kingdoms, Spain ſerving them only for a paſſport, we ſhould then have that plenty, increaſe of people, ſtrength, and other advantages we are now deſtitute of, by the deſertion and decay of the manufactures above-mentioned, and which it is in our power to revive, enlarge, and improve, by granting ſome indulgences, and making a *judicious reform of the duties upon exports and imports.* For though the commodities now exported from Spain are few, there would then go abroad large quantities; and, were they to pay no higher duty than 2 ½ *per cent. of their value, the cuſtoms would yield more than at preſent.* Nay, as the country would be rendered more populous by means of the manufactures, there would enſue an increaſe of the revenue, ariſing out of the more frequent ſales and purchaſes, and a large conſumption of commodities and fruits: and, what is a natural conſequence, a better cultivation and produce from our lands, and an improvement in all *mechanic arts.* To all which ought to be added, as a ſure and ſettled principle, that, though the treaſury ſhould not be ſo viſibly augmented, and go hand in hand with the wealth of the ſubjects, it would not be poſſible, under the obligation and tender regard we have for the king, to leave him poor, while we ourſelves are rich.

MORE-

Moreover, let us always recollect, when we think of this eſſential point, of re-eſtabliſhing and enlarging our manufactories, that we ought not to be diſcouraged by the language of certain low-ſpirited perſons, that believe there is not a ſufficient number of people in Spain to execute this *grand project*; for it ſhall be demonſtrated, that, by means of thoſe that now are here, and ſuch as commerce will always bring along with it, there will be a ſufficient number for this, and other proviſions for the relief of the kingdom."

This is a ſketch only of what is about to be done in Spain; and ought it not to rouze and alarm us?

We ſhall now conſider what mighty advantages we have obtained by the commerce of Spaniſh America, and particularly by that intended to have been carried on in the South Seas, which gave birth to our preſent company of that name.

This company was eſtabliſhed by act of parliament, in the ninth year of the late queen Anne, entitled, An act for making good deficiencies, and ſatisfying the public debts, and for erecting a corporation to carry on a trade to the South-Sea, and for the encouragement of the fiſhery, &c.

Many of the moſt judicious in comercial affairs looked on this company, conſidered as a joint-ſtock corporation for carrying on trade, as a chimerical project; and ſo it proved at length; but not from the nature and deſign

of

of the inſtitution as a trading ſociety, if the ſame had been wiſely projected, and its trade carried into execution as it ought to have been. For ſuch a powerful company would have paved the way for an immenſe ſcene of trade to have been cut out into the South-Seas, which might have been carried on by ſeparate traders, to no leſs benefit to themſelves than the nation, when it might have been neceſſary to have diſſolved this company, as a trading one, excluſive of all other his majeſty's ſubjects. For this, and this only, is the motive for our ever favouring any joint-ſtock monopolies for foreign trade; and this idea I intreat the reader he would always take with him, when he obſerves me to ſay any thing favourably of ſuch like trading corporations.

THE preamble to the eſtabliſhment of this company, in relation to its trading capacity, runs thus: " Whereas it is of the greateſt conſequence to the honour and welfare of this kingdom, and for the increaſe of the ſtrength and riches thereof, and for the vending the product and manufactures, goods and merchandizes of or brought into this kingdom, and employment of the poor, that a trade ſhould be carried on to the SOUTH-SEAS, and other parts in America, within the limits herein after mentioned; which cannot be ſo well carried on as by a corporation with a joint ſtock EXCLUSIVE OF ALL OTHERS: now, for the better encouragement

ment of all and every the perſon or perſons, &c."

Is it not plain from hence, that the company, by its firſt inſtitution, was to have an excluſive trade within the certain limits particularized in the ſaid act? and that our people of Jamaica, by the very act, were to be deprived of the trade to the South-Seas, which was, before this, carried on greatly to the advantage of themſelves and the nation? But ſo wiſely did the Spaniards manage this matter, that they got this company in England converted from a trading corporation (which they apprehended might too much benefit England, and too greatly detriment them in the Spaniſh Weſt India commerce) into a mere Aſſiento for negroes, and a 500 ton annual ſhip. Was not this giving up the certain profits of our Jamaica trade to thoſe imaginary ones, with which the nation were only amuſed?

It is true, the Jamaica traders were not excluded, but only from Buenos Ayres, ſouthwards, and from the South-Sea; they had ſtill left the places in the Atlantic ocean for themſelves: but the profit they and the nation before annually derived from the South-Seas was conſiderable; and Spain found means, by tampering with the miniſters of thoſe days, to have all theſe advantages given up to the company, as an expedient, that the company, as ſuch, might be the more eaſily brought to give them up to Spain; which

which the nation would never have done; had it not been for this chimerical amuſement of mighty things to ariſe from this company. Hereby we loſt the ſubſtance for the ſhadow, and what did Spain give us as an equivalent? Why truly that court very liberally beſtowed upon us a ſcandalous and ruinous Aſſiento contract; a contract to ſell the Spaniards 4,800 negroes per annum, together with a permiſſion to ſend 500 tons of goods to Porto Bello! Thus all our ſolid advantages, that we might have reaped from a South-Sea trading corporation, vaniſhed into this paultry Aſſiento! an Aſſiento abounding with ſtipulation contrived purpoſely by the court of Spain to quarrel with us whenever they thought proper; for ſo greatly did the Spaniards over-reach us herein, that they were ſure always to have the company's merchandiſes in their poſſeſſion; which were often kept three years in the king of Spain's warehouſes, and under his own lock and key. Hereby did one half of the company's goods often periſh in ſo hot a climate, and how could they ever be expected, under ſuch reſtrictions, to be brought in the general to a good market? Or how could the Aſſientiſts ever hope for profit from their negroes, that were to pay a heavy load of duties to the king of Spain? A treaty could ſcarce have been contrived of ſo little benefit to the nation.

Would not one have thought, that after thoſe pompous declarations, which we have ſeen

ſeen in the preamble to the South-Sea act, that ſome attempt at leaſt ſhould have been made, by way of experiment: but ſo amazingly were we duped by the court of Spain, in concert with their fellow-treaty-makers, the court of France, that we wickedly gave up all our pretenſions of trading to the South-Seas, as well from Jamaica as by the company, for an Aſſiento chimera! Is not this the more remarkable, ſince neither the Dutch, nor the French, nor any other nation, has reſtrained their ſubjects from trading to thoſe parts; nor did they neglect to carry on a trade thither with a great profit to themſelves; whilſt the ſubjects of Great Britain, by means of the South-Sea company, were denied this!

HAD the South-Sea company put their original plan in execution with vigour and honour, it would certainly have proved a benefit to the kingdom, by the increaſe of our exports and navigation; but the ſending an annual ſhip under ſuch limitations as was done, though a new method of trade, could not poſſibly prove of national benefit, it leſſening our exports, at the ſame time, by the way of old Spain. Cadiz, Seville, Port St. Mary's, before the South-Sea company was erected, were the places where our Spaniſh merchants, trading to the Spaniſh Indies, informed themſelves what ſpecies and quantities of goods were ſhipped off from time to time; but on ſending of the annual ſhips by the South-Sea company, they were under

ſuch

ſuch uncertainties, that they very greatly declined dealing in our manufactures by thoſe channels. This gradually and inſenſibly gave our rivals in this trade an open opportunity to eſtabliſh houſes of trade or factories at theſe ports; and by exerciſing the commerce to the Spaniſh Indies, in a way the moſt agreeable to the court of Spain, laid the foundation to ſupplant us ſo greatly as they have done, not only in the Spaniſh Weſt-India trade, but in the whole trade of old Spain.—This was not the eſſential fault of an Aſſiento, but the fault of being over-reached in the ſtipulations thereof, that we have become ſuch ſufferers thereby.

BUT even this Aſſiento, however beneficial it might have been rendered, both to the nation and the company, if the court of England had duly ſupported her dignity with that of Spain, was, by miſmanagement, rendered quite otherwiſe; it was for many years like the dog in the manger, it neither traded itſelf, nor ſuffered thoſe who would have done ſo in the like branch of commerce. The act for erecting this company deprived Jamaica of trading to the South-Seas; but the Aſſiento contract ſhut them out of the commerce of the Spaniſh Indies. Thus Spain got their ends by excluding us out of the trade of the South-Seas, and at length has deprived us alſo of the Aſſiento contract, which we weakly ſuppoſed was to make us more than an ample compenſation for giving up the whole South-

South-Sea trade, which we intended to eſtabliſh, *riſum teneatis!* Whoever conſiders the coaſts, countries, and iſlands, the product, trade, and the then ſtate of all the places within the limits of the act of parliament, which conſtitutes the South-Sea company, muſt allow the aim was great, and the benefits might have proved no leſs ſo: but what a ridiculous exchange did we make for ſuch an Aſſiento? In a word, it is apparent, from this plain and impartial ſtate of the caſe, that our miſunderſtanding with the court of Spain may be juſtly attributed to thoſe who made the Aſſiento, and the treaty of Utrecht; all which might have been avoided, if the nature of the Spaniſh Weſt-India and South-Sea trades had been then better underſtood by our miniſters of thoſe days. But it is no eaſy matter for ſubſequent miniſters to rectify ſuch capital miſtakes, committed by their predeceſſors. And theſe things being candidly and diſpaſſionately recommended to conſideration, may help to guard us againſt being thus impoſed on in future.

THOUGH I do not at preſent intend to enter into the cauſes of the late war with Spain, yet there is one particular that may be neceſſary juſt to mention: that at the making of the late peace, and before we had abſolutely ſettled the buſineſs of the Aſſiento with the court of Spain, it was a little unhappy that the *logwood affair* alſo had not been finally ſettled, that being one cauſe of the late war,

war, and may be productive of ill blood hereafter. If we have no right to carry on that trade in any ſhape, it would have been better to have explicitly renounced ſuch a claim by treaty, than to leave the matter doubtful, that our traders therein might know upon what footing they ſtood in that reſpect: if we have a right to cut logwood, it is to be lamented that ſuch right has not been expreſſly aſcertained by treaty.

We have never heard that the French or the Dutch pretend to any ſuch claim to this trade as the Engliſh have; and yet, while I am writing theſe papers, we have an account, it ſeems, of a French ſhip being taken in coming from the Miſſiſſippi, that has a large quantity of logwood on board. So that this logwood trade, as carried on by the French, we find is winked at by the Spaniards, while we have had frequent accounts that they threaten to deſtroy all our people who are any way concerned in this commerce.

We have for ſome time been amuſed with the Spaniards entering into a ſtrict neutrality during the preſent war. I am afraid that we ſhall not be greater gainers by their neutrality than we are by thoſe of the Dutch, the Hamburghers, Danes, &c. For hereby will not the ports of Spain be free and open to export all Spaniſh commodities to Great Britain, and a great part in their own bottoms too, ſince they have commenced an active

com-

commerce; while the Spaniards ſhall carry, and cover under Spaniſh names, all French commodities? For there is no end of the deceits practiſed by neutral carriers in times of war. In a word, as our commerce is circumſtanced, in regard to that of France, (with relation, I mean, to the difference in price between their commodities and ours) the neutrality of maritime carriers muſt prove very deſtructive to the trade of England, becauſe thoſe neutral powers will not traffic in Britiſh goods, as I have elſewhere obſerved, while they can in French to much greater advantage. Beſides, ought it not to be conſidered whether the neutrality of Spain may not prove far more beneficial to France than even Spain declaring war againſt us likewiſe may be? For may they not, under colour of ſuch neutrality, ſupply them with the treaſures of the Spaniſh Indies to ruin us? I am much afraid that a Spaniſh neutrality, and a French war will prove more deſtructive to Great Britain than a war both with France and Spain.—But I ſhall not enter into a diſcuſſion of this important point: I cannot, however, avoid expreſſing my fears, and leaving the matter to the animadverſion of thoſe, whoſe duty it is more than mine to enter deeply into thoſe delicate concerns.

We have ſhewn, on another occaſion, how large a fleet Spain has now ready for action; and if they ſign a neutrality, will this preclude them from ſelling their ſhips of war to France?

Or

Or, will it be reckoned an infraction of ſuch neutrality for Spain ſome how to diſpoſe of this fleet for the aſſiſtance of France? Can we ſuppoſe the Spaniards ſo weak as to put themſelves to ſuch great expence for nothing? Let us only ſuppoſe (for I would not preſume to go farther than bare ſuppoſition) that France propoſed to Spain, after they have ſigned a neutrality, to give them up Minorca, if they will give them an equivalent in men of war, and the naval ſtores they have now ready for action. Could ſuch an agreement be conſtrued a violation of the Spaniſh neutrality? Minorca is, by conqueſt, at preſent the abſolute property of France, and they can diſpoſe of it as they pleaſe; they may give it, or ſell it, to whatever power they ſhall think proper; and why not to Spain, for what they may think a valuable conſideration? If the neutrality of Spain takes place, I wiſh this may prove imaginary. But the ſhort queſtion is, whether this policy is not far more for the mutual intereſt of France and Spain, than Spain to join with France againſt England? If they find it ſo on deliberation, I make no doubt but we ſhall ſoon hear of a Spaniſh neutrality. But from whoſe inſtigation is this neutrality to take place? We can hardly believe it can proceed from the court of England.—Would not this betray our weakneſs as well as our dread, no leſs than the diſtraction of our ſyſtem? Is the Antigallican prize to be made the tub to decoy us into theſe ſnares? Or, is advantage to be taken of the

the preſent unhappy ſituation of our domeſtic affairs? Or, have we not reaſon enough to believe that France has made ſecret overtures to Spain to come into a neutrality? Let it proceed from whatever cauſe it may, if Spain makes choice of ſuch a part, we muſt certainly be ſtone-blind not to diſcern that this is brought about by the councils of France and Spain acting in ſecret concert. But what is the cover? Where lies the deception upon poor old England? Here it lies, I am much afraid--the Antigallican affair, and ſome other pretences, are to be made the motives to England for ſuing to Spain for her own deſtruction!

It will be aſked, perhaps, why ſhould we dream of Spain's exchanging her royal navy to France, or ſigning a neutrality? From ſome motive or other, we will not ſay what. —If not from thoſe we have ſuggeſted, are there no others to induce Spain to aſſiſt France in her trade, and even with her marine, under the pretext we have mentioned? And may it not be ſecretly agreed between thoſe two courts, on conſideration of ſuch artful aſſiſtance on the part of Spain, that France ſhall exert ſuch Spaniſh naval ſtrength, in conjunction with their own, to wreſt Gibraltar out of our hands, as they have done Minorca? And, after the affair was over, would it not be very eaſy for thoſe two powers to make an exchange again; the French to give up Gibraltar to Spain, and Spain return Minorca to France? And may not all this be done under cover of a neutrality! But while France and Spain were playing this game, could not Spain underhandedly aſſiſt them alſo by land in the acquiſition of Gibraltar, while France were acting by ſea with the combined fleets? And if England complained of this, as a violation of the Spaniſh neutrality, what ſatisfaction would ſhe have by it? The buſineſs might be over before our remonſtrances might be liſtened to at the court of Madrid; or ſo delayed as not to prevent the execution of the ſcheme projected. And Spain then would declare war againſt England alſo, and bid us defiance. In this manner may Great Britain be duped out of her moſt invaluable rights and poſſeſſions, and out of the whole commerce of the Mediterranean, the Turkey, and Levant trades: and after this, what might not the combined powers effect, by ſuch artful machinations? Are not theſe powerful motives for France and Spain thus to unite ſword and purſe, if not ſword and ſword, to obtain theſe great points? Can we ſtill be weak enough to amuſe ourſelves that we have the leaſt favour or friendſhip to expect from Spain, either from her neutrality or otherwiſe? But why are we to expect ſuch tenderneſs from Spain as ſome people flatter themſelves with? Have we had the leaſt experience of it ſince the peace of Utrecht to the preſent tenſe? Ah, but ſhe is a great gainer by the trade with us, and not with France, and ſhe will not quarrel with us. Nothing more true; ſhe is a much greater than ſhe deſerves to be, by a nation

ſhe

ſhe has ſo much inſulted, and on whoſe traders ſhe committed ſuch ſcandalous depredations, without provocation any way adequate to the reſentment ſhewn. Well! but ſay others again, though in contradiction to the former, we are ſo great gainers by the trade of Spain, that it is not our intereſt to quarrel with her at any rate. This appears to be a great falſhood, and an egregious impoſition upon thoſe who think ſo; and let any impartial man conſider connectedly what I have ſaid upon this topic, and he will find his miſtake; but I will ſay no more here at preſent: in ſhort, the balance of trade between England and Spain turns daily more and more to our diſadvantage; and it will ſoon appear more conſpicuouſly ſo to the eyes of thoſe who will not ſee at preſent. The great point, however, ſubmitted to conſideration is, whether it may not be more for our intereſt to have a war both with France and Spain, than with France alone, and Spain to remain neuter?

Is it time to ſpeak out, or ſhall we refrain till the nation is undone? However unpaid, or unthanked, I will throw in my mite to ſave the ſinking nation; for ſinking we certainly are, in the opinion of all candid and impartial men; in the opinion of all who will be honeſt enough to ſpeak what they think. But certainly ſome people muſt not think at all, or think only like ſuperlative traitors to their country, who inſinuate, that, for peace ſake, we ſhould not ſcruple even to give

give up Gibraltar itſelf to Spain! How can we expect things to go well with us, while principles of this kind ſhall be adopted? If complaiſance would effectually attach that court to our intereſt, have we not already ſufficiently ſhewn it? Have we not given up the trade of the South-Seas, and alſo that of the Aſſiento contract, to oblige Spain? And have we not been the chief inſtruments of ſettling two Spaniſh monarchs in Italy? And after all, did they not inſult us, and obſtruct our commerce and navigation to and from our colonies to ſuch a degree, as at length forced us into a war with them? Can we ſuppoſe, therefore, that if we were ſo further complaiſant to them, as to make them a preſent of Gibraltar, and Jamaica too, that they would uſe us the better, by reaſon of our greater impotence to reſent their wrongs and indignities? No man can ſeriouſly think ſo. That the miſtakes of ſuch who are really indifferent in regard to Gibraltar, the following reaſons are humbly ſubmitted to their candid conſideration, for our preſervation of that important place.

(1) Because Gibraltar preſerves to us the conveniency, protection, and ſecurity of our commerce to the ſtreights, above that of all other nations, more eſpecially in regard to the Algerines and Salleemen, who are influenced by it to keep their treaties made with us; which they never do longer with any

other

other nation than till they find it their intereſt to break them.

(2.) Because in reſpect to the great advantage which the poſſeſſion of that place hath already given us, when in war with France and Spain; and, conſequently, will always give us again upon the like occaſion, whilſt we continue to keep it.

(3.) With regard to our trade in general up the Mediterranean: for, as it commands the paſſage or enterance of all our navigation into that ſea, both in time of peace and war, ſo it is equally neceſſary, and as much our intereſt, to keep it ourſelves, as for any gentleman to keep poſſeſſion of the gate which leads to his own houſe; it being in the power of thoſe who poſſeſs this port, at all times, to interrupt, annoy, or hinder whom they ſhall think fit in their trade, by keeping a few ſhips of war conſtantly on that ſtation; in the ſame manner almoſt as the Danes, by the poſſeſſion of Elſineur command the paſſage into and out of the Baltic: ſo that, if this port and fortification were in the hands of any other nation, it would be in their power likewiſe either to permit us to navigate our trade within thoſe ſtreights, or not, as they ſhould think fit, unleſs a very ſtrong ſquadron was conſtantly kept at the enterance of the ſtreight's mouth, to ſecure the paſſage, and to be relieved, from time to time, by freſh ſhips, which would put us to a much

greater

greater expence than we are now at in keeping this place.

(4.) BECAUSE, before England was in possession of Tangier, on the opposite side of the streight, we were never able to deal with the Algerines, and other Turkish rovers; who, for near a century, had carried on a successful piratic war against the commerce of this nation, and never could be reduced till, by the situation and our possession of the abovementioned place, we distressed them so much, not only by taking their ships going in and coming out of the streights, but also by retaking such of their prizes as they had taken in the Ocean, that at last they were forced to be content with such a peace as we would give them; the continuance of which is owing to nothing so much as to our having been, for many years passed, and, at present, in the same condition to chastize those rovers, by the possession of Gibraltar, as we were before by the possession of Tangier.

(5.) BECAUSE the security of our Italian, Turkey, and fish-trades entirely depends on our possession of this place; and, should we ever lose it, or part with it, it is very reasonable to believe that both the Algerines and Salleemen would soon break with us again: so that, in such a case, the abovesaid branches of trade would almost wholly fall into the hands of our rivals, the French from Marseilles, who, by their situation, are always

ways ready at hand to furniſh thoſe markets, as ſoon as they are in want, while we, on our part, ſhall be obliged to carry on that trade by the tedious methods of fleets, and convoys, and at laſt, perhaps, come long after the market is ſupplied by our rivals. Beſides all this, the article of inſurance, which would certainly run much higher than uſual under theſe circumſtances, would prove a heavy charge on our goods, more than thoſe of foreign traders, which would thereby very much affect thoſe branches of our trade and navigation.

(6.) BECAUSE the miſchief would not ſtop here: for, as the Algerines, of late years, often cruize at the mouth of our channel, and as ſome of them have alſo heretofore come into our very ports two or three years ſucceſſively; ſo it is poſſible that, if we ſhould loſe Gibraltar, they may become, being ſo well acquainted with our channel, a much more dangerous enemy to us than ever they were formerly, and may attack all our trade in general, as the St. Malo privateers did in the wars of queen Anne, whenever they ſhall find that they can carry home their prizes without any interruption; which is not to be done, unleſs we ſhould be diſpoſſeſſed of Gibraltar, and thereby take the bridle, which has hitherto reſtrained them, out of their mouths.

(7.) BECAUSE, in reſpect to our neighbours, Gibraltar is ſituated in ſuch a manner, that

that it is in the power of the preſent poſſeſſors to cut off any naval communication between one port and another, of each of thoſe very powerful kingdoms: with which we have had ſuch frequent occaſions to be at war for almoſt theſe fifty years paſt; who would ſoon turn the tables upon us, if they ſhould recover this place out of our hands, eſpecially in time of any rupture between us; nothing being more ſelf-evident than that it gives, to thoſe who are maſters of it, eſpecially in conjunction with Minorca, the ſovereignty and command of the commerce and navigation of the Mediterranean ſea, and makes it almoſt impracticable for any other nation to trade there with ſafety, without their leave. And farther, by our poſſeſſion of this place, all nations within the Mediterranean will be obliged to court our friendſhip, or fear our power, particularly, the piratical ſtates, who, beholding vengeance ſo near at hand, will be thereby deterred from attempting to interrupt our trade, while they are deſtroying that of all others.

(8.) Because this advantage is not all that we reap from the poſſeſſion of Gibraltar; for it hath put into our hands occaſionally a great proportion of freight-trade into the Mediterranean, eſpecially, that of the Hamburghers, and Hollanders, who have made uſe of Britiſh bottoms to carry on their commerce in thoſe ſeas, till the Dutch obtained a peace with the Algerines; whereby we loſt one great advantage that belonged to the navigation

tion of Great Britain, which we before enjoyed, whilſt thoſe merchants made uſe of Engliſh ſhips, finding it dangerous to venture their eſtates in any other.

(9.) BECAUSE, laying aſide all other conſiderations, there cannot be a ſtronger proof of the importance which the poſſeſſion of this place hath proved to us, than that it hath been a formidable check to the naval power of France, from the hour of our taking it, to the concluſion of the laſt French war: nor, indeed, could they ever ſend any naval ſtores round about into thoſe ſeas, without an apparent danger of their falling into our hands in going through the ſtreights. And, had not ſuch unhappy miſunderſtandings fell out as did between two admirals in the late war, we ſhould have more feelingly experienced the invaluable benefit of this poſſeſſion, which would have prevented a war for many years to come.

(10.) BECAUSE it's proximity to Cadiz, the great mart and center of almoſt all the riches of Spaniſh America, gives us the greateſt opportunity of commanding that port, and the trade frequenting it from the Weſt-Indies; which, in time of war with Spain, may be reckoned of no ſmall conſideration, or importance.

(11.) BECAUSE, as the advantages of Gibraltar which reſult to this kingdom from the foregoing particulars, are fully confirmed and demonſtrated by the experience of many years paſt, ſo the preſervation of it, at all times, is of of much greater concernment than it was ever before, as will appear by conſidering the preſent ſtate of public affairs: particularly, that many capital manufactures are ſpringing up in moſt parts of Europe, and are grown to a great height as well in Spain as France, and that ſeveral other powerful ſtates are endeavouring to vie with us in commerce and a maritime force; which ought to put us on the ſtricteſt guard, and determine us not to part with a place which is manifeſtly of ſo much advantage, by ſecuring and improving our own trade and navigation, as well as by defeating the attempts of our enemies and rivals therein.

(12.) BECAUSE Spain and France in conjunction, if not others, will ever have their eye upon this poſſeſſion, in order to wreſt the ſame out of our hands, to ruin the whole maritime power of Great Britain.

(13.) BECAUSE Gibraltar lies at hand to intercept their Eaſt-and Weſt-India fleets, with the ſpoil and riches of both worlds: it ſeparates and divides Spain from itſelf, and hinders all communication by ſea from the different parts of their dominions, and, conſequently, muſt keep them in a perpetual dependence, and put them under a neceſſity to court our friendſhip, as well as fear our enmity, if our naval ſtrength is once duly exerted: it gives us an opportunity to pry into all their meaſures, obſerve all their motions, and, without the moſt ſtupid remiſsneſs on our part, renders it impracticable to them to form

any

any projects, or carry on any expeditions against us or our allies, without our having due notice.

(14.) Because it may be made highly useful to check the rise of the naval power of France, which can never be above our match at sea, if uncorruptly exerted, whilst Gibraltar remains in our hands. It hinders the communication between their ports and squadrons in the Ocean and the Mediterranean: it makes it impossible for them to supply their southern harbours with naval stores either for building or repairing of fleets; of which they were so sensible in queen Anne's war, that, as soon as Sir George Rook had possessed himself of it, they saw themselves under a necessity to lay aside their usual caution, and dare him in open battle; and, not meeting the success they hoped for, the very same year, to the unspeakable prejudice of their other affairs, besieged it in form, and lost a French and Spanish army before it, and never afterwards appeared with a fleet upon the seas again during the whole war, but suffered their great ships to moulder and rot in their harbours, for want of the means to fit them out again.

(15.) Because long experience has evinced, that we can never, with security, depend on the faith of France: and, therefore, if Britons are determined never to become vassals to the dominion of that crown, they can never part with any thing that is so substantial a preservation of their maritime power,

and,

and, consequently, of their liberties and properties, as that inestimable fortress of Gibraltar.

(16.) BECAUSE it appears throughout this work, from a series of facts incontestable, that the commerce and navigation of France have been encreasing ever since the time of that great and able minister Mons. Colbert: and that they have now settled the same upon so broad a bottom, and with such peculiar and extraordinary advantage for their daily rise and encouragement, that, if Great Britain gives up Gibraltar, she may be so eternally embroiled in wars with that nation, as to encrease her national debts and incumbrances to a degree so enormous, that her whole trade must inevitably sink under them.

(17.) BECAUSE a right use made of the possession of Gibraltar will always give us reputation and figure in those seas, which are always rewarded with power and riches. It will oblige all nations who trade in the Mediterranean, or have empire there, to court our friendship, and keep measures with us. It will awe even the courts of Rome and Constantinople, and make them afraid to disturb or provoke us.

(18.) BECAUSE the charge and expence of keeping Gibraltar bears no proportion to the advantages we reap by it, and the detriment and injury our trade and navigation must sustain, if ever we part with it.

(19) BECAUSE if Minorca ſhould be reſtored to us, PORT-MAHON cannot poſſibly anſwer all the purpoſes of Gibraltar: which muſt be evident to any one, who but looks into the map; for the iſland of Minorca lies many hundred miles further up towards the gulph of Lyons, and, in truth, out of the road of all ſhips trading to Sicily, the Adriatic, the Levant, or Africa. It is ſituated at ſuch a diſtance from France, and Spain, that the greateſt fleets can eſcape unobſerved, unleſs we keep perpetually before their ports to watch and purſue them; which is exceeding dangerous, if not impracticable in thoſe ſeas. We ſhall be out of a way of all intelligence. But as we have loſt Minorca, there is ſtill a greater neceſſity for our keeping Gibraltar.

(20.) BECAUSE nothing is plainer, than that it will be exceeding difficult, if not impoſſible, to keep the iſland of Minorca, if reſtored, without the poſſeſſion of Gibraltar; at leaſt it will be more expenſive to us than both would be, eſpecially, if France and Spain ſhould join again; which event, I think, we ought to keep always in view, for then Gibraltar will be the only reſource we have to carry on any trade in the Mediterranean, and to prevent the union of the French and Spaniſh fleets with themſelves, or each other.

(21.) BECAUSE all the objections, made againſt the facility of a communication of the different ports of France and Spain with one another,

another, will be ſtronger againſt us; for they have others near to Gibraltar, where fleets may lie ſafe, and have a chance to eſcape us, by catching at favourable opportunities, and the advantage of winds; whereas we muſt run all hazards, and truſt to our ſtrength alone, without any harhour to retreat to, in caſe of ſtorms or other accidents.

(22.) Because we have no means of ſending naval ſtores and recruits to our garriſons, and often proviſions for them, without a port to protect us during a thouſand leagues ſailing. Portugal will not be ſuffered to receive, or relieve us, and then we muſt run the gauntlet by ſingle ſhips, with ſcarce a chance to eſcape, or ſend convoys upon the ſmalleſt occaſions, capable of fighting the united French and Spaniſh power.

(23.) Because we ought not to be ſurprized, if the nations of Europe and Africa ſhould wiſh it in hands leſs potent at ſea, and who could conſequently enjoy it more harmleſsly to it's neighbours: it muſt be undoubtedly an awe to any people who would be our rivals in trade or naval power, or, indeed to any ſtate that aſpires to empire, which can never be accompliſhed without fleets as well as armies.

(24.) Because, if we part with Gibraltar, to what purpoſe have we made war? To what purpoſe beſtowed great ſums, and gained great victories? Did we beat the enemy, and force them to beg peace, and yet muſt bribe

bribe them to accept of it? Have we conquered, and ſhall they give terms, and get towns by loſing battles? Or, if we do not part with Gibraltar for the ſake of peace, pray what conſideration are we to receive for the ſake of Gibraltar? What can be given as an equivalent?

(25.) Because there can be no ſubſtantial reaſons to take ſuch a thorn out of the foot of Spain and France, and to remove ſuch an obſtacle to their greatneſs: the enterprizing genius of the latter is as well known, as it is formidable to all it's neighbours, but, in particular to us. And Spain, we have ſeen, are taking large ſtrides to raiſe manufactures and maritime power. And do we not know by experience, what help we are to expect from our allies, when we have no more millions to give. We are not able to keep great ſtanding armies at home, nor is it conſiſtent with our liberty to do ſo; and, therefore, we ought to take every meaſure to encreaſe our naval ſtrength, and to put new bridles upon thoſe who are, or may ſoon be, our rivals therein.

(26.) Because the nation in the world whoſe power we have moſt reaſon to guard againſt, is that of France; and yet I don't know by what fatality it has often ſo happened, that we have been the unhappy inſtruments of promoting it. Oliver Cromwell gave the firſt riſe to it's greatneſs at land, and king Charles II.

at ſea: the late queen, by an ignominious peace, reſtored it, when it was reduced to the loweſt extremity, and muſt have ſubmitted to any conditions ſhe had thought fit to impoſe. But ſure it will never be ſaid that any Britiſh miniſtry, who profeſs to be the patrons of liberty, the conſtant and declared enemies of thoſe proceedings, ſhould act ſo far in defiance of all their known principles, as, voluntarily and unconſtrainedly, to throw away any part of that national ſecurity, which are the only rewards and recompence of a tedious, ſucceſsful, and glorious war, carried on at an immenſe expence of blood and treaſure, of which we and our poſterity ſhall long feel the ſevere effects.

(27.) BECAUSE there ſeems to be more reaſon for our being tenacious in preſerving this poſſeſſion, at this time, than there ever was ſince we had it; for, it is to be feared, that we are the only maritime power that muſt alone ſtand againſt thoſe of France and Spain, and ſuch allies as they ſhall be able to influence; ſince our old and natural allies, the ſtates-generals of the United Provinces, do not appear to be at all inclined, as heretofore, to unite with Great Britain, and act with vigour, when occaſion may require, but on the contrary are, by their neutrality, greatly aiding to the encreaſe of the commerce of France, and thereby enabling her the better to continue the war.

(28.) BE-

(28.) BECAUSE the Spaniards give more encouragement to the French in their trade, by the way of Old Spain to New Spain, than they do to the English; and, in consequence thereof, our commerce in that channel declines, while that of France advances. And the Spaniards to favour the French in the S——h W——t-I—-a trade, which they carry on from their colonies, to the Spanish main, both from the Mississippi, and St. Domingo, while they are always pecking at the English about a little paultry logwood, which affair they ought long to have finally settled, but have always declined the same.

(29.) BECAUSE the too frequent unkindly treatment of the English in particular, by the Spaniards at present in America, is said by some to be with a view to compel us, at length, to give up Gibraltar; which, for that very reason, we ought to be the more sanguine to preserve.

(30.) BECAUSE Great Britain has already done enough in favour of the court of Spain without sacrificing Gibraltar, to induce them to desist from their obstruction to our trade and navigation to and from our own colonies, even, if we had no right whatever to cut logwood.

THE conduct of Great Britain towards Spain, in order to influence them to preserve a good understanding with them, is notorious to the whole world, and may be chiefly comprehended under the following articles.

(1) Our

(1) Our giving up the trade of the South-ſeas in exchange for the Aſſiento contract. (2) Our giving up the Aſſiento contract itſelf for a ſong for peace ſake. (3) Our being the chief inſtrument of making two Spaniſh ſovereigns in Italy.—To which may be added (4) Our being the beſt cuſtomers for Spaniſh wines, fruits, &c that Spain has to her back. And, if Great Britain ſhould even acquieſce to the creating of a third ſovereign to gratify, and to give up Gibraltar alſo, what ſecurity ſhould this nation have, for the friendſhip of Spain ?

ONE part of the grand ſyſtem of the court of Spain, in the time of Alberoni, was to preſerve the rights of Spain and of the houſe of Parma to Spaniſh princes; and to make a ſettlement for Don Charlos and Don Philip worthy of their birth, out of the ſtates which the emperor poſſeſſed in Italy: and has not this part of the ſyſtem been ſteadily and ſucceſsfully purſued ? But how could theſe ſovereignties be effectually ſecured, ſays a certain princeſs, without the poſſeſſion of Gibraltar ? This, therefore, was a point to be gained, in order the better to ſecure the other. The ſyſtem, at preſent in Spain, is bottomed on the ſame principles; it is not only to provide for a third prince in Italy, or elſewhere, but to fall upon the eſtabliſhment of manufactories, with a view to ſupply their extended American colonies themſelves with their own merchandizes, and thoſe of France, inſtead of taking them from the other nations of Europe.

Will

Will not this affect Great Britain, in proportion to what ſhe now ſupplies Spain with? Some accounts from Spain about two years ſince tell us, that it appeared, by an authentic liſt of the ſhips which entered the Spaniſh ports that year, their number amounted to 1142: of which 643 were Engliſh, 277 French, 148 Dutch, and 74 of different nations.

SUPPOSING this to be true, ſome people may infer from hence, perhaps, that the trade of England muſt be far ſuperior to any of the reſt: ſo it is, indeed! But what ſort of trade are we carrying on with that nation? We are ſending 6 or 700 ſhips or more annually to purchaſe their wines and their fruits, while France ſends between 2 or 300 to carry their own manufactures. If this be the caſe, does not France, therefore, gain far more by their ſmaller quantity of ſhipping, than we do by double the number? The fact is, that we decline in our exports to Spain, and encreaſe in our imports; while France encreaſe in their exports to Spain, and decreaſe in their imports from thence. Have they not allured away our manufacturers and ſhipwrights out of the kingdom, with a view to turn the hands of our own artiſts againſt us?

WHAT is urged in divers other parts of this work, will enable us to judge, whether it can ever be adviſeable to acquieſce in the giving up Gibraltar; and, eſpecially ſo, if we add to theſe conſiderations what we have ſaid alſo in regard to the commercial dominion of

FRANCE:

FRANCE; becauſe we ſhall find, that SPAIN is now following the example of France, in order to ruin the commerce and navigation of theſe kingdoms: for the ſyſtem of the two courts ſeems really to be what is ſaid in a tract lately printed, called the Political Teſtament of cardinal Alberoni. "While the navy of the two crowns [meaning thoſe of France and Spain] ſays the writer, is not ſuperior to that of the Engliſh and Dutch together; while MINORCA and GIBRALTAR are not in poſſeſſion of their proper maſters; while DUNKIRK is not raiſed from the ſtate to which it was reduced by the treaty of Utrecht, a deſcent on the coaſt of ENGLAND and IRELAND, will be always ineffectual, &c."

DIS-

DISSERTATION XXXVI.

Of the neceſſity of Great Britain being more cloſely connected and allied with the continent *than ſhe ever has been, though upon quite different principles, and not at ſuch an* expence, *in times of war, as has been the caſe heretofore.*

IT has, doubtleſs, coſt this nation an immenſe profuſion of blood, as well as treaſure, to preſerve the liberties of Europe, by forming ſuch alliances and confederacies as have been occaſionally neceſſary to withſtand the torrent of arbitrary power of thoſe nations, who have brooded ſchemes of ruin and deſtruction to their neighbouring ſtates.

OUR allies alſo have been at as great a proportion of the expence as they could well afford in the ſame good cauſe, notwithſtanding the large ſubſidies wherewith we have been obliged to ſupply ſome.

THE great public debt, and the burdenſome taxes with which our commerce is hereby become incumbered, to our unſpeakable detri-

detriment, in consequence of those measures, make it necessary for the court of England to change this *old system*, and adopt such other as may exempt her and her allies from those prodigious expences which have hitherto proved necessary. Those potentates who have disturbed the tranquillity of Europe, have been chiefly such who are interested in the cause of arbitrary and tyrannical rule, the enemies of liberty, and the enemies of mankind; and they have been withstood chiefly by the Protestant potentates, the friends of liberty, and the friends of mankind. And the glorious stand made by those states having hitherto preserved the liberties of Christendom, and maintained the balance of power; the expence, be it what it will, is no way disproportionate to the important and invaluable blessings it has hitherto procured. For what avail all the treasures of the earth, if we are deprived of the only solid felicity that life affords; the freedom of thought, the toleration to worship our maker according to the dictates of our reason and conscience, and the full enjoyment of property, and every right and privilege that human nature can wish or desire. Certain then it is, that the expence of this nation, however great it has been, bears no comparison to the inestimable purchase that we have obtained as an equivalent. This no free Briton will gainsay.

The argument, therefore, with respect to our connections with the continent, is reduced

duced to this ſingle queſtion: whether Great Britain could have proved the happy inſtrument that ſhe has been in preſerving the liberties of Europe, at leſs expence than ſhe has been put to? If ſhe could, this is to be laid at the door of thoſe miniſters of ſtate, who have been too profuſe of the public treaſure. Whatever proportion of the expence we have been at, might have been ſaved to the nation, muſt be attributed to the bad meaſures of thoſe who have had the conduct of our public affairs from the revolution to the preſent time: the fault lies not in the cauſe for which we have contended, but in the exorbitant expence to which we have been put; which cauſe might have been as effectually ſupported, in my humble opinion, at a far leſs expence than it has been: no man will undertake to aſcertain exactly how many millions might have been ſaved to this nation, and yet the liberties of this kingdom, and the balance of power in Europe, have been no leſs ſecure than they are at preſent. For my own part, the work * I drew up the laſt year for the public ſervice, ſignifies explicitly enough how many millions, I apprehend, might have been ſaved to the nation by raiſing the ſupplies for carrying on wars within the year, and purchaſing all naval and military ſtores for ſhort credit, or at

* Great Britain's True Syſtem.

a ready money price, as it were. In the ſame tract I have ſhewed my diſapprobation of the meaſures of ſending Britiſh troops to the continent, when we could hire auxiliaries at a much cheaper rate. But the contrary meaſures have certainly proved wrong, as having exceſſively accumulated the expence, and incumbered the nation with an enormous debt, and clogged our commerce with taxes ruinous to it.

As I have ſhewed myſelf an advocate for the contrary meaſures to what have hitherto been purſued in this reſpect from the revolution to the preſent time; ſo the courſe of my ſtudies has led me to conſider every way whereby we can ſupport the liberties of Europe and our own, at the leaſt expence poſſible: and, in my writings, I have entered into a detail of the particular ſteps that I have judged neceſſary for that purpoſe, which need not be here repeated.

But this is not near the full length that I have humbly attempted to go. No: I have endeavoured to form a new foreign ſyſtem; or rather to engraft an entire new ſyſtem upon the old one, whereby one million of money properly raiſed, and properly applied, may go near as far as two millions have been made to do upon the old ſyſtem. And I ſuppoſe, if the court of England could, by the moſt parſimonious meaſures, obtain ſuch alliances upon the continent for one half the

expence

expence that ſhe has been at heretofore, as ſhall prove ſufficient to withſtand the power of the enemies of the Proteſtant intereſt; I preſume no body could, or would, think much of ſuch an expence. As we are the chief Proteſtant potentate in Europe, and it is reckoned that no other can afford to be at ſo great an expence as we can, we muſt expect to bear a greater ſhare of the burden than any other; and eſpecially ſo in the preſent war, ſince we are the principals therein. Indeed, when the religion and liberties of other Proteſtant ſtates become endangered, theſe ſtates then become no leſs principals than we, in regard to theſe points, and as ſuch, it is to be hoped will be excited to act in concert with us for our mutual defence and ſecurity.

When people talk of our not being under the neceſſity of having any connection with the continent, they certainly talk very irrationally and wildly; when they are pleaſed to conſider that our whole commercial intereſt abſolutely depends on thoſe continental connections, becauſe they are our trading cuſtomers, and our reciprocal trafficable dealings require us to cement thoſe connections. Upon what principles of policy elſe are all our treaties of commerce founded? When the court of England is not capable of obtaining allies to contribute to fight their battles for them without ſubſidies, then we have a great lamentation for want of allies; and yet,

yet, in the ſame breath. theſe very complainants will roundly aſſert, that we have no need of any connections with the continent! Can any thing be more inconſiſtent? From whence but from the continent are we to have any allies? Well then, the matter lies here; we are always glad to have good allies in times of danger; and he is the ableſt miniſter who can obtain ſuch at the leaſt expence to the nation. If this is the right ſtate of the matter, then we will hope that the Britiſh miniſtry will act upon this ſyſtem.

WE have ſeen, from a ſeries of the plaineſt and moſt indiſputable *facts*, how formidable the power of France is, and what capacious ſchemes of commercial ſway and dominion ſhe has projected.—We have ſeen likewiſe that the ſyſtem of Spain is perfectly compatible with that of France; that Spain follows as cloſely the Steps of France, as if the miniſters of France were in the cabinet of Spain.—We hear too, and I wiſh it may not prove true, that the Spaniſh miniſter Don Enſeneda is recalled to court, and that our dear friend the queen dowager of Spain has again crept into his Catholic Majeſty's councils, which forebodes no good, perhaps, to Great Britain.—Do we not know likewiſe that Spain has got a pretty formidable fleet? And can we imagine that this court has been at ſuch an expence to parade it only? We have ſeen too the detrimental effects to our

com-

commerce of a Spaniſh neutrality. So that, let Spain take which part ſhe will, have we not all reaſon to connect ourſelves more cloſely with ſome good continental allies than ever we had? With allies who will not only act ſo far in concert with us by land, as may prove preſervative of the Proteſtant intereſt there, but ſhall be induced to unite their maritime power with ours; for I wiſh that we may not have occaſion enough for it. Allies then are certainly neceſſary for us to obtain, and ſuch too as are able and willing to do us, and the Proteſtant cauſe, the moſt effectual ſervices. But what allies can we expect to obtain, according to the old ſyſtem of foreign affairs? The Dutch, we have too long experienced, are immoveable, and we have ſeen their reaſons why. Whether the reaſons aſſigned be real or pretended, it matters little, as to their good offices towards us now in time of need. If the reaſons aſſigned are real, we have it in our power to obviate them; if they mean otherwiſe than they ſay, it is our buſineſs to penetrate that meaning, and remove their moſt ſecret articles to a perfect union between us. But if we prevail with them no farther than to fulfil their treaties with us, what dependence can we make on their aſſiſtance? Has not experience ſufficiently taught us? It is manifeſt, therefore, that Great Britain cannot reckon at all on the ſervices of the United Provinces upon the old ſyſtem, eſpecially

cially as affairs are at present circumſtanced between the French and the Dutch. What then becomes the wiſdom of Great Britain to do, in regard to the Dutch? For their neutrality, at preſent, is little leſs detrimental to our commerce than if they threw the weight of their whole power againſt us into the French ſcale. But ſome are inclined to think that the Dutch are quite impotent as a ſtate, and that their power is not worth courting by Great Britain. This is a great miſtake. Were they determined to exert their whole ſtrength, and act in concert with their old and natural ally, as one and the ſame nation: were the Dutch in earneſt to act in conjunction with us to reduce the power of France within the requiſite bounds, and was England reſolved to move in conjunction with Holland upon the ſame principle, and in earneſt alſo to humble France once for all, we ſhould ſoon ſee that the Dutch could figure it as highly and mightily as they ever have done; for their plea of inability is pretence only: thoſe who know their commercial reſources, the true ſtate of that republic, and the millions they have in foreign funds, know that theſe are only ſpecious coverings, and to ſave appearance with the court of London. But if Great Britain becomes once happy enough to have a miniſtry that the Dutch think they can abſolutely depend upon; if they become once convinced that the affairs of the nation will be ſo conducted,

ducted, that if we draw them into an expenſive war againſt France as principals, we ſhall not be able to extricate them from it with honour and advantage: if we ſhall convince them that we are determined at laſt to take Lewis by the whiſkers, we ſhould ſoon ſee the Dutch move with us, and for us, as heretofore.

BUT what muſt be done on our part to convince the Dutch they may ſecurely depend upon us to do all this? Certainly our old ſyſtem, with relation both to our domeſtic as well as foreign affairs, will never make the due impreſſion for this purpoſe upon the United Provinces: we have tried that long enough, and often enough, and it is ſuperlative weakneſs to rely any longer upon it. Is it not then in the power of Britain to form no other ſyſtem that will at once convince the Dutch that they may ſafely depend no leſs upon her ability than her wiſdom, to bring her ſecurely, honourably, and beneficially out of a war, if they came vigorouſly into one with her againſt the enemy? If there is ſuch a ſyſtem of policy to be projected, that ſeems to promiſe fair to anſwer thoſe deſirable purpoſes, has it not a title to be candidly examined into, although it ſhould come from the moſt obſcure and unknown perſon in the kingdom? though it ſhould come from ſo inſignificant a perſon as the writer of theſe papers?

WITH

WITH respect to the domestic system he has endeavoured to recommend and establish, that is openly enough declared in his last work. If the Dutch are once convinced that the court of England is determined to raise the supplies necessary to carry on the war within the year; if our ancient and natural ally shall once be made sensible that we are able to carry on a war without farther increasing our public debts and taxes, this measure alone we have seen from the declaration of their cabinet will remove some of the essential objections against their joining with us heartily against France.—If they shall find also, that such is the wisdom of his majesty's councils, that all parsimonious ways and means are fallen upon, both in the expending as well as raising of the public money; if the Dutch once experience that our public credit shall be established upon a rock, and that instead of augmenting their public debts and taxes, that we shall infallibly get into the certain road of reducing both; what weight will not this domestic step have with the states of Holland to induce them to listen to our remonstrances?

THOUGH these may be the proper preliminary steps requisite to be taken to convince the Dutch that our measures, and not only our ministers are changed; yet these alone will not have all the due influence with that state to bring them sanguinely into an offensive war against France. No: the court of England,

England, I humbly apprehend, muſt ſtill go greater lengths: they muſt alſo change their foreign ſyſtem, in order to induce the Dutch to throw up ſo lucrative a neutrality as they at preſent enjoy.—But how to accompliſh this is the great point!

DOES it become the wiſdom of any ſtateſman to affirm roundly, that he does not think it poſſible for the ſyſtem of foreign affairs to be ſo changed, as to induce the Dutch to give up their neutrality, and join the whole weight of their power with Britain againſt France? If men had been diſmayed from their reſearches into things from a prepoſſion of the impoſſibility of the diſcoveries which they have attempted, what advance in ſcience could we have expected? When people in authority ſhall declare the moſt important attempts to be impoſſibilities in their eye, can any thing prove a greater obſtruction and diſcouragement to the increaſe of knowledge of any kind? Who can undertake to aſſert with infallibility that it is impoſſible for the human underſtanding to diſcover this or that? Is there leſs preſumption in ſuch an infallible declaration, that an attempt to diſcover the ſuppoſed impoſſibility? Men of ſcience, I believe, will be of opinion, that the preſumption on the part of the one, is far more injurious to ſociety than any modeſt attempts on the ſide of the other to diſcover uſeful and important truths of any kind. But does not the progreſs of arts and

ſciences

ſciences ſhew, that the great ſeeming impoſſibilities have proved the moſt eaſy and palpable truths? If ſuch like authoritative caveats had been pronounced againſt all the diſcoveries that have been made, would there not long ſince have been a ſtop put to all the mathematical and philoſophical ſciences, which abound with numberleſs truths that appear at preſent greater impoſſibilities to thoſe who do not underſtand them, than the diſcovery of the political problem affirmed to be an impoſſibility by a late certain great man?—I am concerned for the gentleman's honour that he ſhould be ſo raſh in making ſuch an haſty declaration; but the goodneſs of his heart, with me, will attone for all the miſtakes of the head; for I greatly honour him, notwithſtanding his haſty determination in regard to a matter which has not fell under his conſideration.

LET it be ſuppoſed, however, that it is even impoſſible for the court of England to bring the Dutch into any new ſyſtem to act vigorouſly againſt France; is the court of England to ſet ſtill, and not endeavour to make any other alliances, in order to ſtem the torrent of popiſh dominion? No true Briton will ſay, that England ſhould attempt to act alone againſt France and Spain, as may ſoon prove the caſe. But leſt ſuch an event ſhould happen, does it not become the wiſdom of England to guard againſt ſo great an evil, if poſſible; becauſe, if England was capable of ſupporting a war to her advantage againſt both

both thoſe great potentates for a time, the number of neutral powers who would commence maritime carrier for Spain as well as France would ruin the commerce of England, and protect that of her enemies.

To what a degree the trade of France is, at preſent, promoted by the neutrality of the Dutch, the Danes, the Swedes, and the Hanſe towns, I have already repeatedly ſhewn; and who knows but ſome of thoſe neutral powers may endeavour to ſkreen Spaniſh, in caſe of a war with Spain, as they do, at preſent, French property. I am afraid this will prove the caſe, unleſs England can form a ſyſtem that will draw off thoſe powers from their neutrality. I will not ſhow how this may be done, leſt I ſhould put miſchief into the enemy's head, which they may not ſo readily fall upon. It follows then, if we conſider this point in whatever light we can, that England muſt make good alliances with the next beſt natural friend, ſhe can obtain, if ſhe cannot draw the Dutch into her circle of policy. And who are our natural allies next to the Dutch? Is it not happy for England that ſhe can have Pruſſia and Hanover to ſupply their place? If we cannot obtain theſe to act effectually againſt France and her allies, at ſo eaſy an expence as we could wiſh, is theſe not the greater neceſſity to raiſe the ſupplies within the year, and to purſue a ſteddy ſyſtem of domeſtic oeconomy, the better to enable us to ſupport our

allies,

allies, that they may give all the diverſion poſſible to the French power in Germany, which has proved the devouring grave of thoſe our enemies?

BUT theſe allies cannot give us any maritime aſſiſtance againſt the enemy. Why, therefore, ſhould we not endeavour to gain what maritime aſſiſtance we can from others? But theſe alliances will be very expenſive to us, if we are to purchaſe them at the rate we have heretofore done. I do not ſay, That ſhould be the caſe; but, if we cannot, or will not attempt to change our foreign as well as our domeſtic ſyſtem, that muſt be the caſe, let it coſt what it will; and, if we keep only from encreaſing our public debts and taxes, it will be happy for us if we can make no greater change in our general ſyſtem than *That*, it will prove of extraordinary help, and enable us the better to carry on the war, and procure an honourable peace. However, as I have ſaid, there is ſtill a much greater change needful then this alone, I mean a change in our whole foreign ſyſtem; ſuch a change as I humbly apprehend promiſes fair to bring in the Dutch, as well as our other next natural maritime allies into the war againſt France; and, which I conceive to be practicable upon far leſs expenſive meaſures than have been purſued from the revolution to the preſent time.

INSTEAD of being unconnected with the continent, as ſome would have, we ſtand in need

need of being more closely connected therewith than ever we yet were; but those connections should be founded rather upon interesting than expensive principles; and, as a trading nation we have more reason to be connected with the continent than the continent has to be with us. In regard likewise to our security both by land and sea, though an island, we may, in times of danger, stand in no less need of the aid of continental allies than they may occasionally do of ours; for, can any thing be more weak and ridiculous than to think ourselves omnipotent, because we are islanders, when we have experienced that neither our fleets by sea can infallibly protect our commerce, or our possessions abroad, nor our fleets and armies jointly preserve us from panicks at home? How absurd is it to imagine that an island, which depends upon commerce for it's wealth, should be emancipated from the continent, by which it subsists, and should establish it as a part of their political creed, that they will neither give to, nor receive from their continental friends any succour when their very Being depends upon their reciprocal support, and defence? However omnipotent by sea as well as land we might be formerly, the scene is now changed; our enemies have as greatly improved in the arts of war by sea and land as they have in the arts of commerce. This is one cause of our ill success. The marine as well as military system of France is greatly improved to what ours is in many eſſential reſpects, and it is no wonder that they prove more ſucceſsful than formerly.

VARIOUS are the arts of the French to divide this nation from all preſervative connections with the continent, they well knowing that if they can but once work us up to ſuch a ſtate of pride and ſelf-ſufficiency, as to think ourſelves independent of all the world beſide; and, in conſequence of ſuch vanity to influence our councils to break off all connections with the continent, they cannot fail to conquer us, or ſo diſtract our affairs as to obtain the end aimed at. Upon this principle it is, that they have left no artifice untryed to divide our continental ally, the Dutch, from our intereſt, which they ſeem to have done pretty effectually—Another point they have laboured not leſs arduouſly, though not ſucceſsfully, is to divide Great Britain from her continental ally, the Elector of Hanover, by employing her emiſſaries to propagate the greateſt falſhoods relating to His Majeſty's German dominions, and in making the people believe, that there are no commercial connections between this kingdom and thoſe dominions to induce us to ſupport them; when I have ſhown *, that thoſe connections are not leſs intereſting than thoſe with moſt other ſtates in Europe?——

* See my Great Britain's true ſyſtem.

They have likewiſe drawn off our continental allies the queen of Hungary, and the empreſs of Ruſſia, and would, if poſſible, detach the king of Pruſſia from our alliance. In ſhort, thoſe anticontinental principles that have been ſo induſtriouſly propagated of late years ſeem to have been coined in the mint of France, and circulated here to anſwer the moſt deſtractive as well as deſtructive views to this nation, and her natural allies. But I hope there is one good end that ſuch gallican politics will anſwer; which is, *that they will promote a ſtricter union between Great Britain and the continent than ſhe ever yet had, though at a far leſs expence than they ever yet did.—This is the* NEW SYSTEM *that will give us and our allies the victory, nor do I believe that any other can do it ſo effectually*; *and, therefore, I humbly hope, that the court of England will ſoon take the ſame into ſerious conſideration, although it comes from no greater a perſon than the humble writer of theſe papers.* Reaſon will prevail without authority, but authority will not prevail without reaſon. "Qui autem requirunt, quid quaque de re ipſi ſentiamus, curioſius id faciunt, quam neceſſe eſt: non enim tam auctoritatis in diſputando, quam rationis momenta quaerenda ſunt. Quin etiam obeſt plerumque iis, qui diſcere volunt, auctoritas eorum, quid ſe docere profitentur: deſinunt enim ſuum judicium adhibere; id habent ratum, quod ab eo, quem probant, judicatum vident. Nec vero probare

bare ſoleo id, quod de Pythagoreis accepimus; quos ferunt, ſi quid affirmarent in diſputando, cum ex iis quaereretur, quare ita eſſet, reſpondere ſolitos, ipſe dixit : ipſe autem erat Pythagoras. Tantum opinio praejudicata poterat, ut etiam ſine ratione valeret auctoritas. *Tul. de nat. deor.*

DISSERTATION XXXVII.

Some general principles whereon the balance of trade is founded; with the application thereof to the present work, in a recapitulation of it's contents; the consideration of which is earnestly recommended to public regard; in order to throw the balance of trade so effectually into the hands of Great Britain as to put the constant balance of power of Europe into her hands also.

THE general balance of a nation's trade is the difference between the amount of what it buys and what it sells abroad. That difference must necessarily be paid in money which is the sole equivalent for what is deficient in the exchange of commodities for commodities.

To receive that balance is the point which every trading nation aims at; and in fact it is the only thing capable of augmenting the positive and relative mass of their metals, of encreasing their populousness, and of giving circu-

circulation that activity which diſtributes eaſe, the uſeful principle of luxury, through every claſs of the people.

THE general balance is the reſult of the particular balances, which are not all immediately advantageous, though the general balance be lucrative. But they are not burdenſome to the ſtate when they are the means of procuring other more uſeful branches of trade, or leſſen the loſs on thoſe without which a nation cannot carry on trade.

TWO things deſerve to be taken particular notice of in the balance of trade: the way to know one's advantage, or diſadvantage; and the means of obtaining advantage.

IF no fraudulent exports or imports were made, it would be eaſy to aſcertain the nature and amount of the particular balances, by the cuſtomhouſe books and regiſters. But care muſt be taken in ſuch valuations not to rate the goods exported by foreign ſhips, higher than their firſt value and the expence of carriage on board; to which muſt be added the value of the freight, if they are ſhipped in national veſſels. It is on the other hand equally proper to value the imports made by foreign ſhips, on the footing of the value of the commodities at the place where they are landed; and on the footing of their firſt value only, when imported by national veſſels.

ANOTHER way to judge in general of the advantage or diſadvantage of the general balance

lance of trade during a year, is to combine the courſes all the exchanges have been at. This method is evidently not ſuſceptible of any poſitive degree of knowledge: nor is it in general of that of the particular balances, becauſe it often happens, that one place, by the trade with which a nation loſes, is employed to make the remittances of another with which it gains, without having any open courſe of exchange with it. But this method is more certain than the other to know whether money comes into a country, or goes out of it, becauſe it embraces every object.

BESIDES, the active and paſſive debts of foreign trade, ſtates have ſometimes others between themſelves.

THESE ſecond debts are the mutual expences of ſubjects who travel to each other's country; the intereſt of ſums put out either with private men, or in the public funds, or government ſecurities; and laſtly, their political engagements.

A BODY-POLITIC is not ſtrengthened by a new ſubſiſtance till all thoſe kinds of debts are mutually balanced. The reſult of thoſe operations cannot be known with any degree of certainty, but by a combination of the exchanges.

BOTH methods may in general be of great help to each other, and afford a reciprocal elucidation; for which reaſon they ought not to be ſeparated.

AN

An advantageous balance is chiefly the fruit of the ſeveral mechanic branches of commerce, which have made a part of the ſubject of this treatiſe: all particular operations ought to tend to four fundamental points, as Sir Joſiah Child very juſtly obſerves. They conſiſt,

1ſt. In conſidering trade as the chief intereſt of a nation.

2dly, In increaſing the number of workmen.

3dly. In increaſing the nation's capital in commodities.

4thly. In making foreigners find their account in trading with her.

Every occupation contrary to any one of theſe four means is dangerous: the commerce of a ſtate will fall ſhort of perfection, in proportion as theſe four means ſhall be leſs extenſively made uſe of.

It is plain that the two firſt naturally lead to the two others, which are the abſolute and neceſſary conſequences of them.

It ſeems equally ſuperfluous to inſiſt on the neceſſity of conſidering trade as a nation's chief intereſt; that maxim we hope having been eſtabliſhed to content.

We have had fewer opportunities of inſiſting on the neceſſity of increaſing the number of workmen, than on the means of occupying the people. One ſtill remains for us to touch upon, after which we will proceed to this important object.

We

We have obſerved that foreigners may contract a ſecond kind of debts with a nation, by the expences they are at in travelling there.

It is to the liberal arts and ſciences that curioſity generally pays that tribute. A double motive for acknowledgment towards ſuch as cultivate them with ſucceſs; towards thoſe great and uncommon genius's, to whom nature has intruſted the art of inſtructing other men, or of leading them on to pleaſure by ſenſations purer and more analagous to that part of us which thinks and knows. They do not only anſwer the intent of their glorious motive with regard to thoſe whoſe intellectual faculties are leſs ſluggiſh and obſtructed; but uſeful and aſſiſting to all that bears the ſtamp of humanity, they procure a more comfortable ſubſiſtance to a rude and ignorant multitude, too much inclined to diſown the favours they receive.

Real talents, ever modeſt, and unambitious of whatever does not conduce to perfection, would alone have but a very ſmall ſhare in the eaſe and convenience that flows from them, if unaſſiſted by the juſtice and liberality of government and princes. A prince cannot build his glory on a ſurer foundation, and that part of the public revenues which he employs therein is an advantageous commerce which he procures his ſubjects. For the ſame reaſon it is right to multiply public

public buildings and monuments, and repositories of ſcarce and valuable things, when the public eaſe admits of it. There it is that artiſts ought chiefly to pique themſelves on ſhewing the extent of their invention, and rivalling nature in all they do, emulate thoſe beauties, whoſe charms, felt by all, command reſpect from the moſt capricious, and the ignorance of leſs happy ages.

To raiſe the curioſity of ſtrangers is, however, not alone ſufficient; it is likewiſe neceſſary to ſeduce them, and prolong their ſtay. Public diverſions cannot be too much varied in a capital, nor too magnificent; and if the national beauties are not ſufficient of themſelves to pleaſe the taſte of every nation that reſorts thither, it is proper to add others to them, but better ſtill to make them one's own by a happy imitation.

Of all allurements the moſt ſeducing certainly are the engaging manners of a people and their cordiality. The French are allowed by all to excel in the firſt; but I cannot help ſaying, that the ſecond, by much the moſt eſſential, is leſs common in their capital. It is quite the reverſe in their provinces, with which foreigners are moſt delighted, when they know them.

The buildings and monuments of a city are ſoon ſeen, the walks and gardens are ſoon run over, as well as the country ſeats about town, and the public diverſions. What can

tempt

tempt a foreigner to ſtay after that, if he has formed no intimacies with the inhabitants? Can he form any, if he be in a manner excluded from ſociety? I am ſenſible that the entrance into that ſociety ought to be difficult wherever a great multitude is collected together, becauſe a greater facility would be an inlet to numberleſs abuſes; beſides that, the continual hurry and agitation in which men are forced to live, does not ſuffer them to attend minutely to objects indifferent in themſelves. Accordingly, foreigners are not ſo unjuſt as to require being ſought after and courted: but it is with reaſon they complain of being ſhunned; of not being excuſed their different air, dreſs, language, and ignorance of particular cuſtoms: nay, even of the jargon, frivolouſneſs and ridiculous affectations of a people, which are, however, the perpetual object of their jokes and laughter.

It would, perhaps, not be beneath the majeſty of a great king to appoint a proper perſon or two, whoſe function ſhould be to do as it were the honours, of a country to foreigners of diſtinction, or ſuch as ſhould be recommended by their miniſters.

It would not require much money to keep two good tables. Thoſe to whom that care ſhould be entruſted ſhould ſtudy to invite men capable of giving foreigners a juſt idea of our manners and politeneſs: of the

better

better bred to all ſtrangers, notwithſtanding the rudeneſs of the vulgar herd; they would thereby be enabled to form acquaintance and connections more eaſily. Such an example would influence the great, who would think it their duty to promote ſuch noble views; they could not themſelves but be gainers by the inſtruction they would learn relating to foreign affairs; and the political intereſts of the ſtate would in all probability likewiſe reap advantage thereby.

It will next be neceſſary to obſerve the means of procuring a ſtate an advantageous balance of commerce, by the increaſe of the number of workmen.

It is plain, that if the ſtrength of commerce be known, if it becomes a nation's chief intereſt, the various kinds of work will multiply of themſelves. But that is not the only means that ought to be made uſe of to increaſe the number of workmen. Sound policy will effect it likewiſe, by drawing over workmen from abroad, and ſeeing in general that men are employed in the beſt manner poſſible.

If the inhabitants of one country enjoy more happineſs than thoſe of others, the latter will reſort to the former of their own accord. The diviſion of Europe into ſeveral ſevereignties, has left policy no other reſource whereby to obtain ſuperiority. The legiſlator would therefore deprive himſelf of

part

part of the fruit of his labours, if he opposed difficulties or indifference to the willingness of useful men desirous to become his subjects. It is highly proper that all who come capable of increasing the number of commodities, or who bring their fortunes with them, should, on conforming to the laws of that country, enjoy all the prerogatives of subjects. If they marry there, it would be unjust, and perhaps more imprudent, either to refuse to naturalize them, or to make that naturalization expensive.

To obtain men is a great advantage; but it is indispensably necessary to employ those we have in the best manner possible. That best employment consists in receiving from them all the assistance that can be gathered from their faculties, both mechanic and intellectual: it is by so much the more important, as every inequality affects population.

It is not enough for the public welfare that every poor inhabitant gets a livelihood; but the manner in which he gets it ought likewise to be useful to society in general.

A great number of beggars may live comfortably, though the body-politic receives no part of its strength from them. It is even weakened by them: for, not to speak of the contagious example of idleness, the substance which compassion and charity allot for the maintenance of those useless members, is partly with-held from other members, who are no longer able to exert all the activity of which they are susceptible.

COMMERCE considered as the chief interest of the nation, and the safety of industry, are the easiest ways of keeping men from a way of life so hurtful to the community. But force alone can break that habit, when once contracted.

WORKHOUSES are as old as industry in nations wise enough to conceive betimes, that the occupation of the subjects was the pledge of their fidelity, the source of population, of national riches and public revenues: in short, the only solid foundation of a well judged foreign power. Those houses have answered two intents of police: at the same time that they root out sloth and idleness, they are a means of punishment to such as disturb the public order, without going such lengths as to deserve to be quite cut off from society; which, by that means, inflicts a proper chastisement on vice, without losing it's right to the labour of vicious men.

IT must not be imagined that such establishments are expensive, or difficult, or fit for some particular countries only. Every county has it's hospitals, it's laborious works, such as hewing stones, felling wood, sawing planks, making ropes, and tow, the first dressing of wool, hemp, and an infinity of other things sufficient to maintain a

man

man againſt whom the laws are juſtly incenſed.

HANDS may likewiſe be tranſmitted from one workhouſe to another, where the country affords more work. Such an eſtabliſhment requires little expence, but great order, and an exact and uniform police.

BESIDES begging, men have other ways of ſubſiſting pernicious to ſociety: and I will again venture to aſſert, that population always decreaſes in proportion to the encreaſe of ſuch kinds of occupation.

THAT amazing multitude of livery ſervants choſen from among the moſt robuſt and beſt made men in the country, can never make amends by their conſumptions for the want of that better degree of culture, which the lands had a right to expect from them. The ſtate loſes on the capital of it's commodities and the balance of it's trade; and the public revenues will be weakened thereby, ſo long as that object of luxury, pernicious fruit of a bad principle, ſhall not be ſubjected to ſuch an impoſt, as ſhall keep it within proper bounds.

TWO or three thouſand, or perhaps more, water-carriers are employed in Paris to do what four hundred carts might perform equally well. The quays, bridges, and ſtreets, of that city are more and more crouded every day with pedlars, old clothes-men, and other ſuch like people, whoſe ſtation in life cannot

well

well be defined, and who live by doing needless things; by hawking about lottery tickets, an invention, perhaps, full, as hurtful to the ease and honesty of the people, as all the other effects of unpunished idleness. All these men, deserters from tillage, navigation, and manufactories, did not want for employment and wages; but they have found out a way of getting more by doing no one useful thing: void of care and without families, they lead a more debauched life, too often supported by larceny.

THOUGH the legislator cannot, nor ought to enter into the particular details of every subject; can it be doubted how much it concerns him to forbid in general by his laws, all public acts that tend to depopulation, and the ruin of society? I do not pretend that a particular plan of life or industry should be laid down for every man, but only that such things as are incompatible with public order, should be suppressed and prevented.

THAT indeed can never be so well effected as when foreign trade shall incessantly procure the totality of the people new riches together with new branches of useful industry.

IF the proper employment of industrious men, is what constitutes essentially the strength of the body politic; it follows, that to multiply the days of that employment is to multiply the resources of the state. It were to be wished as Don Geronimo de Ustariz, the Spaniard,

Spaniard, obſerves, that it were poſſible, without interfering with the public worſhip of God, to provide for the wants of the poor: every holiday is a diminution of at leaſt eight millions of piaſtres out of their wages. It muſt be owned that in thoſe dioceſes where feſtivals are leſs ſtrictly obſerved, all the working people do not profit by it: but that is leſs owing to their zeal and piety, than to their habitual depravity of life. Many, however, make a good uſe of it; it gains ground inperceptibly, and to encourage it ſtill more, it would, perhaps, not be amiſs to oblige all ſhopkeepers to keep their ſhops open when permitted by the ſuperior clergy.

THOUGH all men are born to labour, the the inequality of conditions has introduced among them very reaſonable diſtinctions with regard to the object of that labour. We will here call employment of the intellectual faculty whatever is not the work of the mechanic labour of the body.

THE more the principles of a frivolous education have introduced variety among a people, the more thoſe diſtinctions are become ſhameful and humiliating.

THAT, however, is not the only abuſe: as all endeavour to riſe, men born in a middling ſtation would think they demeaned themſelves, if they ſtooped to the claſs in which their grandfathers were born. If thoſe

those middling classes were more numerous than their proportion with the others could well bear, the multitude of men, whom pride would keep poor and idle, would be as infinite as their pretensions: very few of them would marry, and the celibacy forced upon part of the children would be thought a necessary cruelty on account of the rest.

PUBLIC prejudice would thus encrease daily, together with the causes of depopulation, whilst no body would think of explaining what in the public order is understood by reputable profession and honourable family.

FARMING, navigation, arts, and commerce, not being included in these vague indefinite terms, because none would apply to them for resources, all such as should have grown rich in these four classes would leave them as quick as possible.

IF the admission into the class distinguished by public order could be bought on terms ruinous to the prince's domain, all the rich would have a double inducement to abandon their former state to purchase lands, and live in a manner suitable to the prejudices of their new condition. If their descendants chanced to impoverish themselves, they would hold all kind of work in still greater contempt. The army would be their resource, but the causes of depopulation would not be the less multiplied.

To ſuppreſs the venality of nobility in France might be now a more brilliant than uſeful operation; both on account of the public wants, and, becauſe it is of conſequence not to retrench ſuch objects of emulation as men have been accuſtomed to; and likewiſe becauſe it would be depriving one's ſelf of thoſe extraordinary talents, which chance does not confine to any one claſs, as the national prejudices would have it be; but above all for fear the rich ſhould carry their fortunes over to ſome other country, where they could enjoy what their own refuſed them.

The privileged nobility in France, always ſeparated from the other by a boundleſs ſpace, or, at leaſt, by ſuch a one as great men only can ſtride over, will be forced, as they multiply to confine themſelves pretty nearly to the occupations of the order from which they ſprung: France begins already to find that effect from her multiplying of privileges. If the legiſlator did but add to the firſt expedient, ſome few ſignal favours in behalf of ſuch kinds of occupation as ſhould be judged moſt proper to be preferred, one might hope to ſee prejudices ſoon ſubſide in every proportional claſs of the ſubjects; labour would inſenſibly reſume her rights, and the cauſes of depopulation would diminiſh.

Vanity does not confine to any one claſs of men her oppoſition to the better employment of their mental faculties. She it is that,

backed

backed by too great a number of colleges and academies meerly literary, produces and keeps up, to the prejudice of all ranks of people, wretched poets, insipid novelists, and all the numerous tribe of scriblers and pretended wits and *beaux esprits*. Agreeing among themselves in one point only, their superstitious worship of fancy, they resemble each other in petulance, and in being equally, in the highest degree, useless to society.

THE loss of those men is already inestimable in itself; but, by becoming an object of luxury with the great and rich, they have infected both sexes with their contagious flights. A too fatal imitation has carried the spirit of levity and giddiness even to the mechanic, the whole inheritance of whose widow and children will, perhaps, be to know how to beg their bread in more elegant words.

NOTHING but ridicule and the sharpest criticism can avenge society of such wrongs: for sound criticism is as formidable to a little wit, as it is advantageous to a genius truly great.

LET not a vain indulgence be claimed here: the imperfection of humanity, I grant, is such that it's good things are never without some mixture. Did not the wisest of men deserve the hemlock draught? Humiliating, but useful reflection! Athens justly preferred the preservation of public order, to the life of her best philosophers.

I DO

I DO not after all deſire a law ſhould be paſſed to forbid people from loſing their time in ſcribbling, but only that a proper degree of ridicule be tacked to it. It is not the multitude of bad writers that makes them better: in the career of imagination every man born with but a ſmall genius, will make but a bad author as long as he lives; they are ſynonimous terms. The names of ſuch as are animated by a genius truly great, will live as long as the annals of the nation that has them. But the ſole conſideration of the luſtre it enjoys, will make no ordinary men take up the pen. The works of thoſe great maſters will be the ſtudy of well organiſed heads, and of the ſmall number of ſuch as are worthy to imitate them.

No man can be more ready than I am, to pay to all pleaſing arts that tribute of praiſe which cannot be refuſed them without injuſtice, nor without hurting the real good of ſociety. Several paſſages in this work muſt ſcreen me from any contrary invitation. But many, to whoſe ſentiments I owe the greateſt deference, tax me with having ſeen the abuſe that is made of our intellectual faculties, with too ſevere an eye. I had rather own it, than ſeem to perſiſt in a dangerous opinion. But yet I do not know whether the abuſe of the academies *merely and purely literary*, with which our provinces abound, deſerves ſo little attention as is pretended. It is not the loſs

of

of five or ſix hundred men known to polite literature, that I regret; ſome of them do honour to their country; and others, as manufacturers will always deſerve ſome regard. But with what eye ſhall we look upon the ineſtimable loſs of time of thouſands of young people in every province, whom the frivolous advantage of being thought witty, induces to neglect thoſe ſtudies to which they were deſtined by their birth and family? Can it be thought ſufficient to renounce all wildneſs and levity of mind at the very inſtant when a man enters on a profeſſion? That it is quite eaſy to check an imagination, the flights and ſtarts of which have been long applauded? In ſhort, is not the time when a man enters into life, that wherein he ought rather to act than ſtudy? It is not only in that light that I conſider the abuſe of the mind: let us penetrate into the private tranſactions of families; we ſhall ſee women give up all domeſtic cares, to indulge themſelves in the reading of books, which, far from forming, corrupt their minds; we ſhall ſee them deſpiſe the company and counſels of a huſband, who is only a man of plain good ſenſe, and ſtudy to deſerve a ridiculous character; a mother will conſult the man that amuſes her moſt, about the plan of education, or the choice of a tutor for her ſon. I do not pretend to enumerate all the follies, the affectation of *bel eſprit*, has been productive of in our days: I am content

content to obſerve that it is hurtful, even to the progreſs of learning. The pretended good company, of which the *bel eſprit* is the charm and idol, is fit only to enervate a young author, to fill him with that inconſiderate and raſh confidence, which is a certain ſymptom of neglect of ſtudy, and of very indifferent performances. Let us, in fine, apply to this luxury of mind, the principles that have guided us in our own examination of that which appertains to commerce. It is not to be feared, if it proceeds from a uſeful principle, that is to ſay, from public inſtruction and a general taſte for that well ſeaſoned reaſon in which all true wit conſiſts. I do not ſpeak of the academies where they ought to be, becauſe it is proper there ſhould be diſtinctions there for eminent men, and that every kind of luxury ſhould center there.

If perfection in the ſciences is reſerved to a certain degree of intelligence, ſeldom given by nature, it is at leaſt certain that every degree of knowledge that is acquired, has it's uſefulneſs. Mediocrity in an aſtronomer, a mathematician, naturaliſt, chymiſt, lawyer, and, in ſhort, in any of the ſciences, is ſufficient to qualify a man for numbers of employments in ſociety; for, even that mediocrity always ſuppoſes ſome degree of judgment and application. *Neque enim ita generati*

rati a natura ſumus, ut ad ludum & jocum facti eſſe videamur, ſed ad ſeveritatem potius & ad quaedam ſtudia graviora atque majora. Ludo autem & joco, uti illis quidem licet, ſed ſicut ſomno, & quietibus caeteris, tum cum gravibus ſeriiſque rebus ſatisfecerimus. Cic. de offic. lib. 1.

For many other particulars relating to a knowledge in the balance of trade, the reader may pleaſe to conſult my dictionary of commerce.—Every one will diſcern how far theſe ſentiments of Monſ. Melon, a judicious Frenchman, are applicable to theſe kingdoms. But by what peculiar means the particular balances of trade, and in conſequence thereof, the general balance may be augmented for the benefit of Great Britain, is the intent of the preſent treatiſe.

Wishing, that it might be well underſtood in this nation, from what general as well as particular ſyſtem of police the commercial grandeur of France has proceeded, I thought it my duty, before I laid down my pen, to diſplay the ſame in a connected view: and judging one eſſential cauſe thereof has been owing to the general cheapneſs of their commodities; I have laid the foundation of theſe papers, by endeavouring to ſhow, by what meaſures, I humbly apprehend, we may be enabled the ſooner to compete with this rival kingdom, in that reſpect, which is, by urging the neceſſity of taking more and

more

more land into cultivation, till we ſhould be capable of gradually diminiſhing our taxes, by the gradual leſſening of our public debts. Hereby likewiſe, we conceive, that all future ſcarcity of grain, and other proviſions, in the kingdom, may be effectually prevented; in order to render the neceſſaries of life and labour cheaper, that our arts and manufactures may become ſo, in conſequence thereof.

WE have next taken under conſideration the produce and trade of England, and compared them with thoſe of Scotland, and Ireland, and the Britiſh plantations; and alſo with each other, from a view further to enforce the reaſonableneſs and neceſſity of England's falling into the meaſures before recommended; ſhewing otherwiſe that her lands and her trade are not leſs likely to be ruined by her own dominions than by foreign rivals. This is the tenor of the two firſt diſſertations.

BUILDING much on the greater cultivation of land, it has been judged eligible to give a ſummary of various general principles of agriculture, as founded on experience, for the better improvement of our lands; in order the better to promote that general plenty and proſperity in England aimed at by theſe writings. As connected herewith, we have entered upon the point of eſtabliſhing public and private granaries. Theſe make the ſubject of the three ſucceeding diſcourſes.

FROM hence I have examined into the eſſential connections of trade between Great

Great Britain and Ireland, and the Britiſh plantations, and pointed out ſuch productions, manufactures, and trades, as England, Scotland, Ireland, and the Britiſh plantations ſhould chiefly cultivate; in order to rival and compete with foreign nations, and not with each other; repreſenting meaſures neceſſary to be taken for the joint proſperity of the commerce and navigation of them all. Theſe topics carry on our animadverſions to the Xth diſſertation.

We begin next with our conſiderations on the neceſſity and advantages that will ariſe to Great Britain in general, from a proper union between her and Ireland. This ſubject is continued in divers lights to the XIVth diſcourſe; the next beginning, as having affinity with the preceding, on the point of annexing the Iſle of Man to Great Britain, and thereby to lay the axe to the root of the infamous practice of ſmuggling carried on from thence.

From conſidering the commercial ſtate of our concerns in Europe, we next take a ſuccinct view of the conſtitution of the Britiſh plantations in America, and of the condition wherein they have many years been; pointing out the chief and diſregarded cauſes of their becoming the preſent ſeat of war; with reflections how they may recover their ſtrength and ſtability, and become a match for our enemies. This is the tenor of our

endeavours

endeavours from the XVIth to the XIXth diſcourſe.

To corroborate our humble ſentiments on thoſe concerns, we have ſubſequently taken a review of the conduct of France, in relation to the North-American colonies. On this capital point we have endeavoured to give a compariſon between her management of her American affairs, and that of Great Britain. This ſubject carries us to diſſertation XXI.; when the next enters upon a matter no leſs intereſting at this juncture—and I call it the ſyſtem of the French with regard to their African trade; wherein will appear by what police they have become ſo ſucceſsful therein, and obtained the advantage ſo greatly over us. This is continued to the XXIId diſcourſe; beginning next, as the reader will diſcern the reaſon, with a ſummary review of the commerce of France in the Eaſt-Indies; ſhewing by what gradations they have advanced the ſame, and how Great Britain ſtands in contraſt with them in that reſpect. Diſſertation XXIV. treats of the policy of England with regard to her management of the African trade; with conſiderations how the ſame might have been better conducted, and far more extended for the general intereſt of the nation; with a farther compariſon between our management and that of France, reſpecting the ſame: and by what means our Eaſt-

India

India company may be rendered inſtrumental to the ſecurity and advancement of this commerce. The XXVth diſcourſe continues the preceding ſubject. I next conſider, in the XXVI. the increaſe of the naval power of France and Spain, by the means of their FISHERIES, and ſhow the neceſſity of England balancing that degree of naval power, by the carrying of her fiſheries to the full extent they will admit of. And to the end that the reader may have before him in full view the preſent ſtate of the commercial connections of France, we have taken a ſurvey of her trade with all the European nations, which finiſhes the XXVIIth diſcourſe.

AFTER this, we enter more minutely, in the XXVIIIth diſſertation, into the eſſential principles of navigation in general, and fiſheries in particular, and ſhew how they contribute to give the balance of commerce, and conſequently of power.—And in order to apply thoſe maxims to the ſtate of affairs in the times of war, we have next taken into our conſideration the beſt methods of ſtationing our convoys and cruizers for the ſecurity and protection of our trade and navigation, and for the annoying thoſe of the enemy. This is the purport of diſcourſe XXIX. And that our naval force may not be obſtructed in its full exertion to the utmoſt public benefit and advantage, I have ſhewed the

ill

ill policy of our insuring the ships and merchandizes of the enemy in times of war: with considerations on the detrimental consequences to our trade, and the advantages to that of France, arising from so many neutral maritime carriers. This point finishes the XXXth dissertation; and the subsequent topic is an enquiry how long France may be presumed to carry on the war from the present state of affairs, according to the old system of conduct.

In our next discourse, we have given a summary of general maxims regarding the prosperity of our national commerce, as founded on experience, and the sentiments of the most knowing and judicious.

That what has been urged throughout these discourses may be the better relished by the reader, and make the desired impression upon his understanding, we have next given a recapitulation of fundamental principles, whereon the national trade may be promoted in every branch. This concludes dissertation XXXII; and is introductory to what is urged in the subsequent discourse, of arts and manufactories.

In order to render this work the more seasonable at this critical conjuncture of public affairs, we afterwards make an enquiry into the reasons why Holland has changed her system of late years towards the court of England; giving an abstract of a genuine remarkable speech

ſpeech ſaid to be made at a conference by the G——d P———r of Holland, in the year 1742, before certain Britiſh lords, who were ſent on an embaſſy to engage the Dutch in Britiſh meaſures: with remarks ſhewing that Holland expects Great Britain ſhould change her ſyſtem towards that republic, before ſhe can alter hers; with ſome intimation how Great Britain may change her ſyſtem to gain the Dutch, and ſeveral other her natural allies, as principals in the preſent war againſt France; and that at little expence to this nation in compariſon to what it has coſt heretofore. This ſubject finiſhes the XXXIVth diſcourſe.

After that I have animadverted on the conduct of the court of Spain towards that of Great Britain, ſince the peace of Utrecht; with remarks on the extraordinary friendſhip that we may reaſonably expect from that nation at preſent: with this ſubject ends the XXXVth diſſertation.

In the ſubſequent diſcourſe, we enter upon the neceſſity of Great Britain being at preſent more cloſely connected and allied with the continent than ſhe ever has been, though upon quite different principles; and not at ſuch an expence in time of war, as has been the caſe heretofore. Here ends the XXXVIth diſcourſe.

I next enter upon the general principles, whereon the balance of trade is founded; with the application thereof to the preſent

work

work, in a recapitulation of it's contents; the consideration of which is earnestly recommended to the public regard, in order to *throw the balance of trade so effectually into the hands of Great Britain, as to put the constant balance of power in Europe into her hands. Discourse* XXXVII.

FINIS.